THE NAVAL MUTINIES OF 1797
UNITY AND PERSEVERANCE

Portsmouth Harbour looking North [from Spithead]. Oil painting by Captain R. J. Elliott, working in Portsmouth c.1790.
Copyright Portsmouth City Museum & Records Service, reproduced by kind permission of Portsmouth City Museum & Records Service.

The Naval Mutinies of 1797
Unity and Perseverance

Edited by

Ann Veronica Coats and Philip MacDougall

THE BOYDELL PRESS

First published 2011
The Boydell Press, Woodbridge

ISBN 978 1 84383 669 8

The Boydell Press is an imprint of Boydell & Brewer Ltd
PO Box 9, Woodbridge, Suffolk IP12 3DF, UK
and of Boydell & Brewer Inc.
668 Mount Hope Ave, Rochester, NY 14620, USA
website: www.boydellandbrewer.com

A catalogue record for this book is available
from the British Library

The publisher has no responsibility for the continued existence or accuracy of URLs for
external or third-party internet websites referred to in this book, and does not guarantee
that any content on such websites is, or will remain, accurate or appropriate.

Papers used by Boydell & Brewer Ltd are natural, recyclable products
made from wood grown in sustainable forests

Printed and bound in the United States of America

Contents

List of Illustrations	vii
List of Tables	ix
Preface	xi
About the Contributors	xiv
Acknowledgements	xvii
Abbreviations	xix
Introduction, Analysis and Interpretation	1
Ann Veronica Coats and Philip MacDougall	
1. Spithead Mutiny: Introduction	17
Ann Veronica Coats	
2. The Delegates: A Radical Tradition	39
Ann Veronica Coats	
3. What Really Happened On Board HMS *London*?	61
David W. London	
4. The Spirit of Kempenfeldt	79
David W. London	
5. Voices from the Lower Deck: Petitions on the Conduct of Naval	
Officers during the 1797 Mutinies	98
Kathrin Orth	
6. Crew Management and Mutiny: The Case of *Minerve*, 1796–1802	107
Roger Morriss	
7. The 1797 Mutinies in the Channel Fleet: A Foreign-Inspired	
Revolutionary Movement?	120
Ann Veronica Coats	
8. The Nore Mutiny: Introduction	142
Philip MacDougall	
9. The East Coast Mutinies: May–June 1797	147
Philip MacDougall	
10. Reporting the Mutinies in the Provincial Press	161
Philip MacDougall	
11. A Floating Republic? Conspiracy Theory and the Nore Mutiny	
of 1797	179
Christopher Doorne	

12. Lower Deck Life in the Revolutionary and Napoleonic Wars   194
        Brian Lavery

13. 'Launched into Eternity': Admiralty Retribution *or* the
        Restoration of Discipline?   209
        Ann Veronica Coats

14. Discipline, Desertion and Death: HMS *Trent* 1796–1803   226
        Nick Slope

15. 'We went out with Admiral Duncan, we came back without him':
        Mutiny and the North Sea Squadron   243
        Philip MacDougall

16. The Influence of 1797 upon the *Nereide* Mutiny of 1809   264
        Jonathan Neale

Select Bibliography   280
Index   297

Illustrations

Cover Portsmouth Harbour Looking South (towards Spithead)
Captain R. J. Elliott c.1790
Copyright Portsmouth City Museum & Records Service, reproduced by
kind permission of Portsmouth City Museum & Records Service.

Frontispiece Portsmouth Harbour looking North (from Spithead)
Captain R. J. Elliott c.1790   ii
Copyright Portsmouth City Museum & Records Service, reproduced by
kind permission of Portsmouth City Museum & Records Service.

1. True Blue! Or Britain's jolly tars paid off at Portsmouth, 1797
by Isaac Cruikshank   xx
Copyright Philip MacDougall.

2. Chart of St Helen's Road, Spithead, Portsmouth and Langstone
Harbours 1783 Lieut. Murdoch Mackenzie Junr.   18
© National Maritime Museum, Greenwich, London, reproduced by
permission from the Trustees of the National Maritime Museum,
Greenwich, London.

3. Sir John Carter, d.1808   34
Copyright Portsmouth City Museum & Records Service, reproduced by
kind permission of Portsmouth City Museum & Records Service.

4. Lord Howe's Fleet 1794: 'The Town and Harbour of Portsmouth'   36
Copyright Portsmouth City Museum & Records Service, reproduced by
kind permission of Portsmouth City Museum & Records Service.

5. View of the Prizes Taken on the 1st June [1794] by Earl Howe, at
Anchor at Spithead Lithograph N. Pocock and R. Pollard   38
Copyright Portsmouth City Museum & Records Service, reproduced by
kind permission of Portsmouth City Museum & Records Service.

6. Broadside 'To a Loyal and Discerning Nation', The Seamen's
    Manifesto, from 'The Loyal and Humane Tars of His Majesty's
    Fleet at St. Helen's. Queen Charlotte, May 13, 1797.'   62
    Copyright Trustees of the National Museum of the Royal Navy
    reproduced with permission from the Trustees of the National Museum
    of the Royal Navy.

7a and 7b. Local Trade Token obverse and reverse 1793   121
    Copyright Portsmouth City Museum & Records Service, reproduced by
    kind permission of Portsmouth City Museum & Records Service.

8. The Downs and the Nore: centres of naval mutiny in 1797 Kent   142
    Copyright Philip MacDougall.

9. The blockade of the Thames. Position of Nore ships on 8 June 1797
    after the government removed the navigational buoys
    in the Thames   146
    Copyright Philip MacDougall.

10. Richard Parker, President of the Committee of Delegates for the
    Redress of Grievances.   160
    Copyright Philip MacDougall.

11. The fifth-rate frigate Beaulieu, 1809   171
    Copyright Philip MacDougall.

12. 'Mutiny at the Nore – Ill-treatment of Officers' by Colonel C. Field
    RMLI 1924   210
    © Trustees of the Royal Marines Museum, reproduced with permission
    from the Trustees of the Royal Marines Museum.

13. Admiral Duncan from a contemporary print   244
    Copyright Philip MacDougall

Tables

1.1 Summary of Spithead Demands, Granted or not Granted   27

1.2 Naval Ships and Seamen at Spithead April–May 1797   32

2.1 Spithead Delegates, April–May 1797   44

2.2 Delegates in Sir Roger Curtis's Squadron April–May 1797   44

2.3 Plymouth Delegates, April-May 1797   45

7.1 Irish Seamen as a Percentage of Ships' Companies from the Muster
    Books of leading Ships in the Spithead Mutiny, April–May 1797   138

14.1 Flogging Statistics on HMS *Trent*, 1796–1803   231

14.2 Recorded Offences on HMS *Trent*, 1796–1803   231

14.3 Discipline and Death on HMS *Trent*, 1796–1803 (Seamen only)   233

14.4 Discipline and Sickness on HMS *Trent*, 1796–1803   234

14.5 Discipline and Desertion on HMS *Trent*, 1796–1803
    (Seamen only)   234

14.6 Discipline and Nationality on HMS *Trent*, 1796–1803
    (Seamen only)   235

14.7 Discipline and Recruitment on HMS *Trent*, 1796–1803
    (Seamen only)   235

14.8 Discipline and Quality on entry into HMS *Trent*, (Seamen only)   237

14.9 Discipline and Promotion on HMS *Trent*, 1796–1803
    (Seamen only)   238

14.10 Discipline and Captains on HMS *Trent*, 1796–1803   239

Preface

The Naval Mutinies of 1797: Unity and Perseverance does not aim to replace Conrad Gill's definitive work on the mutinies of 1797, but to complement his scholarship and re-examine some of his conclusions.[1] His extensive range of sources has been mined by subsequent historians, but *The Naval Mutinies of 1797* is a meticulous exploration of documentation and nuance. While this multi-authored work lacks a single author's unity of theme, research method and interpretation, multiple specialist authors offer wider searches and insight. Each chapter explores a separate area of debate. Were the mutinies a struggle over 'arrears of pay' or a 'revolutionary movement'; were there one, four or more mutinies? Emphasis is placed on documentary evidence, especially from the lower deck. What emerges predominantly is a desire for peace and unity on the part of the majority, together with a fundamental loyalty and internal discipline. After the mutinies the Admiralty aimed to restore peaceful relations to a *status quo ante* Spithead, but some writers indicate that it prompted an examination of officer discipline. A scrutiny of leadership as such is not central to this volume, but is demonstrated to be relevant to overall discipline. The original spelling and punctuation of quoted documents has been retained throughout except where noted to the contrary, to convey an authentic voice.

The mutinies of 1797 were of singular importance, resonating long after the year ended. When else has the most powerful navy in the world, with ships stationed in every ocean, found itself paralysed by the combined actions of so many seamen? To stimulate historical re-scrutiny in 1997, the editors convened two bicentenary conferences and designed two exhibitions.[2] What has emerged from those initial papers is a profoundly lateral and innovative study. While focusing on the events of 1797, later mutinies deemed to have been inspired by 1797 are also examined, as is subsequent Admiralty policy regarding conditions on board naval ships.

Reviewing writings since 1997, John Hattendorf reminds us that ships for centuries have been 'the most complex technological devices that humans have ever devised', requiring 'an organized and disciplined relationship between a ship's officers and crew', further complicated by an adverse environment and war.[3] Yet, with few exceptions, this momentous historical event, which occurred at a crucial point in the war with revolutionary France and her allies,

1 C. Gill, *The Naval Mutinies of 1797* (Manchester, 1913).

2 Initial papers were presented to conferences held in the Royal Naval Museum Portsmouth and Chatham Historic Dockyard Chapel in 1997 and 'Reactions to Revolution Colloque', Université de Caen, December 1997. The Public Record Office, Kew (now the National Archive) and Portsmouth City Museum sponsored two exhibitions in 1997.

3 J. B. Hattendorf, Foreword, in C. Bell and B. Elleman, eds, *Naval Mutinies of the Twentieth Century: An International Perspective* (London, 2003), p. xiii.

has not featured greatly in naval histories.[4] The twentieth century witnessed, after Gill, only two full accounts, those of Manwaring and Dobrée (1935) and Dugan (1966), with only the former drawing upon new source material.[5] Others, in attempting to place the mutinies within a wider historical context, have seen their work challenged, the subsequent debate weakened and unresolved by this same lack of overall research. Some generalised observations made by E. P. Thompson and Roger Wells have been challenged by N. A. M. Rodger and writers in *The Naval Mutinies of 1797*.

The threat to national defence posed by the mutinies was of vital interest to government, shown in many of the chapters, thus placing this book within mainstream political history. Events are also contextualised within history, culture and society. In 2003 Rodger argued for an explanation of 'the naval influence on, or contribution to, political, social, economic ... history.' Citing Carew and Capp in 1995, he contended that 'Historians of trades-unions or radical social movements may not be able to tell us everything about life at sea, but they can tell us a great deal which conventional naval historians have hitherto missed'.[6]

In 2003 Rodger highlighted 'the lack of research' into the naval mutinies. He contended: 'The time is therefore not yet ripe to attempt any serious reconsideration of the significance of the mutinies' but qualified this by saying that 'this does not mean that is impossible to say anything at all about the 1797 mutinies'.[7] The editors of *The Naval Mutinies of 1797* are in the unusual

---

4   The *Annual Register, 1797* and the *Journal of the House of Lords* detail Pitt's payments of specie to his European allies against the advice of the directors of the Bank of England, leading to the suspension of cash payments on 26 February 1797. Exports to 'Germany', the largest recipient, were 96,980 ounces of silver in 1794; 31,069oz 13dwts (pennyweights) of gold and 1,239,882oz, 18dwts of silver in 1795; 4,119oz 4dwts of gold and 706,757oz 10dwts of silver in 1796. On 'the 9th of February, 1797, the directors ordered the governor to inform the minister, "that under the present state of the bank's advances to government here, to agree to his request of making a farther advance of 1,500,000l. as a loan to Ireland, would threaten ruin to the bank, and most probably bring the directors to shut up their doors."' *Annual Register, 1797* (London, 1800), pp. 178–206; the *Journal of the House of Lords*, volume 41 (1797), p. 253.
5   Gill, *Naval Mutinies*; G. E. Manwaring and Bonamy Dobrée, *The Floating Republic* (London, 1935) and James Dugan, *The Great Mutiny* (London, 1966).
6   N. A. M. Rodger, 'Mutiny or Subversion? Spithead and the Nore' in Thomas Bartlett, *et al.,*, eds, *1798: A Bicentenary Perspective* (Dublin, 2003), pp. 549–564; See E. P. Thompson, *The Making of the English Working Class* (Harmondsworth, 1963), p. 184; R. Wells, *Insurrection: The British Experience, 1795–1803* (Gloucester, 1986), p. 99; Rodger, 'Considerations on Writing a General Naval History', in J. B. Hattendorf, ed., *Doing Naval History* (Newport, Rhode Island, 1995), p. 123; fn. 23: A. Carew, *The Lower Deck of the Royal Navy 1900–39: Invergordon in Perspective* (Manchester,1981); Capp, B., *Cromwell's Navy: The Fleet and the English Revolution* (Oxford, 1989).
7   Rodger, 'Mutiny or Subversion?', pp. 549, 550; N. A. M. Rodger, *Command of the Ocean* (London, 2004): A. Coats: 'Spithead Mutiny: Introduction'; 'The Delegates: A Radical Tradition'; 'The 1797 Mutinies in the Channel Fleet: A Foreign-Inspired Revolutionary Movement?'; C. Doorne: 'A Floating Republic? Conspiracy Theory and the Nore Mutiny of 1797'; P. MacDougall: 'The East Coast Mutinies: May–June 1797'; '"We went out with Admiral Duncan, we came back without him': Mutiny and the North Sea Squadron'. Also see C. J. Doorne, 'Mutiny and sedition in the Home Commands of the Royal Navy,

position of having had six draft chapters from this book evaluated by Rodger
before its publication, as the authors made them available preparatory to his
chapters in *1798: A Bicentenary Perspective* and *Command of the Ocean*.
They believe that important new conclusions may be drawn from their re-
examination, to stimulate further detailed research. This volume also collates
new sources and presents new images.

This need for new research into the empirical detail and interpretation of
these mutinies inspired this publication, which collates and correlates recent
research from leading naval and social historians. While individual conclusions vary, this cohesive, definitive and comprehensive analysis of documents
will clarify previous uncertainty. From intensive examination of court martial
papers, muster books, petitions, logbooks, subsequent remarks of naval officers, writings from the lower deck and witnesses, new conclusions are ad-
duced by Coats, London, Morriss, Orth, MacDougall, Doorne, Lavery, Slope
and Neale. Longitudinal case studies scrutinise particular vessels: Morriss the
40-gun frigate *Minerve*, Slope the 36-gun frigate *Trent* and Neale the 36-gun
fifth-rate *Nereide*. As a correlative to particular events, Lavery's 'Lower Deck
Life in the Revolutionary and Napoleonic Wars' provides an excellent empirical datum of shipboard organisation which underpins the significant changes
affecting seamen's conditions and discipline in this period.

Like Manwaring and Dobrée, in this book the editors aimed to invoke some
documents 'which [Mr Gill] passed by', and to discover 'many others which
throw an entirely new light on uncertain incidents and characters'.[8]

Ann Veronica Coats and Philip MacDougall

1783–1803' (Ph.D, University of London, 1998).
8 Manwaring and Dobrée, *Floating Republic*, Preface.

About the Contributors

ANN VERONICA COATS recognised in 1995 that the 1797 naval mutinies should be commemorated and their history reassessed. She organised the Spithead mutiny conference at Portsmouth Royal Naval Museum in 1997 and designed jointly an exhibition at the National Archive, Kew: '"To prevent the unbounded oppression": The Naval Mutinies of 1797'. She also created the Spithead Mutiny Bicentenary Exhibition at Portsmouth City Museum: 'A state of democracy and absolute rebellion'. While researching 'The Economy of the Navy and Portsmouth: A Discourse between the Civilian Naval Administration of Portsmouth Dockyard and the Surrounding Communities, 1650 to 1800' (D.Phil., Sussex, 2000), Ann jointly founded the Naval Dockyards Society and is currently its Secretary. The Society has published six volumes of *Transactions* to date (see www.navaldockyards.org). As publisher, Ann has jointly published three maritime books. Since 2000 she has taught at the University of Portsmouth on the MA Maritime Studies and M.Sc. Heritage and Museum Studies courses. She has written articles on naval administration, dockyards, convicts and mutiny, including mutineers Richard Parker and Valentine Joyce (*ODNB*, 2004), and 'Bermuda Naval Base: Management, Artisans and their Enslaved Workers, 1795–1797 – the Heritage of the 1950 Bermudian Apprentices' (*The Mariner's Mirror*, 2009).

CHRISTOPHER DOORNE attended Royal Holloway College, where he obtained his Ph.D. in 1998 with the thesis 'Mutiny and Sedition in the Home Commands of the Royal Navy, 1793–1803'. From 2002–4 he worked for Colchester Archaeological Trust. Since 2004 he has been a Workers' Educational Association tutor in the Eastern region, specialising in historical mysteries, folklore and military and naval history, 1793–1945. He is currently researching a book on Britain's global struggle against France 1807–12, provisionally entitled *The Lion and the Ogre*.

BRIAN LAVERY was a curator at the National Maritime Museum, Greenwich, for fourteen years after working at Chatham Historic Dockyard. He is the author of numerous books on maritime history including *Ship of the Line*, *Nelson's Navy* and *Shipboard Life and Organisation*. He was consultant on the replica of the *Susan Constant* in Virginia and the *Endeavour* built in Freemantle, and historical adviser on the film *Master and Commander*, and television series *Masters of the Seas*. He has appeared in many television programmes including *Timewatch*, *Time Team* and *Wreck Detectives*. He is a member of the *Victory* Advisory Technical Committee and is now a freelance author and consultant.

DAVID W. LONDON gained his Ph.D. at King's College London with his thesis 'Mutiny in the Public Eye: The Role of Newspapers in the Mutiny at Spithead'. He has been Assistant Professor at E. W. Scripps School of Journalism, Ohio University, Associate Lecturer at the University of Portsmouth, Assistant Professor at Central Michigan University and is currently Assistant Professor at the American University in Cairo. Dr London has written and lectured extensively on the subjects of propaganda and manipulation of the media.

PHILIP MACDOUGALL edited the section of papers devoted to the Nore Mutiny and organised the bicentenary Nore Mutiny conference held at Chatham in 1997. A much-published naval historian with a particular interest in social conditions, both on board ship and the related shore industries, he first gained an interest in the mutinies of 1797 while living on the Isle of Grain and in close proximity to those events that ultimately led to the execution of Richard Parker. A distant relative of his also had a more direct connection with the mutinies, employed by Nelson as his shipboard secretary during that period. In continuing to research the social history of the navy, Philip has analysed the extent to which the British navy, during the eighteenth and early nineteenth centuries, was dependent on ethnic minorities. Part of this research has appeared in his book *Settlers, Visitors and Asylum Seekers* (Portsmouth City Council, 2007). A former lecturer at the University of Kent, and now teaching at Portsmouth College, Philip has also written extensively on the industrial and social history of North Kent and the Medway towns.

ROGER MORRISS gained his Ph.D. in 1978 with a thesis on the British Royal Dockyards during the French Revolutionary and Napoleonic Wars which was enlarged into a book on the period 1793–1815, published in 1983. Since then he has written a biography of the naval officer Sir George Cockburn (1772–1853), completed a Navy Records Society volume, *The Channel Fleet and the Blockade of Brest, 1793–1801* (2001), and written *Naval Power and British Culture, 1760–1850: Public Trust and Government Ideology* (2004). He began his career as a teacher but worked at the National Maritime Museum from 1979 to 1995 where he was mainly concerned with the care of the manuscript collections and in 1994 produced a *Guide to British Naval Papers in North America*. Since 1995 he has taught maritime and naval history at the University of Exeter. He has been General Editor of the Navy Records Society since 2000.

JONATHAN NEALE is senior lecturer in creative writing at Bath Spa University. He holds a B.Sc. in social anthropology from LSE and a Ph.D. in social history from Warwick. He has written ten books, including *The Cutlass and the Lash: Mutiny and Discipline in Nelson's Navy* on eighteenth-century naval mutinies; *The American War: Vietnam, 1960–1975*; *Tigers of the Snow*, a history of Sherpa climbers; and, most recently, *Stop Global Warming: Change the World*.

KATHRIN ORTH is a naval historian who has worked for several museums in Germany, most recently for the International Maritime Museum Hamburg, which opened in 2008 and the Historical Museum Bremerhaven, where she has been working since 2010. She completed her MA thesis on 'Crime and Punishment in the Royal Navy during the Revolutionary and Napoleonic Wars: The Mediterranean Fleet in 1803–1805' at Humboldt University, Berlin. She contributed a biographical essay about Sir John Orde to the *British Admirals of the Napoleonic Wars: The Contemporaries of Nelson*, edited by Peter Le Fevre and Richard Harding (2005). Currently, she is completing her Ph.D. on the U-boat and E-boat arms of the Germany navy in the Second World War. In the course of her research on the subject she has published several articles on the motivation and morale of the German U-boat arm at the end of the Second World War.

NICK SLOPE is an independent naval historian and archaeologist specialising in the archaeology of the Middle East and the social history of the Royal Navy of the Revolutionary and Napoleonic Wars. Nick recently led an excavation rescuing the threatened remains of Nelson's sailors from the Battle of the Nile (1798) and the British Egyptian Expedition (1801). He is Commissioning Editor of the Nelson Society's journal *The Nelson Dispatch* and Honorary Secretary of the Anglo-Israel Archaeological Society. His writings include *Serving in Nelson's Navy: A Social History of Three Amazon Class Frigates Utilising Database Technology, 1795–1811* (Ph.D., 2006); 'Royal Navy Officer Development in the Age of Nelson', *The Bicentennial Edition of the Nelson Dispatch* (Nelson Society, 2005); *The Trafalgar Captains: Their Lives and Memorials* (1805 Club, Chatham, 2005); *Volunteer Landsmen Recruits to the Royal Navy 1795–1811: The Case of Three Thames-built Frigates* (Thames Built Ships Symposium, 2003); *HMS Emerald's First Commission 1795–1803: A Case Study Utilising Database Technology* (Freemantle conference, 2001).

Acknowledgements

The Naval Mutinies of 1797: Unity and Perseverance is the product of sixteen years' work. When the editors realised in 1995 that no plans to commemorate the 1797 mutinies were contemplated they resolved to initiate new and timely research for bicentenary conferences in 1997. Ann's D.Phil. supervisor Dr Colin Brooks agreed it had to be done and she effectively took two years out of her doctoral research to organise the conferences. Since then much new research and interpretation has supplemented the authors' knowledge, reflected in the historiography.

The editors acknowledge their gratitude to the many maritime historians within the research nexus of the National Archive, National Maritime Museum, National Museum of the Royal Navy, Institute of Historical Research, Society for Nautical Research, Navy Records Society, the Diggers in the Storehouse and the Naval Dockyards Society with whom they discussed this draft project, particularly Dr Peter Le Fevre and Dr David Davies. Conference speakers emerged, and the editors are extremely grateful to those authors who extended and updated their research. The ambience of the conferences was greatly enhanced by Pete Watkinson and the Portsmouth Shantymen's custom-made tape of songs, *Mutiny 1797: Songs from the Spithead & Nore Mutinies* (1997).

Sponsorship and academic support for the conferences in the National Museum of the Royal Navy in 1997 were given generously by director Campbell McMurray, curators Colin White and Matthew Sheldon and administrator Sue Goodger. Sources were found by librarians Andrew Trotman, Allison Wareham and volunteer R. E. G. Harris.

Chris Carrell, Portsmouth City Arts Officer, and Museums and Records Officer Sarah Quail, Local History Curators John Stedman and Katy Ball of the Portsmouth City Museum and Records Service are thanked for supplying sponsorship, images and advice, while Exhibition Officer Ian Chappell refined the design for the exhibition 'A State of Democracy and Absolute Rebellion', assisted by Sid Whatcott and Geoff Coats.

Chatham Dockyard Historic Trust and Chatham Dockyard Historical Society, especially Peter Dawson, are also thanked for sponsorship of the 1797 Conference in Chatham Dockyard Chapel in 1997. The editors are also grateful to the National Archive for its generosity in hosting the 1997 exhibition: '"To Prevent the Unbounded Oppression": The Naval Mutinies of 1797', produced through the hard work of Jamie Beveridge and Alan Alstin. One paper was presented to 'Reactions to Revolution Colloque', Université de Caen, December 1997. The editors thank these institutions and Portsmouth City Council for sponsoring the project in 1997.

We thank Portsmouth City Museum and Records Service for permission to reproduce Captain R. J. Elliott's *Portsmouth Harbour looking South and Portsmouth Harbour looking North*, the portrait of Portsmouth Mayor Sir John Carter, a view of Lord Howe's Fleet 1794: *The Town and Harbour of Portsmouth*, the *View of the Prizes Taken on the 1st June* [1794] *by Earl Howe, at Anchor at Spithead*, and the obverse and reverse of a defiant local trade token depicting Earl Howe in 1793, with the particular assistance of John Stedman, Katy Ball and Nick Thompson. We are grateful to the Trustees of the National Maritime Museum, Greenwich, Dr Nigel Rigby, Head of Research at the National Maritime Museum and Picture Librarian Melanie Oelgeschlager for generous assistance and permission to reproduce the chart of St Helen's Road, Spithead, surveyed 1783. We thank the Trustees of the Royal Marines Museum for permission to reproduce *Mutiny at the Nore – Ill-treatment of Officers* by Colonel C. Field RMLI, with the generous assistance of Director Chris Newbery and Photographs and Paintings Librarian John Ambler. Thanks also go to Trustees of the National Museum of the Royal Navy for permission to reproduce the broadside 'To a Loyal and Discerning Nation', The Seamen's Manifesto, from 'The Loyal and Humane Tars of His Majesty's Fleet at St. Helen's. QUEEN CHARLOTTE, May 13, 1797', and for assistance from Matthew Sheldon and Stephen Courtney.

Finally, greatest thanks are due to Professor Michael Duffy of the University of Exeter for preserving the original electronic manuscripts, and subsequently to Boydell & Brewer editor Peter Sowden for his belief that the book should be brought to completion. The editors greatly valued the comments of N. A. M. Rodger in previewing six of the chapters in 'Mutiny or Subversion? Spithead and the Nore', in Thomas Bartlett *et al.*, *1798: A Bicentenary Perspective* (Four Courts, Dublin, 2003) and *Command of the Ocean* (Allen Lane, London, 2004) and observations made by J. D. Davies on the Introduction, Analysis and Interpretation. Allison Wareham and Matthew Sheldon of the NMRN, Dr David Davies of the NDS and Isobel Kilgallon of the University of Portsmouth helped crucially in checking references. As is customary, the editors accept full responsibility for their individual conclusions.

Ann Veronica Coats and Philip MacDougall

Abbreviations

Add. MS.	Additional Manuscript
BL	British Library
CSPD	*Calendar of State Papers Domestic*
HMSO	Her Majesty's Stationery Office
HRH	His Royal Highness
LCS	London Corresponding Society
NMM	National Maritime Museum
NMRM	National Museum of the Royal Navy
NRS	Navy Records Society
ODNB	*Oxford Dictionary of National Biography* (Oxford, 2004), www.oxforddnb.com
OED	*Oxford English Dictionary*
Parl. Hist.	*Parliamentary History*, Wiley Interscience, ISSN 1750–0206
RMLI	Royal Marines Light Infantry
RMM	Royal Marines Museum
SCI	Society for Constitutional Information
TNA	The National Archive, Kew

1. *True Blue! Or Britain's jolly tars paid off at Portsmouth, 1797.* A contemporary cartoon drawn by Isaac Cruikshank attempting to portray 'the jolly jack tar' in a very different fashion from that claimed by the writers of the petitions that were emanating from both Spithead and the Nore. Cruikshank was part of a carefully orchestrated campaign – which reached particular intensity at the time of the Nore mutiny – to undermine the considerable national support that was initially given to those in mutiny.

Copyright Philip MacDougall.

Introduction, Analysis and Interpretation

Ann Veronica Coats and Philip MacDougall

> Never had British seamen more Reasonable demands nor a
> favourable Opertunity of rendering themselves a Respectable
> Body of men then the preasent but if they are Deverted or
> amused by false alarms or fair but vain Speaches or Promises
> from their preasent Glorious and Rightious Resolution of doing
> themselves Justice after haveing so long fought for the Intrest of
> Others – neglecting their own, Dreadfull is the Consequence. the
> Success is shure.[1]

The naval mutinies of 1797 were unprecedented in scale and impressive in their
level of organisation. Crews on board a majority of ships of the Royal Navy's
fleet in home waters, while invasion threatened, after making clear demands,
refused to sail until their demands were met. It was an all-encompassing event
that affected the crews of over one hundred ships in at least five different anchorages. Furthermore these same actions were replicated elsewhere, with seamen
in the Mediterranean Sea and Atlantic and Indian Oceans following suit. This
chapter describes the 1797 mutinies briefly and examines recent scholarship
and interpretation to introduce themes that will recur throughout *The Naval
Mutinies of 1797*. The title echoes Conrad Gill's comprehensive work, prosaic
but unambiguous.[2]

The Spithead mutiny was initiated in February 1797 when seamen in the
Channel Fleet moored at the Spithead anchorage in the Solent sent eleven
anonymous petitions seeking a pay increase to Admiral Richard Howe, their
nominal commander.[3] Due to his failure to respond to their satisfaction,
when the Channel Fleet returned to Portsmouth in March from blockading French ports, the seamen found that no action had been taken. Further
failures of communication between the Admiralty, Howe and Admiral Lord
Bridport, acting commander, led to the seamen's refusal to sail on Easter
Sunday, 16 April 1797. Thirty-two delegates from sixteen ships of the line

---

1 Statement from *Queen Charlotte* on the first day of the Spithead Mutiny, 16 April 1797.
TNA, ADM1/5125.
2 Conrad Gill, *The Naval Mutinies of 1797* (Manchester, 1913).
3 TNA, ADM1/5125; ADM3/136. But ADM1/107, Bridport to Nepean, 17 April 1797
suggests that petitions were first sent in December 1796.

met in *Queen Charlotte*'s cabin that evening and drew up rules to govern their behaviour.

The news reached London on Easter Monday, 17 April. Earl Spencer, First Lord of the Admiralty, left for Portsmouth with a party of commissioners. Following the seamen's rejection of their first offer, on 20 April the Admiralty party consulted Lord Bridport, three admirals and sixteen captains and agreed to most of the seamen's demands. On 21 April the delegates on *Queen Charlotte* insisted on a pardon from the King before returning to duty. Admiral Gardner accused the seamen of cowardice and hypocrisy, leading to a breakdown in negotiations. Spencer left Portsmouth immediately, obtained the King's pardon and despatched it to Bridport. On 23 April it was read to the fleet and on 28 April most of the Spithead fleet sailed to St Helen's to await a good wind for Brest, but was wind-bound. *Marlborough*, *Minotaur*, *Nymphe* and *Ramillies* had unsettled grievances with their officers, so stayed at Spithead with *London*. The *London* incident on 7 May (analysed in detail by David W. London in Chapter 3, 'What Really Happened On Board HMS *London*?') led to a further crisis, which prompted resolution of most of the seamen's demands.

Meanwhile, on 26 April *Porcupine* reached Plymouth with the news from Spithead and a pre-arranged supportive mutiny broke out among ships of the Channel Fleet stationed there. The seamen refused to go to sea, and set their officers ashore. On 27 April *Atlas* was designated 'the Parliament Ship' and a boat was chartered to send a delegation to Spithead, where the Channel Fleet accepted the Spithead terms on 15 May.

The mutiny at the Great Nore anchorage, where the River Medway merges with the River Thames, was declared on 12 May when the crew of the 90-gun *Sandwich* gave three cheers and raised the red flag. Before then a significant amount of organising had been undertaken by committees elected on board most (if not all) of the warships lying in the anchorage, with some twenty warships declared to be in mutiny. Unlike the ships at Spithead, this was no organised fleet but an assortment of vessels awaiting stores, men or repairs, conducting local patrols or, in the case of *Sandwich*, a receiving ship. Richard Parker emerged as a figurehead 'president', but real power lay in the hands of other delegates who maintained a much lower profile. Although at its outset the Nore mutiny supported the Spithead mutiny, it soon took on a momentum of its own. After the Spithead mutiny ended on 15 May, the seamen of the Nore devised a more extensive set of demands that focused on the removal of unpopular officers, more equal distribution of prize money and alterations to the Articles of War. Without the arrival of Admiral Duncan's North Sea Squadron, also in mutiny, it is likely that the Nore mutiny would have collapsed at the end of May. Reinvigorated, however, those at the Nore held out until mid-June, their additional demands unmet by a government refusing to negotiate further. Parker was hanged on 30 June, with a dozen or so mutineers (out of a total of sixty condemned) receiving the same punishment. Many of the supposed leaders appear to have escaped punishment, some fleeing to revolutionary France.

Conrad Gill in 1913 identified three mutinies: two at Spithead and one at the Nore; but in 2003 N. A. M. Rodger distinguished four mutinies: the first and second Spithead mutinies, the Nore mutiny and that of the North Sea Squadron, each with different causes. He epitomised naval historians' dichotomies of 'benign' and 'unpolitical' (Spithead) or 'malign' and 'political' (East Coast) mutinies. He noted their perception of Quota men as introducing an alien political element. In 1795 and 1796 five Quota Acts obliged local authorities to raise army and navy recruits, many of whom would have been landsmen. He also observed E. P. Thompson's 'romantic socialist' view that the mutinies were part of the rise of the English working class, a peace movement and an embryonic revolutionary movement. While writing from different standpoints, the assumption shared by these diverse historians was that the English could not achieve insurrection unaided. Rodger cited Marxist historians Jonathan Neale and J. P. Moore who argued a contrary opinion, and praised Neale's 'handling of the evidence' within his Ph.D. thesis as 'exemplary'.[4] Rodger accepted the evidence in Coats, Chapter 2, 'The Delegates: A Radical Tradition', which concludes that the Spithead mutiny was not led by Quota men. Rodger also examined partisan claims that Irish personnel, whom some writers have equated with the rebel United Irishmen, amounted to a quarter of the seamen and thus provided an external motivation for revolution.[5] In Chapter 7 of this volume Coats shows that while around a quarter of the Channel Fleet was Irish-born, no Spithead mutiny actions derived from Irish republicanism. It would have been surprising to find a smaller proportion of Irish seamen and marines, given recruitment policies and estimates of the Irish population as half that of Great Britain.[6] Turning to the mutinies at the Nore, Rodger agreed that a rift existed within the leadership and that those who escaped were possibly more extreme than many of those who were punished. This latter point is explored specifically by Doorne and MacDougall in their respective chapters.[7]

---

4 Rodger, 'Mutiny or Subversion?', pp. 550, 554–6. J. Neale, 'Forecastle and Quarterdeck: Protest, Discipline and Mutiny in the Royal Navy 1793–1814', Ph.D, University of Warwick (1990); J. P. Moore III, '"The Greatest Enormity that Prevails": Direct Democracy and Workers' Self-Management in the British Naval Mutiny of 1786', in Colin Howell and William Twomey, eds, *Jack Tar in History: Essays in the History of Maritime Life and Labour* (Fredericton, 1991).

5 Rodger, 'Mutiny or Subversion?', p. 561. The United Irishmen were an Irish parliamentary reform society on the 1780s who became a revolutionary republican group in the 1790s. Under its leader, Wolfe Tone, they mounted the Irish rebellion of 1798 to gain independence from Britain.

6 Census Act 1800 (41 Geo. III c.15). The 1801 census estimated the population of England as 8.3 million, Wales 0.54 million and Scotland 1.6 million, totalling 10.5 million for Great Britain. This figure excluded naval and merchant seamen and marines, soldiers and militia, and convicts, who totalled 0.47 million. There was no census in Ireland until 1821. Anderson estimates the population of Ireland as 5–5.2 million, following K. H. Connell, *The Population of Ireland* (Oxford, 1950). Anderson estimated England 8.7 million, Scotland 1.6 million and Wales 0.6 million in 1800, giving Great Britain a population of 10.9 million. M. Anderson, 'Population Change in North-Western Europe,1750–1850', in M. Anderson, ed., *British Population History from the Black Death to the Present Day* (Cambridge, 1996), pp. 120, 211.

7 Rodger, 'Mutiny or Subversion?', p. 558. See Chapter 9, MacDougall, 'The East Coast Mutinies: May–June 1797' and Doorne, Chapter 11, 'A Floating Republic? Conspiracy Theory and the Nore Mutiny of 1797'.

Countering the interpretation of alien Quota men inspiring the mutiny, Rodger contends crucially that 'Professional seamen like the delegates of the fleet at Spithead were the heirs of an ancient tradition which owed nothing to outside tutelage'. It is a debate to which Doorne, Chapter 11, also gives attention. In Chapter 2 Coats indicates that merchant seamen were historically engaged, through their articles, in shipboard management, so the majority of trained seamen were accustomed to collective organisation. In 1999 Cheryl Fury had confirmed Elizabethan traditions which stressed continuity of experience, a clear hierarchy of skills and high rates of literacy amongst merchant officers and seamen.[8] Rodger concludes that the events 'have to be understood in their own terms'.[9] An emphasis on seamen and events in their own terms drives *The Naval Mutinies of 1797*.

Rodger also touches on the economic and political perspectives deriving from recruitment via impressment, whereby a large proportion of naval seamen had originally been merchant seamen. The writings of Captain Philip Patton are cited to show that if seamen had remained in the wartime merchant navy they would have been earning four times as much as they did in the Royal Navy. The navy had increased from 16,600 men in 1793 to 123,000 in 1797 to address increased naval requirements, deaths, disease and desertion. Professor Baugh makes the shocking point that between 1793 and 1813 around one hundred thousand naval personnel died: 6.3 per cent by enemy action, 12.2 per cent by shipwreck or other disasters, but 81.5 per cent by disease or accident.[10] While some 31,000 Quota men had been recruited 1795–97, the majority of this increased navy were volunteers who were already trained seamen, such as Valentine Joyce, or impressed merchant seamen.[11] This influx provided a powerful motivation for peace, as these impressed (or impressed men subsequently entered as volunteers) believed peace would mean a return to higher wages.[12]

The editors of this volume seek to refine the analysis of 'mutiny'. Bell and Elleman, in *Naval Mutinies of the Twentieth Century: An International Perspective* (2003), provide an excellent discussion, comparing British and American usage of mutiny. In their view 'academic historians' have taken less interest than 'popular' writers, whose concerns have been 'simplistic and romanticized'. Their analysis of international and chronological definitions leads to a spectrum of mutinies, from Hannay's '"so-called mutinies" that were "in fact simply strikes" and cases "of mutiny pure and simple, when men broke loose from all discipline and seized, or tried to seize, a ship"'. They address the emotive aspects of mutiny and focus on multiple-ship mutinies

---

8   Cheryl Fury, 'Training and Education in the Elizabethan Maritime Community, 1585–1603', *Mariner's Mirror*, 85, 2 (May 1999), pp. 148–9, 151, 154. She has also written *Tides in the Affairs of Men: The Social History of Elizabethan Seamen, 1580–1603* (Connecticut, 2002).

9   Rodger 'Mutiny or Subversion?', pp. 563–4.

10 D. Baugh, 'The Eighteenth Century Navy as a National Institution' in J. R. Hill, ed., *The Oxford Illustrated History of the Royal Navy* (Oxford, 1995), pp. 138–40.

11 Rodger 'Mutiny or Subversion?', pp. 559.

12 Paradoxically their peacetime wages would be lower than in wartime, due to a larger supply of seamen.

rather than single-ship mutinies, which 'tend to stem from simple and obvious causes and offer fewer lessons'. Their aim is to 'identify the dynamics at work in their outbreak, development, and resolution'.[13] Rodger compliments their volume as 'a pioneering effort to impose intellectual rigour on a subject which is important both for social and political history'.[14]

Hattendorf declares that before Bell and Elleman, 'mutiny has rarely been subjected to scholarly analysis of any kind', both comparative and internationally over time. He raises the imprecision of the word itself, praising them for 'establish[ing] clearly the distinct shades of meaning involved in the term'. Their 'study of this extreme form of naval protest' is certainly relevant to the events of the 1790s examined here. Hattendorf focuses on leadership, both at the top and throughout the chain of command, which reflects contextual social attitudes. He highlights seamen's dual military/civilian occupational traditions and emphasises that mutiny is regarded as a 'failure in the necessary reciprocal relationship between officers and men'.[15] These are underlying themes of this volume.

Geoffrey Till, editor of the Cass Naval Policy and History Series which published *Naval Mutinies of the Twentieth Century*, warns against generalisation: 'Mutinies have such a wide variety of causes and aspirations that it is dangerous and usually simplistic to seek general causes, but there are certainly common elements.' Ambiguously, despite a reference to egalitarianism, Till considers that the officers 'presumably knew rather more about what was actually going on and [their] views therefore had greater authority'.[16] The Spithead mutiny demonstrated, however, that most officers did not know it would happen and lost some degree of power for its duration.

In many mutinies, as demonstrated by both Gutteridge in a general history of naval mutinies and Bell and Elleman in their more defined period, a replication of authority's failure to enter into a dialogue is frequently witnessed. In 1931, to take one example, the British Royal Navy saw a further mass refusal of members of the lower deck to obey their officers, affecting the Home Fleet anchored in the Cromarty Firth near Invergordon. Those on board had lost faith in the established grievance procedure. Admiral Sir John Kelly's inquiry into the cause of that mutiny considered that 'a request put in today may be investigated and answered in two years['] time is obviously an anachronism' and one that needed to be removed.[17]

---

13 Bell and Elleman, *Naval Mutinies*, pp. 1–6. For the Royal Navy in the 1790s the relevant text is the Articles of War. See D. Baugh, 'The Eighteenth Century Navy as a National Institution' in J. R. Hill, ed., *The Oxford Illustrated History of the Royal Navy* (Oxford, 1995); N. A. M. Rodger, *Articles of War* (Hampshire, 1982); D. Hannay, *Naval Courts Martial* (Cambridge, 1914), pp. 111–4.

14 N. A. M. Rodger, Review: C. Bell and B. Elleman, eds, *Naval Mutinies of the Twentieth Century: An International Perspective*, in *Journal of Military History*, 68, 1 (January 2004), pp. 297–8.

15 Hattendorf, Foreword, Bell and Elleman, eds, *Naval Mutinies*, pp. xiii–xvi.

16 G. Till, Series Editor's Preface, Bell and Elleman, eds, *Naval Mutinies*, p. xviii.

17 L. F. Gutteridge, *Mutiny: A History of Naval Insurrection* (Naval Institute Press, Annapolis, 1992); Bell, 'Invergordon Mutiny, 1931', in Bell and Elleman, eds, *Naval Mutinies*, p. 184, citing J. Kelly's 'State of Discipline in the Atlantic Fleet', 9 November,

While it was outside the scope of Bell and Elleman's book to make connections with 1797, Invergordon and Spithead shared many characteristics. Both involved the majority of the fleet, a pay dispute as the cause, the government in a weak financial position facing external problems and internal threats, failure by the Admiralty to recognise their seriousness, their leadership by senior ratings, government use of surveillance agents, detailed coverage by the press, wide-ranging enlistment bringing in non-traditional recruits and the men's fear, and their belief that their actions were justified.

Bell's chapter on Invergordon dismisses a claim that it was caused by 'social tensions which were threatening to erupt into class warfare' as 'exaggerated'. Rodger echoes his assessment: that its 'importance ... has been over-estimated' and it was 'essentially [a] minor incident ... which cannot bear the weight of interpretation which has been piled on [it]'.[18] However, Lionel Yexley's warnings about lower-deck unrest and systemic class issues are documented from 1907.[19] Bell alludes to the surprise of both Admiralty and officers as proof of a lack of communication between the ranks, and the failure of grievance procedures to satisfy the men, as at Spithead. He concludes that Invergordon was a 'spontaneous reaction to drastic pay cuts that threatened the well-being of senior ratings and their families'. Similarly, in 1797 unequal pay rates between naval seamen, officers and other armed forces had not been addressed. Whereas Bell cites few lower-deck words, relying almost entirely on Admiralty and officer comments, *The Naval Mutinies of 1797* aims to balance lower-deck and officers' words.[20]

In 2004 Rodger's foreword and bibliography in *Command of the Ocean* generously acknowledged the conclusions of six draft chapters of this volume, particularly on the impact of Irish and Quota men. He notes that a survey of 4,474 men on Plymouth-commissioned ships in 1804 and 1805 showed that 29 per cent were Irish. He also considers the effect of single-ship mutinies upon the 1797 mutinies, particularly *Culloden* in 1794, when the Admiralty revoked what was believed to be Captain Pakenham's word that there would be clemency; and *Hermione* in 1797, caused by 'inconsistent and irrational brutality'. He emphasised the seamen's collective and personal loyalty to officers. Crucially he distinguished between the officers' immediate feelings of uncertainty and the long-term effects of the mutinies. He characterised mutiny leaders invariably as 'petty officers or long-serving leading hands, the natural aristocracy of the lower deck'.[21] Chapters in *The Naval Mutinies of 1797* investigate the interactions and their consequences for officers and men.

David Hannay doubted in 1891 whether the 1797 mutinies 'have ever received

---

1931, TNA ADM178/111.

18 Bell, 'Invergordon Mutiny, 1931', in Bell and Elleman, eds, *Naval Mutinies*, p. 170, citing A. Ereira, *The Invergordon Mutiny* (London, 1981). Rodger, Review: Bell and Elleman, eds, *Naval Mutinies*, p. 298.

19 L. Yexley *Our Fighting Seamen* (London, 1911); Royal Naval Museum Portsmouth, Lionel Yexley Papers, 2007, p. 49.

20 C. Bell, 'Invergordon Mutiny, 1931', pp. 170–92. D. Divine, *Mutiny at Invergordon* (London, 1970), pp. 47–8, 77, 120, 196, 203, 208.

21 Rodger, *Command*, pp. 444–53, 723–4, 794, 801.

the attention which they deserve'. He observed that the 'general historian is too busy to look into their causes and consequences. To naval writers they have not been an agreeable subject. Contemporary officers avoided talking of them'. He judged them 'worthy of attention … because they supply within manageable limits, and in singular perfection of development, the history of the rise, the explosion, the degradation, and the end of a sedition'.[22] With some naval historians reluctant to examine mutiny because it was shameful to officers, an essential element of shipboard life and organisation, ultimately affecting naval command and administration, risks remaining opaque.[23] Reflecting hierarchy and the weight of documentation, historians tend to focus on officers rather than men, although there are notable exceptions.[24] How disposed are historians to address mutiny in the twenty-first century? Till recognises that 'in our more egalitarian times, lower-deck attitudes have become an object of academic study'. The experience of other ranks 'provides another angle' and 'round[s] out our concept of naval history.'[25] An admittedly unsystematic but representative survey of the biographies of serving naval officers of the 1790s in the *Oxford Dictionary of Biography* is revealing. Mutiny is not mentioned in the case of some officers who were involved in or wrote about mutiny: Edward Brenton, Robert Calder, Sir Thomas Bladen Capel, Sir Roger Curtis, William Hotham, Sir Samuel Hood, Cuthbert Collingwood, Sir Philip Durham or Edward Pellew. Sir Alan Gardner is reported as second-in-command of the Channel Fleet, but there is no discussion of his role in the negotiations. There is an account of the mutinies' effect upon Adam Duncan's strategy at the Texel in 1797; of Sir William Hargood being put ashore on the Isle of Wight during the mutiny but *Leopard* being regained by its officers; also that Sir Richard Goodwin Keats and Sir Israel Pellew were put ashore at Plymouth and that Sir John Duckworth was ousted from his ship. Sir Richard Onslow is confirmed as assisting Duncan by quelling mutiny on *Nassau* and *Adamant*, while Sir John Orde subdued mutiny in Plymouth and presided over the Nore courts martial at Portsmouth.

However, there is a detailed description of Sir Nesbit Willoughby's behaviour which led to mutiny on *Otter* in 1808 and Robert Corbet's leadership of *Nereide* which instigated mutiny in 1809.[26] The role of Alexander Hood, Viscount Bridport, as commander of the Channel Fleet is treated at length. It is noted that he 'consistently took the part of the mutineers' and the delegates were grateful for his '"open and generous manner"' and his '"humanity"'. Richard, Earl Howe, has a section devoted to the Spithead

---

22   D. Hannay, 'The Mutinies of 1797', *The Saturday Review* (June 6, 1891), p. 677.

23   Alan Pearsall, personal information, 1997. Alan (1925–2006) was an historian at the NMM for thirty years and a generous mentor to researchers until his death. Roger Knight, 'Obituary, Alan Pearsall', *Mariner's Mirror*, 92, 3 (2006), pp. 260–1. Also see TNA, ADM178/133, 'Mutiny in the Royal Navy', II, chapter 13.

24   See J. D. Davies, *Gentlemen and Tarpaulin: The Officers and Men of the Restoration Navy* (Oxford, 1991); B. Capp, *Cromwell's Navy: The Fleet and the English Revolution* (Oxford, 1992).

25   Till, Series Editor's Preface, Bell and Elleman, eds, *Naval Mutinies*, p. xviii.

26   See Neale, Chapter 16, 'The Influence of 1797 upon the *Nereide* Mutiny of 1809'.

mutiny, acknowledging his belated recognition of the initial petitions and his unhelpful speech in Parliament, and the fleet's welcome when he brought the King's pardon. John Jervis, Earl St Vincent, is described as 'suppress[ing] every manifestation of mutiny with unbending severity', keeping the fleet active off Cadiz and court-martialling mutineers promptly in 1797 and 1798. Sir John Colpoys's order to his officers on 7 May to fire on his crew, causing three deaths on *London*, is reported; also that he took responsibility for these events. Sir Thomas Pakenham's involvement in *Culloden*'s mutiny is recorded and his report of the men's dissatisfaction to Spencer in December 1796. Philip Patton's entry refers to a mutiny on board his ship *Prince George* in 1779 and an extended section on his *Observations on Naval Mutiny*, sent to Spencer, Pitt, Dundas and Wilberforce in 1795. He highlighted the likelihood of a general naval mutiny and preventive measures, focusing on the improvement of pay and conditions of senior ratings and warrant officers. This was ignored, but when the Spithead mutiny broke out he presented Spencer with another copy. With severe constraints on word limits, authors dealt with mutiny if it had a major impact upon the officer's career or if it defined their lives, particularly in the case of Richard Parker and Valentine Joyce, but not as an aspect of leadership.[27]

From the same pool of historians only the editors and four of the fourteen writers in *The Contemporaries of Nelson* tackled mutiny. Its editors comment on the consequence of the 1797 mutinies upon fleet effectiveness and as a shock to individual officers. Lambert, writing about William, Lord Hotham, reported that he 'gave way' to 'collective action by the lower deck' of *Windsor Castle* but exerted physical force to put down a later mutiny on *Terrible*. Lambert indicates that Hotham was more sensitive to lower-deck feelings than First Lord of the Admiralty Earl Spencer, but does not discuss seamen's collective memory of how these mutinies were put down.[28] Davies devotes a complete section to Admiral Duncan's handling of the Yarmouth mutiny, describing his initial successful attempts to quell it and his sympathy for their cause. Duncan was unable to overcome its second outbreak, despite his personal popularity, so his Texel blockade was handicapped severely by having only two ships of the line.[29] Rae's biography of Sir Edward Pellew refers to a subsequent mutiny at Berehaven on *Impétueux* in 1799, attributed to 'disaffected Irishmen'. Pellew seized the initiative and the ringleaders, and was praised by St Vincent for preventing a larger fleet mutiny in Bantry Bay.[30] Colin White refers to Sir Richard Goodwin Keats being turned out of *Galatea* during the mutiny, and that Keats wrote about it as '"an event which he looks back to with the deepest concern"', originally drafted as '"horror"'.[31] These

27 All the above are articles from the *Oxford Dictionary of Biography* (Oxford, 2004). NMM, WYN/109/7/14. Philip Patton, 'Observations on Naval Mutiny Presented April 1795'.
28 Peter Le Fevre and Richard Harding, eds, *British Admirals of the Napoleonic Wars: The Contemporaries of Nelson* (Chatham, London, 2005), pp. 10, 30–1.
29 Ibid., pp. 54–5.
30 Ibid., p. 284.
31 Ibid., p. 352.

writers do treat mutiny as a facet of leadership. David Syrett's 2006 biography of Howe uncritically described his actions regarding the initial Spithead petitions while increasingly debilitated by gout and seeking retirement. Having finally retired on 10 April 1797, Howe's 'last service to the Royal Navy' Syrett celebrates: to achieve reconciliation and 'convince mutinous seamen to return to duty' (as in the 1783 mutinies following the American War), dependent on his reputation as 'an even-handed disciplinarian'.[32]

The editors of *The Naval Mutinies of 1797* agree with Rodger that there remains considerable room for further research. In particular, greater use of muster books will provide a more subtle understanding of those who led the mutinies or crewed particular vessels which espoused, resisted or drove mutiny forward. More material is undoubtedly waiting to be uncovered in muster books and correspondence, shown by recent articles in *The Mariner's Mirror*. Anthony Brown searched the muster books for proof of the influence of Quota men, Irish and radicals at the Nore. He confirmed that Irish and Quota men were not disproportionate among the leaders. He also suggested Americans as possible radical instigators. Brown offers a new interpretation of 'poor communication between the fleets' and a desperate intransigent leadership.[33] This is considered unlikely by MacDougall, who suggests that charismatic leader McCarthy would not have persisted without being confident of further action by the Channel Fleet.[34]

Ann Hawkins and Helen Watt have produced a detailed account of the actions of one particular crew on *Inspector*. They base their article on hitherto unused captain's letters held in Admiralty files at the National Archive (Kew). Although it is known that such letters are likely to exist, the two researchers demonstrate the value of continuing to comb these and other collections in search of further contemporary letters and reports. Their evidence also corroborates evidence from Spithead muster books that active mutineers were long-serving skilled seamen, so their 'manner of joining the navy was not an issue'.[35]

In tandem with the need to undertake further research, there is a need to consider theories of mutiny, as 'convincing theoretical structures' are lacking among naval historians, according to Rodger.[36] This is an aim of this volume. It is this lack of methodology that has led to confused and often contradictory conclusions proposed by some historians of the mutinies of 1797. Leonard Smith, in 1994, felt that the way forward was through 'a methodology that could connect the microcosmic and macrocosmic features of the problem'.[37]

---

32 D. Syrett, *Admiral Lord Howe* (Spellmount, Stroud, 2006), pp. 150–1, 159.

33 Anthony Brown, 'The Nore Mutiny – Sedition or Ships' Biscuits? A Reappraisal', *Mariner's Mirror*, 92, 1 (February 2006), pp. 60–74.

34 Philip MacDougall, 'The Nore Mutiny, Correspondence', *Mariner's Mirror*, 93, 1 (February 2007), pp. 96–8.

35 Ann Hawkins and Helen Watt, '"Now is our time, the ship is our own, huzza for the red flag": Mutiny on the *Inspector*, 1797', *Mariner's Mirror*, 93, 2 (May 2007), pp. 156–79.

36 Rodger 'Considerations', p. 119.

37 Leonard V. Smith, Review of Leonard F. Gutteridge, *Mutiny* in *Journal of Military History*, 58:3 (July 1994), p. 523. Quoted in Bell and Elleman, eds, *Naval Mutinies*, p. 1.

Bell and Elleman, considering a broad range of twentieth-century naval ship and fleet mutinies, have devised a typology. At one end of the spectrum are those mutinies that have sought only to improve service conditions while at the other are those that were overtly political from the outset and sought far-reaching government changes, following the conventional strike versus politics analysis.[38] Such a developed typology, drawn from an examination of all types of mutinies from all types of navies, will lead to a clearer understanding of the dynamics of a warship operating in isolation or in a fleet situation. Bell and Elleman demonstrate the tendency for demands to escalate when an initial marginalisation of defined leadership allows 'the more politically minded sailors to fill the void'. This is especially apposite when applied to the Nore and Spithead mutinies and the controversy surrounding levels of outside political influence that may or may not have existed. Bell and Elleman add that some mutiny leaders, lacking confidence in a favourable settlement, subsequently determine upon the 'the overthrow of the government' as possibly their 'only way to avoid punishment'.[39] They also note that mutinies rarely occur during wartime, but when it happens the men usually stress their loyalty.[40] In fact, the number of courts martial arising from mutiny was much higher in 1796–98 than before 1796 or after 1798 during the period of French wars (1793–1801, 1803–15); but loyalty and willingness to go to sea if the enemy appeared was emphasised constantly throughout the Spithead mutiny. Bell and Elleman also characterise authoritarian regimes, seeing them as a systemic threat, as being more likely to experience mutinies than democratic ones.[41]

The academic process of considering a range of mutinies over a wide historical period may also reveal other useful analytical comparisons. Fundamental to twentieth-century mutinies, and clearly apparent in 1797, is the response by the authorities to the grievances expressed from the lower deck. As Coats points out in Chapter 1, 'Spithead Mutiny: Introduction', those in authority did not act upon petitions from the lower deck ; instead 'they had merely ignored the warning voices because it had not suited their interests to do so'. This is also examined in detail by Orth in Chapter 5, 'Voices from the Lower Deck'.

Relevant to Neale's Chapter 16, David Featherstone has analysed the court martial of *Grampus*, involved in the Nore mutiny, to establish 'assertive subaltern political identities'. In a similar fashion to Neale's analysis of Captain Corbet's court martial, he characterises court martial testimonies as sailors' attempts to 'recover their often hidden and marginalised forms of identity and agency'. He emphasises that 'knowledge was mobilised' by seamen from 'power-laden routes and connections that were central to emerging forms of maritime governance and administration in the late-eighteenth century'.[42]

---

38   Bell and Elleman, 'Naval Mutinies in the Twentieth Century', in Bell and Elleman, eds, *Naval Mutinies*, p. 266.

39   Ibid., p. 270.

40   Ibid., pp. 267–8.

41   Ibid., pp. 270–5.

42   D. Featherstone, 'Counter-Insurgency, Subalternity and Spatial Relations: Interrogating Court-Martial Narratives of the Nore Mutiny of 1797', *South African Historical Journal*, 61, 4 (December 2009), pp. 766, 768, 770, 775.

Featherstone highlights the disputed accounts possible within the court martial context which did not always produce 'docile, repentant roles', but continued contestation.[43] He stresses the seamen's 'particular understandings of
justice, just conduct and common ways of constructing grievances', and their
dislike of officers' '"arbitrary power"' which feature in Chapters 1, 2, 5, 12, 15
and 16. He also examines the influence of the Corresponding Societies upon
the political organisation of the mutineers.[44]

The editors propose a typology applicable to any mutiny from the sixteenth
to the twentieth centuries. Context is always relevant: conditions in the six-
teenth-century navy were vastly different from the nineteenth, so concepts of
what is normal, reasonable and acceptable change over time.

Typology

- Mutiny is a state-derived term for both a seamen's strike and a
  political act.

- A mutiny can be a political act, a labour dispute or both.

- Mutiny has more serious ramifications in a large permanent state-run
  navy.

- Within a state-funded navy, mutiny invariably becomes a political issue.

- Seamen, when part of the military state, are not allowed to withdraw
  their labour as they are inevitably committing an act of rebellion.

- Mutinies are led by experienced senior ratings whom men trust.

The degree of state concern varies according to whether:

- its stability is threatened;

- it is financially straitened;

- it is at war/under threat of invasion;

- it fears losing ships to the enemy;

- it fears political revolution;

- it fears its seamen will join other navies;

- the mutiny becomes a public issue.

Causes

- Failed logistics.

- Imbalance of discipline.

- Incompetent leadership.

- Pay arrears/actual or effective pay cut.

---

43 Featherstone, 'Counter-Insurgency', pp. 772–3, 784.
44 Ibid., pp. 774–6, 778–80. This is also discussed in Doorne, Chapter 11.

- Unfair distribution of prize money.
- Poor/dangerous ship seaworthiness.
- Unreasonable cruelty goes unpunished.
- Unacceptable food.
- Abnormal disrespect shown to the men.

Perpetuation of mutiny
- Initial prevarication by the authorities leads to further demands.
- Discipline is undermined in the short- and long-term, although resolution of the issues can be redemptive.

There is a major distinction between single-ship and fleet mutinies. Lessons learnt by British seamen during single-ship and fleet mutinies in the 1780s and 1790s had taught the fleets to act collectively. Lessons learnt during the 1797 Spithead mutiny honed seamen's organisational skills and encouraged them to raise their demands. Single-ship mutinies, especially those of *Bounty* (April 1789), *Windsor Castle* in Corsica (November 1794), *Culloden* at Spithead (December 1794), *Terrible* in St Fiorenza Bay, Corsica (September 1795) and *Hermione* (1797), reinforced the message that punitive measures were inflicted on seamen with grievances on individual ships.[45] For this reason the editors disagree with Bell and Elleman that single-ship mutinies 'offer fewer lessons about why mutinies occur or, just as important, why they sometimes spread'.[46] The mutinies of 1783 occurred when ships returning from the American War wished to be paid off quickly in their home ports so the seamen could resume their merchant occupations. They had taught the seamen a lesson 'in the power of concerted resistance to authority on a large scale as a means of having grievances put right'.[47] They also demonstrated that collective memory was a powerful motivation for the Spithead mutiny. Howe, with the benefit of hindsight, came to the same conclusion:

> The occurrences in 1783, when I was first put at the head of the Admiralty, and when the same steps were taken by several ships' companies to emancipate themselves from the control of their officers, excited my fears and expectations that the experiment would be renewed before the remembrance of the effect had ceased.[48]

45 J. McArthur, *Principles and Practice of Naval and Military Courts-Martial*, II (London, 1813), pp. 440–1 for *Bounty*'s inquiry and court-martial, 1790 and 1792; Laird Clowes, *Royal Navy*, IV, pp. 167–8, 240–1, 246–7, 269–74; TNA, ADM178/133, Cdr J. H. Owen, 'Mutiny in the Royal Navy 1691–1919' (Admiralty, 1933), pp. 45–50; ADM2/607, September–November 1794; ADM2/608, November 1794–January 1795; ADM2/1117, 1789–February 1797; ADM51/1130, *Culloden* November 1794–November 1795; ADM106/1866, 1790–94; ADM106/1867, 1795–96.
46 Bell and Elleman, eds, *Naval Mutinies*, p. 3.
47 TNA, ADM178/133, 'Mutiny in the Royal Navy', I, p. 45.
48 16 August 1797. J. Barrow, *Life of Earl Howe* (London, 1838), pp. 247–8.

A recent book which examines the 1797 naval mutinies within the social and moral context of the late eighteenth century is Richard Blake's *Evangelicals in the Royal Navy, 1775–1815*. Blake examines the influence wielded by 'Blue Lights', a group of naval evangelicals who complied individually with *Regulations and Instructions for His Majesty's Service at Sea* (1731 and subsequent editions) and their influence upon naval discipline reforms after 1800, following the mutinies. In his analysis of the mutinies Blake contends that the Blue Lights promoted religion to 'elevate the self-respect of the lower deck'.[49] However, it could be argued that the mutinies had already articulated the seamen's self-respect.

Blake claims undeniable 'religious elements in the mutinies, even though not specifically evangelical. It is noteworthy that the Spithead mutineers used an oath to bind loyalty'.[50] As this volume's Spithead chapters demonstrate, the mutineers expressed themselves in god-fearing language and used oaths because that reflected their culture. Blake equates naval officer piety with reform and a high rate of worship with good leadership, citing eighty ships as supporting 'praying groups'.[51] Adam Duncan is named as an exemplar, his flagship *Venerable* performing worship thirty-one times in an eighteen-month period including the North Sea mutiny. He also sent a memorandum to the Admiralty calling for more fresh food, more regular pay, fairer distribution of prize money, the end of impressment, less physical punishment and more leave, with better pay for petty officers. He was initially successful in dealing with the mutiny, through good relations with his men, and he obtained pardons for his men after the mutiny. Blake quotes Duncan as regarding the mutinies as a 'chastisement ... for a warning to mend our ways'.[52]

Blake also cites the Nore leader Richard Parker as an exemplar of religious expression before his hanging, but this derived from his early education.[53] While Blake contends that the sermons of 'cultivated, educated' clergy 'might well be incomprehensible to the bulk of his hearers', Valentine Joyce, Spithead spokesman, was not unique on the lower deck in being able to write and speak fluently due to a nonconformist upbringing.

In reporting that the officers knew nothing about the Spithead mutiny Blake notes that Captain Philip Patton 'reported to the Admiralty that something was afoot, but neither he nor they had any idea of the true seriousness'.[54] On the contrary, Philip Patton had given Earl Spencer a detailed report on how to improve the allegiance of leading ratings in 1795 but had been ignored.[55] A

49   Richard Blake, *Evangelicals in the Royal Navy 1775–1815: Blue Lights and Psalm Singers* (Woodbridge, 2008), pp. 87–9, 93–5.

50   Ibid., pp. 94.

51   Ibid., pp. 2, 34, 72–4, 103–4, 134–7.

52   Ibid., p. 137, citing Duncan to Nepean, 23 May 1797, from R. A. P. H. Camperdown, *Admiral Duncan* (London, 1898), p. 122.

53   Ibid., 94; J. K. Laughton, rev. Ann Coats, 'Parker, Richard', *ODNB* (Oxford, 2004).

54   Blake, *Evangelicals in the Royal Navy*, p. 91, p. 103; Ann Coats, 'Joyce, Valentine', *ODNB* (2004) www.oxforddnb.com.

55   NMM, WYN/109/7/14, Philip Patton, 'Observations on Naval Mutiny Presented April 1795'. Blake may be referring to Charles Patton, Philip's brother, who reported the impending mutiny on 13 April 1797.

group of officers had also recommended a pay increase in 1796 but had been rebuffed by Spencer. Blake speculates that communication between ships could have been spread by a 'Christian underworld' of Methodist prayer groups, overlooking the fact that official messages were carried from ship to ship and stores were taken onboard frequently in harbour and during blockade, creating many opportunities for seamen to pass messages.[56] Trusted seamen were also sent ashore on errands.

Blake concludes that the Blue Lights promoted humane reforms and less harsh penalties, asserting that captains such as Duncan and Sir Charles Penrose 'listened to the grievances of the lower deck and advocated changes which – if implemented sooner – might have stopped the mutinies from happening'.[57] The Admiralty certainly implemented reforms at the beginning of the nineteenth century. On 28 April 1806 an Admiralty Order abolished running the gauntlet and pay was further increased.[58] In 1808 First Lord of the Admiralty Lord Barham (Charles Middleton, an evangelical) issued printed orders that men were not to be treated 'with cruelty or oppression' by inferior officers and punishments could only be ordered by the captain. On 15 June 1808 a proclamation allocated prize money more fairly, giving half rather than a quarter to the ship's company.[59] Starting with a rope's end was forbidden by the Admiralty in 1809 (although it persisted after then), perhaps in reaction to the mutinies on *Otter* and *Nereide* analysed here by Neale in Chapter 16. Punishment returns were instituted in 1811.[60] In November 1814 an Act of Parliament awarded pensions for long service 'to Seamen not disabled' (previously only disabled seamen had received pensions) and in 1815 cessation of the war effectively ended impressment. More humane attitudes gradually permeated forms of discipline, but more research is needed to investigate incidents of starting and to link decreased punishments to the 1797 mutinies.

In contrast to Blake's clear and relevant use of the 1797 mutinies as a tool for assisting his analysis of the impact of religious piety on the navy of this period, is the failure by John D. Byrn to acknowledge them where they would seem to have unquestioned relevance. *Naval Courts Martial, 1793–1815* is a recently published collection of transcribed naval courts martial papers drawn from the National Archive.[61] Given the uncompromising nature of the title, it is difficult to understand such an omission. Admittedly Byrn is concerned primarily with the complexities of 'military jurisprudence in the late eighteenth and early nineteenth centuries' and chose examples that best met that particular objective. But it seems perverse that the Nore mutiny, a rare example of mass action which resulted in a series of courts martial, did not merit

---

56 Blake, *Evangelicals in the Royal Navy*, pp. 93–4.

57 Ibid., pp. 34, 95, 131–3, 153–5, 165–70, 180–1. See Michael Lewis, *The Navy in Transition, 1814–1864: A Social History* (London, 1965), pp. 122–3.

58 Rodger, *Command*, pp. 492–3.

59 In May 1797 magistrate Aaron Graham had called for a more 'reasonable Distribution of Prize Money', BL, Add. MS. 37,877, Windham Papers, vol. XXXVI, folios 72–73v, May 1797; R. Hill, *The Prizes of War* (Royal Naval Museum/Sutton, Stroud, 1998), pp. 201–5.

60 Rodger, *Command*, pp. 492–3.

61 John D. Byrn, ed., *Naval Courts Martial 1793–1815* (NRS vol. 155, London, 2009).

the inclusion of a few sample trials. The choice of those brought before the courts clearly shows that procedures were different from the sample courts martial that Byrn draws upon. Instead of selecting all those deemed to have infringed the Articles of War, those court-martialled for their actions at the Nore were, as MacDougall points out, 'the ten most guilty' on board each vessel.[62] Presumably, in an attempt to mitigate this inherent unfairness, for the guilt of the first man on board one ship might well have not even achieved tenth status on board another ship, the majority of those tried were pardoned. In fact, of four hundred men detained for punishment, only twenty-nine were hanged, a further twenty-nine imprisoned, with nine flogged. Following the trial of those on board *Defence* in 1798, a further significant court martial ignored by Byrn, some nineteen seamen were executed for mutiny. If this same approach had been applied to the crews of the leading ships at the Nore, then the number of executions would have approached a three-figure number. Such idiosyncrasies of legal theory and practice should surely have featured in a book written from the premise that such a study can 'contribute to our understanding of military jurisprudence in the late eighteenth and early nineteenth centuries' while also furthering 'our knowledge of Georgian and Regency criminal law in general'.[63]

The mutiny at Spithead was simply the largest naval mutiny within the merchant or royal navies in history. The event was not unusual, its extent was. The seamen had tried traditional methods to pursue their grievances, with no response from the authorities. Mutiny was their last resort.[64] It was followed by subsequent outbreaks of the initial mutiny, defined by the particular circumstances of each respective fleet and location. *The Naval Mutinies of 1797* is an intensive examination of the extraordinary events at Spithead and the Nore, followed by an examination of their effects on individual ships, and an evaluation of underlying continuities of leadership styles, officers' and men's attitudes to punishment and the loyalty of the men to their ships and officers. The notion examined in Chapter 6, that the level of punishment tended to diminish with the length of a commission and was a facet of paternalism, is speculative and may not have been typical. *The Naval Mutinies of 1797* transmits human stories, drama and humanity. Many officers were loved by the men and many officers were sympathetic to their cause.[65] As well as the personal, political ramifications are also considered.

The leaders of the mutinies were not Quota men, but long-serving able seamen and senior ratings.[66] This was the class of seamen whose pay Admiral Patton had advised First Lord of the Admiralty Earl Spencer in 1795 should

---

62 See Chapter 9, MacDougall, 'The East Coast Mutinies: May–June 1797'.
63 Byrn, *Naval Courts Martial*, p. xvii.
64 TNA, ADM178/133, 'Mutiny in the Royal Navy, I, 1691–1919', p. 3, *passim*; P. Burke, *Celebrated Naval and Military Trials* (London, 1866); Rodger, *Safeguard of the Sea*, pp. 401–3; Capp, *Cromwell's Navy*, pp. 25, 228–9, 248–9, 274; J. Hattendorf, *British Naval Documents 1204–1960* (London, 1993), pp. 131, 281–2; N. A. M. Rodger, 'Jolly Tars Were Our Men?' in *Mutiny on the Bounty 1789–1989* (Greenwich, 1989), pp. 16–7.
65 See Coats, Chapter 2 and Orth, Chapter 5.
66 TNA, Muster books; Manwaring and Dobrée, *Floating Republic*, pp. 262–3.

be increased by a third to ensure that 'the best seamen in every Ship will be attached to the Service of their Country, and those very men who now excite mutiny will be most ready to repress it'.[67] His view was that 'Seamen cannot be supplied from the body of any Nation, being of a profession of difficult, and tedious acquirement'.[68] Further research is needed into county returns and returns from the Port Act of 1795.[69] Similarly, Irish, French or American republican control of, or significant influence upon, the mutinies have not been proven from the sources. Oaths were perceived by the authorities as dangerous symptoms of rebellion or republicanism and legislation was passed swiftly, forbidding them.[70]

Evidence does suggest that institutional attitudes towards discipline changed gradually but significantly after the naval mutinies of 1797, but more research is needed to collate evidence and if possible, motivations, to link such changes back to the mutinies.

While traditional dichotomous analyses have characterised the 1797 mutinies as strike or political act, benign/malign, 'arrears of pay' or revolutionary movement', *The Naval Mutinies of 1797* focuses on process and new research. It addresses interpretational imbalance by looking at historically assessed sources leading to a new synthesis – self-determination – the seamen on their own terms.

---

67   NMM, WYN/109/7/14, fols 5, 15. Patton made six proposals to increase their benefits and numbers on each ship. See the Earl of Galloway's similar suggestion in 1813, H. Richmond, *Statesmen and Sea Power* (Oxford, 1946), pp. 347–9.
68   NMM, WYN/109/7/14, fol. 2.
69   Rodger, 'Mutiny or Subversion?' p. 560, fns 56–8, names counties whose returns have been analysed or considered in published research (Essex, Kent, Lancashire, Leicestershire, Lincolnshire, London, Northumberland, Nottinghamshire, Sussex, North Riding of Yorkshire) and cites TNA, ADM7/361–2 and ADM30/63/8 as sources for Essex, London and the Isle of Wight returns which have not been studied. The Port Quota Act 1795 (35 Geo III c.9).
70   Unlawful Oaths Act 1797, 37 Geo. III c.123. See Coats, Chapters 2 and 7. It was the Act by which the Tolpuddle labourers were convicted and transported in 1834.

Spithead Mutiny: Introduction

Ann Veronica Coats

In the Month of February the following Petition was Drawn out on board H.M. Ship Queen Charlotte and forwarded to the rest of the Fleet at Spithead and about a Dozen Coppys was sent to Admiral Earl Howe Just at the time the fleet was Ordered to sea and after being out one month and Laying a forthnight at Spithead.[1]

These chapters represent the most recent research into the conditions of naval seamen in 1797 and the causes and consequences of the Spithead mutiny. The Spithead and Nore mutinies of 1797 have been comprehensively investigated by historians, from a variety of ideological perspectives, but textual and contextual dimensions have not been examined exhaustively. The mutinies had such a deep psychological effect on the Royal Navy during the nineteenth century, reinforced in the twentieth century by the 1931 Invergordon mutiny, that they have received wide, although sometimes shame-faced historical coverage in the biographies of officers concerned. However, the sheer scale and subtlety of the events has not yet been portrayed fully. Some conclusions of the following writers at the start of the twenty-first century vary markedly from those of earlier historians, informed by detailed research.

The four most comprehensive works on the mutinies to date are:

- W. J. Neale, *History of the Mutiny at Spithead and the Nore* (Tegg, London, 1842);

- Conrad Gill, *The Naval Mutinies of 1797* (University of Manchester Press, 1913);

- G. E. Manwaring and B. Dobrée, *The Floating Republic* (Geoffrey Bles, London, 1935);

- James Dugan, *The Great Mutiny* (London, 1966).

Their accounts vary in political perspective and emphasis. Neale's work,

1 February and March 1797. TNA, ADM1/5125, April 1797, papers of *Queen Charlotte*.

St. HELEN'S ROAD
SPITHEAD
PORTSMOUTH and LANGSTONE
HARBOURS

despite some inaccuracy and bias against Pitt (pointed out by Gill), and considering his restricted access to Admiralty documents, is an informative, ironic and fluent account of the mutinies. He analysed the political situation quite succinctly:

> But when the surprise of the moment had ceased, and men began to weigh the causes and probable results of this disastrous intelligence, party spirit undertook to interpret the views of the sailors, and to attack or defend the ministers, according to its particular bias.[2]

Neale's reformist principles were expressed in the dedication to Sir Francis Burdett, and his sympathies for the seamen in the introduction. He distinguished the seamen as unanimous, humane, determined and disciplined; believed Quota men were their leaders; and dismissed claims that 'a republican leaven had been secretly introduced by designing and traitorous politicians into the vitals of the navy'.[3] Concisely, he explained the public's

> loss to understand the spirit of determination which seemed all of a sudden to inspire the seamen, and to make them doggedly indifferent either to the honour or the safety of the country, except upon their own terms, and therefore it was generally, though foolishly inferred, that the intrigues of the Jacobins – not the real pressure of real and intolerable wrongs – had knit together this formidable confederacy.[4]

Gill's 1913 work most systematically covered a massive array of documents, for which subsequent researchers are indebted to him, but in my view he

---

2 W. J. Neale, *History of the Mutiny at Spithead and the Nore* (London, 1842), p. 15.
3 Ibid., pp. 15–8, 30–1.
4 Ibid., pp. 23–4. In 1790 'Jacobin' described those who maintained and propagated the principles of extreme democracy and absolute equality. By 1793 in England it was used to identify an extreme radical in politics, and by 1800 any political reformer. *OED*.

Left: 2. Chart of St Helen's Road, Spithead, Portsmouth and Langstone Harbours, surveyed in 1783 by Lieutenant Murdoch Mackenzie Jr. It shows the fathom depths of channels between the sandbanks, denoting the narrow channel to the harbour mouth which protected Portsmouth from attack by enemy ships. The large Spithead Anchorage may be seen clearly. After Admiral Gardner threatened on 21 April 1797 to hang every fifth man in the fleet, the mutineers were concerned that they might be fired upon from the guns of Southsea Castle and Fort Monkton, so moved further east. After the first pardon was read to the fleet on 23 April most ships sailed to St Helen's Road to await a westerly wind but *Marlborough*, *Minotaur*, *Nymphe* and *Ramillies* had unsettled grievances against their officers, so remained at Spithead under the eye of HMS *London*. The *London* incident occurred on 7 May.

wrongly assigned to Quota men a leading role in the mutiny not proven by the sources. Publishing in 1935, Manwaring and Dobrée wrote in the aftermath of the Invergordon mutiny which had many parallels with Spithead. They quote a seaman who compared bureaucratic reactions in 1932 to the 'rumblings of discontent' of 1914 and 1916–17 with those leading to 1797. They also quoted *The Times* in 1934 which criticised the Admiralty for not flying to Invergordon in 1931 for dialogue:

> The situation at Invergordon had many features in common with the naval mutiny of 1797, but in 1797 the Board of Admiralty faced the situation for which they were responsible.[5]

Manwaring and Dobrée were avowedly sympathetic to the aims of the seamen:

> Mr. Gill seems to have had less sympathy with the sailors than we have, and thus we have arrived at conclusions different from him, conclusions which we feel may be of use in approaching certain aspects of our day.

They characterise 'the naval mutiny' as 'alarming', 'dramatic' and 'mysterious', but 'ordered with rigid discipline, a respect for officers, and unswerving loyalty to the King'. By being 'rationally grounded' it significantly not only achieved 'the betterment of the sailor's lot, but also began a new and lasting epoch in naval administration'. They acknowledge the publication of new sources (*Spencer Papers*) unavailable to Gill and the subjectivity of document selection: 'we have used some which [Mr Gill] passed by, and … we have discovered many others which throw an entirely new light on certain incidents and characters.'[6] From their researches in the muster books they established the delegates', and in particular Valentine Joyce's, accurate background, and presented a truer picture of the long-term composition of the Spithead Fleet and its limited revolutionary and Irish input.[7] By naming their book *The Floating Republic*, they encompassed both the mutinies' self-perception and their assessment by the government's Committee of Secrecy.[8] Their appraisal of Neale as 'too emotional' can be applied to their own generic pronouncements that the 'food was disgusting', the drink was 'nauseating' and officers

---

5   G. E. Manwaring and B. Dobrée, *The Floating Republic* (London, 1935), pp. 254–5, 260–1, citing Sidney Knock, *Clear Lower Deck: An Intimate Study of the Men of the Royal Navy* (London, 1932), pp. 148, 14–21; Manwaring and Dobrée 254–5, citing *The Times*, 1 August 1934.

6   Manwaring and Dobrée, *Floating Republic*, Preface, pp. vii–viii, 252, 254. See G. J. Marcus, *The Age of Nelson* (London, 1971), p. 88: 'The mutineers at the Nore, unlike those at Spithead, had no clear objective in view and never put forward any specific demands.' *The Private Papers of George, 2nd Earl Spencer, First Lord of the Admiralty 1794–1801*, 4 volumes, ed. J. S. Corbett and Rear Admiral H. W. Richmond (London, 1913, 1914, 1923, 1924).

7   Manwaring and Dobrée, *Floating Republic*, pp. 101–2, 262–3.

8   Ibid., 'An attempt was made to give to the ships in mutiny the name of "The Floating Republic."' From the Report of the Committee of Secrecy, 1799. Front pages.

tyrannical.[9] Their differentiation between the two mutinies has been responsible for later cruder condemnations.[10]

Dugan, whose sympathy for the seamen was conveyed in his chapter 'The Humble Petition', very usefully integrated the social, cultural and political context from British and French perspectives. However, his text hurtled pell-mell at the reader: a succession of images bereft of citations. He perpetuated, like Gill, the *canard* that Valentine Joyce was a Belfast clubman sent to the fleet to stir up support for the United Irishmen, even though magistrate Aaron Graham's evidence called this assumption into question.[11] He also followed Gill in attributing the instigation of the Spithead mutiny to Quota men: 'the tremendous influence of Paine's ideas was now transmitted by the quota men to the ignorant Jack'.[12] This insulting view of the majority of seamen misrepresented the true significance of the Spithead mutiny: that long-serving seamen, part of the social and political milieu of the 1790s, could successfully organise and execute a collective action.

Two more recent works have devoted specific chapters to examining the Spithead and Nore mutinies from the point of view of United Irish and revolutionary involvement:

- M. Elliott, *Partners in Revolution* (Yale University Press, London, 1982), Chapter 5;

- R. Wells, *Insurrection: The British Experience, 1795–1803* (Gloucester, 1983), Chapter 5.

Elliott argued that Valentine Joyce administered United Irish oaths, but an examination of the oaths sworn at Spithead shows that they differed significantly from United Irish or Defenderist oaths.[13] Wells also accepted that Valentine Joyce had a history of sedition.[14] He conflated evidence from *Pompée*'s court martial in June 1797 with the Spithead mutiny, surmising: 'The involvement of *Mars*, "manned principally by Irishmen", and among the most militant ships at Portsmouth, suggests United Irish participation in these events.'[15] In fact, *Mars* had the lowest number of Irish-born seamen among

---

9   Ibid., Preface, pp. vii, 245.

10 Ibid., pp. 147–8, 153, 158, 169, 248–9, 251–5.

11 James Dugan, *The Great Mutiny* (London, 1966), pp. 63, 162.

12 Ibid., p. 63.

13 See M. Elliott, *Partners in Revolution* (London, 1982), pp. 42, 143, 149; and T. Pakenham, *The Year of Liberty* (London, 1969), pp. 255–6 for United Irish and Defenderist oaths. Compare with the oaths in TNA, ADM1/5125 and ADM1/5339, *Pompée*'s court martial. See Thomas Bartlett *et al.*, eds, *1798: A Bicentenary Perspective* (Dublin, 2003); J. L. McCracken, 'The United Irishmen' in T. D. Williams, ed., *Secret Societies of Ireland* (Dublin, 1973), p. 66; T. Bartlett, 'Defence, Counter-insurgency and Rebellion: Ireland, 1793–1803', in T. Bartlett and K. Jeffery, eds, *A Military History of Ireland* (Cambridge, 1996), pp. 277, 278; H. Murtagh, 'Irish Soldiers Abroad, 1600–1800', ibid., pp. 307, 310. Defenders were a Catholic secret society who supported the Irish Rebellion of 1798.

14 R. Wells, *Insurrection: The British Experience, 1795–1803* (Gloucester, 1983), p. 92.

15 Ibid., p. 101.

the Spithead ships, at 14.9 per cent.[16] Moreover, her crew sent a letter on 13 May to the *Portsmouth Gazette*, responding to reports that they were 'the only dissatisfied ship in the Fleet, which information we positively contradict'.[17] Muster books of fifteen leading ships at Spithead give an average of 25.7 per cent Irish among the ship's companies.[18] Numbers of Irish on ships does not prove United Irish involvement. See Coats, Chapter 7, for a detailed discussion of these aspects.

Elliott and Wells perpetuated the assumption that Quota men were instrumental in organising the Spithead mutiny.[19] Wells inferred from the symbols and methods employed by the seamen, and common to all groups who were critical of the government, that they were directly controlled by the secret societies of the 1790s.[20] Rather, they were part of their own collective traditions and part of the social, political and economic context of the 1790s. This lack of faith in the seamen's own abilities is not justified by the evidence in the archives.

N. A. M. Rodger's *Command of the Ocean*, Chapter 29 in particular, corrects these inaccuracies surrounding the leadership and recruitment context of the Spithead and Nore mutinies, acknowledging the conclusions of several writers of this volume. Specifically the numbers of Quota men (around thirty thousand) and United Irishmen (just 115 United Irishmen in the Royal Navy, 1795–97) do not justify claims of their high influence. Crucially he notes the effect of previous single-ship mutinies such as *Culloden* in 1794, where 'an essential bond of trust had been severed'. He cites praise of the mutineers' conduct by contemporaries Edward Brenton, Philip Beaver and Nelson, but demonstrates some subsequent loss of confidence by officers, partly restored by Admiral St Vincent's pro-active leadership at Cadiz.[21] Events at Spithead herald all the elements of the subsequent mutinies: grievances, lack of communication, leadership, humanity and inhumanity and resolution.

The seamen acted according to the accustomed rules. In February and March 1797 the Channel Fleet sent eleven anonymous petitions in traditional form seeking a pay increase to their popular Commander-in-Chief, Admiral Richard Howe.[22] Citing a rise in the cost of living of 30 per cent, they were sent from *Queen Charlotte*, *Royal George*, *Formidable*, *Ramillies*, *Minotaur*, *Audacious*, *Juste*, *Theseus*, *Sans Pareil*, *Triumph* and *Bellerophon*. Some of these ships differed from those later active at Spithead because of the constantly shifting nature of the Channel Fleet: some ships were on blockade, some sailing to or from Brest, some in Plymouth or Torbay, while others were refitting at Portsmouth. They were acting collectively.

---

16 TNA, ADM36/12233.
17 *Portsmouth Gazette and Weekly Advertiser*, 15 May 1797.
18 Elliott, *Partners in Revolution*, p. 138; Wells, *Insurrection*, p. 82. See Coats, Chapter 7, 'The 1797 Mutinies in the Channel Fleet: A Foreign-Inspired Revolutionary Movement?'.
19 Elliott, *Partners in Revolution*, 136; Wells, *Insurrection*, pp. 81, 83, 84.
20 Wells, *Insurrection*, pp. 84, 96, 101.
21 N. A. M. Rodger, *Command of the Ocean* (London, 2004), pp. 443–53, 724, 794, 801, 836.
22 TNA, ADM1/5125.

Howe had been on extended sick leave with atonic gout since spring 1795 and, aged seventy-one, actively wished to resign his post. He was unreceptive to the men's complaints, because they were not signed or forwarded by officers.[23] However, there are many unsigned petitions to the Admiralty in the National Archive. A precedent for the seamen to petition had been set in 1654, when the Council of War under John Lawson decided 'that it was lawful for the seamen to present their grievances by way of petition'.[24]

A feud between Howe and Lord Bridport meant that Howe chose not transmit the petitions to Lord Bridport, acting commander-in-chief of the Channel Fleet. On 22 March Howe gave the petitions to Admiralty commissioner Rear Admiral Lord Hugh Seymour, asking him 'to ascertain whether or not any discontent did really exist in the fleet'. Seymour told Howe that the 'plot' was the 'work of some incendiary' and forwarded them to the Board of Admiralty, which ignored them. A pay rise would have required an Act of Parliament and the navy debt had reached £12 million in the autumn of 1796.[25]

On 30 March the seamen in the Channel Fleet returned to Spithead from blockading Brest to find that no notice had been taken of their petitions. Spithead is an anchorage situated between Portsmouth and the Isle of Wight, protected from the prevailing westerly winds by the island and from the enemy by narrow channels between sandbanks, necessitating experienced navigational skills. The fleet could moor there to take on men and supplies more quickly than if it entered Portsmouth Harbour, and avoid the risk of men deserting. Bridport went ashore to transact 'some material Business' until 10 April and many other officers were granted leave.[26] The command style of Admiral Lord Bridport, aged seventy, was quite unlike the tight control exercised by Admiral John Jervis (Earl St Vincent) in the Mediterranean Fleet at Cadiz, and contributed to the lack of foreknowledge of the mutiny. Bridport's officers were accustomed to taking leave while ships were refitting and storing in Spithead.[27]

The seamen were not allowed ashore, but could communicate with each other and maintained contact with the shore via 'bum boat' women and slop sellers.[28] Thus the seamen had ample time to execute their plan of December 1796. Observant captains, through their spokesman, Captain Thomas Pakenham, had in December 1796 urged a wartime pay rise for able seamen to 30s a month to First Lord of the Admiralty Earl Spencer, but he had rejected it.[29]

On 13 April 1797 Captain Charles Patton, a Transport Board agent, noted signs of impending mutiny on *Queen Charlotte* and *Royal Sovereign*. He told

---

23 TNA, ADM1/136, 19 April 1797.
24 TNA, ADM1/5125. H. W. Hodges and E. A. Hughes, eds, *Select Naval Documents* (Cambridge, 1936), pp. 67–8; W. Laird Clowes, *The Royal Navy*, II (London, 1996), p. 105.
25 TNA, ADM3/136, 14 April 1797.
26 BL, Althorp Papers, G191, Bridport to Spencer, 30 March 1797.
27 TNA, ADM1/107, January to April 1797.
28 TNA, ADM1/5125, *Nymphe*, 22 April 1797; for an exaggerated description of a bum-boat woman see C. N. Parkinson, *Portsmouth Point: The Navy in Fiction 1793–1815* (London, 1948), pp. 103–4.
29 Marcus, *Age of Nelson*, p. 82; BL, Althorp Papers, G187, Pakenham to Spencer, 11 December 1796, Spencer to Pakenham, 12 December 1796.

Bridport, who sent a message by shutter telegraph to the Admiralty, seeking instructions about the petitions and 'disagreeable combinations'. On Good Friday, 14 April, Vice Admiral Peter Parker, Port Admiral of Portsmouth, told the Admiralty that on Tuesday 18 April *Queen Charlotte* and *Royal Sovereign* would 'refuse doing their duty till their wages is increased'.[30] Spencer sent Howe's eleven petitions to Bridport. On 15 April he returned them to Evan Nepean, Secretary to the Admiralty, asking why he had not been informed earlier, enclosing three more petitions from *London*, *Royal George* and *Queen Charlotte* and stating that answers should be given before the fleet sailed. Sir Peter Parker told captains to sleep on board. The seamen sent further petitions to Nepean and Charles James Fox, leader of the opposition. *Royal Sovereign* sent a letter to *Defence* declaring they would 'take charge of the ships'.

On Easter Sunday, 16 April, Bridport reluctantly ordered his second-in-command, Vice Admiral Alan Gardner, to take his squadron to sea, precipitating the men's plans. Gardner's flagship, *Royal Sovereign*, did not move and the sailors on *Queen Charlotte* gave three cheers and sent a boat to tour the fleet. *Royal George* (Bridport's flagship) sent a boat telling each ship to send two delegates to *Queen Charlotte* (Howe's flagship). Bridport asked the men to state their grievances. That evening two delegates from each of the sixteen ships of the line met in *Queen Charlotte*'s cabin and drew up rules to govern their behaviour and maintain unity.

The different Ships Boats retained on Board of the Queen Charlotte in the Evening where they agreed to the following Rules and Orders
~
First Every Ship shall Diligently keep a Quarter watch and any man found below in his Watch shall be severely punished. ~

Secondly every Ship shall give three Cheers at 8 O Clock in the Morning and at Sun set in the Eavning. ~

Thirdly no woman shall be permitted to go on Shore from any ship but as many come in as Pleases. ~

Fourthly any Person attempting to bring Liquor into any Ship on any Pretence whatever or any found Drunk to be severely punished. ~

Fiftly the greatest attention to be paid to the Orders of the Officers any person failing in Respect Due to them or neglecting their Duty shall be severely punished. ~

Sixtly Every Seaman and Marine in the fleet to take a Oath of Fiddelity not onely to themselves but to the Fleet in General. ~

Sevenethly that no ship shall lift an anchor to Proceed from this Port untill the Desire of the fleet is satisfied. ~

Eighthly that there shall be no Liberty from ship to ship Until all is Regularly settled. ~

The Form of Oath was taken by the fleet every man swore by his maker that the Cause we have Undertaken we Persevere in till accomplished. ~

In case of Disturbance on board any of the ships a Red flag at the fore

30 TNA, ADM1/1022.

top Gall.t Mast head and tow lights at Night one above the Other a Boat with the Delegates to Repair Immediately to that Ship. ~[31]

The news reached London on Easter Monday, 17 April. Bridport wrote to Nepean:

> I have been informed, that this plan was to have taken effect before the Fleet sailed from Spithead in Dec. last, and it is reported to me that Petitions were presented six months ago, for an increase in pay, of which I was totally ignorant, 'till I wrote my first letter on this subject.[32]

Spencer left immediately for Portsmouth with the Admiralty commissioners. They arrived at 11a.m. on 18 April and issued their offer to the delegates through Admirals Gardner, Colpoys, Pole and Sir Peter Parker.[33] *The Times* reported that 'we think it is highly probable that this unpleasant business was amicably settled yesterday, through the intervention of the Lords Commissioners'.[34] However, on 19 April *The Times* correspondent feared 'it will be difficult to comply with all the demands of the sailors, who have been evidently set upon by villains who are known traitors to their King and Country'. The editorial blamed the opposition: 'Let any man compare the language of some of our Opposition prints with the disorderly proceedings now going on at Portsmouth, and say whether there is not a very close affinity between the two parties.' On 20 April the Admiralty party consulted Lord Bridport, three admirals and sixteen captains and agreed to most of the seamen's demands.[35] On 21 April the delegates on *Queen Charlotte* insisted on a pardon from the King before returning to duty.[36] Admiral Gardner accused the seamen of cowardice and hypocrisy, knowing the French were ready for sea and were afraid to meet them. He threatened to hang every fifth man in the fleet.[37] The meeting broke up, the red flag was hoisted and the General Assembly declared the delegates would return to their ships.[38] They stated:

> that it is a firm Resolution that untill the Flour in Port be removed the Vegetables and Pensions be augmented the Greavences of private Ships be redressed an act Passed, and His Majesty's gracious Pardon for the fleet

31   TNA, ADM1/5125, 16 April 1797, Delegates' Rules and Orders, Papers from *Queen Charlotte*.

32   TNA, ADM1/107, Bridport to Nepean, 17 April 1797.

33   Printed in TNA, ADM3/136, fol. 372; see ADM1/5125, 18 April 1797, *The Times*, 21 April 1797. The first offer was 4s a month rise to able seamen; 3s to ordinary seamen; 2s to landsmen.

34   *The Times*, 18 April 1797.

35   TNA, ADM1/5125; ADM3/136 fol. 400.

36   TNA, ADM3/136 fol. 372.

37   Marcus, *Age of Nelson*, p. 85.

38   The red flag was a signal for battle. See *Saturday Review*, 6 June 1891, p. 678. T. Wilson, *Flags at Sea* (Greenwich, 1986), p. 108, 'Bloody flag. A red flag, otherwise known as the "flag of defiance", used by European warships and corsairs in action in the 17th century.' Also see *The Times*, 9 May 1797 and 24 April 1797.

now lying at Spithead be granted, that the fleet will not lift an anchor; and this is the finall and total Answer.[39]

At midnight on the 21st Spencer realised he needed to obtain the King's pardon and left Portsmouth immediately with the Board. On Saturday 22 April *The Times* printed another petition sent to Parliament, signed by thirty-two delegates, asking for a pay rise, fairer distribution of prize money, better food and better treatment for the sick and wounded. The Admiralty party arrived in London on the 22nd and met Prime Minister William Pitt and the Privy Council. At 5p.m. Spencer went to Windsor with Pitt, Foreign Secretary Lord Grenville and the Lord Chancellor Lord Loughborough, obtained the King's pardon at 9p.m., and despatched it to Lord Bridport at 10p.m.[40] On 23 April the pardon was read to the fleet.[41] On 28 April most of the Spithead fleet sailed to St Helen's to await a good wind for Brest, but were wind-bound. *Marlborough, Minotaur, Nymphe* and *Ramillies* had unsettled grievances against their officers, so stayed at Spithead with *London. Nymphe*'s petition complained:

> as to Flogging it is carried on to Extremes One man rec.[d] three Dozen for what was termed Silent Contempt which was nothing more than this. after being beat by a boatswains mate the man smiled this was the Unpardonable crime. another man was flogged for not going up the Riggin Quick Enough and another for not sending him down as was supposed smart enough[.][42]

The *London* incident occurred on 7–8 May because the seamen were worried that their grievances were not being redressed by Parliament and Admiral Colpoys misinterpreted the Admiralty order of 1 May.[43] Three seamen were killed on *London*, Admiral Colpoys was seized and further officers were put ashore.[44] This crisis prompted Parliament to pass the Act for increase of pay and provisions on 9 May, with George III giving his assent the same evening. On 14 and 15 May Admiral Howe visited the ships and led celebrations in Portsmouth. The fleet finally sailed on 17 May.[45]

Meanwhile, on 26 April *Porcupine* had arrived at Plymouth with the news from Spithead. A supportive mutiny broke out as planned, involving *Atlas, Saturn, Majestic* and *Edgar*. It spread to the Hamoaze, involving *Leviathan* and *Gibraltar*. The seamen refused to go to sea and set officers ashore. On 27 April *Atlas* was designated 'the Parliament ship' and a boat was chartered to send a delegation to Spithead, where they accepted the Spithead terms.[46]

---

39 TNA, ADM1/5125, 21 April 1797.
40 *The Times*, 24 April 1797. Grenville was also Pitt's cousin. P. J. Jupp, 'Grenville, William Wyndham', *ODNB* (Oxford, 2004) www.oxforddnb.com
41 TNA, ADM1/1022, 23 April 1797, Peter Parker to Evan Nepean.
42 TNA, ADM1/5125, 22 April 1797.
43 TNA, ADM2/133, Instructions, 1 May 1797; *London Chronicle*, 9–11 May 1797; *Morning Post*, 10 May 1797.
44 *Portsmouth Gazette and Weekly Advertiser*, 15 May 1797.
45 *The Times*, 16 May 1797. See *Gentleman's Magazine*, 67, 2 (1797), pp. 1091–3.
46 TNA, ADM1/1022, 18 April 1797; ADM1/811, Orde to Nepean 28 April, 2 May.

To apply the term 'mutiny' to Spithead is to view the event through the eyes of the authorities. Mutiny, as defined by Admiralty and the government, was to refuse submission to discipline or obedience to the lawful command of a superior; revolt against or openly resist a superior.[47] As one eighteenth-century seamen expressed it: 'All that you are ordered to do is duty. All that you refuse to do is mutiny.'[48] But Admiral Collingwood accepted officer responsibility: 'Mutiny, Sir! mutiny on my ship! If it can have arrived at that, it must be my

Table 1.1. **Summary of Spithead Demands, Granted or not Granted**

Demanded	Granted **Y**; Not granted **N**
Rise to 1s a day, giving 30s to able seamen, to be paid every three months in cash	18 April the first Admiralty offer was 4s a month to able seamen, 3s to ordinary seamen and 2s to landsmen.
	20 April the second Admiralty offer was made (below)
	23 April the seamen accepted this offer and the King's pardon
	9 May Act passed by Parliament
	20 May its provisions were to take effect, as promised by Lord Bridport
	5s 6d to able seamen (totalling 29s 6d per lunar month)
	4s 6d to ordinary seamen (23s 6d per lunar month)
	3s 6d to landsmen (21s 6d per lunar month).
Pension increase from £7 to £10 a year	**N**
More equal shares of prize money	**N**
Marines to have same allowances on shore as paid on board	**Y**
Provisions raise to 16 ounces a pound*	**Y**
Care or pension for injured seamen	**Y**
Full pay for sick or injured seamen	**Y**
Removal of named officers	**Y** 113 officers removed

* Resulting from a petition of 1776 the purser was allowed to deduct an eighth of the value of his stores to cover wastage. C. Lloyd, 'Victualling of the Fleet in the eighteenth and nineteenth centuries', in J. Watt, E. J. Freeman, W. F. Bynum, eds., *Starving Sailors* (NMM, Greenwich, 1981), p. 11.

47 OED.
48 Cited in M. Rediker, *Between the Devil and the Deep Blue Sea* (Cambridge, 1989), p. 211.

fault and the fault of every one of the officers. It is a charge of the gravest nature, and it shall be most gravely enquired into.'[49] Although he also blamed the Quota men and bounty men, his private criticisms of Howe and Bridport were scathing:

> It is impossible that Lord Howe can justify his not having taken proper notice of the memorials and petitions of the seamen which were sent to him, and which neglect was the sole cause of this great national calamity which has shook the constitution of England, and given a wound to naval discipline which will require a length of time and the most delicate treatment to heal.
>
> ...I had no idea of Lord Bridport's tamely submitting to the indignities he suffered, and allowing Lord Howe to sap the foundations of all future discipline while he commanded the fleet.[50]

The disciplinary framework was clearly set out by the 1749 Articles of War:

> If any Person in or belonging to the Fleet shall make or endeavour to make any mutinous Assembly upon any Pretence whatsoever, every Person offending herein, and being convicted thereof by the Sentence of the Court-martial, shall suffer Death.

The offence of 'endeavouring to stir up Disturbance on Account of unwholesomeness of Victual' was also tried by court martial:

> If any person in the Fleet shall find cause of Complaint of the Unwholesomness of the Victual, or upon other just Ground, he shall quietly make the same known to his Superior or Captain or Commander in Chief.[51]

The seamen were therefore using language carefully. They were redressing 'grievances' against 'hardships and oppressions' and referred to them as 'discontents'.[52] Admirals Bridport and Howe also saw it as a labour dispute, reporting 'Combinations' among the seamen.[53] In the view of 'V.V.', writing to Lord Chancellor Thurlow in June 1797: 'Mutiny it cannot be called; for there was neither mutiny nor riot.'[54] The seamen were uniting for a common

---

49   G. L. Newnham Collingwood, ed., *A Selection from the Public and Private Correspondence of Vice-Admiral Lord Collingwood: interspersed with memoirs of his life* (London, 1828), p. 55.

50   Collingwood to his sister, 7 August 1797. E. Hughes, ed., *The Private Correspondence of Admiral Lord Collingwood* (London, 1957), pp. 85–6. Bounties of around £5, paid to encourage naval enlistment, were announced in the *London Gazette*. See B. Lavery, *Nelson's Navy: The Ships, Men and Organisation 1793–1815* (London, 1989), pp. 120, 124, 129; An Act for procuring a Supply of Men, 35 Geo. III, c.9, 1795.

51   N. A. M. Rodger, *Articles of War* (Havant, 1982), p. 26. N.B. More articles were directed at the discipline of the officers than the men.

52   Throughout TNA, ADM1/107, ADM1/5125, ADM1/5339.

53   TNA, ADM1/107, Bridport to Spencer, 13 April 1797.

54   V.V. to Lord Chancellor Thurloe, 9 June 1797, in A. A. Miles, 'A Letter on the Naval

purpose, not withdrawing their labour.[55] Their own rules clearly said that 'the greatest attention to be paid to the Orders of the Officers' and that anyone 'neglecting their Duty shall be severely Punished'. What they refused was 'to lift an anchor to Proceed from this Port untill the Desire of the fleet is satisfyed'.[56]

Selection of the most significant causes and events of the Spithead mutiny is necessarily subjective. The most obvious and longest standing complaint concerned wages, which had not been increased since 1653. This formed the basis of the seamen's initial demand.[57] Captain Philip Patton, a commissioner of the Transport Board from 1794 and elder brother of Captain Charles Patton (also a Transport Agent), citing respective wages before the start of the French wars, stated that the seamen had been 'obliged to relinquish nearly half the profits of their labour'.[58]

An underlying cause of discontent was erosion of the seamen's status and decision-making role during the eighteenth century. The seventeenth-century Commonwealth had recognised the vital part played by the seamen in defending the vulnerable republic, and had deliberately raised their pay and improved their conditions in order to retain them in the service.[59] During the early eighteenth century captains of merchant ships and privateers regularly consulted the seamen as a body on the running of the ships.[60] By the end of the eighteenth century, however, despite the divisional system which linked a section of the crew to a specific lieutenant and midshipman, first-, second- and third-rate battleships were so large that potentially divisive social barriers between the officers and the men were exacerbated by the inconsistent application of punishment (shown in the chapters of Kathrin Orth and Nick Slope), and the variable quality of officers.[61] This 'difference of opinion' between officers and

---

Mutinies of 1797', *Mariner's Mirror*, 78, 2 (May 1992), pp. 200–1.

55   OED.

56   TNA, ADM1/5125, 16 April 1797, Papers from *Queen Charlotte*. Also ADM1/107, *Ramillies*, 7 May 1797; Ibid., Seamen to Bridport, 23 April 1797.

57   Wages had been raised on 1 January 1653: able seamen from 19s to 24s a month, ordinary seamen remained at 19s. The act of Charles II was cited because that was the last occasion that Parliament had set wage rates, but they were the same as the Act of 1 January 1653. Manwaring and Dobrée, *Floating Republic*, p. 23 citing *CSPD*, 1652–53, p. 43; Clowes, *Royal Navy*, II, p. 98. BL, Althorp Papers, G187, Pakenham to Spencer, 11 December 1796. Patton, NMM, WYN/109/7/14, fol. 5, April 1795. Also see R. Davis, *The Rise of the Shipping Industry in the Seventeenth and Eighteenth Centuries* (London, 1962), pp. 137, 323, 325; D. Baugh, 'The Eighteenth Century Navy as a National Institution', in J. R. Hill. ed., *The Oxford Illustrated History of the Royal Navy* (Oxford, 1995), pp. 138–9.

58   NMM, WYN/109/7/14, Philip Patton, 'Observations on Naval Mutiny Presented April 1795', drafted in 1790. P. K. Crimmin, 'Patton, Philip', *ODNB* (2004) www.oxforddnb.com.

59   J. B. Hattendorf *et al.*, eds, 'Propositions for the Encouragement of Seamen, 20 December 1652,' *British Naval Documents 1204–1960* (London, 1993), pp. 274–5; Clowes, *The Royal Navy*, II, pp. 104–5. For the sixteenth century see N. A. M. Rodger, *The Safeguard of the Sea* (London, 1997), p. 322.

60   Woodes Rogers, *A Cruising Voyage Round the World* (London, 1928), pp. 22–3.

61   N. A. M. Rodger, *The Wooden World* (Glasgow, 1990), pp. 216–17. See W. James, *Old Oak: The Life of John Jervis* (London, 1950), pp. 104, 112, 126, 147–55; J. S. Tucker, ed., *Memoirs of Earl St Vincent*, I (London, 1844), p. 306; B. Lavery, *Nelson's Navy* (London, 1989), p. 217.

men was acknowledged in Chaplain J. J. Fresselique's sermon to celebrate the victory of 1 June 1794.[62] The high proportion of impressed merchant seamen in wartime increased militancy, as they brought their tradition of striking to further wage demands.[63] This view of the mutiny as an attempt by seamen to regain lost rights is confirmed by the continuing labour disputes in the royal and merchant navies immediately after the official ending of the Spithead mutiny, mainly concerned with the condition of their ships or pay arrears. These were treated by the authorities as labour disputes, not as mutinies, and were negotiated accordingly.[64] Later mutinies in the Channel Fleet and at Cadiz were dealt with immediately by courts martial.[65]

The immediate context for the seamen's grievances was the relentless demand from 1793 for British seamen to fight in the French revolutionary wars. The number of seamen and marines borne on the books jumped from 16,613 in 1792 to 69,868 in 1793. By 1797 the number was 123,041.[66] The Admiralty had resorted to impressment, quotas and bounties to raise men to sail the ships and provide replacements for those who had deserted or were killed, injured or diseased.[67] The numbers of Quota men actually mustered is still a matter of debate and leads to differing interpretations. Further research is required to determine numbers across the UK.[68] Most naval seamen had been impressed from merchant ships and knew that their rate of pay would drop dramatically, that they would not in fact be paid for months or years.[69] Their living conditions would become more overcrowded and they would be 'kept more like convicts then free Born Britons', at sea for an indefinite period without being allowed on shore to see their families.[70]

---

62   NMRN, J. J. Fresselique, *Sermon for the Late Victory 1794* (Gosport, 1794), p. 15. Also see N. A. M. Rodger, 'Jolly Tars Were Our Men?' in *Mutiny on the Bounty 1789–1989* (Greenwich, 1989), p. 16.

63   Dugan, *Great Mutiny*, p. 88.

64   TNA, ADM1/1023, May–June 1797.

65   See W. Laird Clowes, *The Royal Navy*, IV (London, 1997), pp. 176–80; C. Gill, *The Naval Mutinies of 1797* (Manchester, 1913), pp. 252–3; Tucker, *Memoirs of Earl St Vincent*, I, p. 300.

66   Numbers in the Royal Navy: 1794, 87,331; 1795, 96,001; 1796, 114,365; Lavery, *Nelson's Navy*, pp. 118, 128; C. Lloyd, *The British Seaman* (London, 1968), pp. 288–9; TNA, ADM8/73, May 1797.

67   See Lavery, *Nelson's Navy*, pp. 117–28. For numbers dying, see C. Lloyd, ed., *Health of Seamen* (NRS vol. CVII, 1965), pp. 176, 198; Baugh, 'The Eighteenth-Century Navy', p. 140.

68   See C. Emsley, 'Recruitment of Petty Offenders during the French Wars 1793–1815', *Mariner's Mirror*, 66 (1980), pp. 199–208 and J. Ehrman, *The Younger Pitt* (London, 1996), p. 19. Both cite C. Oprey, 'Schemes for the Reform of Naval Recruitment 1793–1815' (MA thesis, Liverpool, 1961), pp. 41, 127–8. See Rodger, 'Mutiny or Subversion? Spithead and the Nore' in Thomas Bartlett, *et al.*, *1798: A Bicentenary Perspective* (Dublin, 2003), p. 560, fn. 56 and Rodger, *Command*, pp. 443–4, 722–3, 788, 804–5, 838 for sources.

69   In 1797 *Nassau* had not been paid for nineteen months. J. S. Corbett, ed., *The Private Papers of George, 2nd Earl Spencer, First Lord of the Admiralty 1794–1801*, II (London, 1914), p. 145. In 1801 *Audacious* had not been paid for four years. Lavery, *Nelson's Navy*, p. 131.

70   Davis, *Rise of the Shipping Industry*, pp. 324–5; TNA, ADM1/5125, *Nymphe*, 22

A lesson in tactics had been learned by the seamen in 1783 at the end of the American War. They organised a fleet mutiny to speed up being paid off on their return to Spithead. Their success, achieved by remaining firm and united, was contrasted with the executions of the leaders of the single-ship mutinies of *Culloden* in 1794, *Terrible* in 1795 and the eventual tracking down and courts martial of the *Bounty* mutineers of 1789. At least two naval officers in the 1790s had articulated the danger of a general mutiny if the leading seamen were not more highly rewarded and increased in number.[71]

The immediate cause of dissatisfaction in the fleet was the government's blatant disregard for the seamen's interests, compared with those of the army, militia and naval officers who had been awarded pay rises in 1795 to counter inflation. Britain's vulnerability to attack by French and Batavian forces, political instability in Ireland, and the government's financial problems in 1797 provided the most opportune moment for the seamen to press their case. While they were willing to exploit the moment to achieve their ends, these did not include overthrowing the government or aiding the French. However, as the Admiralty's preconceptions of seamen convinced it that they were incapable of such sophisticated planning and language, it saw outside influences from French or revolutionary groups. This was instrumental in widening the dispute into a protest about conditions. The Admiralty's concern was to restore discipline, not to deal with the issues being raised. It planned to isolate the ringleaders, grant a few concessions and get the ships back to sea. When it became obvious that this would not work, admirals attempted 'Perswasions threatings and all other means in their Power', but the men remained resolute.[72] The seamen used the press astutely to secure wide propagation of their case to an influential newspaper-reading public. The Admiralty had to accept that their options were limited, they had lost the propaganda battle, and had to concede virtually all the men's demands in a damage-limitation exercise.[73]

The sheer size of the Spithead mutiny has been missed by previous histories. During April and May 1797 there were more than eighty ships at Spithead, manned by thirty thousand men: a quarter of the total manpower of the navy and a sixth of its ships. This does not include Sir Roger Curtis's squadron of ships stationed at Plymouth, part of the Channel Fleet and privy to the original planning of the mutiny. The Channel Fleet was a long-established body of ships and men in the Royal Navy, accustomed to the 'anxious and fatiguing service' of blockading the French navy in their ports.[74] Of the crews

April 1797. In 1797 *Intrepid* had been at sea for four years without her crew having leave. Corbett, *Spencer Papers*, II, p. 143.

71 NMM, WYN/109/7/14, Philip Patton, 'Observations on Naval Mutiny Presented April 1795'; BL, Althorp Papers, G187, Thomas Pakenham to Earl Spencer, 11 December 1796. Also see Rogers, *A Cruising Voyage*, pp. 4, 33.

72 TNA, ADM1/5125, 21 April 1797.

73 TNA, ADM1/107, 23 April 1797, Seamen to Bridport; TNA, ADM1/107, 15 April 1797, Bridport to Nepean; ADM1/5125, see the Spirit of Kempenfeldt letters, April 1797, analysed by David W. London in Chapter 3, 'What Really Happened On Board HMS *London*?'

74 *Naval Chronicle*, I, January–June 1799, p. 22.

Table 1.2. Naval Ships and Seamen at Spithead April–May 1797

April 1797	Total no. ships at Spithead	67	Total no. seamen at Spithead	25,713
May 1797	Total no. ships at Spithead	54	Total no. seamen at Spithead	18,828
April & May 1797	Total no. ships at Spithead	82	Total no. seamen at Spithead	29,669
April 1797	Total no. ships in the Navy	508	Total no. seamen in the Navy	121,481
May 1797	Total no. ships in the Navy	529	Total no. seamen in the Navy	123,041

Sources

The National Archive, Admiralty Disposition Book ADM8/73, April and May 1797 and Admiralty correspondence in the National Archive, Kew: ADM1/107, ADM1/579, ADM1/1022, ADM1/1023, ADM1/5125; British Library, Add. Ms. 35197.

The ships, and hence numbers of men at Spithead varied from day to day, because the Channel Fleet was regularly patrolling between Portsmouth, Plymouth and the Brest blockade, so the monthly Disposition Book cannot give a completely accurate picture.

of the leading ships at Spithead, with complements of 600–850 men, most had mustered together since before 1796.

Manwaring and Dobrée emphasised the professionalism and experience of the seamen who led the Spithead mutiny. These were without exception leading seamen, midshipmen and petty officers: men who held the respect of their fellows, who were already the leaders of the lower deck and who had the experience to handle an extremely sensitive and dangerous campaign.[75] The wide range of aims among the ships' companies, from ultra-loyalism on *Garland*, to the peace movement and pro-French sentiments on *Pompée*, can be assessed from letters, petitions and court-martial evidence.[76] Their success lay in being able to maintain 'Unity and Perseverance' in the face of these conflicting aims and pressure from the authorities.[77] Their accounts, together with their handbills and newspaper reports, provide a rich understanding of their motives and methods. The mature and disciplined behaviour of the Spithead delegates won support from the community of Portsmouth: printers published their proclamations, the opposition Whig Mayor Sir John Carter allowed the three killed *London* seamen to be buried with dignity by their shipmates. Even magistrate Aaron Graham, sent by the Home Secretary to find Jacobin links, acknowledged their loyalty and determination. This will be examined in more detail in Chapter 2, Coats, 'The Delegates: A Radical

---

75 Manwaring and Dobrée, *Floating Republic*, p. 262–3; Lavery, *Nelson's Navy*, p. 131. Also see Rodger, *Safeguard of the Sea*, pp. 319, 320, 324.

76 TNA, ADM1/5125, 1 April 1797; ADM1/5339, *Pompée* court martial.

77 TNA, ADM1/5125, 27 February 1797.

Tradition' and Chapter 7, Coats, 'The 1797 Mutinies in the Channel Fleet: A Foreign-Inspired Revolutionary Movement?'.

Nineteenth-century naval historians accepted and perpetuated the propaganda of Pitt, Home Secretary the Duke of Portland and *The Times*, 'that some of the mutinies were assisted, if not actually fomented, by French agents'.[78] Chapter 2 demonstrates that the organisation of the Spithead mutiny drew on the ancient collective traditions of naval and merchant seamen and pirates from the seventeenth century: red flags, 'round robins', delegates, loyalty oaths and reference back to the main body of the ships' companies.[79] It sets the Spithead mutiny within the context of seamen's disputes in the eighteenth century. The Admiralty enforced discipline through the Articles of War and by increasingly separating the ranks, but the merchant navy was acknowledged to be the nursery of the Royal Navy and in wartime the majority of seamen were recruited from the merchant navy. The codes of merchant seamen provided a context for naval seamen's expectations. While they were prepared to sacrifice their interests for the national interest, they were acutely aware that their conditions were significantly worse in terms of pay and freedom than those of the people they were defending.[80] They had followed the established procedure of petitioning for a pay increase. They felt justified, and knew they had the power to achieve their ends. Ironically, not only did Pitt and Spencer acknowledge the justice of their cause (the pay rise cost only £472,000 in 1797), but the government awarded the Army another pay rise only weeks after the seamen's was awarded, afraid that disaffected soldiers would attack London.[81]

David W. London's Chapter 3, 'What Really Happened On Board HMS *London*?' focuses on the treatment by the London newspapers of the only deaths which occurred during the Spithead mutiny. He analyses news reports, seamen's and government proclamations and editorial comments by ministerial and opposition newspapers to measure their impact upon the determination of the seamen and the events of the mutiny. As the drama unfolded in the Channel Fleet, it had echoes and repercussions in the dramatic debates in Parliament, reported in the press on 4 May, which contributed to the tragic killing of three seamen on *London*. Circumstances surrounding these events revealed bureaucratic blundering, Vice Admiral Colpoys's insensitivity, the seamen's determination and the delegates' restraint. For perhaps the first time, newspaper reporting had such an impact on the consciousness of participants and observers of a national event that it altered the course of history.

---

78 Laird Clowes, *Royal Navy*, IV, p. 167. See Ehrman, *The Younger Pitt: The Consuming Struggle* (London, 1996), pp. 119, 470; E. Rhys, ed., *Orations of the French War by William Pitt* (London, n.d.), p. 233; *The Times*, 23 May 1797.

79 See Rodger, *Safeguard of the Sea*, p. 401.

80 TNA, ADM1/5125, 'Caution from the Delegates to the Fleet'; NMM, WYN/109/7/14, fol.5, Philip Patton, Observations on Naval Mutiny,' April 1795.

81 *The Times*, 25 May 1797; Supplies granted by Parliament for the year 1797, *Annual Register* (London, 1800), Appendix, p. 166. Gill, *Naval Mutinies*, pp. 97–8, citing TNA, ADM1/107, J180, states that it was dated initially from 24 April, but Bridport had promised it would begin on 20 April. Gill states the additional pay amount for a whole year was £351,000, plus an additional cost for increased provisions as £185,000, hence a total increase of £536,000 a year.

3. Sir John Carter, d.1808. He was knighted in 1773 during George III's visit to Portsmouth and was elected Mayor in 1769, 1772, 1779, 1782, 1786, 1789, 1793, 1796, 1800 and 1804. The extended Carter family comprised wealthy merchants and brewers. Sir John was also a landowner and a member of the South Hants Agricultural Society, which encouraged agricultural improvement. He was one of a group of local politicians that in the 1770s and 1780s successfully asserted the town's independence from the Admiralty, which had previously nominated who should be elected the town's MPs. Portsmouth Corporation was predominantly Whig and nonconformist, led by Sir John Carter, Mayor during the mutiny. They campaigned for electoral and religious reforms and had social and political links with radical skilled workers from the Dockyard.

Kathrin Orth's Chapter 5, 'Voices from the Lower Deck: Petitions on the Conduct of Naval Officers during the 1797 Mutinies', describes the normal procedures followed by seamen in petitioning to have grievances redressed and the resultant investigations by the Admiralty. It is notable that, when presented with identically worded petitions for a pay increase, Admirals Howe and Seymour were not concerned with investigating the justice of the seamen's claim, but in establishing whether there had been a conspiracy. Orth reveals that the seamen's petitions were not complaining about the issue of physical punishment (apart from specific excessive floggings), but rather about the level of lesser punishments and abusive language inflicted by inferior officers, which exacerbated conditions of physical discomfort and undermined their self-respect. Her evidence also shows that the mutiny provided an opportunity of ridding ships of unpopular officers on an unprecedented scale.

Roger Morriss's Chapter 6, 'Crew Management and Mutiny: The Case of *Minerve*, 1796–1802', describes the immediate response of *Minerve*'s crew at Madeira in June 1797 to the arrival of *Thames*, which brought with it the mutinous spirit of Spithead and the Nore. In examining the reasons why there were only 'marginal' instances of mutiny on *Minerve*, Morriss analyses both revolutionary and stabilising factors in the operation of the ship, defining Captain Cockburn's appreciation of the duality of discipline as crucial to the establishment of harmony. By analysing the composition of the crew, he reveals a core of long-serving mature seamen and competent officers and petty officers, who 'maintained stability of relations, discipline and morale'.[82] Like Nick Slope in Chapter 14: 'Discipline Desertion and Death: HMS *Trent* 1796–1803', Morriss examines punishment records as an indication of the command and disciplinary styles of the captain. He concludes that continuity, stability and the captain's commitment to providing the best available care for the seamen were crucial in preventing a serious outbreak of mutiny on *Minerve*. Reduced numbers of punishments were possibly due to the crew becoming more aware of the standards of a particular captain.

A twentieth-century Admiralty staff study stated:

> Mutiny is a combination of two or more persons to defy Authority, either with or without violence. It ranges from the passive refusing of duty to the wholesale usurping of power by the mutineers. ... It has in its passive form certain analogies to a workmen's strike, having as its object the simple redress of grievances, when men believe it is their only way to find justice or do not know any other way of bringing their grievances to light. But it may also amount to rebellion against the State...
>
> The cause of discontent may be a matter of pay, food, or leave; it may be neglect or harsh and unsympathetic treatment by an individual officer. As a rule, it is something tangible. Men do not often concern themselves with the abstract.[83]

---

82 R. Morriss, Chapter 6, 'Crew Management and Mutiny: The Case of *Minerve*, 1796–1802'.

83 TNA, ADM178/133, 'Mutiny in the Royal Navy', I, 1691–1919 (unpublished, Admiralty, 1933), p. 3.

The TOWN and HARBOUR of PORTSMOUTH.

4. Lord Howe's Fleet 1794: 'The Town and Harbour of Portsmouth'

A black-and-white view showing Lord Howe's Fleet in 1794, from a point on Portsdown Hill overlooking the Harbour. Viewed from a point close to where Fort Nelson now stands, it illustrates the capacity of Portsmouth Harbour and fortifications at its mouth. Spithead was a spacious anchorage for ships preparing to sail into the Channel, sheltered from the enemy and prevailing westerly winds by the Isle of Wight. Here they could receive minor repairs and take on men and stores from Portsmouth Dockyard. These aspects made Portsmouth the chief military embarkation point during the French wars The Channel Fleet comprised about 24,500 men in around 60 ships and vessels. The total of men in the navy in 1797 was about 122,000.

Copyright Portsmouth City Museum & Records Service, reproduced by kind permission of Portsmouth City Museum & Records Service.

The author, a serving officer, appreciated the continuity of experience felt by mutinous seamen from the seventeenth to the twentieth century, an experience expressed movingly by participants of the Invergordon mutiny in a 1997 BBC television documentary.[84] Pakenham and his fellow captains were more in tune with the feelings on the lower decks than most fleet commanders and London politicians. The fact that 30 shillings was also the sum requested by the seamen showed either the coincident thinking of these officers and the men, or reflected lower-deck discussions overheard by officers.

The Spithead mutiny should never have happened, but the fact that it did, and was followed by further mutinies, condemns Admiralty thinking as inhumane, blinkered and unable to accept the consequences of its own actions until forced into a corner. The mutinies of 1797 were a blood-letting experience which did not heal ailments in the navy, but revealed the causes of its infirmity and in the long term may have induced a more sympathetic attitude towards

84   BBC2, *Mutiny in the Twentieth Century*, 5 April 1997.

the seamen by the Admiralty. These chapters represent the beginning of a fresh examination of mutiny as the only option available to seamen to express their grievances when other options were denied.

View of the Prizes taken on the 1st of June by E. Howe, at Anchor at Spithead.

5. *View of the Prizes Taken on the 1st June* [1794] *by Earl Howe, at Anchor at Spithead*. Lithograph on paper with the following beneath the left-hand of the image 'N. Pocock del.' and below the right hand 'R. Pollard'. The image shows a large group of men-of-war, some missing parts of their masts and some with the Union flag flying over the Tricolor, at anchor, with a rock promontory in the foreground on the left, on which some men are standing looking at the ships. A fishing boat passes the rock. The return of Howe's fleet caused great public celebrations, equalled by the celebrations following the negotiated and peaceful end to the Spithead Mutiny.

Earl Howe arrived in Portsmouth on the morning of 10 May 1797 and was rowed to St Helen's, where he addressed ships' companies and met delegates. On the morning of 15 May 1797 the delegates landed at the Sally Port, and marched up to the Governor's House with a band of music, playing alternately 'God save the King' and 'Rule Britannia'. Howe and the delegates then visited all the ships, reading out the king's Pardon. At six in the evening Lord Howe landed at the Sally Port, amidst the acclamation of the largest concourse of people ever assembled at Portsmouth.

Copyright Portsmouth City Museum & Records Service, reproduced by kind permission of Portsmouth City Museum & Records Service.

2

The Delegates: A Radical Tradition

Ann Veronica Coats

> we have not the least Dout but by Unity amongst ourselvs and a
> steady Peaceable perseverance to Carry our Point[1]

The delegates, elected leaders of the Spithead mutiny, were men of deserved influence with a sophisticated understanding of the issues involved in their action. They understood the political context, the strategic dimensions, and the vulnerability of Pitt's government. The Channel Fleet, the largest in home waters, comprising eighty ships and thirty thousand men, pursued their action on behalf of the entire Royal Navy.[2] The majority of these crews had mustered together for at least two years, some far longer.[3] They were experienced seamen professionals who knew and trusted each other. They selected as their leaders men whom they respected as seamen and whom they believed would successfully present their case and conduct their negotiations. They understood the terrible risks these men faced: the almost inevitable capital punishment inflicted upon the 'ringleaders'. The seamen determined that the whole fleet would act in unison to prevent this outcome.

The term 'delegate' had been used in the *Culloden* mutiny of 1794, suggesting to Admiral Howe both American and French revolutionary and political practices, but the concept was far older.[4] In 1647 the New Model Army mutinied over Parliament's plan to disband the army and non-payment of wages. To seek redress of grievances, first soldiers and then officers elected two Agitators from each regiment to speak for the whole army. They also addressed '"all honest seamen", explaining their objects and asking for support', and assembled at a rendezvous in Newmarket for Parliament to reconsider its proposals.[5] Unpopular captains were expelled from some regiments, but most

---

1   Charlottes, February 1797, TNA, ADM1/5125.
2   TNA, ADM8/73, ADM8/74, disposition books, April, May 1797.
3   TNA, ADM36, muster books.
4   J. Barrow, *Life of Earl Howe* (London, 1838), p. 302.
5   J. R. Powell and E. K. Timings, eds, *Documents Relating to the Civil War 1642–1648* (1963), pp. 265–6; H. N. Brailsford, *The Levellers* and the English Revolution, ed. C. Hill (Nottingham, 1976), p. 216 and chapter 10.

officers supported the men. Brailsford commented: 'There had been nothing like this spontaneous outbreak of democracy in any English or continental army before this year of 1647, nor was there anything like it thereafter', until 1917.[6] He argued that the army's appeal 'failed to move the seamen', but Capp has shown that on 11 December 1648 a letter from the admiral's flagship sent support to the army, and on 24 December four captains including Robert Moulton and Richard Haddock affirmed support from officers in the Downs and elsewhere.[7]

Levelling doctrines had clearly penetrated the navy: in February 1649 'The Remonstrance of the Navy' called for 'yearly election' of all officers of the Fleet, and for 'agents' to monitor those chosen.[8] Generals Blake and Popham searched Thames warehouses for Leveller writings in 1649, but Blake's own flag-captain, Charles Thoroughgood, wrote to John Lilburne, the imprisoned Leveller leader, in 1650.[9] The pro-royalist 1648 naval mutiny (led by petty and warrant officers), stimulated the Navy and Admiralty Committees to purge the officer corps of royalists and pay attention to the grievances of the men.[10] As a result, 'the navy became a stronghold of political and religious radicalism', where, significantly, 'officers kept order by fostering a sense of harmony and community rather than by imposing a ferocious disciplinary regime'.[11] Capp concludes that in naval discipline 'the brutality of the 1790s was the exception, not the norm', and Blake's opinion that 'officers and mariners were all fellow-servants to the government' became a powerful legend.[12] There is convincing evidence that Leveller ideas and writings persisted into the nineteenth century.[13]

By 1797 'delegate' was the accepted term for elected representatives of the London Corresponding Society and other democratic organisations.[14] In the navy its role in a collective form of organisation and sharing of responsibility was a pragmatic response to the traditional Admiralty practice of separating . and punishing the ringleaders and pardoning the rest. The Articles of War of 1749 clearly stated that any seaman that 'shall make or endeavour to make any mutinous Assembly upon any Pretence whatsoever ... shall suffer Death'. For complaints about 'the Unwholesomness of the Victual ... he shall quietly make the same known to his Superior or Captain or Commander in Chief'.[15] Therefore the delegates presented their pay grievances and later complaints about provisions through petitions, to avoid the risks of being accused of mutiny and hanging.

---

6   Brailsford, *Levellers*, p. 181.

7   Ibid., p. 216; B. Capp, *Cromwell's Navy* (Oxford, 1992), p. 44.

8   Brailsford, *Levellers*, p. 224; Capp, *Cromwell's Navy*, p. 118.

9   Capp, *Cromwell's Navy*, pp. 118–9.

10   Ibid., pp. 2, 4, 25, 45, 400.

11   Ibid., pp. 396, 400.

12   Ibid., pp. 400, 401.

13   F. K. Donnelly, 'The Levellers and Early Nineteenth Century Radicalism', *Bulletin for Social Study in Labour History*, 49 (1984), pp. 24–8.

14   BL, Add. MS. 35,143, fol. 24; TNA, PC1/42/A, fol. 143, reproduced in H. Alves, *The Adam of a New World* (Universidade do Minho, 1985), p. 283. I am grateful to H. Alves for sending me this book.

15   Rodger, *Articles of War*, p. 26.

The thirty-three delegates at Spithead were experienced and skilled seamen. They comprised five midshipmen, six quarter masters, one quarter master's mate, two quarter gunners, one gunner's mate, one yeoman of the powder room, four yeomen of the sheets and thirteen able seamen.[16] They usually met in the captain's cabin on *Queen Charlotte*.[17]

The delegates at Spithead were radicals because they enacted the most fundamental principles of political reform.[18] They practised democratic principles which reformers in Parliament merely mouthed. They were not revolutionary, because the overthrow of government was never their aim, but their methods were more radical than those of their successors at the Nore because of their transparently democratic practices in pursuing the campaign to improve their conditions. They initiated the campaign to redress the seamen's grievances; subsequent mutinies followed where they led. The belief that the Nore mutineers were more 'political' arose from overtly Jacobin, revolutionary and United Irish references at the courts martial and papers found at the Nore. There were no courts martial at Spithead, so there are no comparable documents, only rumours and reports of Jacobin intentions, substantiated by courts martial evidence from later mutinies in the Channel Fleet.[19] The delegates organised a campaign unanimously supported through the confidence of the seamen. Their demands for pay increases wisely included the marines, whose interests and conditions were interlinked with their own, thereby preventing this force being used against them.[20] The marines on board *Duke* promised: 'The Oath we took we will Stand by while one Drop of blood Circulates in our veins.' The marines on board *Queen Charlotte* averred:

> Impressed with the strongest sense of Gratitude for the good wishes of the Seamen towards us we do Return them our Thanks with every Assurance of Steadyness to their Cause. We Offer our Services and do Assure them that we will assist them in Recovering their Lawfull Rights at this time or any Other Whatsoever[.][21]

Radical Traditions of Seamen

Expectations of discipline, officer roles, and collective decision-making were established during seventeenth-century wars, influenced by privateering, paternalism and growing professionalism.

16 These consisted of two delegates each from sixteen of the leading ships at Spithead. See Manwaring and Dobrée, *Floating Republic*, pp. 262–3. One of *London*'s original delegates, Alexander Harding, was replaced by John Fleming after three seamen were killed. Delegates were also elected on *Monarch*, on Sir Roger Curtis's squadron, and on Plymouth ships. For the traditional importance and skills of these ratings, see Rodger, *Safeguard of the Sea*, pp. 319–20, 324.
17 TNA, ADM1/5125.
18 OED.
19 TNA, ADM1/5339, Courts martial: *Calypso, Artois, Pompée*, June 1797.
20 See M. Lewis, *A Social History of the Navy* (London, 1960), p. 121.
21 TNA, ADM1/5125.

Heirs of a tradition of rule by consensus, seamen expected their voices
to be heard and mutinied if they were not, especially on privateers where
they regarded themselves as being in some sense shareholders in the
voyage.[22]

Discipline implied the subordination of seamen to officers, but the corollary
was that officers were expected to exhibit professionalism and a willingness
to share the hardships of the men. The sea was a levelling occupation, where
'base-born mariners' such as Drake rubbed shoulders with nobles such as
Lord Howard, to 'mould a united ship's company which transcended social
divisions, however wide'.[23]

War imposed great burdens on seamen. They were forced to work in constantly dangerous situations and were invariably neither adequately supplied
nor paid on time. In 1628 poor food, clothing, health and pay provoked mutinies in Plymouth and Portsmouth, where one hundred and fifty men, 'refusing
to weigh anchor', went ashore with a flag to call out the rest of the fleet.[24] In
Rodger's opinion: 'It is not surprising that these years saw the first examples
of the round robin, and the classic cry of the mutineer, "one and all".'[25]

Seamen's disputes of the seventeenth and eighteenth centuries reveal a tradition of negotiation and ever refined tactics.[26] Naval and merchant seamen were
the same men: naval seamen were merchant seamen who volunteered or were
impressed. Spithead petitions included merchant and East India Company
seamen in their demands for an increased Greenwich Hospital provision, 'as
This in Time of Peace must be paid by your Petitioners, we trust will give a
convincing Proof of our Disinterestedness and Moderation'. The increased
pension was required,

> as we know by Experience that there are few Sailors employed by them
> but what have been in the Royal Navy and we have seen them with our
> own Eyes after Sickness, or other accidents has disabled them without
> any Hope of Relief or Support but from their former Services in the
> Navy.[27]

Apart from areas around dockyards and ports, naval recruitment most frequently drew on merchant shipping. The navy required recruits to train from
boyhood, or to be experienced able seamen who had learnt their skills in the
merchant navy.[28] Numbers of naval seamen rose with each war of the eight-

22 Rodger, *Safeguard of the Sea*, p. 322.
23 Ibid., pp. 297–8, 302–3.
24 Ibid., p. 403.
25 Ibid., p. 403.
26 See Davis, *Rise of the English Shipping Industry* (London, 1962), pp. 135–8, 153–6; M.
Rediker, *Between the Devil and the Deep Blue Sea* (Cambridge, 1989), pp. 6, 166, chapters
2, 5; W. Rogers, *Cruising Voyage round the World* (London, 1928), pp. 4, 22, 33; N. Uring,
Voyages and Travels (London, 1928), p. 178.
27 TNA, ADM3/136, fol. 373, 'The Seamen's' Reply', 19 April 1797.
28 See Lavery, *Nelson's Navy*, especially 124, and chapters V, VI, passim; A. T. Mahan,
Seapower in Its Relations to the War of 1812, I (London, 1905), pp. 9–13.

eenth century: 49,000 in 1714, 59,000 in 1746, 84,000 in 1762, 107,000 in 1783, reaching a peak of 129,000 in 1802.[29]

Royal Navy traditions therefore reflected the traditions of Britain's merchant seafaring communities. The muster books of the ships involved in the Spithead mutiny show that the majority of personnel came from the seaboard counties of the British Isles. Their communities invariably supported them because families and shopkeepers relied on their wages. Throughout the eighteenth century merchant seamen participated in many strikes. At the end of the Seven Years' War economic hardship resulted from the release of labour and inflation in the 1760s. In December 1762 Liverpool seamen struck for a minimum wage of 40s a month. Those arrested were liberated from Ormskirk gaol by a sympathetic crowd. In the North East, seamen demonstrated for higher wages in April 1768. Authorities tried to maintain employment protection and keep down the price of food by enforcing the Assize of Bread.

Another seamen's strike broke out in Liverpool in August 1775 when a wage cut was attempted. Trade was hit by embargoes, imposed at the start of the American War, and the simultaneous end of the whaling season. The sailors immobilised *Derby*, a slaver, and were supported by a crowd who paraded behind a red flag demanding the restoration of their wages. The sailors picketed the docks, dissuaded other sailors from working, and negotiated with the merchants in the Exchange. Arrested sailors were released by a crowd of two thousand townspeople. After merchants had attacked and killed unarmed sailors, the strikers seized firearms and two guns from a whaler. Behind a red flag, and wearing red ribbons, they attacked the Exchange and the houses of merchants who opposed them. They did not disperse until troops arrived from Chester a week later.[30]

Another powerful group of seamen from Tyne and Wear had diverse experiences and destinations: the London coal trade, Baltic naval supplies, the Mediterranean, West Indies and Americas, and Greenland fisheries in spring and summer. As Tony Barrow has pointed out, this made them 'hardy and competent mariners with an awesome reputation for toughness and riotous behaviour'. Their unpleasant living conditions and physical dangers paralleled those of naval seamen. Their militant campaigns to maintain wage levels 'depended on the solidarity of the sailors, and their acceptance of the discipline of their elected representatives'. They frequently detained colliers needed in London from sailing to press their case.[31]

Similarly, keelmen of the Tyne and Wear rivers often used 'collective bargaining by riot'. The term 'mutiny' was applied to their strikes in the seventeenth century. They petitioned, withdrew labour, and threatened violence to

---

29 Lloyd, *British Seaman*, pp. 286–9. See Lewis, *Social History of the Navy*, p. 121.

30 These accounts were taken from J. Stevenson, *Popular Disturbances in England 1700–1832* (London, 1992), pp. 155–7 and R. B. Rose, 'Red Flag over Liverpool: 1775 – A Liverpool Sailors' Strike in the Eighteenth Century', in B. Blick and L. Patsouras, eds, *Rebels against the Old Order* (Youngstown State University Ohio, 1994), pp. 63–70. I am very grateful to R. B. Rose, for sending me this article.

31 T. Barrow, 'The Greenlanders at Shield 1760–1830: A Labour Elite', *North East Labour History*, 24 (1990), pp. 2, 6–7. I am grateful to Tony Barrow who sent me this article.

Table 2.1. Spithead Delegates April–May 1797

Ships	Guns/Rate	Delegates
Royal George	100 1st	Valentine Joyce, John Morrice
Queen Charlotte	100 1st	Patrick Glynn, John Huddlestone
Royal Sovereign	100 1st	Joseph Green, John Richardson
London	90 2nd	Alexander Harding, William Riley, John Fleming
Glory	90 2nd	Patrick Duggan, John Bethell
Duke	90 2nd	Michael Adams, William Anderson
Mars	74 3rd	Thomas Allen, James Blithe
Marlborough	74 3rd	John Vassie, William Screaton
Ramillies	74 3rd	Charles Berry, George Clear
Robust	74 3rd	David Wilson, John Scrivener
Impétueux	78 3rd	John Witney, William Porter
Defence	74 3rd	George Gallaway, James Berwick
Terrible	74 3rd	Mark Turner, George Salked
Pompée	84 3rd	William Potts, James Melvin
Minotaur	74 3rd	Dennis Lawler, George Crossland
Defiance	74 3rd	John Saunders, John Husband
Monarch	74 3rd	John Hollowood, John Bennet

Sources
I. Schomberg, *Naval Chronology*, III (5 vols, Egerton, London, 1802), 11.
G. E. Manwaring, B. Dobrée, *The Floating Republic* (Geoffrey Bles, London, 1935), 262–3.
TNA, ADM36 Muster Books: ADM1/5125.

Table 2.2. Delegates in Sir Roger Curtis's Squadron April–May 1797

Ships	Guns/Rates	Delegates
Prince	90 2nd	John Linsday, James Ramsay
Juste	84 3rd	Thomas Redpath, James Scully
Hector	74 3rd	Edward Cavanagh, William Cass
Caesar	84 3rd	John Gilder, William Oliver
Ganges	74 3rd	Henry Edwards, John Nows
Formidable	90 2nd	William Ingram, George Horser
Russell	74 3rd	James Willson, Robert Sinclair
Thames	32 5th	John Cristell, John Hyland

Sources: TNA, ADM1/4172, 15 May 1797; ADM8/73, April, May 1797.

Table 2.3. Plymouth Delegates April–May 1797

Ships	Guns/Rates	Delegates
Atlas	90 2nd	Edward Williams, Hugh Carr
Edgar	74 3rd	John Wilson, Alexander Plantain
Majestic	74 3rd	Patrick Cook, Benjamin Greenland
Saturn	74 3rd	John Cole, James Peage
Cambridge	80 3rd	John Lemon, Andrew Mackenzie
Leviathan	74 3rd	George Hoggan, Richard Mumford
Magnanime	44 5th	John Roberts, William Thorn
Cerberus	32 5th	John Johnstone, John Snowdon
Artois	38 5th	Thomas Mein, Nicholas Pearce
Gibraltar	80 3rd	George Walter, James Parkinson
Concorde	32 5th	John Wishart, Alexander Inglis
Galatea	32 5th	James Payne, Neil MacCarthy
Greyhound	32 5th	George Elphinstone, Samuel Atchison
Zealand	64 3rd	John Roberts, Ryan Preed

Sources: TNA, ADM1/811, 30 April 1797; ADM1/812, 6 June 1797; NMRN, 1988.500(295); ADM8/73, Jan-May 1797.

support their wage demands, combining the manpower of these two rivers. Their sheer weight of numbers (nearly three thousand in 1719) was too great for the civil powers to subdue by force, so the authorities had no choice but to negotiate a return to work. Until the early nineteenth century strikes continued to erupt over rates of pay and volume of work, often only ended by the use of troops.

In 1968, McCord and Brewster published, in Tony Barrow's words, 'one of the earliest scholarly attempts to make a connection between the seamen's strike and their opposition to impressment in 1792–93 and the naval mutinies in 1797'.[32] The parallels are inescapable. One was the reaction of the authorities, who

> firmly believed that to yield to the demands of the seamen was not simply to lose an industrial dispute, but to contribute to the over-turning of that due subordination which was an essential ingredient in the established order of society.[33]

32   Tony Barrow's comment on N. McCord and D. E. Brewster, 'Some Labour Troubles of the 1790s in North East England', *International Review of Social History*, XIII (1968), pp. 365–383. I am grateful to Tony Barrow for sending me this article. This point might be contested by R. B. Rose, whose article was originally published in *Transactions of the Lancashire and Cheshire Antiquarian Society*, 68 (1958), pp. 85–92. Dugan, *Great Mutiny*, pp. 88–9, also refers to seamen demonstrating for higher pay in 1792 in Scottish and East Anglian ports.
33   McCord and Brewster, 'Some Labour Troubles of the 1790s', p. 369.

Another parallel with Spithead lay in the tactics of the seamen who para-lysed Tyne harbour for weeks, preventing ships from sailing. They were 'not a body lightly to be tackled', and the shipowners did not attempt force to end the strike. Civil powers attempted conciliation, while assembling a naval and military force.[34] The seamen's behaviour in managing the strike and avoiding 'major provocations' was crucial:

> [T]he leaders of the seamen were in full control of their followers, and there was very little violence; the only assaults recorded are the mild meas-ures taken by the strikers to enforce discipline in their own ranks.[35]

Rowland Burdon, Durham MP, assured Evan Nepean, then Under Secretary at the Home Office, in November 1792 'that the Sailors appear heartily at-tached to the Government of the Country'.[36] In December, they demonstrated their lack of animosity to the naval force assembled against them by pulling *Martin* off a shoal in the river, where she had grounded.[37]

In 1793 the Tyneside seamen attempted to counter the hardships imposed by a vigorous Impress Service by petitioning Parliament for a pay rise for naval seamen, supported by a local publicity campaign and strenuous opposition to the press gangs locally. Like the 1797 seamen's proclamations, the language of the handbill, directed at their fellow seamen (but also aimed at the public at large), emphatically expressed their loyalty to their country, explained their dire economic position and the hardships imposed on their families when men were forced to join the navy at such low wages. They wished to remedy these 'Calamities', 'not to <u>create disturbances</u>'.[38]

Despite extensive lobbying by the seamen and by the Impress Captain on their behalf to the Admiralty, their petition was rejected by the House of Commons on 25 February 1793, and a scheme to regulate seamen's wages proposed by MP Rowland Burdon was not taken up by the government.[39] Confrontation between the Impress Service and North-East seamen per-sisted until 1797, as problems of '"Augmentation of Wages"' and the lack of 'some easy Mode of remitting a part home to their Families"' were not addressed.[40]

There is conclusive evidence, therefore, for saying, as Rose does, that

> each outbreak expressed a common tradition of resistance among sea-going men. By 1797 a fivefold wartime expansion had transformed the professional navy with an influx of newly enrolled civilians, and had thus

---

34 Ibid., pp. 369–70.
35 Ibid., p. 370.
36 Quoted in McCord and Brewster, 'Some Labour Troubles of the 1790s', p. 381.
37 McCord and Brewster, 'Some Labour Troubles of the 1790s', p. 373.
38 Seamen's handbill, 'Friends and Fellow Seamen!', 2 February 1793. I am grateful to T. Barrow for sending me a copy of this handbill.
39 McCord and Brewster, 'Some Labour Troubles of the 1790s', p. 380.
40 James Rudman, Mayor of Newcastle, to Home Secretary Dundas, quoted in McCord and Brewster, 'Some Labour Troubles of the 1790s', p. 381.

made its personnel more broadly representative of British seamen as a whole.[41]

The naval seamen of 1797 were well aware of the fourfold difference in pay rates between themselves and merchant seamen, of the increases to the army, militia and officers in 1795 which unfairly discriminated against them: 'That is a Truth every Seaman knows and a certain Loss they endure, with all the Patience of Subordination, and all the Zeal of Patriotism.'[42]

Naval Precedents

A series of labour disputes in the navy from the 1780s determined both the pattern of expectations and discontents from the seamen, and the pattern of Admiralty reactions. The mutinies which accompanied the conclusion of the American War in 1783 foreshadowed the methods used by the 1797 mutineers and the reactions of the Admiralty. Prompted by mutinies in January 1783 amongst soldiers embarking reluctantly from Portsmouth for the East Indies, mutiny spread to ships returning from America. The Navy Board delayed payments in the outports because it would 'occasion great increase of business to the clerks' and wished to 'guard against double payments'.[43] On 11 March 1783, six weeks after peace preliminaries had been signed, the 'people' on *Janus* were 'in a mutinous state'. On Sunday 16 March, 'Lord How came on board and Harangued to the Ships Company'. Despite being paid prize money on 24 March, *Janus* was still mutinous the following day, but on the 26th 'the People returned to their Duty'.[44]

In all, twelve ships mutinied, and Earl Howe, First Lord of the Admiralty, was sent down with the 'fullest approbation' of George III.[45] He reported that some ships were protesting against being sent to the East Indies, while others wanted to be paid and discharged and others wanted an advance on their wages to buy requirements for going abroad.[46] At first Rear Admiral Hood (later Lord Bridport), Commander at Spithead, reported:

---

41   Rose, 'Red Flag over Liverpool', p. 69.
42   NMM, WYN/109/7/14, fol. 5, Captain Patton; BL, Althorp Papers, G187, Pakenham to Spencer, 11 December 1796.
43   TNA, ADM178/133, 'Mutiny in the Royal Navy', I, 1691–1919 (unpublished, Admiralty, 1933), p. 11.
44   TNA, ADM51/4226, *Janus*, Captain O'Hara's log.
45   TNA, ADM178/133, 'Mutiny in the Royal Navy', I, 36. Ships from home waters were *Egmont, Janus, Cambridge, Triumph, Pégase, Ganges, Goliath, Queen, Portland, Princess Royal* and *Bombay Castle. Raisonable* returned from the West Indies in June 1783. Ibid., chapter IV.
46   TNA, ADM1/982, *Atlas*, 18 Jan 1783. Pye reported to the Navy Board that the captains felt that the men were entitled to the advance, particularly Captain Elphinstone of *Atlas*, who wrote to Pye that only 26 had had the advance, leaving 460 who had not, and that the crew were also entitled to six months' pay, which they understood they would not get yet. Captain Elphinstone was in command of *Monarch* during the 1797 mutiny.

The people remain … quiet, and do the duty of the ships without murmurs, but with a serious, silent, and fixed determination not to proceed to sea, but to the ports where their ships may be paid off.[47]

Howe visited the Spithead ships again because the men still had not been paid off and were refusing to obey orders. He promised that each would be first to go into Portsmouth Harbour, then returned to London, reporting to the Cabinet that the paying off should proceed 'with caution'.[48] This exacerbated the situation by introducing the risk that the men would carry their ships into harbour themselves. The Admiralty sent firm orders to pay off five ships of the line, twelve frigates and two sloops. The port admiral, Sir Thomas Pye, sent in the largest ships first, on 30 and 31 March, and they were paid off in two weeks, but not without further disturbances from later ships.

Raisonable, returning from the West Indies, wished to be paid off in Portsmouth rather than Chatham. The Admiralty's reaction presaged its 1797 behaviour: Lord Keppel, succeeding Howe as First Lord, decided that enough had been conceded:

[I]f they gain their point, every ship's company that does not chose to go round will refuse, especially as they have so late an example before their eyes.

This time … is not like the first breaking out of the mutiny in the fleet, and this is only a single ship. Some example must be made to put a stop to it in future.[49]

Portsmouth's new port admiral, Sir John Montagu, planned to fire on the ship and sink her if the men tried to bring her in.[50] Thomas Sneeden, captain of the forecastle on *Raisonable*, was virtually in command of the ship, although a letter from the mutineers said 'there are no ringleaders amongst us; it is all the ship's company's projection. Thomas Sneeden is appointed by the people as speaker and transactor'. After one day and two nights Captain Hervey regained control, arresting and hanging Sneeden with two colleagues at Chatham.[51]

These mutinies taught the seamen 'the power of concerted resistance to authority on a large scale as a means of having grievances put right'.[52] It also reinforced the Admiralty's approach to discontent: that ringleaders would be picked out and scapegoated. Single-ship mutinies: *Windsor Castle* and *Culloden* in 1794 and *Terrible* in 1795, reconfirmed that individual offenders would be punitively penalised. In 1794 *Windsor Castle*'s crew complained of excessive ill-treatment and demanded fresh officers. Despite the captain's court martial which cleared him, the crew was pardoned and the captain replaced

---

47 TNA, ADM178/133, 'Mutiny in the Royal Navy', I, p. 37.
48 Ibid., p. 37.
49 Ibid., p. 41.
50 Ibid., p. 42.
51 Ibid., p. 43.
52 Ibid., p. 45.

when they continued to mutiny. On *Culloden* fear of sailing in an unseaworthy ship, and on *Terrible* grievances over bad biscuit, caused mutinies. Five men from *Culloden*, and five from *Terrible* were hanged, the latter's captain telling the crew 'it should not be a *Windsor Castle*'s business'.[53]

Spithead Radicalism in Action

Among Admiralty documents are petitions, letters and proclamations from the ships' companies involved in the Spithead mutiny.[54] These provide a clear indication of the seamen's planning and reactions to events throughout the mutiny. From the start, their approach and methods were democratic:

> A boat from the Queen Charlotte with tow [*sic*] men Impowered to act for the ships Company went on board every ship in the fleet and as they were Boarded they chose tow men and followed in their own boat.

The thirty-three delegates, at least one of whom had sent an allotment of his wages home to his family, had served on their ships for between two and four years.[55] In the evening of 16 April they agreed their rules.[56] The Admiralty saw sedition in the sixth rule: that 'Every Seaman and Marine' was to take 'an oath of Fiddelity not onely to ourselves but to the Fleet in General': every man 'swore by his maker that the Cause we have Undertaken we Persevere in till acomplished'. Messages confirming that the oath had been taken were sent by *Nymphe*, *Duke* and *Defiance*. It was agreed that a red flag at the fore top gallant mast, or two lights at night, one above the other, would signal the alarm for the delegates to assemble on any ship. Rose interpreted this 'as the colour of rebellion and solidarity'.[57] It was the invariable signal for going into action, but because of its alternative association with pirates and corsairs, was known as the 'bloody flag' or 'flag of defiance'.[58] The Spithead mutineers undoubtedly used the flag dually: as a warning signal and, like their predecessors since 1628, as a defiant rallying symbol. To government loyalists, however, it was 'the signal of Mutiny and Defiance'.[59]

Early misunderstandings were swiftly clarified. The second rule, designed to reinforce their unity, was that 'every Ship shall give three Cheers at 8 O Clock in the Morning and at Sun set in the Eavning',[60] but apparently not all ships immediately realised this. *Pompée* and *Duke* assured *Queen Charlotte* if they had known the 'Perticulars' they would have 'Cheered you yesterday and you

---

53 Ibid., p. 49.
54 Mainly in TNA, ADM1/5125, ADM1/107 and ADM3/136.
55 G. E. Manwaring and B. Dobrée, *The Floating Republic* (London, 1935), pp. 262–3; TNA, ADM36, Muster Books.
56 Transcribed in Coats, Chapter 1, 'Spithead Mutiny: Introduction'.
57 Rose, 'Red Flag over Liverpool', p. 69.
58 T. Wilson, *Flags at Sea* (London, 1986), p. 77, and see pp. 46, 61, 79, 108.
59 Rodger, *Safeguard of the Sea*, pp. 402–3; *True Briton*, 27 May 1797.
60 TNA, ADM1/5125, 16 April 1797.

may rely on our being true on every Occation'. It was also used to alert the fleet to problems on individual ships. The crew on *Nymphe* were denied a boat and cheered to attract attention. *Megaera*'s crew were prevented from cheering by their master, and when told by the *Royal George* delegates that they need not cheer, still expressed their 'desire to be Zealous to the Cause'. Cheering had historic celebratory associations, enacted when agreement was reached with the Admiralty on 23 April.[61] Some ships' companies were clearly still being kept under strict control by their officers as a letter from *Royal William* on 20 April showed: 'we have reason to beleve that lett.ⁱˢ has been sent to us from you as we beleve they have been sent Into the wardroom'. They also asked why they had not been visited by the delegates, pleading: 'let us here from you as soon as Possable'.[62]

Correspondence revealed the breadth of the seamen's convictions: they were submitting the petitions 'on behalf of themselves and the Rest of their Bretheren on board of the fleet at Spithead or Elsewhere'. *Queen Charlotte*, Lord Howe's flagship, took the initiative.[63]

> In the Month of February the following Petition was Drawn out on board H.M. Ship Queen Charlotte and forwarded to the rest of the Fleet at Spithead and about a Dozen Coppys was sent to Admiral Earl Howe Just at the time the fleet was Ordered to sea and after being out one month and Laying a fortnight at Spithead.[64]

Her ship's company drew up and sent out the original petitions to Lord Howe because he was their commander-in-chief.[65] They revered him because, commanding *Queen Charlotte* at the Battle of the First of June in 1794, he had led them to victory. Lieutenant Philip Beaver, *Monarch*, also recalled on 17 April 1797: 'After the battle of the 1st June Lord Howe hinted, if he did not actually promise, that he would endeavour to get the seamen's pay increased.'[66]

London's seamen fully supported *Queen Charlotte*, returning 'their harty thanks for your kind Intentions. the Resolutions is generous, the Intention

61 Rodger, *Safeguard of the Sea*, pp. 325–6; TNA, ADM1/5125.

62 *Royal William* was Sir Peter Parker's flagship, moored in Portsmouth Harbour as a receiving ship. It was therefore isolated, although visible to the fleet at Spithead.

63 TNA, ADM1/107, Bridport to Spencer, 13 April 1797, Bridport to Nepean, 15 April 1797; BL, Althorp Papers, G191, Bridport to Spencer, 23 April 1797, 24 April 1797; Portsmouth City Museum, 'Lines composed on Board His Majesty's Ship LONDON', C571, loaned by John Pounds; Lady Spencer to William Windham, 20 April 1997, in Earl of Rosebery, ed., *The Windham Papers*, II (London, 1913), p. 49.

64 February and March 1797. The following references are from TNA, ADM1/5125, April 1797, papers of *Queen Charlotte*.

65 TNA, ADM1/5125, documents from *Queen Charlotte*. The petitions all repeat the claim to be acting for the whole fleet.

66 Lieutenant Philip Beaver, *Monarch*, 17 April 1797, in E. H. Moorhouse, ed., *Letters of the English Seamen: 1587–1808* (London, 1910), p. 180. An increase in the full and half pay of naval lieutenants was awarded in 1795 'in consequence, it is believed, of a petition'. E. P. Brenton, *The Naval History of Great Britain*, I (London, 1837), p. 46; TNA, ADM178/133, 'Mutiny in the Royal Navy', I, p. 10.

noble. In short It is worthey of the Conquers of the Glorious first of June'.[67] They argued that it was not sufficient just to send it to the Admiralty. As it is a 'Nationall affair', and as they are the 'purse Bearers of the nation', the petition must also go to the House of Commons. They ended: 'Proceed in Caution peace and good behaviour. Let no Disorder nor tumult Influence your proceedings. Most Affectionately London'.

After six weeks with no reply, the delegates drew up further petitions to the Admiralty and to the House of Commons and 'Determined not to go to sea till they got what they aimed at on Saturday the 15.th April, the day apoint:d for sending the Petitions away'. In these the seamen refined their negotiating techniques:

> our Reason for Adressing the Lords of the Admiralty in percuence to the house of Commons was this. the Board of admiralty are all Professionall men and might take Umbrage at not having the Compliment Paid to them first.

Naïvely, they envisaged the Admiralty's swift approval and response to their petition: 'if they adopt the prayers of our Petition they will soon pass a Motion in concequence and bring it before the house with all the Ministral party to back ... it and thereby take the merit to themselves'. They trusted that even 'if through their means It should Misscarry', once it reached the House of Commons, 'with all force of Opertunitys on our sides..., we have not the least Dout but by Unity amongst ourselves and a steadey Peaceable persever-ance to Carry our Point.'

Again, their petition was couched deferentially: 'we beg leave to Remind your August assembly' that the cost of living had risen 30 per cent since the last Act relating to their pay, passed in the reign of Charles II, and requested a revision to 'Enable your Petitioners and their Families to live In the same Comfortable manner as Seamen and Marines could do at that time'.[68] Alluding 'with Jelousey' to the pay rises awarded to the Army and Militia, they pro-fessed themselves as 'Loyal to our Sovering and Zealous In the Defence of our Countary' as those forces. [69]

To the Admiralty, they recalled the 'many hardships and Opressions we have Laboured under for many years' and their 'worth and good Serveis both in the American war and the preasent war'. They asked for 'the Respect due to us' and 'do not in the least dout but your Lordships will comply with our Desires

---

67 A reference to the leading role played by *Queen Charlotte* as Howe's flagship in June 1794.

68 The rate of pay had actually been raised during the Interregnum to the current level as an 'encouragement' for 'mariners, to induce them to come in cheerfully and speedily to the service'; on 1 January 1653, able seamen's pay rose from 19s to 24s a month, ordinary seamen's remained at 19s. *Calendar of State Papers Domestic, 1652–53*, p. 42. The Act of Charles II was cited because that was the last occasion that Parliament had set wage rates, and Charles II's government had not endorsed the Commonwealth's statutes, but they were the same as the Act of 1 January 1653. Manwaring and Dobrée, *Floating Republic*, p. 23; W. Laird Clowes, *The Royal Navy*, II (London, 1996), p. 98.

69 Awarded in 1795.

which are in every way Reasonable'. Their first grievance was over pay. By the second round of petitions they had extended their list of grievances to six more:

1. Their allowance of provisions to be raised from fourteen ounces in the pound to sixteen ounces (to eliminate the purser's eighth) and to be improved in quality.

2. While in harbour to receive more fresh vegetables and meat (and no flour to be served in port).

3. Improved care of the sick.

4. Greater 'opportunities to tast the sweets of Liberty on shore when in any Harbour'.

5. Injured men to be paid in full until cured or discharged.

6. Grievances from individual ships to be redressed.

The perspicacity of the delegates was eloquently revealed in a Caution to the fleet:

> The Settlement of a business of such vast Importance as the preasent is the most Critical, and ought to be attended to with the Greatest wisdom, as ourselves and Carracters Depends on our preasent conduct.

It set out their bargaining positions:

1. That all the requests in their Petition should be granted.

2. That only a written statement of what will be passed into law will satisfy them.

3. That an Act of Parliament be passed to increase the pay.

4. That a pardon be granted from the King.

It ended by reassuring the fleet that the moment for action was right:

> Never had British seamen more reasonable demands nor a favourable Opertunity of rendering themselves a Respectable body of men then the preasent but if they are Diverted or amused by false alarms or fair But vain Speeches or Promises from their Preasent Glorious and Righteous Resolution of doing themselves Justace after haveing so long fought for the Intrest of Others, neglecting their own, Dreadfull is the Consequence, the Success is shure.

During the protracted negotiations over the details of the pay award, the strength of the seamen was tested on 22 April by Admirals Gardner, Colpoys and Pole, who 'tried by Persuasions threatings and all other means in their power to Perswade the Delegates to agree to the Proposals'. They tried to cajole *Queen Charlotte*'s ship's company into accepting another paper 'which was said to be agreed to by the Dellegates but this Fraud was useless for the People was Determined and showed their Disapprobation by hissing and other marks of Contempt'. While the three admirals informed the rest of the fleet that *Queen Charlotte* had agreed, *Royal George* hoisted the red warning flag so that all the ships sent boats to her and discovered the admirals' 'Duplicity'. After Lord Bridport's flag was hauled down from his flagship *Royal George*, his ship's company wrote to him personally to explain the reason for their actions. They firmly blamed Vice Admiral Gardner for trying to 'sew division in the fleet' and expressed their conviction that 'we have nothing to depend upon but our own vigours Exertions to obtain redress of Greavances'. They assured him, however, that the whole fleet was 'universally and Zealously Attached' to Bridport and regarded him as 'their Father, their Friend, and in short as a Nobleman willing to assist and further our Endeavours'.

Duke and *Nymphe* wrote to ensure that the delegates would 'not be led Astray' by these 'False Insinuateing Desings', saying, 'we hope, Brothers, you will not Desist from your Former Resolution but Continue it untill all is Granted'. *Defiance* encapsulated the crux of their campaign:

> We smile at the Simplicity of our Officers In attempting to divide us. We know the Consequence of our oath and value it Equal to our lives.
>
> Redress we will have Seduced we will not be we can Plainly foresee by the Papers that was Read on [sic] Yesterday on board of our Ship it seamed only a desing to keep us in the Preasent state of Pay and Provisions unless Passed into an act of Parlement for you might Plainly see by the act Passed in the Reing of King Charles the Second that unless this is Passed Into an act of Parlement the Admiralty the Parlement or the whole nation at Large may promise to take our Grevences into consideration and after that trample them and us under their feet when we are divided so brothers we will never flinch from you in this Preasent Cause[.]

Even the marines of *Queen Charlotte*, *Duke* and *Royal George* expressed their 'Steadyness to their Cause' and promised their assistance.

The seamen saw the setback as a prelude to an attack from the Admiralty. Gill stated that 'throughout the mutinies the seamen showed an extraordinary readiness to believe any suggestion against the government. Their suspicion, however, was natural'.[70] From their perspective, the most probable outcome of a breakdown of negotiations was physical force. However, in 1795, Captain Philip Patton had warned Earl Spencer that 'no force of which the state is possessed, Ships of War only excepted, can reduce Mutinous Seamen who are in possession of Capital Ships'.[71]

The extent to which the ships' companies were prepared to go to enforce their case was expressed by *London*: any ship

---

70 Gill, *Naval Mutinies*, p. 51, fn. 1 and see p. 56.
71 NMM, WYN/109/7/14, fol. 4.

that dares to deviate from these our Determined Resolutions we will at the Hasard of our lives send them to such immediate Destruction as we are well capable of and as their Crimes Most justly Disarve.

Also from the *Duke*: 'Brothers, this is to let you know that we are all Readey perpared for anything that can happen. we have got Possession of the small arms and Everything that is necessary to our Preservation.' *Minotaur* assured the delegates that they were 'still willing to Part with the last drop of our Harts Blood to maintain the cause we now labour under and not to flinch untill the Act … is Passed'. *Royal George* advised the delegates that the ships moored to the west, that is, nearer to the mouth of Portsmouth Harbour and the shore batteries, ought to 'drop down to Eastward to be secure from any attempt', and also to 'shot the Guns as we have allreadey done'.

The perseverance of the seamen was rewarded when the King's pardon was eventually read out by Captain Lock on board the *Queen Charlotte* on 23 April, but they received it cautiously. He

> Desired the People to give three Cheers which was done by some of the People and the Officers, but the Majority of the Ships Company not being satisfyed, and it being Sunday and none of the Dellegates on board, the Signal was made and all the boats from Each ship came on board of the Queen Charlotte and the same had been read on board of Every Ship in the fleet but the People not being satisfyed because nothing was mentioned Concerning the Greavences at large the Dellegates went into the Cabbin as Usuall to Consult upon it and were Dubious, fearing it to be a fraud, therefore it was agreed to send to the Royal George for the Impression of the Seal that was on the Packet.

Four delegates brought back the seal carried by Admiral Pole, who was reluctantly (recalling his last visit with Vice Admiral Gardner) allowed on board. The delegates were satisfied that redress of grievances would be made and took the news back to their ships. The discussions then began on each ship:

> Various were the Oppinion in the Charlotte till at last by the Preswasions of the most senseable part of the ships company they were all brought to Understand it and agreed to put an End to all Disturbances If the rest of the fleet was satisfyed, and the Signal being made for the Dellegates, the all came on board again and the word they brought back was they would stand by the Queen Charlotte.

This occasion: Sunday 23 April, was marked by every ship manning their yards and every man 'Dressed in Blue jackets and White Trowsers which made a beautiful Sight'.

With agreement reached between the Admiralty and the seamen, most of the fleet went to St Helen's to wait for an easterly wind to take them to Torbay, where a supportive mutiny had broken out.[72] Only *London* remained

---

72 News of the Spithead mutiny had reached Plymouth via *Porcupine*. Mutiny broke out

at Spithead with *Marlborough* and *Nymphe* because of further grievances.[73] Two weeks passed, however, with no easterly wind, and no news of the Act of Parliament. On the isolated ships at Spithead seamen read disturbing reports of unsatisfactory Parliamentary debates in the newspapers and the new quantities of provisions were not served. Rumours abounded that the seamen's cause was forgotten and ships remaining at Spithead were to be picked on individually. An ambiguous order sent by the Admiralty on 1 May led to the tragedy on *London* on 7 May, examined in detail in David W. London's Chapter 3, 'What Really Happened On Board HMS *London*?'

It may be deduced that no influence was exerted upon Spithead delegates by French revolutionaries or United Irishmen, because their proclamations made no such references. Pro-peace and pro-French sentiments were expressed in the Channel Fleet, however, within a month of the Spithead settlement, revealing a keen awareness of opposition politics and the possible outcome of the Spithead mutiny if it had not been carefully restrained by the delegates. On *Pompée* a plan to circulate a petition for peace which would 'go from ship to ship when they got into harbour' was discovered in June 1797. The plot also involved *Mars*, *Duke* and an unnamed fourth ship. The leaders spoke of the reform of Parliament and

> that upwards of Sixty thousand People in London had Petition for Peace, which Petition had been rejected and that it could only be brought about by the Sailors, and that instead of applying for an Increase of Wages, and an Addition to the Provisions, he would have been for a Peace, ... by the Saylors petitioning for Peace they would be doing an Act of Charity to the Nation, and if they the Sailors would petition for Peace the Nation at Large would be highly Indebted to them.[74]

They argued that peace 'could not be done without dismissing the Ministers'.[75] One of the leaders, William Guthrie, 'pointed his Hand through the Port towards France and said it is not our Enemys that live there it is our Friends'.[76]

Pompée's oath, 'To ever stand true till Death in promoting the cause of Freedom with Equity, while any Probability of furthering its progress remained', sworn so that 'we shall not deceive each other', concerned the Admiralty so much that in July 1797 an Act was passed against such unlawful oaths.[77] Since 'divers wicked and evil-disposed persons have of late attempted to seduce persons serving in his Majesty's forces by sea and land ... and to incite them to acts of mutiny and sedition' by imposing 'the pretended obligation of oaths unlawfully administered', these would in future be liable to seven

---

on 26 April and followed the same pattern as at Spithead. The seamen would not return to their duty until assured that the Spithead dispute was settled satisfactorily.
73   TNA, ADM1/5125.
74   TNA, ADM1/5339, *Pompée* court martial, June 1797, evidence of William Guthrie.
75   Ibid., evidence of James Addison.
76   Ibid., evidence of James Addison.
77   Ibid., evidence of Dr. Josiah Packwood, James Callaway and Thomas Ashley.

years' transportation.[78] It is clear from evidence concerning the oathtaking on 'a Book about the size of a small Bible' that those involved considered the action serious and binding.[79]

Most significant on *Pompée* were not the revolutionary activities, but the fact that the debates raged among the ship's company for three days before the officers were informed. Two parties 'discoursed on the subject', with only eighty-six signing in favour (many under duress).[80] The plan was revealed to the officers on Sunday 4 June by loyalists, because 'there was a murmering that they were going to take the Ships Company into a French Port'.[81] The majority opinion, articulated by John Sweet, Sergeant of Marines, was that 'we all wished for a peace but we were not the People who ought to make peace'.[82] To conspirators Thomas Ashley and William Guthrie, 'Liberty' was a political concept, but to most of the crew it simply meant 'Liberty to go on shore'.[83] The activists obtained signatures by intimidation, showing that support for this issue was far from universal. *Pompée*'s Spithead delegates, James Melvin and William Potts, significantly, were among the majority opposing the plan.[84]

At Spithead the delegates' actions were designed to maintain a dialogue with the Admiralty, but not to sacrifice any of their concrete demands nor incur any penalties. Their sense of self-respect, pride, self-discipline and loyalty were overwhelmingly expressed in their writings and actions. Admiralty correspondence made no adverse comments on their behaviour. Even Colpoys, writing to Secretary of the Admiralty Evan Nepean on 8 May while uncertain about his future, reported the delegates saying 'We shall shew – as we have the power – that we can use it with discretion.'[85] Two decisions illustrate their commitment to these aims. When *Romney* refused to accompany a convoy, in accordance with the oath not to lift an anchor, the delegates decided that she should sail, 'as we would in no wise wish to bring the Injury of Country in our Cause'.[86] After the *London* shootings delegates Valentine Joyce and Patrick Glynn visited the injured seamen and marines in Haslar Hospital, and in order to maintain discipline in the volatile situation, appointed a seaman who was a patient, Alexander Tutton, 'to keep good order amongst them'.[87]

78 An Act for more effectually preventing the administering or taking of unlawful Oaths, 37 Geo. III c.123, 19 July 1797, *Statutes Revised*, III (London, 1872), p. 443.

79 TNA, ADM1/5339, *Pompée* court martial, evidence of John Kelly. Also that of George Long, who took his 'Hatt off' and James Kirkwood, who kissed 'the Book'.

80 Ibid., evidence of Isaac Stewart and Michael Bowen.

81 Ibid., evidence of James Kirkwood.

82 Ibid., evidence of John Sweet.

83 Ibid., evidence of Thomas Ashley, John Dewar and John Livingstone.

84 TNA, ADM3/137, 'An Address from Pompée', 6 June 1797.

85 TNA, ADM1/107, 8 May 1797.

86 TNA, ADM1/1022, 17 April 1797.

87 TNA, ADM1/1472, Graham, 22 May 1797.

Valentine Joyce, Delegate[88]

Chief spokesman for the Spithead mutineers, and delegate from *Royal George*, Valentine Joyce has been the most misrepresented character of the mutiny. Among the principal secondary sources Temple Patterson was sceptical of the accepted view that Joyce was a career seditionist, held by all the rest except Neale and Manwaring and Dobrée.[89] Gill was apparently the starting point for these modern misconceptions, citing 'Joyce had been imprisoned for sedition' as evidence for his statement that 'at Spithead there were many Irishmen who had come from prison'.[90] Later he stated that Joyce had entered the navy as a Quota man and 'had been imprisoned for seditious practices'.[91] Despite reading magistrate Aaron Graham's comments on Joyce, Gill did not recognise that his own interpretation was both unlikely and inconsistent with naval requirements.[92] Wells stated that Joyce was '"well" known to the Home Office for his political work', while Elliott declared that he 'administered the United Irish oath'.[93] Lewis argued that Joyce was 'too well educated to have been a professional seaman'.[94] Dugan stated that he 'had served a sentence for sedition, lost his tobacco shop in Belfast as a result, and had recently come aboard in the quota'. Like Gill, he ignored evidence of Joyce's circumstances which should have made him recognise this *canard*.[95] Manwaring and Dobrée came closest to the truth, because they examined muster books and accurately interpreted Aaron Graham's evidence. They described Joyce as 'a sound, experienced, authoritative sailor, or he would not have been Quarter Master's Mate' whose 'family lived in Portsmouth'.[96] They cited the opinions of Burke that Joyce was a seditious Belfast clubist, to show how ready such politicians were 'to sniff sedition anywhere'.[97]

Joyce may have been confused with someone else, or deliberately libelled as a subversive Irishman to discredit the delegates: the libel was given wide circulation in the London press. He was aware of the attempt to malign him, and confronted his accuser through the *Portsmouth Gazette*.

I beg leave to say, that in the Sun of the 11th instant [May], the Editor is pleased to mention my name jointly with a suppositious one of <u>Evans</u>, and

---

88 See Ann Coats, 'Joyce, Valentine', *ODNB* (Oxford, 2004) for more details of his life.
89 Gill, *Naval Mutinies*; M. Elliott, *Partners in Revolution* (London, 1982); R. Wells, *Insurrection: The British Experience, 1795–1803* (Gloucester, 1983); Manwaring and Dobrée, *Floating Republic*; Dugan, *Great Mutiny*; Neale, *History of the Mutiny*; A.T. Patterson, *The Naval Mutiny at Spithead*, Portsmouth Paper, 5 (Portsmouth City Council, 1978).
90 Gill, *Naval Mutinies*, p. 255.
91 Ibid., p. 317.
92 Gill, *Naval Mutinies*, p. 313; TNA, ADM1/4172, Graham, 12 May 1797.
93 Elliott, *Partners in Revolution*, p. 143; Wells, *Insurrection*, p. 92.
94 Lewis, *Social History of the Navy*, p. 125.
95 Dugan, *Great Mutiny*, pp. 63, 162.
96 Manwaring and Dobrée, *Floating Republic*, pp. 35, 68.
97 Manwaring and Dobrée, *Floating Republic*, pp. 98, 101., citing J. P. Gilson, ed., *Correspondence of Edmund Burke and William Windham* (Cambridge, 1910), pp. 144-5, 10 May 1797.

to describe me as a Tobacconist of Belfast in Ireland, who for seditious
harangues, had been shipped on board a tender by Lord Carhampton.

The above statement is totally erroneous – I am now twenty-eight years
old, and have been seventeen years in his Majesty's Navy – am a <u>Seaman</u>,
who from his soul, wishes well to his King and Country, and whose conduct,
I flatter myself, has and will free his character from the effects of malice or
misrepresentation[.][98]

Muster books substantiate this statement, showing that he was born (c.1769),
in Jersey. Instead of Dugan's mistaken inference that his family was 'apparently
stranded on parish charity', the truth was that his father, also named Valentine
Joyce, was serving in the Garrison invalid corps in Portsmouth. Magistrate
Aaron Graham met his mother, Elizabeth Joyce, and knew of a sister also living
in Portsmouth.[99]

In 1797 Valentine Joyce was a quarter master's mate, a skilled and experienced rating. He had served continuously on *Royal George* since 1793. His
naval career can be traced back to 1788, when he entered *Perseverance* in
Portsmouth as an able seaman. He was, as he claimed, a professional naval
seaman, having joined in peacetime aged nineteen, already sufficiently skilled
to be rated able seaman. His education and eloquence were a result of his
Unitarian upbringing. This substantiates his statement that he had served in
the navy for seventeen years, since about 1781, and completely refutes the *Sun*
statement.

Valentine Joyce and John Fleming (*London* delegate, also in his twenties),
were undoubtedly the most influential delegates at Spithead. Their courage
and coolness on board *London* after the shootings prevented further bloodshed and the risk of more serious retribution from the Admiralty. In the days
following, their determination that the seamen should act rationally and hu-
manely eventually ensured peaceful transition from mutiny to duty.

Conclusion

Gill attributed the 'authorship' of the Spithead mutiny to the 'unusual number
of quota-men – volunteers who had been recruited by the civil authorities'.[100]
From the fact that they were 'generally persons of comparatively good education', and 'had been used to happier conditions' he deduced that they were
'more discontented than those who were seamen by trade', and 'it has been
shown that the men who were the best fitted to contrive the mutiny and to
incite the others to join their conspiracy, were those who had adopted the
political ideas of the Revolution'.[101] His theories supported his conclusions
but the facts do not: that political activists had been deliberately infiltrated

98 *Portsmouth Gazette and Weekly Advertiser*, 10 July 1797, letter from Valentine Joyce
to the Editor, dated 15 May 1797. This story was also printed in *The Times*, 12 May 1797.
99 Dugan, *Great Mutiny*, p. 162; TNA, ADM1/4172, Graham, 12 May 1797.
100 Gill, p. 315
101 Gill, *Naval Mutinies*, pp. 316, 312.

to stir up revolution among the more politically sophisticated landsmen and Quota men.[102] His vague identification of political activists such as Evans at Spithead and Lee at Plymouth, substantiated by no concrete evidence from the sources, place Gill in the 'must have been' school of history, a school generously endowed by Edmund Burke, the Duke of Portland, William Pitt and the Commons Committee of Secrecy, who all overtly ascribed the mutiny to outside influences.[103]

Dugan, Elliott and Wells are more recent students of this school, also attributing the cause of the mutinies to Quota men, Elliott stating that 'over 100,000' seamen recruited in the three years before 1797 were 'primarily products of the Quota Acts of 1795 and 1796'.[104] This is far in excess of Lavery's presentation of less than ten thousand from inland counties, of which the traditional seafaring counties bore a high proportion; or Ehrman's thirty-one thousand in 1795 with fewer in succeeding years.[105] Wells was more conservative, estimating fifteen thousand, but as a proportion of one hundred and thirty thousand men, this hardly represents a 'revolution in the social composition of the lower decks'.[106]

The delegates' place of origin cannot be correlated with revolutionary activity. Of the thirty-three delegates from the sixteen ships listed by Manwaring and Dobrée, just four were Irish-born: 12 per cent.[107] Far more than outside influences, the general political climate in the country affected seamen as an occupational group of 122,000 men. They read newspapers and spoke to people ashore.[108] They had time to discuss politics in their messes. Seamen were cosmopolitan: American, Dutch, Scandinavian, German, French, West Indian, Russian, many held against their will.[109] Newspapers, both ministerial and opposition, propagated the myth that revolutionary ideas were invading Britain.[110]

Resentment played a part. As *Nymphe*'s petition complained, 'we are kept more like convicts then free Born Britons'.[111] The navy was a melting pot of ideas with the organisation and opportunity to achieve the seaman's aims.

---

102 Ibid., pp. 317, 355 and generally in chapters XXII, XXIII, XXIV, XXVI.
103 Gill, *Naval Mutinies*, pp. 78, 307–9, 318; TNA, ADM1/579, Howe to Nepean, 12, 13 May 1797; *The Times*, 1 June 1797; *True Briton*, 2, 29 June 1797. I. R. Christie, *Wars and Revolutions* (London, 1982), p. 218.
104 Dugan, *Great Mutiny*, pp. 61–3, Elliott, *Partners in Revolution*, p. 136; Wells, *Insurrection*, pp. 81, 83.
105 Lavery, *Nelson's Navy*, pp. 126, 128; Ehrman, *Younger Pitt: The Consuming Struggle*, p. 19 and fn. 3. Also see C. Emsley, 'The Recruitment of Petty Offenders during the French Wars 1793–1815', *Mariner's Mirror*, 66 (1980), pp. 199–208, esp. 204, fn. 22.
106 Wells, *Insurrection*, p. 83. Also see Lewis, *Social History of the Navy*, pp. 116–27.
107 TNA, ADM36/11634; ADM36/11704; ADM36/11715; ADM36/11724; ADM36/11759; ADM36/11769; ADM36/11865; ADM36/11978; ADM36/12233; ADM36/12345; ADM36/12482; ADM36/12824; ADM36/11908; ADM36/12830; ADM36/14344; ADM36/14794.
108 TNA, ADM1/107, Gardner to Nepean, 8 May 1797.
109 Lewis, *Social History of the Navy*, pp. 127–133.
110 E.g. *The Times*, 23 May 1797, citing Lear III, p. 1.
111 TNA, ADM1/5125, 22 April 1797.

Their initial quest for a pay rise expanded into a wider campaign for the restoration of their working conditions and care of the sick and wounded. Magistrate Aaron Graham knew that suspect books and handbills had been distributed to Spithead ships, but failed to obtain proof, distanced by his class and hampered by opposition Whigs in Portsmouth Corporation.[112] Naval officers were not in a position to search seamen's quarters for such material. Graham was an astute observer, however, who found 'that there is not a man in the fleet whose attachment to the King need be doubted or who would not rejoice in an opportunity of meeting and fighting the Enemy'.[113] A forthright communicator, he accurately assessed that their aims were primarily material, and not motivated by disloyalty.[114]

The Spithead mutiny was a justified campaign to redress seamen's grievances, responding to British social, economic and political conditions of 1797: Pitt's government financially overstretched, peace wanted for economic reasons, and the opposition exploiting every ministerial weakness for its own ends. As a result, the Spithead mutiny was the largest and most successful radical event in British history since the civil wars, its success directly related to the democratic way in which the delegates represented the seamen.

---

112 TNA, ADM1/4172, Graham, 11, 12, 22 May 1797.
113 TNA, ADM1/4172, Graham, 12 May 1797.
114 TNA, ADM1/4172, Graham, 22 May 1797.

3

What Really Happened On Board HMS *London*?

David W. London

On 7 May 1797, when nearly everyone assumed the recent discontents had been amicably settled, a new disturbance broke out in the Channel Fleet. Those in government insisted it was the result of misrepresentations of parliamentary debates in the London newspapers. Those in opposition argued this second mutiny was caused by ministerial delays in confirming the promised wage increase. In truth, there was no second mutiny. From 16 April the men of the Channel Fleet insisted they would not weigh anchor, until an Act of Parliament confirming their pay increase was passed and the King's pardon was secured.

Until the afternoon of 7 May, the disturbance could be (and was) accurately described as a 'discontent' or a 'spirit of unwillingness'. There was no violence: all courtesies were extended and, with one obvious exception, all orders were obeyed. All this changed when the delegates of the fleet rowed from St Helen's to Spithead, where they sought permission to meet in convention on board HMS *London*. Believing he was acting on Admiralty instructions to maintain discipline and prevent mutinous assemblies, Vice Admiral Sir John Colpoys refused permission to board. What happened next has been debated for two hundred years. While the episode is well documented, few of the accounts agree. The facts are reasonably clear:

- Vice Admiral Colpoys's efforts to maintain discipline failed.

- A heated exchange of words escalated into a heated exchange of bullets.

- Colpoys and his supporters were overpowered, confined and nearly hanged.

What follows compares and analyses the various accounts in an attempt to provide a clearer idea of what actually happened on the day a 'discontent' became a 'mutiny'.[1] On 8 May 1797, the *Morning Herald* offered some curious, yet rather pointed, observations about the causes and probable consequences of the mutiny at Spithead. They appeared as the latest in a series of public letters to Earl Spencer, First Lord of the Admiralty, and began:

---

[1] This involves more than a mere question of semantics. While the Admiralty clearly defined *any* disobedience or refusal to obey orders as mutiny, the men saw their actions, not as a revolt against authority, but as the means to an end (i.e. a pay increase). Whereas political expediency governed the 'interpretations' of politicians.

To a Loyal and Discerning Nation,

THE FOLLOWING LINES ARE HUMBLY SUBMITTED.

As various Reports have been propogated by malicious and unprincipled Men, We, the Seamen of His Majesty's Fleet, under the Command of ADMIRAL LORD BRIDPORT, *Knight of the Bath, &c. think it a Duty incumbent on ourselves to publish at large our just and moderate Requests;—Grievances which were promised to be Redressed;—Snares laid to to entrap our Loyal Brethren, such as were deemed Heads of our Proceedings;—the Particulars of the unfortunate Affair which happened on Board the London, the 7th Instant;—unjust Aspersions thrown on our Characters as British Seamen, by an Honorable Member in the House of Commons, with Observations on the same;—and our particular Reason for not proceeding to Sea, that our grateful Countrymen might not be deceived, or ourselves prejudiced by false Reports.*

WE requested an Augmentation of our Wages, which was complied with, though reluctantly on the part of Ministers. Our late Wages were,

	l.	s.	d.	
Able Seamen, -	1	2	6	per Month.
Landmen, -	0	17	6	

the present is,

Able Seamen, -	1	10	0	per Month.
Ordinary Seamen,	1	2	0	
Landmen, -	1	1	0	

there being now three Classes. We requested likewise, that the Purser's Eighths should be taken off, which was complied with;—the Weight of the different Articles were as follows:

Bread, - - - -	14 Ounces.
Cheese, - - - -	9 ditto.
Butter, - - - -	12 ditto.

of Spirituous Liquors and Small Beer, the Purser had an Eighth out of each Gallon, those Eighths are now taken off, and we have the full Weight. His Majesty's Pardon was then requested to exempt our Brethren from having any Punishment inflicted on them for trivial Misdemeanor, and our non-compliance to the Order given for going to Sea;—His Majesty was pleased to grant the same;—we then returned to the Ordinary discharge of Duty, as desired, but from that we never deviated during our Perseverance, except weighing Anchor, which we positively refused, excepting our Requests were complied with. We then went to St. Helens, distant from Spithead about three Miles, on the Signal being made by the Admiral (excepting three Ships of the Line, which had not their private Grievances redressed, viz. London, Marlborough and La Nymph.) The Wind did not favour our proceeding to Sea, during our Silence, for by this we wish to be understood we were in a State of Suspence, as there was no sign of an Act being passed;—we could not be deceived in that Point, as the Freedom of the Press is allowed, and several of us in the Fleet can read. Our Reasons are obviously, not confined alone to the Act not being passed, although it laid Dormant for fourteen Days;—private Instructions were sent to each Commander in the Fleet, of which we are not Ignorant, as will be found in the Sequel. Full Allowances was granted to some Ship's Companies, supposed to be the leading ones, and not to others, which caused a Suspicion throughout the whole Fleet. The Ships remaining at Spithead had not their private Grievances redressed, though many Days had elapsed, nor any sign of their being redressed: be it understood by Private Grievances—trying by a Court Martial such Officers as had, repeatedly, behaved in a Tyrannical and Oppressive Manner, unbecoming the Character of Gentlemen and the dignified Station they filled. Private Murmurings was heard,—at length, the Breasts of Seamen, fired with Indignation, at being neglected, Burst forth on the 7th Instant. It was then, Oh! Horrid to relate! that we found out the Schemes laid out to Sacrifice some of the brightest Gems that ever adorned this or any other Country. Permit us, grateful Countrymen, to ask a few Questions on the Occasion, and as you are at a considerable Distance from us at present, and Ignorant of the Particulars, permit us also to return the Answers, and we will cheerfully submit the whole to your mature Consideration.

Were we not united in one Cause? *Answer.*—Yes.

Were we not bound by Oath to persevere in our Resolution of not going to Sea until our just and moderate Requests were attained, and the Sanction of Parliament given for the Performance of the same?—Yes.

Did we not solicit our most Gracious Sovereign's Pardon for any excesses committed by our Brethren during our late Perseverance?—Yes.

Was it not granted?—Yes.

No sooner that Pardon granted, but, in direct Contradiction to that His Royal Proclamation, were Individuals selected for the express Purpose of sacrificing them to Malice and private Resentment.

Are then poor, but loyal Individuals, Lives to be sacrificed for the mere Sport of Tyrants?—Not, according to the Laws of civilized Nations?

Is such the Recompence for meritorious Service tendered to their amicable Sovereign and benevolent Nation?

To whom, are we to look or apply for Protection?

We cannot surmise, since all Laws, Humane or Divine are trampled under foot, Miserable, indeed, then is the Situation of the loyal, but unfortunate Tars, whom their Country at large Adores, but whom tyrannical and malicious Men in Office seek, basely seek, to betray and sacrifice; if a National Bond is not given, such [illegible] be the Disaster some will Experience. Will [illegible] the following melancholy Catastrophe, evince [illegible] whole World of our Assertions:—On Sunday the 7th Instant, ever to be recorded, a gallant Chief, (not indeed so, but as such represented, by an Honourable Member, Mr. *Whitbread*;—perhaps the Honourable Member committed a Mistake, it was surely his Gallantry with the Fair Sex he alluded to, for his Country is ignorant of any gallant Action by him performed) with his Officers in Consort, espied the Boats of the Fleet proceeding on board the Marlborough, which was fortunate enough on their side, as the London's Officers, had the Quarter Deck Guns loaded with Grape and Cannister Shot ready to Fire into them. Admiral Colpoys had all hands sent aft, and informed them their was something amiss amongst the Ships at St. Helens, and desired them to go below, run in the Lower Deck Guns, and lower the Ports;—and then part of them to return on Deck and Hoist in the Boats, which was complied with. The same being done, all Hands were ordered below, at the same time the Officers appeared armed, and the Marines were armed and accoutred, with Bayonets fixed, and Pieces loaded. Four of the Main Deck Guns were ordered to be loaded with Grape and Cannister Shot, run in as far as the Breechings would allow, to be ready to point forward on the Ship's Company. Before they People could well comply with the Orders of going below, [illegible] Captain ordered Lieutenant *Bover* to Fire [illegible] of the People that were forward under the [illegible]ecastle, which he did not immediately comply with, upon which Captain *Griffiths* presented his Pistols to him, and swore he would put him to Death that Moment if he did not instantly comply with his Orders;—in this dilemma, the Lieutenant fired, and Wounded two Men. The Ship's Company being now all below, and hearing there were some Boats alongside, they expressed their wish to know what they wanted, but in vain, the Hammocks and Spars from the Booms were thrown on all the Hatchways, and the Officers putting the Hammocks a little aside, so as to give Room, fired aslant down the Hatchways on the unarmed Men below, and Wounded several severely, part of which are since Dead;—in the mean time the little Midshipmen were busily employed, with proper Implements, prepared for the Purpose, to cut away the Port Ropes of the Middle Deck, well knowing that the Heart of a Seaman could not Hurt a Boy. At last, irritated with seeing so much Blood spilt, we were determined to Force the Gunner's Store-room, to procure Small Arms; they then drew Cartridges from some of the Lower Deck Guns, to supply them with Powder, taking Care to secure the Magazine with proper Centinels. Thus armed they were determined to gain the Main Deck, to confer with the Officers, on which the Marines were summoned to take the Oath of Allegiance to the Officers, but they, provoked at premediated Murder, did not consent, nor would they Fire, but went and joined their unhappy Shipmates. The Upper Deck was then stormed in spite of Opposition—the Officers called for Quarter and then Fled. The Heat of Passion by this Time subsided, and they were used with much more Humanity than the most part of them deserved. This is an impartial Account of the unhappy Affair, and we trust will be a Warning to Officers of the Navy to use the Men with less tyrannic Sway.

	No.
Seamen dangerously Wounded and since Dead	3
Marines slightly Wounded - - - - - - -	1
Officers Wounded (one in the Arm, and has since suffered Amputation) - - - -	2

Thus ended the first Action that ever the brave Admiral Colpoys, as some are pleased to call him, was in; and had it not been owing to the kind Interference of the Delegates and the Boat Crews, which arrived at the Time they had got the better of the Officers, that *gallant* Officer, with all his Associates would have fell Victims to an enraged Crew, which their Rashness justly merited. They were then confined, each to his separate Cabin, to be tried when they arrived at St. Helen's. It was the general Opinion of the Seamen, and much to their Credit be it spoken, on the Ship's arrival at St. Helen's, to deliver the Officers, except Admiral Colpoys, whom they were certain was the Instigator of the whole, up to the Civil Law. On the 10th it was proposed, that the Opinion of each Ship's Company should be given in Writing, folded up, and not to be opened until the whole of the Opinions were delivered on board the London, and the Delegates from each Ship present. A Signal was then made by the London for all the Delegates to attend (*May* 11) and deliver their respective Ships Opinion, when there appeared,

In his Favour, at least that he should be left to his own Ship's Companys' Mode of Punishment - - - -	12
For immediate Execution - -	5
Majority in his Favour - -	7

the Admiral and his Officers were then delivered up to the Portsmouth Magistrate.

In the beginning of our Narrative, we mentioned the Aspersions thrown on our Characters as British Seamen. The following concerns the Mars alone—whose Crew, evil-minded Men were pleased to say corresponded with French Agents; but they are as groundless as they are Malicious. Her Crew, we do not Deny, were more Headstrong than those of other Ships. Treachery or Republican Principles they, like the Crews of the whole Fleet, disavow. The following Aspersions allude to us all, and are taken from an Honourable Member's Speech in the House of Commons, inserted in the *Sun* of the 19th instant, Parts of which we have quoted, with necessary Remarks on the same, beginning with the following, his express Words:—"There must be a point in which the Demands of the Seamen must cease." Can that Hon Member entertain a doubt but we maturely weighed within our Bosoms the Boon we solicited, nor took Advantage of our distressed Country at the present momentous Crisis, when so many Millions were voted away for chimerical Purposes. He condesends to say, "What has been granted to us, appeared to be no more than what justice required; but he could not avoid declaring his Disapprobation of the Mode we adopted—it was not consistent with that high Character which British Seamen always maintained." It is beyond our Comprehension what Measures he would adopt as plight Faith was forfeited. He farther say, and on the bare Reflection of which, he migh Blush, if ever a Blush adorned his Cheek. "I fear they have been worked upon by some Interference of the foulest, basest and most treacherous Nature." Treachery! as British Seamen, we detest the Thought. "If there were Men who, upon other Occasions, considered themselves as being oppressed, there was at least something of Dignity and Openness in complaining at the Moment; but if they wished to obtain Revenge," says he, "by Endeavouring to sap and destroy the Bulwark of the Country, they were the basest and foulest Traitors that ever disgraced a Country." Dignified we are, for the Service tendered to our Country on every Occasion, when we had to dispute with the Enemy (superiority of Numbers not excepted) the Empire of the Main, of which this Country retains the Asendency. Openness of Heart and frankness of Mind are the general Characteristic of a British Seaman. "He never could have believed, that while the Fleet of the Enemy was preparing for Sea, English Sailors would remain in Port disputing with Government; they were the last body of Men from whom he should suspect such Conduct." Oh! *Sheridan*, if this by mean Opinion of British Seamen, thou knowest little, very little, of Seamens' Sentiment. Our Requests were moderate and just. Why then should Government, (who know our Deserts) dispute with us? We are not tainted with Republicanism; on its Agents we would not deign a Look. Impute any Thing to us thy mean Soul can dictate but Treachery; its Principles we disavow. What Revenge does he suppose we could wish to take of the Country which gave us Birth. If any Revenge was our Aim, it would have been on those who opposed us, private Individuals, not our grateful Country. That Honourable Gentleman thinking he had defeated the Chancellor attacked the poor but loyal Tars. He will not find them easily defeated; opposed to a foreign Foe in particular. That Hon. Member's struggles are great—a good Salary he wants—then (like an Honourable Friend of his Bosom) he will be Silent, with Ministers in particular.

Dear Countrymen, we presume you will no longer remain Ignorant, therefore beg Leave to conclude our Narrative, and remain

The Loyal and Humane Tars
of His Majesty's Fleet, at St. Helens.

QUEEN CHARLOTTE, May 13, 1797.

My Lord, the statements I have hitherto made, of the probable consequences of so relaxed a state of our marine discipline, have been too pro-
phetic of the calamity which has now befallen the country. The revolutionary triumph of the Portsmouth Mutineers has completed the catalogue of
its misfortunes. That a confederacy of such magnitude should have been
planned, and organised into a controlling power, without the knowledge of
Government, is to suppose a new course in the history of human events.[2]

The author was the prominent opposition leader Lord John Russell. He described the concessions made to the seamen as 'sanctifying treason' and asked
why their demands had not been 'redressed as a boon', before they could be
'extorted as a right?' To Lord Russell, the mutiny represented the breakdown
of discipline, not only in the Channel Fleet, but also in the entire navy – a
breakdown for which he held the Admiralty and Pitt's government responsible. Russell saw no reason to tolerate the seamen's unruly behaviour. Instead,
he argued that the no nonsense approach of Vice Admiral Sir Alan Gardner,
'generally supported, and with equal firmness', would have been a far more
effective remedy than 'a pusillanimous compliance with the mutineers demands'; although he conceded Gardner's actions were 'indiscreetly timed'.

Gardner's Indiscretion

The indiscretion in question occurred on 21 April; and was, ironically, the
result of Gardner's efforts to comply with an Admiralty admonition to restore

---

2 *Morning Herald*, 8 May 1797, p. 3.

Left: 6. Broadside 'To a Loyal and Discerning Nation', The Seamen's Manifesto,
from 'The Loyal and Humane Tars of His Majesty's Fleet at St. Helen's. QUEEN
CHARLOTTE, May 13, 1797.'
    Issued from Earl Howe's flagship, used by the delegates as their HQ, this set out
a chronology of events to correct 'various Reports ... propagated by malicious
and unprincipled men'. It begins:
    We the Seamen of His Majesty's Fleet, under the Command of ADMIRAL
LORD BRIDPORT, Knight of the Bath, &c. think it a Duty incumbent on
ourselves, to publish at large our just and moderate Requests; – Grievances which
were promised to be Redressed; – Snares laid to entrap our loyal Brethren, Such
as were deemed Heads of our Proceedings; – the Particulars of the unfortunate
Affair which happened on Board the London, the 7th Instant; – unjust Aspersions
thrown on our Characters of British Seamen, by an Honourable Member in the
House of Commons, with Observations on the same; – and our particular Reason
for not proceeding to Sea, that our grateful Countrymen might not be deceived, or
ourselves prejudiced by False reports.
    Copyright Trustees of the National Museum of the Royal Navy, reproduced
with permission from the Trustees of the National Museum of the Royal Navy.

discipline.[3] The trouble began nearly a week before, when, according to the *Star*, 'a spirit of unwillingness has manifested itself throughout the fleet'.[4] During the first two weeks of April, letters complaining of 'the smallness of their pay' had been presented to Admiral Lord Bridport, the newly confirmed commander-in-chief of the Channel Fleet.[5] They were forwarded immediately to the Lords of the Admiralty, who ignored them – as they had ignored the petitions forwarded to them in March by Admiral Richard Howe and the various warnings of discontent they had received since the previous December.[6]

Instead, the Admiralty ordered the fleet to sea. At sea, it was assumed, the men would be too busy to engage in further 'mischief' and the fleet would be too dispersed to pose a general threat. Quelling the disturbance and restoring discipline were the Admiralty's primary concerns. The legitimacy of the seamen's complaints was barely considered. However, for the men of the Channel Fleet, their complaints were their only concern. They had exhausted the traditional channels of redress. Coupled with their frustration was a tremendous sense of pride and a keen awareness of their worth to the nation. They knew the strength of their position; but they knew its weakness. They surmised that their only hope lay in unity. Every member of the fleet had sworn an oath of fidelity, pledging not to lift their anchors 'to Proceed from this Port untill the Desire of the fleet is satisfyed'.[7] After refusing to obey the order to sail, most of the ships at Spithead sent petitions to the Admiralty, to Parliament and, most significantly, to London newspapers.

The petitions were, according to *The Times*, 'couched in the most respectful terms'. They requested an increase in pay, similar to that given to the army two years before, from 9¾d to a shilling a day. While the editorial decried that the 'demand held out for an immediate answer before they go to sea', it conceded that 'in other respects, nothing can exceed the general good behaviour and submission of the Seamen'. *The Times* even went so far as to suggest that such conduct provided 'a strong recommendation to grant them some further mark of his Majesty's favour'; and concluded that 'no doubt this unpleasant business will soon be terminated to the satisfaction of all parties'.[8] It might well have – but for Gardner's heavy-handed attempts to restore discipline.

Gardner's initial report on the mutiny revealed how indifferent he was to their complaints and how thoroughly he underestimated their resolve:

---

3   TNA, ADM1/107, 220, Spencer to Gardner, 21 April 1797.
4   *Star*, 18 April 1797, p. 3. Throughout the mutiny, ministry newspapers were reluctant to describe the 'disturbance' as a 'mutiny'. Opposition papers revelled in the embarrassment the suggestion caused; while the delegates carefully avoided the word.
5   *The Times*, 18 April 1797, p. 2.
6   *Annual Register*, 1797 (London, 1800), p. 208; TNA, ADM1/5125, 'Detail of Proceedings on Board the Queen Charlotte'; Pakenham to Spencer, 11 December 1796, J. S. Corbett, ed., *The Private Papers of George, Second Earl Spencer, First Lord of the Admiralty 1794–1801*, II (London, 1914), pp. 105–107; NMM, WYN 109/7/14, Philip Patton, 'Observations on Mutiny Presented in April 1795'.
7   TNA, ADM1/5125, Delegates' Rules and Orders, 16 April 1797.
8   *The Times*, 18 April 1797, p. 2.

I gave the necessary orders this morning to prepare the Ship for sea, and to hoist the launch in, which orders the Ship's Company have absolutely refused to obey, and to a man they have declared, that it is their determined resolution and the resolution of the Seamen and Marines of the whole of your Lordship's Fleet, not to proceed to sea until such time as their grievances are redressed and the prayer of their petition attended to. When the Ship's Company were all upon deck, and standing around me I made use of every argument in my power to convince them of the impropriety of their conduct, and stated to them in the strongest manner I was able, the disgrace and mischiefs they were about to bring upon themselves and their Country, and the encouragement which this very extraordinary and unexpected conduct would give to the Enemy, and I am sorry to say, my admonition and friendly advice was rejected in a manner which has hurt my feelings exceedingly.[9]

After an abortive attempt at negotiation, the Admiralty conceded most of the seamen's demands. They insisted, however, that with the concessions there should be an immediate return to discipline. They advised the officers presenting those concessions:

if the men from the several ships now assembled in the Queen Charlotte do not immediately accede thereto (they being all well known) they may rely upon it that they will be brought to condign punishment and suffer the utmost vengeance of the law. But, on the contrary, should they submit with alacrity, they will experience the forgiveness for which the Board of Admiralty have publickly pledged their faith to them.[10]

Most officers understood the objective, but recognised the volatility of the situation and realised that diplomacy was required. Admiral Gardner chose a less tactful approach. He addressed the crew and delegates on board *Queen Charlotte*. All but four of the delegates were present. The men seemed pleased with the Admiralty's concessions. The Admiral seemed pleased with himself or, at least, was until the missing delegates returned. Having been spared his harangue, they focused instead on the Admiralty's offer – declaring that, without the King's pardon and ratification by Parliament, it was an empty promise. Gardner lost his temper. He accused the sailors of being 'skulking lubbers' who, 'knowing the French were ready for sea, were afraid to meet them'.[11] According to an eyewitness, 'he seized one of the Delegates by the collar, and swore he would have them all hanged, with every fifth man throughout the fleet'.[12] The upshot was not so much a new set of demands as a restatement of the original ones. The delegates accepted the Admiralty's offer, expressed their gratitude, but issued a clear warning: 'we beg leave to remind your Lordships, that it is a firm resolution, that until an Act of Parliament is passed and His

9   TNA, ADM1/107, 202, Gardner to Bridport, 16 April 1797.
10   Conrad Gill, *The Naval Mutinies of 1797* (Manchester, 1913), p. 372.
11   *Morning Herald*, 8 May 1797, p. 3; *Morning Chronicle*, 20 April 1797, p. 2.
12   *Star*, 4 May 1797, p. 3.

Majesty's gracious Pardon is granted, the Fleet will not lift an Anchor. This is
our total and final answer.'[13] They attributed their intransigence to Admiral
Gardner's 'endeavours to sow division in the fleet and in fact to separate our
interest'; and, referring to Lord Howe's apparent failure to forward their
original petitions, declared 'this second instance of the failure of an Officer
all most believed to be the Seamen's Friend has convinced us that we have
nothing to depend upon but our own vigorous exertions to obtain redress of
grievances'.[14]

In addition to this public warning, the delegates issued a private warning to
the Fleet – cautioning them against 'the fair speeches and designs of men who
will use all their eloquence to defeat our glorious and laudable intentions'.[15]
Those intentions were limited to what could be justified and would appear
reasonable. Their behaviour was restrained and governed by strictly enforced
rules. Throughout the 'disturbance', discipline was maintained. Infractions
(like smuggling alcohol on board) resulted in swift, harsh punishments. The
delegates understood not only the strength of their position, but also how
easily it could be undermined.

To Lord Russell the seamen's intentions were irrelevant. He did not consider
their behaviour to be restrained. It was mutiny. Given the political mileage to
be gained, the volatility of the situation simply was not a concern. His letter
closed with what seemed to be confirmation of the seamen's worst fear:

> And now, my Lord, it may reasonably be asked, in what state of security is
> placed the British Navy, in consequence of this degrading submission made
> by its rulers? The delegate mutineers still remain on board their respective
> ships, and you have neither ventured to separate, nor remove them. Should
> it be necessary, on any future occasion, to attempt to enforce punishment
> on the ringleaders, or remove them, or their co-equalisers from their re-
> spective ships, will not the delegate flag of defiance be rehoisted? Will it be
> safe to trust the fleet, so commanded off the enemy's coast?[16]

After suggesting that the Admiralty might renege on its promises and re-
nounce the King's pardon, Russell insulted the seamen's pride by declaring
that it was not 'safe to trust the fleet'. This led him to reveal perhaps more than
he intended, in expressing the fear that seemed to preoccupy those in power:

> You, my Lord, know well enough the effect of power gained by a departure
> from public principle, to decide whether men, so intoxicated with its ex-
> torted sweets, are likely to return with cheerfulness to the sober duties of
> dependence, and subjection? or whether the people of England can rely on
> seamen so transmuted, for their future defence and protection?[17]

---

13 TNA, ADM1/107, 224, 'The Seamen's Second Reply', 22 April 1797.
14 Ibid.
15 TNA, ADM1/5125, 'A Caution from the Delegates to the Fleet'.
16 *Morning Herald*, 8 May 1797, p. 3.
17 Ibid.

Alone, Lord John Russell, MP, occasional contributor to the *Morning Herald*, and brother of the equally outspoken Duke of Bedford, was unimportant. His views, however, were important – because they were widely shared by many in positions of authority – including ironically the objects of his scorn, the Lords of the Admiralty. They remained far more concerned with restoring discipline than redressing any grievances. To that end, they instructed the captains and commanders of the fleet to 'be particularly attentive to the conduct of the men under their command, and that they be ready, on the first appearance of Mutiny, to use the most vigorous means to suppress it, and to bring the ring-leaders to punishment'.[18] While it was later argued that these instructions applied only to future disturbances, on the afternoon of 7 May, Vice Admiral Sir John Colpoys assumed he was acting under Admiralty orders when he ordered his marines to fire on his crew.

Further Indiscretions

In the same issue as Russell's letter, the *Morning Herald* also announced the renewed outbreak of mutiny at Spithead. For the first time, however, they reported the disturbance was attended 'with the most alarming violence'.[19] Blood had been shed. The editors saw nothing inconsistent in now criticising the Pitt ministry for not satisfying the seamen's demands and bringing the matter before Parliament more expeditiously. To the opposition press, such delays and procrastination were the cause of the second outbreak. To the ministerial papers, it was the result of misrepresentations in newspapers of speeches made in the House of Lords. No one dared to mention the true cause.

It began with a seemingly innocent, but actually incendiary question from the Duke of Bedford. On 3 May he rose to ask 'whether any of his to Majesty's Ministers had it in charge, to make any communication upon the recent important transactions which had occurred in the Marine department?'[20] Spencer responded that 'he had it not in command from his Majesty to make any communication to the House on that head, nor did he believe he should have'.[21] His response may have offended his Grace, but it would have meant little to the seamen of the Channel Fleet. More likely, their fears were aroused by the comments and the calls for silence that followed.

Admiral Howe, stung by rumours that he had neglected his men, rose to defend his honour. He offered to postpone his comments and encouraged 'their Lordships to be extremely cautious how they entered into any discussion on the subject'.[22] Then, ignoring his own advice, he voiced the one thought, which almost everyone present shared, but had the good sense not to say aloud:

18 *Morning Post*, 10 May 1797, p. 4.
19 *Morning Herald*, 8 May 1797, p. 3.
20 *London Chronicle*, 22–25 April 1797, p. 392.
21 *Morning Post*, 4 May 1797, p. 2.
22 Ibid.

> Either they must approve of transactions which there was no man who did
> not wish had never happened, or they must withhold that approbation,
> and thus acknowledge that they have made concessions under the pressure
> of the moment which they think improper to confirm.[23]

As if to make sure everyone got his point, he expanded upon it:

> If they came to any resolution approving of the demands of the Sailors, it
> would materially affect the future discipline of the Fleet, by conveying an
> acquiescence to their conduct. If they disapproved it by any resolution, it
> would convey to the Seamen of the fleet an idea that the promises which
> had been made to them were not meant to be performed.[24]

The fact that he added 'all engagements made to them should be punctually
complied with' in no way compensated for the enormity of his gaffe and was,
in fact, lost in the controversy that ensued.[25] Lord Grenville and peers from
both sides of the aisle quickly rose to control the damage. Ignoring what the
aged admiral had actually said, Lord Grenville 'agreed entirely with the Noble
Earl of the inexpediency and impolicy of bringing the subject under discussion, and entreated their Lordships to allow matters to rest as they were'.[26]
Unfortunately, the only 'personage' present with less tact or a poorer sense
of timing than Howe, His Royal Highness the Duke of Clarence,[27] 'rose to
deplore further discussion'; but managed to stumble into the same trap by
adding that: 'It was a question that deeply involved the material point of naval
discipline. It appeared to him, in the arrangement that had taken place, with a
view to the fundamental rules of discipline, to be improper to have complied
with the demands of the seamen'.[28]

Following such statements, it was hardly surprising the seamen suspected
that 'the promises held out by the Board of Admiralty were not meant to be
fulfilled by Government'.[29] They were well informed of the exchange by the
newspapers.[30] Vice Admiral Gardner acknowledged that 'Public Newspapers
are read by almost everyone in the fleet'.[31] There was no need to 'misrepresent'
what was said. The truth was damaging enough.

---

23 *Star*, 4 May 1797, p. 2.
24 *Morning Post*, 4 May 1797, p. 3.
25 Ibid.
26 *Morning Chronicle*, 4 May 1797, p. 4. William Wyndham, Lord Grenville, was Foreign
Secretary 1791–1801, and a cousin and ally of William Pitt. P. J. Jupp, 'Grenville, William
Wyndham', *ODNB* (2004).
27 Later William IV, the 'Sailor King'.
28 *Star*, 4 May 1797, p. 2.
29 *Morning Herald*, 8 May 1797, p. 3.
30 Throughout the mutiny, the seamen of the Channel Fleet had free access to newspapers
– both to monitor the situation and to publicise their views. Significantly, such access was
restricted by the authorities at the Nore.
31 TNA, ADM1/107, Gardner to Nepean, 8 May 1797.

A Second Mutiny or the Continuation of the First?

The *Morning Herald* began its coverage of the second outbreak with a report that the French fleet at Brest was about to put to sea or had already done so in great force. The report, like so many other fleet sightings reported during the mutiny, was false. But it served as the pretext for again ordering the fleet to sea. And again, Bridport's signals were 'universally disregarded'. They reported:

> The several crews, after having given their accustomed mutinous cheers, assembled the delegates of the fleet, and sent their High Mightinesses to confer with the sailors on board the *London*, the flagship of Admiral Colpoys. On their approaching the *London*, Admiral Colpoys gave orders to his men to prevent them from coming on board his ship, which the crew obstinately refused to obey. The marines were then ordered up, and, all remonstrance proving ineffectual, the Admiral commanded them to fire upon the sailors.[32]

The editors were 'at a loss to ascertain' whether or not his order was obeyed, as letters 'varied extremely upon the subject'. They hoped 'the whole affair will prove to have been greatly exaggerated, if not grossly misrepresented'.[33] However, exaggerations and misrepresentations ruled the day. Newspapers depended on letters from eyewitnesses, or at least, those who had spoken to eyewitnesses. When communications with the ships proved impossible, eyewitnesses were unavailable. Second- and third-hand accounts degenerated into rumours and rumours fed speculation. Lacking any perspective, editors could not separate accurate from inaccurate accounts. Consequently, they published conflicting accounts and hoped the truth was buried somewhere within them. However, despite getting the facts wrong and occasionally losing a sense of chronology and logic, these early reports somehow conveyed a clearer sense of what was happening than many of those that followed. Later, artful wording and fabrications concealed the truth. Editors became more selective and published only letters that fitted their preconceptions or political prejudices. Thus, in its first report of the outbreak, the *Star* offered an emotional account providing almost no detail, but giving a clear sense of the atmosphere in Portsmouth:

> With heart-rending pain we announce to our readers the distressing intelligence, that the mutiny in the fleet at Spithead and St. Helen's had broken out again with much alarming violence. Already some blood has been spilt both on the side of the officers and of the men.[34]

The *Star* reported that 'terror and consternation' prevailed in the streets of Portsmouth; and suggested 'the present alarming discontents' had:

> originated from a conversation that occurred a few days ago in the House of Lords, from which the men considered that the faith pledged to them

---

32 *Morning Herald*, 8 May 1797, p. 3.
33 Ibid.
34 *Star*, 8 May 1797, p. 2.

had been broken, as no steps had been taken in Parliament to carry into execution the solemn promise that had been made to them in the name of his Majesty. They thought it indispensable to their security that an Act of Parliament should be passed before they proceeded to sea; and they have ever since talked of the unaccountable delay of Ministers in not bringing forward the business. They also said that the language of Ministers in the House of Lords was not satisfactory, as they had said that the matter was not to be discussed or that it was too delicate for discussion, or words to that effect.[35]

This view undoubtedly made politicians uncomfortable, because it focused on the true issue: the possibility of a breach of faith. Long memories and active imaginations were not required for the seamen to suspect a betrayal. Just three years before, promises of amnesty were offered to the crew of the *Culloden* (who refused to sail because they considered the ship to be unseaworthy). After a negotiated settlement involving Colpoys and Bridport, the ringleaders were identified – five of whom were hanged.[36]

Ministerial papers continued to argue that the second outbreak was caused by misrepresentations of what had been said in the House of Lords – misrepresentations that had led the seamen to believe their bill had been thrown out. They failed to mention what had been misrepresented.

Rather than risk exposing the indiscretions of a revered Whig admiral or a member of the royal family, the opposition's *Morning Post* focused on the 'calls for silence on the subject' which were so 'strongly recommended by Ministers and their friends'.[37] These calls for silence, they argued, convinced the seamen there was 'a design of deceiving them' and led them to suspect that the 'Ministers had no serious intention of endeavouring to have their demands sanctioned by Parliament'.[38] This, they suggested, was why they refused to obey the order to sail and 'resolved to hold a Convention of Delegates on board the *London*'.[39] They reported that as the delegates' boats came alongside Colpoys's flagship, the admiral 'cautioned them against acting as they had formerly done. He told them they had asked a great deal, and obtained much, and he would not suffer them to demand more. If they offered to meet in convention, he would order the Marines to fire on them'.[40] However, in this version of the events, the marines remained loyal to the admiral, the admiral's behaviour was restrained, and it was one of the delegates who fired first. The paper even added currency to the rumour that Colpoys had been hanged. Thus the *Morning Post* provided its

35 Ibid.
36 TNA, ADM1/107, 224, Nichols to Bridport, 21 April 1797; Gill, *Naval Mutinies*, pp. 366–7.
37 Although Fox's Libel Act of 1792 restored to juries the right to determine what constituted libel, any public comment that questioned the Hanoverian succession, ridiculed the royal family or attacked the government's foreign or military policy was by definition libellous. The penalties for newspaper publishers who took the risk were severe. A. Aspinall, *Politics and the Press: History of 'The Times', c.1780–1850* (London, 1949), 37; J. Feather, *A History of British Publishing* (London, 1991), p. 89.
38 *Morning Post*, 9 May 1797, p. 2.
39 Ibid.
40 Ibid.; *Star*, 9 May 1797, p. 3.

readers with a vivid picture of the melancholy business – one that was probably the least accurate report to be found in any paper that day.

The *Star* also sought to salvage Colpoys's reputation, first by suggesting that it was Lieutenant Bover who gave the order to fire, then casting the admiral in the heroic role of saving Bover's life by telling the men he had acted on his instructions, which he, in turn, had received from the Admiralty. Showing less regard for the truth than how the truth might affect public opinion, *The Times* carefully avoided leaving the impression that Colpoys had given the order to fire on his own men.[41]

The truth, however, was inescapable. Letters in the same papers contradicted the editorials. They made it clear that Colpoys had given the order to fire – albeit with great reluctance and only to quell the disturbance. The *Oracle and Public Advertiser* 'recreated' the admiral's speech to the crew as they were about to hang Lieutenant Bover, in which he chastised them for their lack of discipline and offered to take the lieutenant's place.[42] It was a charming invention, which Colpoys himself contradicted.

The admiral provided some valuable, though hardly unbiased, insights in a series of letters written while he was held in captivity on board *London*. The first advised 'in consequence of my endeavours to suppress a disturbance on board here, four of the people who adhered to the officers have been badly wounded'.[43] As though it was of little consequence, he also mentioned that four of the men were wounded 'in the between decks' as they endeavoured 'to force their way on deck'. Three of them later died – the incident's only fatalities. At this point, Colpoys appeared more concerned with preserving his career than his life. He implied he had responded to rather than provoked the disturbance. He failed to mention who had fired first; and certainly did not admit giving the order. He carefully crafted his comments to preclude accusations that he had exceeded his authority or the Admiralty's instructions. He argued that 'I have done no more than my duty', but added that he felt 'very bad' about the result.[44] In his next letter, he expressed the hope 'their Lordships and the Community at Large will do me the justice to believe that my conduct has not proceeded from hasty or tyrannical motives'.[45]

Colpoys continued that, on learning of the disturbance at St Helen's, he addressed the crew. He asked if they had any grievances remaining. They said none. He then pledged to look after their interests, if they would follow his advice. He then ordered them to hoist in all boats, secure the deck guns and lower the ports, and 'to remain quietly below'. He then ordered marines and the officers under arms. When the delegates' boats arrived, 'our people below began to make a stir & shewed a disposition for coming up, which the officers at the hatchways prevented'.[46] Suggesting that it was more implicit than explicit, he finally accepted responsibility for giving the order to fire:

41 *Star*, 9 May 1797, p. 3.
42 *Oracle and Public Advertiser*, 13 May 1797, p. 2.
43 TNA, ADM1/1023, Colpoys to Parker, 7 May 1797.
44 Ibid.
45 TNA, ADM1/107, 269, Colpoys to Nepean, 8 May 1797.
46 Ibid.

They then began to unlash middle deck guns, point them aft & up the hatchways and on the officers – who called to me, saying the men were forcing their way up – & must they prevent them by firing on them? I said, 'Yes, certainly they must not be allowed to come up till I order them.'[47]

After shots were exchanged and blood was spilt, the marines threw down their arms and joined the men. Too late, the admiral realised the futility of the situation and, 'to prevent further bloodshed', surrendered. The crew cried for revenge. Lieutenant Bover, the officer who had fired the first shot, 'was immediately seized and carried forward on the forecastle. And as soon as a yard rope could be rove, they began to place it about his neck'.[48] According to Colpoys, he was granted another opportunity to address the men. He argued that Bover should be spared as he had only been following orders 'And that I only did my duty that I had ever felt it my duty to resist such proceeding, but more especially just now, having received very recent Instructions & Orders from their Lordships for the conduct of officers toward the men'.[49] He apologised to their Lordships for having surrendered those orders (1 May Order) to the men. In his next letter, written in a style that suggests it was dictated to him, Colpoys presented the terms of his release: 'their Admiral had formerly been their friend, but now, as he was become their foe, he might have his life – which could be no compensation for the valuable ones that were taken away by my orders – but that he must also strike his flag'.[50] This condition signalled a flood of other unpopular officers being sent ashore.

The entire fleet debated the admiral's fate. According to the Colpoys, the debate became so heated that it actually 'came to blows'. However, the issue was not whether (or not) to hang him; but whether they should organise a fleet court martial or turn him over to 'the civil power' – which, in the end, they did in the naïve expectation that he would be tried for murder.

The day after the incident, Parliament held its own heated debate – during which many points were scored, but few were actually made. Predictably, members ignored the real issues – arguing instead about whether misrepresentations, calls for silence, delays, or procrastination caused the second outbreak. In calling for the immediate passage of the bill, Lord Grenville asked that there be no discussion of its particulars, thus making the preparations that were said to account for the delays entirely moot. He justified this unusual request by referring to 'the shameful and scandalous misrepresentations that had been made, and industriously circulated' of the last discussion on the subject.[51]

The Duke of Bedford bristled in response, saying 'he knew of no misrepresentations made on the subject, either scandalous or shameful'. He then asked 'Whether it was the intention of his Majesty's Ministers to grant the sailors

---

47   Ibid.
48   Ibid.
49   Ibid.
50   TNA, ADM1/107, 273, Colpoys to Nepean, 9 May 1797.
51   *The Times*, 10 May 1797, p. 2.

everything that had been promised them by the First Lord of the Admiralty?'[52] Grenville responded with 'considerable warmth' that it always had been their intention 'to execute the promises of the Admiralty to their full and utmost extent'.[53] He then condemned Bedford for bringing the subject into public discussion and the press for compounding such indiscretions in print. He suggested these 'gross and shameful misrepresentations were maliciously fabricated to pervert the public mind, and prejudice it against Government'.[54]

In the Commons, Richard Sheridan, a prominent opposition Whig and playwright, argued that the Admiralty's own correspondence made it clear 'they did not expect the Fleet to return to their duty upon their promise alone; nor was it likely they should rest upon a promise, which might be disavowed'.[55] Acknowledging the legitimacy of the seamen's complaints, Sheridan criticised their behaviour and lent his support to a conspiracy theory. He argued their methods were 'inconsistent with the brave, generous and open character of British Seamen'. On this 'evidence' alone, he concluded 'there had been a foul interference with them, and means of the basest nature used to induce them to take the steps which they had taken'.[56]

The playwright may have been carried away with his own rhetoric. He may have forgotten that his extra-parliamentary audience included the seamen. He may actually have believed what he said. Or those reporting his remarks may have 'misrepresented' them by adding their own interpretations. Regardless, his comments, as reported in the public press, wounded the seamen deeply. Sheridan continued: 'when men secretly and insidiously endeavoured to sap and destroy the very bulwark of the country, who did not dare to stand forward and run the chance of the consequences, such men must be considered as the basest, the vilest Traitors that ever a country was curse'd with.'[57] Borrowing Admiral Gardner's 'skulking lubbers' theme, Sheridan added an implication of cowardice to that of treason:

> [I]t was impossible, it was not in the nature, not in the character of British Seamen, that when the fleet of an enemy of their Country was known to be at sea, preparing for the Invasion of their Country, they should be induced to avoid their duty from considerations of a personal nature, such considerations had never existed among that brave and meritorious description of men, the Sailors of Great Britain, and some foul means unknown to the House must have been used to exasperate them to such conduct.[58]

These suggestions of 'foul interference' were lost on the men of the Channel Fleet. They saw no 'foul interference', no 'designing men' who had deluded them. Sheridan's efforts to shame them back to their duty, to distance them

---

52 Ibid.
53 *Morning Chronicle*, 10 May 1797, p. 2.
54 *Star*, 10 May 1797, p. 2.
55 *True Briton*, 9 May 1797, p. 2.
56 *Star*, 10 May 1797, p. 3.
57 *Morning Post*, 10 May 1797, pp. 1–3.
58 Ibid.

from their 'ringleaders' were no more effective than those of Gardner or
Colpoys. All Sheridan succeeded in doing was distancing them from himself.
He compounded the insult by describing Colpoys, whom they expected would
be brought to justice, as a 'great and gallant admiral, whose worth and character he bore testimony to'.

After everyone in both Houses had their say, they unanimously passed an
Act of Parliament and secured the King's pardon. A hundred copies of both
were quickly printed and rushed to Portsmouth. Other than the final negotiations (which centred on disposing of unpopular officers) and celebrations
(conducted in a sublime sense of irony by Lord Howe), the mutiny ended the
next day; but though the mutiny had ended, the controversy surrounding it
had barely begun.

Circulated with Fatal Effect

A week after everything appeared to have been settled the *Oracle and Public
Advertiser* published what became known as 'The Seamen's Manifesto'. It
was the only paper to do so. The manifesto was addressed to 'a Loyal and
Discerning Nation' and claimed to be a response to the 'various reports ...
propagated by malicious and unprincipled men'. It began with the comment:

> WE THE SEAMEN OF HIS MAJESTY'S FLEET think it a duty incumbent
> on ourselves, to publish at large our just and moderate requests – griev-
> ances which were promised to be redressed – snares laid to entrap our loyal
> brethren, such as were deemed heads of our proceedings – the particulars
> of the unfortunate affair which happened on board the London the 7th in-
> stant – unjust aspersions thrown upon the characters of British Seamen, by
> an Honourable Member in the House of Commons, with observations on
> the same – and our particular reason for not proceeding to sea, that our
> grateful countrymen might not be deceived, or ourselves prejudiced by false
> reports.[59]

As promised, the manifesto detailed both their original grievances and the
agreement reached with the Admiralty. It was remarkably precise in that it
contained details that had not been published. It indicated that the Fleet was
'in a state of suspense', when there was 'no sign of an Act being passed by
Parliament'. Their suspicions were aroused by the Admiralty's Order of 1 May
and confirmed when Colpoys used them to justify his actions on 7 May. To
them, this proved 'schemes had been laid out to sacrifice' their leaders.

The manifesto offered a description of what had occurred on board *London*
which coincided in minute detail with other eyewitness accounts, but provided
a radically different interpretation of what had actually happened. It began
with Colpoys ordering *London*'s officers to load the quarterdeck guns with

---

59 *Oracle and Public Advertiser*, 19 May 1797, p. 4; NMRN, 8/1996, 19598, 6.10.3; a similar version may be found in TNA, ADM1/5125, 'An Impartial Account of the Proceeding
on Board H. M. Ship *London*, Tuesday the 7th of May 1797'.

grape and canister shot and be ready to fire into the delegates' boats. He then addressed the crew, telling them there was 'something amiss' with the ships at St Helen's. As in other accounts, he ordered them to run in the lower-deck guns, lower their ports, hoist in the boats, and then go below. While the crew was carrying out the first three orders, the officers and marines were armed.

According to the manifesto, he then he ordered 'Four of the main deck guns be loaded with grape and canister shot, run in as far as the breechings would allow, to be ready to point forward on the ship's company'. Before the crew had time to get below, Captain Griffith ordered Lieutenant Bover to fire on them. When Bover hesitated, the captain 'presented his pistols to him, and swore he would put him to death that moment, if he did not instantly comply with his orders, in this dilemma the Lieutenant fired, and wounded two men'. At this point (not before), the delegates' boats arrived. Upon learning a convention was intended, the crew tried to force their way back on deck. In response, the officers began firing on the 'unarmed men below'. The crew forced the gunner's storeroom, procured small arms, and 'drew cartridges from some of the lower deck guns to supply them with powder'. They forced the hatchways. The manifesto argued that the marines, 'provoked at premeditated murder', refused to fire and 'joined their unhappy shipmates'. After a brief exchange of small arms fire, the officers surrendered and

> thus ended the first action ever of the brave Admiral Colpoys, as some are pleased to call him. Had it not been owing to the kind interference of the Delegates, that *gallant* Officer, with all his associates would have fell victim to an enraged crew, which their rashness justly merited.

As for Sheridan, they declared, 'It is beyond our comprehension what measures he would [have them] adopt as our plighted faith was forfeited'. To his suggestion they had been worked upon by some 'foul interference', they responded:

> Oh! Sheridan, if this be your mean opinion of British seamen, thou knowest little, very little, of Seamen's sentiment. Our requests were moderate and just. Why then should the Government (who know our deserts) dispute with us? We are not tainted with Republicanism; on its agents we would not deign a look. Impute anything on us thy mean soul can dictate but treachery; its principles we disavow. What revenge does he suppose we could wish to take of the country which gave us birth? If any revenge was our aim, it would have been on those who opposed us, private individuals, not our grateful country.

The *Oracle* was the only London newspaper to publish the manifesto and was roundly condemned for doing so. Sheridan dismissed it as a 'scandalous forgery'. He declared: 'I have seen a copy of this gross libel, which affects to be the manifesto of the sailors. I believe it to be forgery, and I think it could be proved to be so from internal evidence'.[60] Apparently, this 'internal evidence'

---

60 *Morning Post*, 24 May 1797, p. 1.

was his opinion that its language was more that of 'a circulating library than that of the forecastle'.[61] Of course, he ignored the fact that other public statements by the delegates were equally articulate. Beyond question, the manifesto was prejudicial, libellous, irresponsible and inaccurate in many of its details. However, it was so startlingly accurate in other details that could only have come from someone with first-hand knowledge of the circumstances. While it seems unlikely to have been a forgery, neither was it likely to have come from the delegates, nor did it represent the thinking of the fleet in general. More likely, it came from a disaffected minority, who, having won their point, were unwilling to leave well alone. Forgery or not, Sheridan was right in suggesting that handbills and newspapers containing the manifesto had 'circulated with the most fatal success' at Sheerness.[62] On 24 May, the *Oracle* published an explanation that came short of a retraction. However, they made it clear they regretted publishing it.[63]

Who Saved Lieutenant Bover?

One mystery can be solved: 'Who saved Lieutenant Bover?' At the time, both ministerial and opposition newspapers seemed anxious to give Colpoys the credit. The manifesto and other accounts from the seamen flatly denied it. Lieutenant Peter Bover himself provided the answer. The day after the incident, in a letter home, he wrote: 'I have been in a most critical situation, but all is well again. I was, fortunately, much beloved by several of the ship's company, and that alone has saved me'. Publicly he did not say a word and as a result, enjoyed Colpoys's patronage. In another letter home, he offered a rather pragmatic, albeit cynical, assessment of his situation:

> Unfortunate as it may have been, it has bettered my prospect of promotion very considerably, from the circumstance of my having been placed in a distinguished situation by the Admiral and Captain at the time when it was first determined to endeavour to compel the mutineers to subordination. I was fortunate enough to give the Admiral so much satisfaction by my behaviour then, that he has declared his intention of making a point of my being promoted.[64]

Within the year, Bover received his reward and was given his own ship.[65] In another letter, he acknowledged (without naming) that he had been saved by a common seaman:

---

61 *Morning Chronicle*, 27 May 1797, p. 1.
62 *Morning Post*, 27 May 1797, p. 3.
63 *Oracle and Public Advertiser*, 24 May 1797, p. 2.
64 *Gentleman's Magazine*, 113, 1843, part 2, Lieutenant Bover's Letters, p. 32.
65 Ibid. The above indicates he was appointed to *Hecla* and fought at Camperdown, appointed commander on 14 February 1798. See D. Syrett and R. L. DiNardo, *The Commissioned Sea Officers of the Royal Navy 1660–1815* (London, 1994), p. 44.

he was principally instrumental in saving my life when I had fifty pistols levelled at my head, and the yard rope round my neck, and it was by his manly eloquence procured a pardon from the delegates for the Admiral and Captain when every one conceived it impossible that they could be saved.[66]

This uncommon common seaman was John Fleming, a newly appointed delegate. Both Fleming and Valentine Joyce, the leading spokesman for the delegates, pleaded on Bover's behalf. Fleming later wrote a letter to his fellow delegates as they debated Colpoys's fate. This extraordinary letter captured the spirit of the mutiny. It explained why, at a critical juncture, the seamen of the fleet chose to maintain discipline, rather than surrender to the passion of the moment:

Now my brethren, your general cry is 'Blood for blood.' Do you mean that as a compliment to us to assist us in following error after error? If so, it is a poor compliment indeed; or do you, let me ask you, think it justice? I hope not; if you do, pray, from whence do you derive the authority to sit as a court over the life of even the meanest subject. The only answer you can give me is that you are authorised by your respective ship's companies. But is that authority sufficient to quiet your conscience for taking the life even of a criminal, much more that of a deserving and worthy gentleman, who is an ornament to his profession in every respect? I can almost safely say you will say 'No.' But if you are to be influenced by your ships' companies contrary to your own opinion, I am but a single individual among you, and before this hand of mine shall subscribe the name of Fleming to anything that may in the least tend to that gentleman's [Lieutenant Bover] prejudice, much more his life, I will undergo your utmost violence and meet death with him hand in hand. I am nevertheless, as unanimous as any member in the fleet for a redress of your grievances, and maintain that point with your all, so long as you are contented with your original demands, but the moment I hear of your deviating from these principles, that instant I become your most inveterate enemy.

You see, brethren, I act openly, and am determined to support it, as I will never form a part to do injustice to my country; and for the future, I shall expect that whatever comes before us shall be only conducive to the much wanted and desirable end of restoring this fleet to the confidence of our injured country. Let these be your aims, and you may depend upon every support from me and this ship's company. And be assured, that the life and character of Mr. Bover shall always remain inviolate in our hands; and we think any step to the contrary highly injurious to ourselves as brothers of your community.[67]

---

66 Ibid.
67 Edward Griffith Colpoys, *A Letter to Vice Admiral Sir Thomas Byam Martin, K.C.B. Containing an Account of the Mutiny of the Fleet at Spithead* (London, 1825), pp. 45–6.

'Within the Shell of a Cracked Nut'

Joseph Conrad once observed: 'The yarns of seamen have a direct simplicity, the whole meaning of which lies within the shell of a cracked nut.'[68] There was no need to look for hidden meanings in the Spithead mutiny. It was a labour dispute, not a plot to overthrow the government or a revolution. It was the consequence of years of neglect and insensitivity. It was the last resort of reasonable men who found all other attempts to obtain redress of their grievances frustrated. The seamen were not 'deluded' or 'misled' by 'designing' men. They wanted nothing more than they avowed: better pay, better provisions and better treatment. There was no revolution, no challenge to authority and, ironically, no breakdown in discipline.

However, revolution in France and civil unrest in England did have a profound effect on the mutiny – not on the seamen, but on politicians both in and out of office. It was a period of repressive legislation and curtailment of civil rights. It was convenient, indeed necessary for the government to blame the mutiny on troublemakers and Jacobins. It allowed them to deny responsibility for the problem; and, more importantly, allowed them to deny the possibility (let alone the reality) of independent collective action by the men of the Channel Fleet.

Conspiracy theories abounded. 'Designing men' were said to seek the destruction of discipline in the Royal Navy and the overthrow of government. An editorial in *The Times* declared that the men were 'intrigued and spurred on by traitors who have nothing in view but the destruction of their country'.[69] However, such views (whether offered then or now) are not supported by the words or actions of the delegates. Frankly, it is absurd to suggest that the absence of evidence suggests the existence of a conspiracy. To even contemplate the possibility, there would have to be some indications of radical or revolutionary goals. At Spithead, there were no facts to support such speculation, no confirmation of the rumours, no basis for the argument. It is an error in logic to confuse revolutionary 'means' with a revolutionary 'end'. The means adopted by the men of the Channel Fleet were the product of frustration. Their objectives, their 'end', can only be judged by their statements, by the public and private records that have survived – not speculation based on assumptions or class prejudices. Those who look for radical or revolutionary connections subscribe to the élitist view that such organisation, eloquence, purpose and discipline could only exist with outside interference. In doing so, they rob the mutiny of its meaning and the seamen of their dignity.

In part, the mutiny happened because the government assumed it could not. They allowed it to happen. They feared challenges to their authority so much they refused even to consider the seamen's complaints until it was too late. Even then, their primary concern was not in addressing those complaints, but in restoring discipline. Ironically, the mutiny at Spithead succeeded because there was no breakdown in discipline and because there was no outside interference. Even with the greatest provocation, the men maintained their 'discipline' throughout their 'discontent'.

68 Joseph Conrad, *Heart of Darkness* (London, 1995), p. 18.
69 *The Times*, 12 May 1797, p. 3.

4

The Spirit of Kempenfeldt

David W. London

'A too restricted view of the truth is counter-productive.'[1]

The mutiny came at an awkward moment for Captain Willett Payne. While he was convalescing at the George Inn in Portsmouth his ship, HMS *Impétueux*, mutinied with the rest of the fleet at Spithead. His unspecified maladies were rumoured to be more the product of an extravagant life ashore than the rigours of life at sea.[2] Payne was an intimate of the Prince of Wales. According to John Knox Laughton, he was an 'associate of the prince in his vices and a supporter in his baser intrigues'. Indulging in one of those intrigues during the Regency crisis led the captain to forget his station and make an inappropriate remark about Queen Charlotte; which, in turn, led to his public censure from Jane, Duchess of Gordon, an intimate of her Majesty: 'You little, insignificant, good-for-nothing, upstart, pert chattering puppy, how dare you name your royal master's royal mother in that style!'[3] While his impertinence did not go entirely unrewarded, given his royal patron's limitations, Payne could expect little support in his time of crisis.[4] To make matters worse, his professional patron, Lord Howe, had just retired and his successor, Lord Bridport, given his own circumstances and poor relations with Howe, was unlikely to be sympathetic to Payne's predicament.

Payne was well aware that officers were encouraged to remain on board their ships while at Spithead. Even his new commander-in-chief's presence

---

1 P. Taylor, *Munitions of the Mind* (Stephens, Wellingborough, 1990), p. 103.

2 After years of 'precarious health', he was 'seized with an apoplectic fit' and died on 17 November 1803. *Naval Chronicle*, x (1803), p. 439.

3 Randolph Cock, 'Payne, John Willett', citing J. F. Molloy, *Court Life Below Stairs*, 2 (2 vols, 1885), 209; Christine Lodge, 'Gordon, Jane, Duchess of Gordon', *ODNB* (2004) www.oxforddnb.com. The Duchess of Gordon also served as political hostess for Pitt and his allies from the 1780s until his death in 1806. See A. Foreman, *Georgiana, Duchess of Devonshire* (London, 1998), pp. 219–20, 223, 225–6, 296.

4 Payne was Member of Parliament for the pocket borough of Huntington and received several lucrative sinecures: Treasurer of Greenwich Hospital, Comptroller of the Household of his Royal Highness the Prince of Wales, and Lord Warden of the Stannaries. Cock, 'Payne, John Willett', *ODNB* (2004) www.oxforddnb.com.

was expected. Spencer made his expectations, though not all of his reasoning, clear in a response to Bridport's request that he be allowed to attend to some financial matters ashore:

> We deem it very important to keep all the officers of the Fleet under your command as much together as possible in order that you may be in a constant readiness to put to sea on any occasion which may arise for it & at the shortest notice. Under the circumstances I own that I should have wished your Lordship to have remained with them, as I know of how much efficacy the presence of the Commander in Chief becomes in order to keep everything as it should be, especially in a case like the present, where at any *moment* an urgent call may happen for the sailing of the Fleet. I hope therefore that unless the business to which you allude is of a very pressing nature indeed, your Lordship will not apply for leave of absence, & in case it is absolutely necessary for you to do so, your absence will be very short.[5]

Bridport took this as a suggestion, which he could ignore, rather than an order, which he could not, and absented himself until 10 April. As Bridport later claimed no knowledge of discontent within the fleet, Spencer appeared to allude to a possible sailing of the French fleet. As the First Lord was aware of discontent in the Channel Fleet and of disorder in the French fleet, his allusion was disingenuous.[6] It also revealed the depth of Bridport's ignorance of the seamen's grievances. Irrespective of Howe's failure to inform him of the February petitions, Bridport claimed he was unaware of what was otherwise considered common knowledge. The *Morning Post* reported that when the fleet returned to port on 30 March, 'a gloomy discontent pervaded every crew'; and added that 'in every public house in Portsmouth' the seamen's discontent 'has been the common topic of conversation during many weeks, and the most fatal predictions have been made'.[7]

As matters progressed beyond preventative measures, Evan Nepean, Secretary of the Admiralty, secretly advised Peter Parker, the port admiral:

> Having communicated to My Lords Commrs. Of the Admiralty your Letter of yesterday's date, acquainting me for their Lordship's information of a private intimation having been made to you that the Crews of some of H. M. Ships at Spithead, who had Petitioned for an increase of Wages, were dissatisfied & intended to refuse doing their duty until their request should be

5   BL Add. MS. 35,197, fol. 90, Bridport Papers, vii, 31, Spencer to Bridport, March 1797.
6   Despite numerous reports of the French, Dutch or Spanish fleets being at sea, none were confirmed. In fact, intelligence reports from Brest, Texel and Cadiz made it clear that none of their fleets were in condition to sail. BL, Add. MS. 35,197, 85, Bridport Papers, Spencer to Bridport, 1 March 1797; TNA, ADM1/4172, Nagzininshi to Carter, 7 April 1797, D'Auvergne, 23 April 1797 and 16 May 1797; ADM1/107, Durham to Warren, 29 April 1797; ADM1/6033, Duncan, 17 April 1797; ADM1/3974, The Hague, 28 April 1797. See David W. London, 'Manipulation of the Media: Indiscretions, Misrepresentations and Fleet Sightings', *American Journalism* 24, 4 (2007), pp. 7–36.
7   *Morning Post*, 18 April 1797.

complied with, & that a correspondence is represented to be secretly carrying on between the different ships companies, in consequence of which you
had communicated with Lord Bridport, and would give private directions to
all the Captains to sleep on board their respective ships; I am commanded
by their Lordships to acquaint you that they approve of your doing as you
have proposed, and to signify their direction to you to order the several
Captains & Commanders & every subordinate officer, to remain constantly
on board their respective ships, so far as their necessary Duties will admit,
and upon discovering any disposition to Mutiny amongst the Crews of their
said ships, to take immediately the most vigorous & effectual measures for
checking its progress & securing the Ringleaders, preventing as much as
may be any communication between the Seamen belonging to the different
ships, & also between them & people from the shore who may possibly have
in some degree been instrumental in exciting the present discontent.[8]

The Admiralty's concerns were justified. The fleet's morale had suffered when
they failed to intercept the attempted French invasion at Bantry Bay in December
1796. They suffered the indignity of having their inadequacies lampooned:

> Now fair and strong the south-east blew,
> And high the billows rose;
> The French fleet bounded oe'r the main,
> Freighted with Erin's Foes.
>
> O! where was Hood, and where was Howe,
> And where was Cornwallis then;
> Where Colpoys, Bridport, or Pellew,
> And all their gallant men?
>
> N'er skill nor courage aught avail,
> Against high Heaven's decrees,
> The storm arose and closed all ports,
> A mist o'erspread the seas.
>
> For not to feeble, mortal man,
> Did God his vengeance trust;
> He raised his own tremendous arm,
> All powerful as all just.[9]

Maintaining blockades and convoying merchant ships up and down the
Channel meant demanding conditions, harsh weather and few opportunities
for prize money. The officers shared the hardships with the men, but were
not denied the pleasures of liberty at Plymouth and Portsmouth. As a result,

8 TNA, ADM3/136, Nepean to Parker, 15 April 1797.
9 M. Elliott, *Partners in Revolution: The United Irishmen and France* (London, 1982),
pp. 120–1, citing T. C. Croker, *Popular Songs illustrative of the French Invasions of Ireland*
(London, 1845–47) pp. 46–9.

discipline suffered – not of the men, although it led to resentment, but of the fleet's officers, as it led them to neglect their responsibilities. Upon hearing of the mutiny, St Vincent commented: 'all your disorders have arisen from the total dereliction of the most material part of the duties of Sea Officers'.[10]

Discipline had long been a concern in the Channel Fleet. Sixteen years earlier, Rear Admiral Kempenfeldt had advised Charles Middleton, a like-minded friend on the Navy Board, that the 'one grand object of the Admiralty should be to restore a strict, orderly discipline in the Fleet'.[11] He observed:

> Without discipline is well planned and strictly supported, a military corps or a ship's crew are no better than a disorderly mob; it is a well-formed discipline that gives force, preserves order, obedience, and cleanliness, and causes alertness and dispatch in the execution of business. We want in the navy such a discipline which should be general; and all commanders, &c., required to put it strictly in practice. It has been for want of this that such a spirit of insolence and licentiousness has so daringly showed itself of late upon so many occasions'.[12]

His criticism did not stop at the lower deck. He pointedly suggested: 'Captains should not be absent from their ships, nor lay on shore when at Spithead'.[13] Kempenfeldt was committed to the reform of naval discipline. His own ascetic life and devotion to duty served as an example. To him, it was an organisational problem:

> [I]f six, seven, or eight hundred men are left together, without divisions, and the officers assigned no particular charge over any part of them, who only give orders from the quarter-deck or gangways – such a crew must remain a disorderly mob, business will be done awkwardly and tumultuously, without order or dispatch, and the raw men put into no train of improvement. The officers, having no particular charge appointed them, the conduct and behaviour of the men are not inspected into; they know nothing of their proceedings; and the people, thus left to themselves, become sottish, slovenly and lazy, form cabals, and spirit each other up to insolence and mutiny.[14]

To remedy the situation, Kempenfeldt advocated a divisional system whereby crews would be divided and sub-divided into as many groupings as there were officers and petty officers to oversee them.[15] His colleagues saw

---

10 NMM, NE4, St Vincent to Nepean, 27 May 1797.
11 J. K. Laughton, ed., *The Letters of Lord Barham*, I (London, 1906), pp. i, 299.
12 Ibid., pp. 304–5.
13 Ibid., p. 299.
14 Ibid., pp. 305–6.
15 While Vice Admiral Thomas Smith was the first to formally adopt a divisional system (in 1755) and Howe was an early proponent, Kempenfeldt was its most articulate advocate. In 1779 he wrote to Charles Middleton: 'The only way to keep large bodies of men in order is by dividing and subdividing them, with officers over each to inspect and regulate their conduct, to discipline and form them'. Ibid., pp. 306.

him as a reformer. Yet, while some may have resisted his tactical or signalling innovations or resented his penchant for quoting French naval authorities in French, they did respect him. Although he was a stern disciplinarian, the lower deck had ample reason to appreciate and consider the admiral their friend. Kempenfeldt added to their physical comfort with his measured approach to ship management and to their material comfort with his daring capture of fifteen French prizes off Ushant in 1781 while a large French squadron under the command of de Guichen watched helplessly to the leeward. The King, however, did not share their appreciation and apparently saw both Kempenfeldt and Lord Sandwich as men not quite up to the job:

> Lord Sandwich cannot be surprised at my disappointment in finding Rear-Admiral Kempenfeldt has only taken a few of the French convoy, when the account of yesterday led me to expect something more decisive. I think he ought certainly to have followed them somewhat longer, to have seen whether by manoeuvre he could not have obtained some further advantage. I should think this event will render it necessary to send further reinforcement with the trade to the West Indies; for as every admiral now seems to expect that an English fleet must be equal in numbers to a French one, or else not risk an action, we must eternally go on without a decisive naval blow, which alone can put us again upon our legs; and if that does not soon happen, the run will be so strong that undoubtedly the Admiralty will be obliged to be changed.[16]

However, the King's displeasure did not prevent the Admiralty from adopting most of Kempenfeldt's recommendations – including his signal books and the divisional system. However, having reorganised the lower deck, they found it impossible to impose any sort of discipline on the quarterdeck.[17] When in port, officers continued to use whatever family or political influence they had and found whatever excuse they could to go ashore. Twenty years later, upon assuming command of the Channel Fleet, Earl St Vincent found nothing had changed. He offered an opinion of the fleet's officers that was widely held, but seldom expressed with such candour: 'You cannot conceive how few men are qualified to command ships of the line.'[18] In June 1800, he wrote that his officers' 'dilatory conduct in port annoys me beyond expression'.[19]

In April 1797 Willett Payne had good reason to suspect that, unless he came quickly to be seen as an advocate of discipline and direct action in dealing with the disturbance, his career and public reputation would be ruined. Fate provided Payne with an opportunity for redemption. On the morning of the 18th, 'between eleven and twelve o'clock, Earl Spencer, with three other Lords

---

16   G. Barnes and J. Owen, eds, *The Sandwich Papers*, IV (NRS vol. 78, London, 1938), pp. iv, 77–8.

17   Ironically, by delegating power to petty officers, the divisional system facilitated the planning and implementation of the mutiny.

18   W. James, *Old Oak: The Life of John Jervis* (London, 1950), p. 149.

19   B. Tunstall, *The Anatomy of Neptune* (London, 1936), p. 265.

of the Admiralty, arrived at Mr. Fielding's, the Fountain Inn, Portsmouth'.[20]
The captain sent a hasty missive from his sickbed, a few hundred yards away:

> Weak as I have been, I could not help putting my thoughts upon paper that
> I might make an offering of them to your lordship, on the present unhappy
> posture of our fleet. I meant to have shaped those loose thoughts, but as
> they are only meant for your own private eye, I cannot let slip the opportu-
> nity of your being upon the spot of sending them as they are.[21]

His loose thoughts began with a bold attempt to shift responsibility, declaring, 'The character of the present mutiny is perfectly French.' He supported
this remarkable conclusion with an observation he had been in no position
to make: 'The singularity of it consists in the great secrecy and patience with
which they waited for a thorough union before it broke out, and the immediate establishment of a system of terror'.[22]

There was no terror at Spithead and no need to import systems from France.
Those required emerged from several hundred years of English labour disputes
and particularly from the past hundred years of merchant and naval seamen's
disputes. The need for secrecy and patience were obvious, as the men knew that
as they passed a certain point in seeking redress of their grievances their actions
could be interpreted as mutiny. And, while mutiny may have been considered an
acceptable form of protest before the revolution in France, afterwards it was not.

Payne's evocative phrasing did not describe what was actually happening. Comfortably ensconced in Portsmouth, he was in no position to know.
Rather, he described what was feared; and in doing so, provided the Lords
of the Admiralty (and himself) with a plausible diversion from what might
otherwise be seen as negligence. His argument was specious, but seductive. He
also offered insights into handling the disturbance:

> It cannot be dealt with like mutinies in individual ships. System and man-
> agement must be met with the like, nor can anything be executed with
> success till some apparent disunion is created in the Fleet[.]

Payne understood the men's strength and resolve. He also saw what most
contemporary observers and historians of the mutiny missed: 'They are perfectly sensible that their force arises from agreement, and the principle of it,
namely, the increase of wages is so seductive that they cannot probably [be]
divided thereon'.[23] Having made such a useful observation, Payne negated its

20 *Star*, 19 April 1797. Actually, there were only two other Lords, Arden and Young, and
the Second Secretary, William Marsden.
21 BL, Althorp MS. G197, Payne to Spencer, 18 April 1797.
22 Ibid.
23 William Johnson Neale came close to recognising Payne's point when he observed:
'The grievances themselves were of such a nature as ought never to have been permitted to
exist in any well-regulated department of the public service; and their reasonableness was
at once admitted, when presented in a form and in language which could not be slighted
without danger.' Neale/Roberts, *History of the Mutiny at Spithead and the Nore: With an*

value with a suggestion that proved irresistible: 'holding out the impropriety of increasing the lowest classes of seamen with the higher ones, would tend to spread difference of opinion, and call on the higher to keep down the claims of the lower orders'. Payne stated no more than the obvious, but understated a crucial warning: 'Irregularities will be sure to produce schisms, but delay may produce serious mischiefs'.[24] He continued to suggest ways of dividing the indivisible, but saw some ships – other than his own – as irredeemable.

> If any thing could be proposed that could satisfy one ship only to express a satisfaction, it would run through the fleet with the exception of the *Queen Charlotte*, *Royal George*, and *Royal Sovereign*, which are seriously in revolt, and should certainly be punished, if possible in the most serious manner. The first might afterwards be sent to the West Indies.[25]

Payne offered another observation he was in no position to make – coupled with further insights that were ignored:

> The disgust shewn by many ships at Spithead (though at present stifled) might be gradually fomented, and no means should be omitted to excite it. No deviation, however, has taken place among the crews on the original compact respecting wages. No assistance can be depended upon from the marines, who are recruits, and never had any habits of military life or discipline from the seamen, [who] are one class with them. This is one of the evils of keeping the establishment of that corps so low in peace.[26]

Perhaps Payne's most significant point – one taken by contemporary observers, but missed by historians – was that 'the mutinous state of the Fleet is not the greatest enormity that prevails'. It was not the disorder, but the order of the seamen's actions that worried him. Discipline was maintained and the business of the fleet continued – with the delegates, rather than the fleets' officers in charge:

> It exercises executive functions. It stops convoys, directs their sailing, distributes orders to the fleet; and the frigates at sea, that have gone from hence, is by their direction, so that they not only throw off all obedience to the Admiralty, but usurp their authority. It is therefore a revolution of the fleet, and should be opposed with the whole vigour of the country. Parliament should come to animated resolutions on it, and the country be advised to address, particularly the trading towns, whose commercial interests must hereafter suffer (by the employment of these mutineers in the merchants' service) should the ringleaders be allowed to escape.[27]

Enquiry into Its Origin and Treatment and the Suggestions for the Prevention of Future Discontent in the Royal Navy (London, 1842), pp. 29–31.

24 BL, Althorp MS. G197, W. Payne to Spencer, 18 April 1797.

25 Ibid.

26 Ibid.

27 Ibid.

He suggested the fleet at Plymouth might, if approached carefully and given the proper incentive, be turned against their brothers at Spithead:

> If the fleet at Plymouth or elsewhere could be brought, jointly, to express their abhorrence of the proceedings of the first rates here in particular, without being called upon to give up their petition for the increase of wages, which might (if proper) be held out to them at the same time, it might have the best possible effect, and partly remove the stain on the navy.[28]

Payne also did not hesitate to threaten violence or cut off allotments:

> I cannot help thinking that this should be accompanied with mounting mortars on the batteries and Fort Moncton, and as much appearance of vigorous preparation – this would alarm all the well disposed, who dread a civil conflict, on account of their families – all allotments might be stopped from this squadron, and they would rally round their officers.[29]

Recognising the importance of securing public sympathies and alienating the seamen from their friends and families ashore, he closed with a suggestion:

> It is even worth while to procure the insertion of plain written papers in the *Star*, expressive of the indignation of the country, and to awaken the pride of the good seamen. There have, I know, been measures taken from the fleet to have no other paper sent off which is generally read.
>
> With grounds like this to act upon, much useful and effectual exertion might be made by the officers of the fleet, which would now be only misspent, and serve rather to raise suspicion and excite mischief in the respective ships, and cripple the influence which may be exercised hereafter, when exertions may be attempted with success.
>
> Great assiduity should be used to explore the root of the existing evil, and the present irregular communication with the *Queen Charlotte* will throw light upon that subject hereafter, and the naval difficulties will never be thoroughly adjusted until the Jacobin springs that now direct it, are fairly disclosed and removed; and our best security is, that the fleet is generally so well affected, that I have no fear of their embracing such doctrines when fairly exposed.
>
> It is necessary, however (in my humble opinion), that they should not be irritated, immediately, into any act of violence, by which they should be united on a more criminal and dangerous principle than the present bond that unites them. I have no doubt of the vigour of the officers, when called into action, with anything of support.

The result of Payne's letter, according to some historians of the mutiny, was a squib[30] bearing the *soubriquet* of the 'Spirit of Kempenfeldt' and appearing in a newspaper on the afternoon of 18 April. Though convenient, the connection is

---

28 Ibid.
29 Ibid.
30 A lampoon, sarcastic or satirical composition. *OED*.

not supported by the facts. The squib appeared on the day Spencer's entourage arrived at the Fountain Inn and the day Payne sent his missive from the George Inn. Instead of being followed, Payne's suggestions had been anticipated.

The Hireling

Payne was anticipated by John Heriot. Considered more adept and certainly more involved in manipulating public opinion, Heriot not only pre-empted Payne, but added a touch of his own – a dramatic reference to a tragic loss of the *Royal George* in 1782. This was far from subtle, as the wreck remained a navigational hazard, its masts and bowsprit protruding from the anchorage at Spithead.

The squib appeared in the government's *Sun*, not the opposition's *Star*.[31] The *Sun* was not merely pro-government. It was – at least at its inception – government owned. Its editor and proprietor, John Heriot, was and for some time had been in government service. He held no office; but he was paid by government to perform a definite service. Heriot was a hireling – the sort of person William Pulteney had in mind when he described journalists as

> contemptible scribblers of ministerial vindication: a herd of wretches, whom neither information can enlighten nor affluence elevate; low drudges of scurrility whose scandal is harmless for want of wit, and whose opposition is troublesome from the pertinacious of stupidity, why such immense sums are distributed amongst these reptiles it is scarce possible not to inquire; for it cannot be imagined that those who pay them expect any support from their abilities. If their patrons would read their writings, their salaries would quickly be withdrawn, for a few pages would convince them that they can neither attack nor defend, neither raise any man's reputation by their panegyric, nor destroy it by their defamation.[32]

Of course, the 'reptiles' saw their activities in a different light. John Heriot saw no dishonour in what he did:

> No pay can be more honorable than that which is given in exchange for services calculated or at least aiming to uphold the Government and Constitution of the country against those whose object it was to overturn both. This is the very principle of military pay and service, and it matters not whether a man achieve this object by his pen or by his sword. It has been my fortune to use both weapons, with what success is not for me to say; I have felt as little consciousness of dishonour in the use of one as in the use of the other.[33]

---

31 Lacking an admission of authorship, it can only be inferred – from its style, content and where it was published – that Heriot wrote the squib. Regardless, it could not have been published in the *Sun* without his explicit and the government's implicit approval.
32 *Parl. Hist.*, pp. xi, 880, 2 December 1740. Pulteney was MP for Shrewsbury.
33 *Annual Biography and Obituary, 1834*, vol. XVIII (London, 1834), p. 45.

Although accounts differ as to who actually owned the *Sun* and the *True Briton*, almost certainly the Treasury supplied the capital.[34] John Heriot served as its editor and publisher.[35] William Cobbett commented: 'The *True Briton* and the *Sun* are, in some sort, the property of the ministers. They are, at any rate, as absolutely at their command as the *Moniteur* is at the command of Bonaparte.'[36] He also saw a flaw in the logic of using a public newspaper as an instrument of propaganda:

> A publication, addressed to the passions and prejudices of the multitude, may raise a mob, and may, in some cases, quiet a mob; it is a desperate remedy that is sometimes made use of to destroy, and sometimes to preserve, lawful authority. But it will never produce a lasting effect; it will never work a change in the temper and feeling of a whole nation; it will never raise that gentle steady flame of patriotism, which alone can lead to great national actions.[37]

W. S. Bourne, founder and editor of the *Observer*, also had no difficulty in discerning the government's purposes:

> A paper has been instituted by Government called the Sun, the real purposes of which are to garble the debates of Parliament and to send them into the world in such a state as to bias the minds of the unwary in favour of whatever measure the ministry may think proper to adopt, and against whatever may derive from real independence. My idea is that a decided opposition should be given to this paper, and my proposals are to change my weekly publication to an every day one – detecting misrepresentation and correcting error.[38]

John Walter, editor and publisher of *The Times*, had reason to be particularly bitter in his criticism of the upstart ministerial papers. In 1789 he had been embroiled in a libel action resulting from an item criticising the behaviour of the Prince of Wales and the Duke of York – a paragraph written by

---

34 George Rose, Francis Freeling, Charles Long, James Bland Burges, George Aust and Lord Kenyon all figure in the speculations. L. Werkmeister, *A Newspaper History of England* (University of Nebraska Press, 1967), pp. 118, 170–1; A. Aspinall, *Politics and the Press: History of 'The Times', c.1780–1850* (London, 1949), pp. 78–9; *History of 'The Times': 'The Thunderer' in the Making 1785–1841* (Office of *The Times*, London, 1935, pp. 68.
35 William Cobbett claimed he was offered the position, but refused. D. Green, *Great Cobbett: The Noblest Agitator* (London, 1983), p. 184.
36 *Cobbett's Political Register*, 21 August 1806. In 1809 Cobbett was sentenced to two years at Newgate for seditious libel stemming from his public defence of the Ely Militia who were flogged following a pay dispute the government chose to consider a mutiny.
37 Green, *Great Cobbett*, p. 212. Fifty years later Disraeli observed: 'a newspaper known to be under the influence of the Treasury ceased to be an authority and became an organ; recognised to be such, it lost much of its moral influence'. Aspinall, *Politics and the Press*, p. 372.
38 Aspinall, *Politics and the Press*, p. 450.

John Heriot had suggested that the wayward princes were less than enthusi-
astic about their father's recovery (presumably from a bout of porphyria).[39]
Walter's bitterness intensified as government printing contracts and advertising, formerly reserved for *The Times*, were given to the *Sun* and the *True
Briton*.[40] The feud became public and increasingly vitriolic – with the *Sun* and
the *True Briton* referring to *The Times* as 'the *Morning Weather-Cock*' or offering empty conceits: '*Tempora mutantur et nos mutamur in illis!*'[41] However,
The Times landed the more telling blows:

> We wish not to trouble our readers with observations on our own, or on
> those newspapers belonging to other proprietors. The Public will always,
> and very properly, judge for themselves. As the paper in question has how-
> ever chosen to give an opinion of this, we shall for once condescend to
> notice it, by observing – that it is a compilation of absurd bombast, ful-
> some panegyric, libellous calumny, and is conducted under the most abject
> servility that ever disgraced a newspaper.[42]

John Heriot made no secret of his success: he served the government. The
ethics of journalism were irrelevant to him. He made his intentions clear in the
True Briton's first issue:

> If ever there was a period when we were all invited to exert ourselves in the
> defence of those Public Principles which we have adopted as the foundation
> of our actions, to counteract the effect of false Theories, and to establish
> those which have stood the test of time and experience, that period is now
> arrived. It shall be our task to perform this useful, and, at the present mo-
> ment, peculiarly necessary duty. No person who feels as a Briton ought
> to feel, can be indifferent to the Public Acts of the Nation, or to those
> events in other Countries with which the state of our own is necessarily so
> intimately connected.[43]

The legend beneath the *True Briton*'s masthead, *Nolumus Leges Angliae
Mutari*, removed all doubts about Heriot's commitment and whom or what
he saw as his master. He continued:

> It is impossible for us to address the Public, without expressing our
> Gratitude for the distinguished favours which have been conferred upon us.
> We trust, that by our perseverance in defence of the Constitution, we shall
> be best entitled to a continuation of such support.[44]

Heriot discovered serving government and resisting change could be combined

---

39 *The Times*, 21, 26 February, 1789.
40 Aspinall, *History of 'The Times'*, pp. 62–63.
41 *True Briton*, 8 February 1793; 31 July 1793.
42 *The Times*, 15 May 1793.
43 *True Briton*, 29 January 1793.
44 Ibid.

in a very profitable enterprise. The evidence can be found both in the *True Briton*'s coverage of the mutiny and the squib from the Spirit of Kempenfeldt.

April Showers: A Week of the *True Briton*

On Saturday, 15 April 1797, the *True Briton* announced:

> The fact is that at no period except the autumn of 1792, was the British Press ever so licentious as it is at present. And, unless, by due exertion of public spirit, some effectual check be speedily imposed on it, the consequences of its licentiousness it is much to be feared, will prove fatal to the country.[45]

It was an unusual position for a newspaper to take. The fact that it appeared nearly two weeks *before* government announced a 75 per cent increase in the newspaper stamp duty was hardly coincidental. Excepting the *Sun* and the *True Briton*, no newspaper – government or opposition – supported a measure so plainly designed to curtail the influence, if not threaten the existence, of newspapers. In fact, no other newspaper even commented on the subject until it was broached in the Commons. On 27 April *The Times* commented:

> We are lost in astonishment at who could be the advisers of such an enormous and impolitic Tax, which must defeat the very purpose for which it was intended. We cannot suppose that it is the wish of the Minister to ruin the property of those who have raised a support for themselves and their families at considerable expense, and at still more considerable labour and risk; such an intention, we are sure, is beneath his consideration; and yet we are at a loss to conceive, what delusion could have prompted him to such a measure. We know very well that his enemies will say of him, that this Tax is intended as an attack on the Liberty of the Press, and to confine the circulation of knowledge; there certainly is ground for suspicion on this head, for the Tax is a complete prohibition of the sale of Newspapers.[46]

On Monday, 17 April, the *True Briton* announced there was a problem in Portsmouth.

> We are very much concerned in hearing, that the seamen on board the fleet at Spithead, have signified their determination not to go to sea, until their wages are raised to one shilling per day; and it is said this determination is universal through the fleet.[47]

The fact that an identical announcement appeared in several other government papers suggests it was inserted by government. It was not the sort of

---

45 *True Briton*, 15 April 1797.
46 *The Times*, 27 April 1797.
47 *True Briton*, 17 April 1797.

news Heriot liked to print. On Tuesday he took premature pleasure in an-
nouncing that he was

> happy in being able to state, that the discontent on the subject of wages,
> which is mentioned in our Portsmouth Letter of the 16th, to have prevailed
> among the Seamen on board some of the Ships at Spithead, had happily
> subsided without any ill consequences having resulted from it.[48]

Not content with misinforming his morning readers; that afternoon – adja-
cent to the squib 'From the Spirit of Kempenfeldt' and beneath the legend:
Solem quis dicere falsum audeat, Heriot confounded his afternoon readers by
reporting that the

> discontents on board the Fleet at Spithead ... had assumed a very serious
> and alarming appearance; but by the firm and determined conduct of Lord
> Bridport, and the respective Officers under his Command, the ferment,
> which seemed to be gaining strength, was speedily allayed.[49]

This was not news. It was not meant to inform readers of what was actually
happening in Portsmouth or allow them to consider or evaluate the action
of government. Instead, it reassured them that all was well. The *True Briton*
published what government wanted the public to think. That it was untrue
was irrelevant. It was propaganda and a theme the *Sun* expanded upon:

> His Lordship on Saturday made the Signal for the Ships under his command
> at Spithead to drop down to *St. Helen's*, but was astonished to find that the
> Signal was not obeyed; and he then learnt for the first time, of the muti-
> nous spirit which had taken possession of the Fleet. On Sunday it shewed
> itself more fully, by several acts of riot and disorder. His Lordship calmly
> expressed his determination to enforce obedience to his orders at what-
> ever personal risk, at the same time recommending it to the Men under his
> Command, if they had any complaints to make, to lay these temperately
> and respectfully before the Admiralty Board, who he doubted not would
> do them ample justice. His Lordship's remonstrances and spirit had their
> desired effect, and discipline and obedience were soon re-established.[50]

The *Sun* concealed the truth. Bridport had, upon learning of the seamen's
intentions, begged the Admiralty not to order the fleet to sea.[51] The Admiralty,
well aware of the seamen's discontent, did so anyway. When Wednesday's
news failed to fulfil Tuesday's wishes, Heriot explained:

> If we have said little upon the subject of the discontent that had shown itself
> amongst the seamen of the ships under the Command of Lord Bridport, it

---

48 *True Briton*, 18 April 1797; *Sun*, 18 April 1797.
49 *Sun*, 18 April 1797.
50 Ibid.
51 TNA, ADM1/107, Bridport to Nepean, 15 April 1797.

was from an impression of the delicacy of the subject, of its importance, in a National point of view; and of the danger of misrepresentation or exaggeration, into which our contemporaries have almost generally fallen from their systematic malignity, or precipitate folly.[52]

Heriot made no secret of his priorities. He sought to resist change and serve government. Fourteen years earlier, he had written to Evan Nepean at the Home Office: 'I can only have one object in view, to serve government by every means in my power, without a wish to obtain what it may be proper & prudent to withhold'.[53] In conveying sentiments rather than news, in seeking to reassure the public, the *True Briton* argued: 'The Admiralty were not ignorant of the sentiments of the seamen or the subject; and several plans have been under consideration, by which some additional advantages might be accorded, without greatly burdening the State'.[54]

For Heriot, the preservation of appearances continued to be more important than the truth. The *True Briton* could not admit that, while discipline was maintained, the officers were not in control.

The combination that had been entered into then became apparent; and though a slight disposition to disorder became apparent, by the firmness of the Officers, its dangerous effects were in a great measure averted. Much praise we understand to be due to the coolness, firmness, and moderation of Lord Bridport, and the Officers under him, who soon brought their men back to a sense of their duty. Their demands were, of course, referred to the Board of the Admiralty; but meanwhile, order and discipline were completely restored.[55]

The charade proved difficult to maintain. In the same article, the *True Briton* baffled those they sought to reassure by declaring:

During the whole transaction, the Sailors expressed, in the strongest manner, their heartfelt attachment to their Sovereign, and the cause of their Country. Though, to gain their object, whether just or not, they thought it necessary, for a while, to throw aside the order and discipline which are the characteristics of the British Navy, yet we are confident, their sense of duty to their King and love for their Country, were never for a moment abated; and that their hearts glowed with those generous and ardent feelings which rang a British Tar as the first of characters.

Heriot knew there was a meeting between the delegates and the Lords of the Admiralty in Portsmouth, but was apparently ignorant of its outcome:

A Petition or Memorial of considerable length was transmitted to the

---

52 *True Briton*, 19 April 1797.
53 TNA, HO42/27, Heriot to Nepean, 10 December 1793.
54 *True Briton*, 19 April 1797.
55 *True Briton*, 19 April 1797.

Admiralty, setting forth the supposed grievances of the Seamen, and representing what their expectations were. Upon the business being discussed with them, however, in a calm dispassionate manner, the generous nature of their character appeared pre-eminent. They unanimously declared, that if their Country could not at present afford an increase of wages, they would be satisfied, and even fight her battles for nothing; but that when a proper opportunity offered, they had no doubt but all their just claims would be attended to. In this confidence they may implicitly repose. The best wishes of the Nation must ever be with those men, who display such heroic conduct in her defence; and there is certainly no reasonable recompense which it can be the wish of any friend to his Country to withhold from a set of men at once so useful and meritorious.[56]

In Friday's *True Briton*, Heriot continued to explore the limits of the public's credulity by reassuring them everything was under control:

We yesterday made a statement respecting the recent proceedings at Spithead which derived from authentic information. To that we have only to add that accounts received in town yesterday, from the Highest Authority at Portsmouth, fully corroborate our statement. The discontents in the Fleet are settled to the perfect satisfaction of all parties concerned.[57]

With complete disregard of the facts, the paper reported:

The Board of Admiralty sat on board the *Queen Charlotte*, the flag ship of Lord Bridport. Complaints were heard with attention and such explanations made as led, we understand, to a conclusion honourable alike to members of the Executive Government concerned and to the good sense and loyalty of British Seamen.[58]

The Squib

On Tuesday, 18 April 1797, the squib 'From the Spirit of Kempenfeldt' appeared on page three of the *Sun*.[59] It did not shower, so much as flood, readers with sentiment. Empty platitudes overwhelmed meagre facts. It had, however, a familiar theme. Its style and syntax marked Heriot as its author. He simultaneously flattered, shamed and berated the men. He assumed they had been misled or misused by 'Banditti, Incendiaries, and Ruffians' whose ultimate purpose was subversion. He trifled with the seamen's pride, patriotism, piety, greed and grief. He provided a familiar mix of conservatism and chauvinism.

---

56 Ibid.
57 *True Briton*, 20 April 1797.
58 Ibid. There was no such meeting, *Queen Charlotte* was Howe's (not Bridport's) flagship and an honourable conclusion was three weeks away. *London Chronicle*, 18–20 April 1797; *Morning Chronicle*, 20 April 1797.
59 *Sun*, 18 April 1797; BL, Add. MS, 35,197, fol. 109.

The squib was a fascinating, self-defeating and not particularly well-conceived propaganda effort. Its essence could be found in the phrase: 'they evinced that obedient fidelity and subordination to their Officers, which have rendered them respectable in the memoirs of discipline'. The mutiny, particularly as it took the form of a well-organised and disciplined collective action, was seen as a threat to established order. Their misbehaviour, they were told, would lead to the 'extinction of Man's dearest Rights'. Allusions, metaphors and melodrama ran rampant. It was simultaneously condescending and confrontational. Other than to ridicule or dismiss them, the squib ignored the men's grievances and dwelt on subjects only marginally relevant to what was happening in Portsmouth. Rather, in Cobbett's words, it addressed 'the passions and prejudices of the multitude'.[60] The squib was neither news nor an editorial. It was propaganda. As such, it proved more of an embarrassment than a service for the government.

This was not what Payne had in mind. By expressing the indignation of the country, he hoped to awaken the pride of the good seamen and create some *apparent* disunion or schisms within the fleet. However, instead of awakening their pride, Heriot incurred their wrath. Instead of isolating and alienating the seamen from their friends, families or the public at large, he invited their response and provided them with an opportunity to clarify their position and secure public sympathies. Instead of creating disunion or schisms in the fleet, the squib united the men and provided an opportunity to resolve their differences. Instead of strengthening the public's resolve to oppose the mutiny, it strengthened the seamen's resolve to continue. Inadvertently, Heriot's propaganda invited the public to consider the legitimacy of the seamen's grievances.

Heriot's efforts were both wasted and counterproductive. He underestimated the perception of the public. Newspapers were an accepted, perhaps even vital, source of information and entertainment, but their shortcomings, vices and biases were understood by readers. To succeed, even to survive, a newspaper had to inform, entertain and appeal to public opinion – while also selling copies. As a result, they were as much influenced by their readers as by their editors and writers.[61] As a hireling, Heriot had no wish to concern himself with the wishes or needs of his readers. His task was not so much to inform, as influence them. However, he did so at the expense of his credibility.

The squib presented a romanticised view of shipboard life – ignoring its unpleasant aspects. It evoked the past to distort the present. It dismisses the seamen's complaints, invites no negotiations – only submission to discipline. In selecting the 'Spirit of Kempenfeldt' as a pseudonym, Heriot could not have made a poorer choice. He assumed the memories evoked would suit the government's purpose – either shaming the seamen into submission or turning public opinion against them. He failed to take into account that the public, the quarterdeck and the lower-deck versions of the tragedy, why it happened and who was responsible for it happening, differed.

---

60 See fn. 37.
61 F. Williams, *Dangerous Estate: The Anatomy of Newspapers* (London: Readers Union, 1958), pp. 11, 71, 74.

Three Tales of a Tragedy

On the surface, it would seem that the sinking of a ship fourteen and a half years earlier and the mutiny had little in common. The connections appear circum-stantial: in 1782 the *Royal George* capsized at Spithead, several of the survivors and many of the witnesses remained in the fleet, while Howe and Bridport had helped construct the official version of what happened. However, the squib in the *Sun* did more than evoke fond memories of a great admiral or grief over a tragic loss. It preyed on lower-deck superstitions. A buoy marked the site of the navi-gational hazard, but, at low tide, the hazard itself protruding from the anchor-age at Spithead to remind those who need no reminder of the hazards of their profession.[62] 'The Spirit of Kempenfeldt' was merely a conceit, but it achieved a far different purpose from that intended. Rather than undermining the seamen's morale, Heriot's squib deepened their resolve and focused their attention on 'a human event of the most extraordinary nature' and lessons not learned.[63]

On 31 August 1782, the *Morning Herald* reported:

> Yesterday morning as express arrived at the Admiralty, from Admiral Lord Howe at Portsmouth, informing the Board of the melancholy disaster of his Majesty's ship the *Royal George* of 110 guns, with most of her crew, being lost at Spithead, about half past ten o'clock in the morning of the preceding day. This unfortunate accident happened while the ship was hove upon a careen, in order to have the water pipe to her cistern repaired, at which juncture a strong squall at NNW came on, and her keel lying across the tide current, she fell suddenly on her beam-ends, and before they could right ship she filled, and went down, her topmasts only appearing at the water's edge! At the time of this calamity 848 officers and seamen were on board, 331 only of which were saved by the boats of the fleet.
>
> Among the officers who perished, it is with the utmost concern we mention that brave and experienced commander, Rear Admiral Kempenfelt, who was writing in his cabin when the ship went down. Mr. Saunders, his first Lieutenant, the fifth Lieutenant, together with Major Graham, and two Lieutenants of the marines, the Surgeon and Carpenter, shared the same fate. The rest of the officers were fortunately saved. What adds to the national loss, on this occasion, is, that the crew of the *Royal George* principally consisted of the best seamen of the whole fleet.[64]

The report suggests the tragedy was an accident, an act of God or a fluke of nature. It served as the basis of William Cowper's celebrated poem 'On the Loss of the *Royal George*' – more commonly known by the line 'The tear that England owes'. The quarterdeck or Admiralty version, provided at the court martial of Captain Waghorn, held that

---

62 In commenting on the *Queen Charlotte*'s role in the mutiny, Bridport observed: 'I have often thought that had she been under the Buoy of the late *Royal George* it would have been a blessing to the country.' BL, Althorp MS. G191, Bridport to Spencer, 24 April 1797.
63 W. Nichelson, *A Treatise of Seamanship and Navigation* (London, 1796), Appendix, 2.
64 *Morning Herald*, 31 August 1782.

It appeared that the ship was not overheeled ... that the Captain, Officers and Ship's Company used every exertion to right the ship as soon as the alarm was given of her settling; and the Court is of the opinion, from the short space of time between the alarm being given and the sinking of the ship, that some material part of her frame gave way, which can only be accounted for by the general state of the decay of her timbers, as appears upon the minutes. The Captain, Officers and Ship's Company are acquitted of all blame.[65]

The lower-deck or Navy Board version argued that a dangerous manoeuvre was attempted to effect an unnecessary repair – against the advice of the Master Attendant at Portsmouth and the warnings of the crew. William Nichelson, the Master Attendant, warned Kempenfeldt against heeling the old and notoriously rotten, fully laden ship in the unprotected and unpredictable waters of the Solent. He suggests he used 'every argument in my power to dissuade my much-esteemed friend from his design in heeling the *Royal George*' by running out the larboard guns and running in the starboard guns.[66] He was equally vehement in opposing the intended repair – replacing a blocked sea-cock – insisting 'it was not a work of necessity, therefore the less to be said for the risk there was to be run in heeling her without an absolute necessity'.[67] The risk was compounded when provisions were taken on board and stacked alongside the larboard lower-deck gunports. The tragedy occurred shortly after the carpenter's warnings and the crew's misgivings were ignored. When the danger was finally admitted, minutes before the *Royal George* sank, Captain Waghorn ordered: 'Beat to Quarters on the Lower-deck, get the Weather Guns out and the Lee ones in and hous'd as soon as possible and send the people aft that are Quarter'd here to get these Guns over.'[68] As a result, the entire crew – over seventy tons of human ballast – immediately moved to the wrong side of the ship. Nichelson's account and analysis of what went wrong were published in an appendix to the 1796 edition of his *Treatise of Seamanship and Navigation*. His implication of negligence was unmistakable:

Providence at times permits us to conduct ourselves in such a manner as to bring on our ruin and destruction, and also that of others, which occurred by the dreadful accident that happened in the loss of that Ship, and so many hundred lives. ... This is what is called an accident; I call it a human event of the most extraordinary nature, and should be held up to posterity as a beacon or sea-mark to them to avoid such danger in similar cases, as it is more profitable to improve by other men's miscarriages than by their own.[69]

---

65   TNA, ADM1/5321, Waghorn court martial, 7 September 1782.
66   Nichelson, *Treatise*, p. 5. To increase the angle of the heel, the starboard guns were removed from their breechings and moved amidships.
67   Nichelson, *Treatise*, p. 5.
68   TNA, ADM1/5321, Waghorn court martial, 7 September 1782.
69   Nichelson, *Treatise*, pp. 2–3.

Nichelson provided confirmation, but the cause of the tragedy was obvious at the court martial. William Murray, a quarter-gunner who helped load the provisions through the larboard lower-deck gunports, testified 'there was a great deal of Water laying in the Larboard scuppers; to the best of my knowledge, I told there was above Fifty Tons fore and aft, and if the Ship was not righted in a few Minutes that we could never right her'.[70] While his testimony was ignored and the officers were honourably acquitted, lower-deck perceptions were less forgiving. And lower-deck memories were long. Fifty years after the sinking, another survivor, James Ingram, recalled the officer of the watch's response to the carpenter's warning:

> 'If you think, Sir, that you can manage the ship better than I can, you had better take the command.' In the waist at the time were a good many men, and they heard what the carpenter said, and what answer the lieutenant gave. They were all aware of the danger, and felt very uncomfortable; there were plenty of good seamen on board who knew what they were about as well as their officers, and certainly much better than the one who had the watch. ... A few minutes afterwards the lieutenant ordered the drummer to be called to beat to quarters, that the guns might be run into their places, that the ship might be righted – he had remained that time doing nothing, merely because he would not be dictated to by the carpenter.[71]

A faulty premise, rather than chance, brought John Heriot to build his squib on the memory of noble sacrifice and tragic loss. Far from achieving Payne's objective of 'expressing the indignation of the country, and awakening the pride of the good seamen', Heriot provided them with a poignant reminder of what could happen when officers neglected their responsibilities and with an opportunity to win the country's support. Like so many others, he made the mistake of underestimating the men.

> Seamen are now a days a thinking set of people, and a large portion of them possess no inconsiderable share of COMMON SENSE, the most useful sense of all; they are capable certainly of judging when they are well treated, whether those in authority over them exercise it with mildness, and in due attention to their comforts; and it is natural to suppose they sit lighter under the yoke of a man who they see knows and does his duty.[72]

---

70 This contradicted Waghorn's statement: 'Mr. Saunders told me he had ordered the two guns ahead of the vessel to be hous'd and the Ports secured, as the spray from the vessel's bow flew in at them'.
71 *Penny Magazine*, 3 May 1834; Julian Slight, *A Narrative of the Loss of the Royal George* (Portsea, 1841), pp. 29–46.
72 Tunstall, *Anatomy of Neptune*, p. 289.

5

Voices from the Lower Deck:
Petitions on the Conduct of Naval Officers during the 1797 Mutinies

Kathrin Orth

Numerous petitions were written by individual seamen and whole ships' companies before and during the mutinies in 1797. They offer a rare glimpse of the ordinary seaman's opinions on discipline and punishment, as well as on the conduct of naval officers. This chapter will concentrate on the petitions submitted by the ships at Spithead in April and May 1797.

In the eighteenth-century navy, if the ship's company had grievances it was customary to bring them to the captain's attention by coming on to the quarterdeck or by putting them in writing. In most cases, the captain would then forward the letter of complaint through the commander-in-chief of the station to the Admiralty. If the captain refused to do so, or was himself mentioned in the complaint, the seamen sent it directly to the commanding admiral or to the Admiralty Commissioners in London. On receiving a petition the Admiralty would invariably order the senior flag officer of the station to conduct an inquiry. He in turn would despatch two or three junior flag officers or senior captains who would question the officers separately, examine the ship's books for excessive use of punishments, and summon the ship's company as a whole to ask their views. Sometimes the complaints were reported to be ill-founded or malicious because no one had come forward to give evidence. It is easy to be cynical about the willingness of ratings to expose themselves by complaining in public against their officers. A number of reports suggest that the majority of ordinary seamen were willing to speak up if they had a genuine grievance. On the other hand, complaints could be made easily and were taken seriously, and therefore offered an opportunity for the men to get unpopular officers into trouble. Undoubtedly, there were a number of malicious or frivolous complaints. However, abuses by officers were also possible. Although justified, a complaint – if not upheld – could cause the petitioner to be severely punished. Sometimes, investigating officers dismissed the charges as being the work of a drunken troublemaker.[1]

This whole range of circumstances can be found on board ships at anchor at Spithead and the Nore in 1797. What makes them especially interesting is the massive concentration of petitions at that time and under conditions that made them a powerful weapon against oppressive and disliked officers.

---

[1] N. A. M. Rodger, *The Wooden World: An Anatomy of the Georgian Navy* (London, 1986), pp. 229–31, 234.

The mutiny broke out among the ships of the Channel Fleet, moored at Spithead under the command of Lord Bridport, in April 1797. It had been preceded by several petitions to the Admiralty concerning pay but no action had been taken to redress the seamen's grievances. On 16 April the men of the flagship, *Queen Charlotte*, refused to weigh anchor, and cheered. Fifteen more ships of the line followed their lead. In several letters to the Lord Commissioners of the Admiralty they repeated their demand for an increase of pay. Two days later a petition composed by the delegates of the sixteen ships was sent to London, now demanding not only higher wages, which had been unchanged since 1653, but that provisions should be increased to the full sixteen ounces per pound, and that they should be of a higher quality. Furthermore, the petition requested that no flour should be served while the ship was in harbour; a sufficient quantity of vegetables should be granted; more attention should be paid to the sick on board; when in harbour, the crew should be granted shore leave; and that wages should be paid for those wounded in action, until they were cured and discharged. The petition closed with the following remark:

> Finally, If any ship has any grievances to Redress, we the Fleet hopes your Lordships will redress them as far as lays in your power to prevent any further disturbances.[2]

The next day, *Robust*'s ship's company was the first to take the opportunity of bringing forward charges against some of their officers.[3] This was followed by many other ships who submitted letters of complaints regarding punishments and the maintenance of discipline on board. It has to be pointed out that these complaints were not part of the initial petitions. Arguably, the Admiralty's neglect to answer the first letters submitted at the end of 1796 and during the first months of 1797 caused dissatisfaction among the seamen resulting in further demands. Furthermore, the unanimity of the mutinous ships' companies gave them greater self-confidence and a more powerful position to support their demands.

Complaints about naval punishments

Analysing the complaints and charges brought forward against naval officers, the most striking feature is the lack of objections against flogging. It appears that most seamen accepted their superiors' claim that there was no alternative to whipping serious offenders. In a letter written by the crew of *Pompée* on 8 May it says:

> My Lord we do not wish you to understand we have the least Intention of encroaching on the Punishments necessary for the preservation of good

---

2   TNA, ADM1/107, no. 208. The petition was signed by the delegates of *Royal George, Royal Sovereign, London, Queen Charlotte, Glory, Duke, Mars, Marlborough, Ramillies, Robust, Impétueux, Defence, Terrible, Pompée, Minotaur* and *Defiance*.
3   TNA, ADM1/107, no. 224.

order and discipline so necessary to be observed in his Majesty's Navy, but to crush that spirit of Tyranny and oppression so much praised and delighted in, by individuals contrary to the Spirit, or Intent of any Laws of our Country.[4]

This statement is supported by the fact that during the mutiny the seamen themselves applied the cat-o'-nine-tails to serious offenders, but with a maximum of twelve lashes. According to the 'Regulations and Instructions', this was the maximum number of lashes that a captain was allowed to administer at his own discretion.[5] What seamen considered to be 'Contrary to the Spirit, or Intent of any Law of our Country' was the severe flogging (three or four dozen lashes) for what they considered to be frivolous crimes. *Nymphe*'s petition mentions a seaman who received three dozen lashes for 'silent contempt', which was nothing more serious than smiling while being severely beaten at Captain John Cook's order.[6]

A physical correction objected to by all petitioners was that of starting, that is beating with a rope's end, a stick, or other such device. According to *Nymphe*'s crew, nearly the whole ship's company was started either by the officers or upon their direct orders and in a very severe manner. 'They beat us', according to the ship's petition, 'at our quarters when engaged with the Enemy off Brest', on 9 March 1797.[7] Sometimes officers are specifically named as being very brutal and eager to provide a 'good starting'. On board *Minotaur*, Lieutenant William Compton, for example, was accused of 'Beating Men Most Unmercyfully, Making them Pull Their Jackets & Ordering two Boatswain's Mates to Start Them, for No Crime Worth Mentioning'.[8]

The practice of starting was abolished in 1809.[9] This decision may be regarded as the first step towards a new attitude concerning corporal punishment in the navy – more important even than the abolition of 'running the gauntlet' three years earlier.[10] Apart from the fact that the latter was becoming infrequent and was seldom the subject of complaint, it was reserved for crimes that affected the whole company such as theft. Starting, on the other hand, was widely abhorred by the ordinary seamen. Although the petitions of 1797 did not lead to the immediate abolition of this practice they may have helped to make officials aware of the increasing significance of the problem.

---

4   TNA, ADM1/4172.
5   *Regulations and Instructions Relating to His Majesty's Service at Sea*, 1st edn (London, 1772), p. 46.
6   TNA, ADM1/107, no. 228.
7   TNA, ADM1/107, no. 228.
8   TNA, ADM1/107, no. 226.
9   The practice of starting was officially prohibited in 1809 following the court martial of Captain Robert Corbet of HMS *Nereide*. However, some captains may have continued to apply this informal punishment for some time. Lavery, Chapter 12, 'Lower Deck Life in the Revolutionary and Napoleonic Wars', suggests it may not have been abolished, as does Rodger, *Wooden World*, p. 215. W. H. Smyth, *The Sailor's Word-Book* (Blackie, Glasgow, 1867) indicates it was definitely abolished by then. See also Neale, Chapter 16, 'The Influence of 1797 upon the *Nereide* Mutiny of 1809'.
10   TNA, ADM2/151, Orders and Instructions, 28 April 1806.

Another punishment that might justly be called specifically naval was to stop or withhold a seaman's daily wine or rum ration. *Cumberland*'s crew suspected the captain of withholding up to one thousand gallons of wine which was due to them. In a letter enclosed in the report of the inquiring officers Captain Rowley explained his policy. He often withheld alcohol when he required a punishment that was more lenient than the usual flogging at the gangway. 'The wine so stopped was applied to the general good of the people', for example, 'by giving it to the people after much fatigue'.[11] Nowadays, this attitude might be judged appropriate and considerate towards the offender. But in the age of sail, with its hardships and limited opportunities for indulgence, the effect felt by the seaman concerned was very different – especially if conducted over a long period of time.

A very different but nonetheless important grievance brought forward by the men was the frequent use of abusive language by commissioned as well as petty officers – a cause of much irritation and ill-feeling among the seamen. John King, boatswain on *Jason*, called the seamen 'rascals and lubbers', 'threatened to cut their souls out, and expressed a wish that some of them were hanged for the business which has lately been agitated in the fleet'.[12]

Villains among Superiors

Having described some of the most important charges regarding the discipline on board brought forward during the 1797 mutinies, the next paragraph will concentrate on the people accused of committing them. As to identification, some letters did name specific persons, while others applied the grievances generically to all the officers on board. The crew of *Marlborough*, for example, requested the removal of Captain Nicholls (among other officers) not only because of the above-mentioned charges but because he hit marine sentinels on their post and punished mates who appeared overly lenient when beating a seaman. Additionally, he was said to have flogged a sick man with eighteen lashes although he was scarcely able to walk. The petition included a number of signatures of which forty-five specifically supported the charges against Captain Nicholls. However, the officers sent by the commander-in-chief to inquire into the grievances came to the conclusion that the complaints were not founded on facts. Nevertheless, they could not help but observe that there was 'a degree of dissatisfaction throughout the Ship's Company'. The report also confirmed that before they left *Marlborough*, five people came forward and declared their intention not to proceed to sea with the captain, the first lieutenant, the surgeon, and the master's mate on board. This was in accordance with the rest of the company. In his letter to the Admiralty Captain Nicholls defended his position and listed a number of benefits he provided for his men. For instance, he carried sheep and vegetables in the ship that were solely for the benefit of the sick. On another occasion he served hot punch to many of the company who were suffering from influenza – paying for the additional

---

11   TNA, ADM1/1023, no. 469; ADM1/5125.
12   TNA, ADM1/107, no. 227.

alcohol from his own pocket. Although the crew generally agreed with the letter's contents, they insisted that Captain Nicholls be removed. The most likely explanation for this contradiction seems to be the fact that the crew acknowledged Nicholls's care for the sick but could not accept his irregular and cruel punishments.[13]

Lieutenants, when named in petitions, were usually accused of ordering cruel punishments and irregular beatings either instigated by their captain, or on their own initiative and without reference to the superior officer. A person frequently mentioned in letters of complaint was the first lieutenant, as was the case on board *Amphitrite* on 17 May. An inquiry revealed that particular instances of beating by Lieutenant Holmes had taken place at least twelve months before. However, due to the strong animosity of the ship's company towards him, it was considered best to remove him from the ship.[14] Another example is the first lieutenant of *Ramillies*, who, in the absence of the captain, ordered the crew to work from four o'clock in the morning until eleven at night. Furthermore, he kept back their allowance of grog and made them carry their hammocks on their backs for two hours.[15] Seamen were particularly irritated when a lieutenant applied the rope's end or stick himself. They considered it to be unworthy of an officer and gentleman.

Apart from a number of commissioned officers, the seamen at Spithead and the Nore requested the removal of petty officers such as masters, gunners and boatswains and their mates. The long list of twenty-five midshipmen turned out of their ships adds to the image promoted by critics of the navy such as 'Jack Nastyface'.[16] In general, they were accused of abusive language, and administering beatings on their own initiative. The ship's company on *Hind* reported that seamen were severely punished as a result of unjust complaints made by petty officers.[17]

It was not only naval officers who were accused of tyrannical and inhuman conduct. Repeatedly, captains, lieutenants or sergeants of the marines were expelled from the ship by their inferiors, such as in the case of *Duke* on 19 April 1797.[18] What is remarkable is to find a surgeon among the rejected officers. In no less than seven cases the petitions pointed out neglectful and inhuman behaviour by medical staff. On board *Pearl*, for example, the surgeon, apart from the boatswain, was the only officer to be turned out of the ship.[19]

13   TNA, ADM1/107, no. 226; ADM1/1022, no. 349.
14   TNA, ADM1/1023, no. 463.
15   TNA, ADM1/5125.
16   J. Nastyface, *Nautical Economy* (London, 1836), pp. 27–8. Jack Nastyface was a pseudonym used by William Robinson, a sailor who fought at Trafalgar in 1805 and later deserted from HMS *Revenge*. Hardly an impartial observer, Robinson published his reminiscences of life on the lower deck in 1836 with a definite political purpose. His all-too-realistic descriptions of press gangs, floggings and poor food were meant to create a scandal to encourage reforms such as severe restrictions of corporal punishment and the abolition of the impress. Pitcairn Jones, C. G., 'On the Identity of Jack Nastyface', *Mariner's Mirror*, 39 (1953), pp. 136–8.
17   TNA, ADM1/4172.
18   TNA, ADM1/107, nos 268, 272; ADM1/1023, no. 426; ADM1/5125.
19   TNA, ADM1/1023, no. 436.

Surgeons and their mates were charged with not caring properly for the sick, as well as withholding part of their provisions. According to *Marlborough*'s petitioners the surgeon failed to prevent punishment of people who were considered to be sick, and accused them of skulking, even though a few days later the same person actually died.[20]

As we have seen so far, petitions provide a valuable insight into life on board naval warships. They reflect the feelings and views of the lower deck and help characterise the different types of naval officers. Many charges are undoubtedly based on facts. However, it should be remembered that some petitions were either untruthful or exaggerated. Therefore, the reports of the inquiring officers, as well as other sources, such as courts martial, should also be considered.

Some of the officers forced to quit their ships may originally have been popular with their subordinates. However, their conduct during the mutinies caused dissatisfaction on the lower deck. The best example of this is the case of *London*, on which three seamen were fatally wounded by shots fired by marines, on the order of Captain Griffith. In a letter, the ship's company stated: 'We cannot think them Capable of Serving after the proceedings on the 7th of May 1797'. Instead, they demanded the removal of several commissioned and petty officers including the ship's captain and Vice Admiral Colpoys.[21]

The ships' companies of *Defiance* and *Terrible* expressed their determination not to accept any officers that were turned out of the ship – not because of cruelty or inhuman behaviour, but because the concerned officers had broken their word and therefore had forfeited the trust of the crew. *Defiance*'s seamen had given all their officers a very good character reference at the beginning of the mutiny, on 17 April 1797. At that time they were promised that after the affair had been settled they would not be reminded of it again. But on their insisting that they should be given what was promised under the Act of Parliament, Lieutenant Dashwood refused to listen. As the seamen were convinced that this affair would not be forgotten and may have consequences for them in the future, they refused to accept the return of the officers.[22]

Later, more complaints were voiced. Even after the formal reconciliation on 9 May, the Admiralty, as well as the Secretary of State, received a number of petitions from the ships at Spithead. One motivation for these may have been the seamen's impression that having realised their major demands, they might use their temporary position of power to get additional grievances redressed. Another reason was the fact that some ships joined the fleet weeks after the mutiny had begun. *Triumph*'s ship's company approached Captain Gower on 22 May to forward a letter of complaint against certain officers of the ship. Although Gower had read out the Act of Parliament, warned the company of possible implications of this 'fresh Act of Mutiny', and promised to inquire into every complaint made against an officer, the people insisted that the officers be removed. Deprived of his power of command, Captain Gower left the

---

20   TNA, ADM1/107, no. 226.
21   TNA, ADM1/107, no. 198, 272, 276; ADM1/4172. See London, Chapter 3, 'What Really Happened On Board HMS *London*?'
22   TNA, ADM1/1024, no. 647; ADM1/4172; ADM1/5125. *Triumph*, ADM1/4172.

ship, although he had not been asked to do so by the crew. On the contrary, the initial petition, as well as a letter written by the crew two days later, makes clear that their dissatisfaction lay with only a minority of the officers: one lieutenant, the boatswain, a mate and five midshipmen. They asked Gower several times to resume command of the ship.[23]

Superiors – Loved and Respected

This example helps prove the hypothesis that a number of officers were respected and loved by their crews. All in all, about one fifth of the officers present at Spithead were sent ashore, among them Vice Admiral Colpoys, Vice Admiral Gardner, ten captains and one hundred other officers. The majority, however, including Admiral Lord Bridport and other admirals and captains remained aboard.[24] Overall, there were only few instances where crews condemned all officers. Usually, they requested the removal of a limited number of persons they had complaints against. *Glory*'s and *Eurydice*'s captains, for instance, enjoyed the same support and respect of their men as did the commander of *Triumph*. When *Eurydice*'s company was forced to go to St Helen's, for fear of being attacked by mutinous *Marlborough*, Captain Talbot left the ship. The men soon wrote to him:

> We the Ships Company of H. M. S. Eurydice which you have the honour to Command, having with pleasure Witnessed your good and tender Conduct, both before and since the present Disturbances, have taken this Opportunity of shewing our Love and Esteem for a Gentleman so Worthy and Deserving of the Confidence of our Family of which you are the Father.[25]

The same reluctance to join the mutinous ships is reflected by the petition of *Pylades* dating from 4 May, when they declared to 'have always behaved with Loyalty and Obedience' and only 'through dread of being fired into' complied with the other ships. According to a letter by Admiral Peyton dated 4 June, the ship's company of *Glatton* even offered 'one hundred Pounds reward for the detection of any Person or Persons, that may attempt to seduce them from their Duty'.[26]

The case of *Royal Sovereign* indicates partial indecision among the mutinous seamen respecting the removal of their officers. On 8 May at 9p.m., Vice Admiral Sir Alan Gardner was asked by the ship's company to leave the ship. The same order was given to Captain Bedford and the other officers, but as it was late at night they were allowed to stay. The next morning, however, the crew insisted on the officers remaining on board, and hoisted Admiral Gardner's flag which had been struck on his leaving the ship. Later that day,

23   TNA, ADM1/1023, nos 485, 486.
24   N. A. M. Rodger, *The Command of the Ocean* (London, 2006), p. 446.
25   TNA, ADM1/1023, no. 426. *Glory*, ADM1/4172; ADM1/5125.
26   TNA, ADM1/727, nos 810, 812; ADM1/5125.

Admiral Gardner received a letter from the ship's company, signed by nine delegates, stating:

> Having exerted ourselves to preserve order & regularity in the Ship, and striving to draw the Ships Company from their rash & immoderate proceedings, we can assure your Honour that our exertions have met with the desired effect, and the Ships Company are desirous you shall return on board, and resume the execution of your functions, as, no Officer is objected to but Mr. Brice.

On 11 May the men even withdrew their objection to Lieutenant Brice and expressed their gratitude to Admiral Gardner for returning on board.[27] The proceedings on board *Royal Sovereign* give an indication of the pressure under which crews of the mutinous ships found themselves. The petitions of the ships at Spithead, made by the individual ship's companies, were based on specific experiences. As a result, the different demands inevitably caused friction between the different mutinous ships. On the other hand, the seamen were anxious to use the newly acquired powers to have their grievances redressed.

Considering the variety of circumstances and situations on board the ships at Spithead and at the Nore, not all the officers who left their ships can be justifiably condemned. Some captains left the ship although they were asked to stay. Other officers were sent out of the ship only for the time of the mutiny. On 8 May, Captain Holloway and all his officers, except two, were sent ashore by the ship's company of *Duke*. The crew's letter to Lord Bridport makes clear that they were determined not to accept these officers on board again, 'except the person with a mark against their names who is to return when any thing is settled to the satisfaction of the fleet'.[28]

In any case, the crew requested that they be put under the command of their former officers who were still in favour, or completely new officers, as soon as possible. They were well aware of the fact that their actions represented a breach of naval discipline. There are signs that seamen considered the situation (although necessary) to be disagreeable and contrary to their notion of honour and respectability. The crew of *Eurydice* wrote to Sir Peter Parker:

> We have further to request of your Honour that until such time that our Captain and Officers may think proper again to take the command that you would appoint us other Officers that our Ship may be put upon the same respectability as other Ships, and that Seamen who have ever shewn themselves ready to step forward in defence of their King and Country may not be left deserted and unprotected by the Officers of his Majestys Navy.[29]

In conclusion, it can be said that the petitions submitted by the ship's companies during the 1797 mutinies reflect a wide range of relationships between the officers and the lower deck. Undoubtedly, there were many justified

---

27 TNA, ADM1/107, nos 275, 293.
28 TNA, ADM1/107, no. 272.
29 TNA, ADM1/1023, no. 486.

complaints against inhuman and cruel captains, lieutenants or petty officers. However, this does not apply to all the ships of the Channel Fleet, let alone the Royal Navy. Moreover, the specific circumstances in spring 1797 – in respect to the Admiralty's policy of neglect and delay as well as the unanimity of the ships concerned – were of major importance for the great number of complaints brought forward at that time. During the mutinies, while some ship's companies requested the removal of certain officers, there were others who expressed loyalty and gratitude towards their superiors. The remark 'sent out of the ship or left the ship' does not necessarily imply the dislike of the whole crew.

When looking at the punishments and accusations of ill-treatment described by the petitioners, one cannot fail to realise that the seamen did not object to the use of corporal punishment in general. Instead, it was excessive use of the cat-o'-nine-tails for 'most trifling crimes' to which they objected. Starting and beating as a form of irregular and arbitrary punishment was also widely despised and rejected. Although written within a relatively short period of time and under pressure of upheaval and mutiny, the petitions address general problems prevailing in the navy. They provide a valuable record of the ordinary seaman's experience in the age of sail.

6

Crew Management and Mutiny:
The Case of *Minerve*, 1796–1802

Roger Morriss

Looking back over the writing that has shaped our attitude to the Spithead and Nore mutinies, the most striking feature of the books by Gill, Manwaring and Dobrée and Dugan is the extent to which they themselves were heirs to the belief that Britain in 1797 was on the brink of revolution. According to their thinking, the whole of Europe was subject to tumult precipitated by revolutionary France. England stood in danger of invasion, Ireland was on the brink of revolt, at which point the Channel Fleet, Britain's shield against invasion, mutinied against appalling conditions of service, brutal discipline, and tyrannical officers.[1] It is a view that has fuelled an empathic and impassioned rationalisation of the mutinies as an element in the politicisation of the whole working community of Great Britain. It was foolish, E. P. Thompson claimed in 1963, 'to argue that, because the majority of the sailors had few clear political notions, this was a parochial affair of ships' biscuits and arrears of pay, and not a revolutionary movement'.[2] It is a view that has been refined more recently by Roger Wells who has revealed that the seamen were both influenced by external democrats and revolutionaries, predominately Irish, and managed by a politically radical but divided minority.[3]

It is not the purpose of this paper to take issue with these beliefs. However it does take notice of two more recent contributions to the naval and political historiography of Britain that have done much to change the ideological context within which the Spithead and Nore Mutinies are considered. First, Nicholas Rodger's *Wooden World* has drastically undercut traditional perceptions of the mid-eighteenth-century navy as 'a floating concentration camp'. He acknowledges 'that the Service which suffered the mutinies of 1797 must have been very different from that of forty years before'. Nevertheless his emphasis on the elements of naval life that made for harmony, as opposed to enmity, inevitably draws attention to the unifying, rather than the disruptive factors of later years.[4] Secondly and almost coincidentally, Ian Christie

---

1 For this view see the cover paper to James Dugan, *The Great Mutiny* (London, 1966).

2 E. P. Thompson, *The Making of the English Working Class* (Harmondsworth, 1968), p. 184.

3 R. Wells, *Insurrection: The British Experience, 1795–1803* (Gloucester, 1983), pp. 79–109, in particular pp. 98, 103–4.

4 N. A. M. Rodger, *The Wooden World. An Anatomy of the Georgian Navy* (London,

in *Stress and Stability in Late Eighteenth-Century Britain: Reflections on the British Avoidance of Revolution* questioned whether Britain really was brought to the brink of revolution in the 1790s. His exploration of the factors of cohesion and social support for working people, along with their processes of protest and defence, emphasised the multifarious and generally overlooked forces making for political and social stability.[5]

These two divergent views in recent historiography – the earlier one assuming a revolutionary situation and the other more recent one emphasising stabilising factors – have informed my examination of the experience of the crew of HMS *Minerve*, a 40-gun frigate, between 1796 and 1802. On the one hand, I was astonished to find echoes of the Spithead mutiny affecting naval vessels so far south as Madeira in the North Atlantic. On the other, I was impressed by the variety of reasons which may have prompted the crew of *Minerve* to reject the opportunity of mutinying themselves. My main source, the papers of her captain, George Cockburn, undoubtedly give a biased view: it was, after all, personally advantageous for a captain to emphasise the order of his own crew in contrast to the disorder suffered by others. Nevertheless, in the current vogue for good management practice, I was deeply struck by the importance of the relationship between the captain of *Minerve* and his crew to the harmony that ship enjoyed throughout the whole period 1796 to 1802.

The disturbing effects of the mutiny at Spithead in mid-April 1797 reached *Minerve* at Madeira on 23 June 1797, brought by the arrival of a convoy of fifty-six merchantmen under the protection of the frigate *Thames*. Her arrival had been preceded by communication of the 'plan for the better encouragement of the seamen and marines serving on board His Majesty's Fleet', embodying the concessions passed by Bill of the House of Commons on 9 May. These had increased the daily rate of pay for each grade of seamen, terminated deductions for leakage and wastage from allowances of provisions without short allowance money, and provided full pay for wounded men until they had recovered, received a pension, or obtained a place at the Royal Hospital for Seamen at Greenwich. Earl St Vincent, off Cadiz, had ordered that these concessions be read aloud to all officers and crew under his command.[6]

However these concessions had done little to improve discipline in *Thames*, even by the time she reached Madeira. A month after the event, Cockburn recounted to Nelson:

> I had heard before your letter arrived too much concerning the mutiny at home by the arrival whilst we were laying at Madeira of a large West India convoy under the protection of the Thames who was in such a state as I suppose no ship ever was before, especially at sea and with so great a charge, the men doing exactly what they pleased and the officers being absolutely afraid to control them. They endeavoured to persuade our

1986), pp. 334–7.
5 I. R. Christie, *Stress and Stability in Late Eighteenth-Century Britain: Reflections on the British Avoidance of Revolution* (Oxford, 1984).
6 St Vincent to Cockburn, 22 May 1797, Library of Congress Cockburn papers, container 13.

people to act like themselves, telling them they turned all the officers they disliked out of the ships and that they did exactly what they pleased in the Channel ships and they even threatened if our people did not mutiny to write against them to the seamen in England; and on being refused leave to come on board of us, they swam under the bows to bring inflammatory papers, which were given up to me by our people. Indeed I had every reason to be very much pleased with the conduct of the majority of our ship's company (in the midst of temptation) who, on my turning them up on account of some suspicions about them, assured me of their firm attachment to their government and officers and offered to prove it by going alongside either of the other frigates that should behave improperly.

That this attitude in the crew of *Minerve* in part arose from Cockburn's management was illustrated by his subsequent observations to Nelson. *Minerve* was accompanied by the 32-gun frigate *Lively* under Benjamin Hallowell and Cockburn went on:

The Lively, I am sorry to say, were not quite so quiet. They broke out one evening (when we [the officers of *Minerve* and *Thames*] were all on board of her) by giving three cheers but they were almost instantaneously quelled and the only excuse they had to urge, or reason to give for their conduct, was that our people [*Minerve*'s] had leave to go on shore and they had not. The fact was Hallowell sent me in some days before he come in himself and according to my usual custom I gave a proportion of my people leave to go on shore; when the Lively arrived, what was at the same time as the Thames, Hallowell did not like to let them go on shore, but gave them leave to have some liquor on board, the fumes of which, added to what they had heard from the Thames, I suppose inflamed them so much they thought they might insist on obtaining liberty. They were however very much mistaken in the issue for most of the ringleaders were most severely flogged and one of them is in irons to be tried by Court Martial. Since this they have behaved with greatest attention and propriety and very much to Hallowell's satisfaction.

Minerve was not totally unaffected by proceedings on board *Thames*. Cockburn admitted to Nelson that in the following month he was informed that 'some few' of *Minerve* 'had been tainted by the Thames, but finding the generality of their shipmates against them they kept silent'. He had proof against only one who was away in a prize, but whom Cockburn intended to write against for a court martial 'for endeavouring to persuade some of the ship's company to revolt and take the ship to England'. Cockburn thought he would have nothing to plead in defence but drunkenness and expected he would therefore be made an example.

As for the disorder on *Thames*, the three captains held an inquiry on board her 'where things came out that Captain Lukin had not an idea of':

It seemed that six or eight of his people had the rest completely under subjection, that they could do with the ship whatever they pleased; and one of these men had said at different times he did not know if he would permit her to go on to the West Indies, but if he did it would be only to make the fleet there mutiny, and he should then carry her home again immediately.

These leading men the captains took out of *Thames* and sent on board a transport in the convoy carrying a detachment of foreign troops in whose charge they were placed. Cockburn expected them to be tried by court martial when they reached the West Indies, as the minutes of the inquiry were also sent on. *Minerve* and *Lively* kept company with the convoy for three days after it left Madeira and, from last accounts, *Thames* 'was behaving in the most orderly manner possible and seemed all to be very happy they had got rid of the above mentioned Terrorists'.[7]

As Cockburn reveals from this letter, he thought in general terms of the happiness of ships' crews and of their intimidation by a small proportion of their total number. So far as he was concerned, intimidation subverted crews from their usual state of allegiance to their superior officers. Obviously, it can be argued that this view was natural to a commanding officer, who was unlikely to make allowance for seamen being made spontaneously mutinous by their conditions of service. As such, it can be regarded as a political view, which now either might be dismissed or endorsed according to our own political views.

However, if we are to understand what mutineers had to disregard or subvert, it may be as well to understand why Cockburn thought in terms of order and happiness, writing of both within the same sentence, almost identifying one with the other. To understand that thinking, one approach is to see why *Minerve* herself as a single ship remained stable in 1797 and operated as an effective warship between 1796 and 1802. To those unconnected with ship operation, there is a tendency to believe that ships operated by magic; that order and happiness came about by serendipity; that a happy ship was chance. If we look at *Minerve*, however, we shall see that order and happiness – but that not without its share of mutiny – was the product of a large amount of conscious managerial effort.

In *Minerve* stability and effectiveness were the product of work in four areas of crew management. Firstly, as a sea-going warship, the officers, both commissioned and warrant, had been selected for their experience and capability, qualities which made their management effective and credible.

As a young captain, Cockburn was probably fortunate. His only previous ship, the 32-gun *Meleager*, had been manned at the outbreak of war and her crew was virtually the same when he joined her in February 1794. Over the following two years her crew was depleted. Though possessing an official complement of 215, by February 1795 she had only 150 men on her books and mustered only 135. Nevertheless that core remained intact until Cockburn left the ship in August 1796.

When Cockburn left *Meleager*, twenty-six seamen went voluntarily with him into *Minerve*. They were replaced by eighteen 'per order' from *Minerve*. These twenty-six 'followers' were all mature seamen or officers and provided

---

7 Cockburn to Nelson, 24 July 1797, British Library, Add. MS. 34,906, fol. 205.

the immediate means of controlling his new crew. Three were master's mates: Jonathan Knapp, aged forty-two, rated as an able seaman in March 1793, whom Cockburn had made second gunner in November 1794, and second master's mate in April 1795; he took the same post again on *Minerve*. So also did Henry Morrison, aged forty-three. Charles Brady, aged twenty-five, had joined *Meleager* in February 1795 as first master's mate and transferred as such with Cockburn. Jonathan Evett, aged thirty-three, had been made yeoman of the sheets in May 1793, a boatswain's mate in May 1794, and transferred in 1796 to become boatswain.[8] Charles Fellows, twenty-seven, had followed a similar course: from able seaman to second gunner in November 1794, to ship's corporal in August 1795 (his predecessor in this post being flogged and reduced for drunkenness and neglect of duty). Fellows took the same post in *Minerve*. Other key posts were taken by Thomas Johnson, thirty-six, yeoman of the sheets; William Markey, thirty-three, carpenter's mate; Robert Taylor, twenty-three, caulker.

While these men took specific posts, at Cockburn's disposal for supervisory purposes were five midshipmen, all of long experience, aged twenty-five, thirty-three, thirty-four, thirty-five and thirty-six. Other experienced men included two able seamen aged twenty-nine and thirty, who would become respectively second master's mate in September and midshipman in November 1796. In addition there was Richard Wilson, an able seaman aged forty, and Jonathan Fells, an ordinary seaman aged eighteen.

More personal was Cockburn's relationship with a handful of other men. Robert Slaper, aged twenty-eight, was the coxswain. Jonathan Renoux, twenty-two, was a French seaman from Marseilles, possibly a refugee, entered as an able seaman in July 1794 and made captain's clerk in August 1794. There was an Italian acting as Cockburn's cook who would be discharged when the English evacuated the Mediterranean in December 1796; also four boys, aged sixteen and seventeen, two of them Italian, at least one of whom was an officer's servant.[9]

Finally, there were Jonathan Culverhouse, *Meleager*'s first lieutenant, then *Minerve*'s first lieutenant; and Thomas Masterman Hardy, who had been third lieutenant in *Meleager* since November 1793 and who became second lieutenant in *Minerve*. *Minerve*, a larger ship than *Meleager*, with potential for greater achievement, provided opportunity for such officers. No doubt Cockburn's interest with Hood and Nelson also influenced their decisions (if they had any choice in the matter) to transfer with him. Hardy at this stage had no patron or interest and only his own ability to commend him. As midshipman and master's mate in *Hebe* in 1791, he had shared a mess with Cockburn when the latter was still a midshipman. For Hardy, Cockburn's friendship and knowledge of his talents probably provided the only foreseeable path to promotion. Hardy was to stay with Cockburn until patronised by Nelson and given his own command after the Battle of Cape St Vincent early in 1797.

For the credibility the management of this ship possessed, one has to refer

8   Yeoman of the sheets: a senior rating overseeing sail operations.

9   Muster books of *Meleager*, 1793–5, and *Minerve*, 1797, TNA, ADM36/13083, ADM36/13135.

to its operational record for the whole of the remainder of the Revolutionary War. For the speed and coordination of officers and men, I refer only to the attempted rescue by Hardy of a seaman who fell overboard while *Minerve* was being chased by Spanish line-of-battle ships through the Gut of Gibraltar early in 1797. A full account may be read in Colonel Drinkwater-Bethune's *Narrative of the Battle of St Vincent*.[10]

The second factor making for relative harmony on board *Minerve* was the experience and apparent commitment to the ship by a large core of her crew. *Minerve* was captured from the French in June 1795, had to be manned from scratch and, even after transfers from *Meleager*, her crew was neither complete nor trained. However three days after Cockburn took command in August 1796, sixty-seven men were brought on board from a French cartel, exchanged for prisoners in British hands; and on 25 October another forty-two were transferred from *Ça Ira*, captured in 1795 and since then a depot ship. By February 1797 *Minerve*'s complement had reached 220, though still far short of her theoretical establishment of 300. Following the battle off Cape St Vincent on 14 February, prize duties reduced her crew as low as 170. Even so, after seven Italians had deserted at Porto Ferrajo in December 1796, the crew was almost totally composed of young British volunteers, the core of which was to remain together until the end of the Revolutionary War.

In April 1798 the crew totalled 241, excluding widows' men, and that number was retained until 1801.[11] There were, to be sure, 102 entries and re-entries in *Minerve*'s muster book over the summer of 1798, and 118 between then and 1801. Quite what proportion of these comings and goings were permanent or temporary is uncertain. But the core was preserved: between May and September 1798, while *Minerve* was refitting, these men were housed in the aptly named hulk *Prudent* in Portsmouth harbour, which maintained stability of relations, discipline and morale. It also kept together a corporate body of skill. Of 241 men that were transferred to a new muster book in 1798, 126 were rated able seamen, thirty-nine ordinary seamen and nineteen landsmen.[12]

Commitment may be said to have accompanied skill. For, of the 241 men still forming the crew by February 1801, only three were recorded as 'prest'. It was in the interests of seamen to volunteer when it was clear they would not escape impressment. Certainly the extent to which this crew had volunteered was probably affected by her captain's policy of allowing shore leave when in port. This in turn may have influenced the disposition of men to avoid desertion. Although others were successful in deserting, between 20 August 1796 and 20 February 1802 only two men were punished for attempted desertion, eight for going on shore without leave, and two for breaking or overstaying their leave.[13]

---

10 Colonel Drinkwater-Bethune, *A Narrative of the Battle of St Vincent* (London, 1797), pp. 13–15.

11 Widows' men were imaginary ratings borne on the ship's books whose wages were paid into a widows' fund for officers' widows.

12 Muster books for *Minerve*, 1797 and 1801, TNA, ADM36/13135 and ADM36/13816. For thirteen months before April 1798 *Minerve* also carried at least one female, the wife of a marine.

13 Numbers of punishments for different offences are derived from Cockburn's logs for

Continuity of service was the third factor making for harmony on board *Minerve*, a factor which was probably vitally important in cancelling the effect of confining a large proportion of young adult males on board the ship. Of 241 men in 1798 only 26 were over the age of forty, 53 were in their thirties, while 162 were younger than thirty. The captain, Cockburn, was himself only twenty-six in 1798. An excess of young adult males might be equated with a surplus of vigour, aggression and repressed (or unrepressed) male sexuality, and there were undoubtedly occasions when relations between seamen were soured. However, from an account of the punishments awarded on the ship, it is quite clear that relations were impaired more frequently between those who shared the crowded lower deck than between the men and their officers. This is evident in the nature of the offences for which Cockburn awarded punishments over the whole period of his command of *Minerve*. Of 212 known punishments for offences, 60 (28 per cent) were for drunkenness, and 51 (24 per cent) for fighting, quarrelling or theft, while 56 (26 per cent) were for neglect of duty or disobedience of orders, and twenty-nine (14 per cent) for contempt or mutiny. Of these punishments, the *majority* (52 per cent) were for drunkenness, quarrelling or theft; that is, for what may be termed anti-social offences. The *minority* (40 per cent) were for those against authority; that is, for neglect, disobedience or contempt.[14] The remaining 8 per cent of punishments were for offences that fell into neither the anti-social nor the anti-authority categories. It was a distribution that tends to suggest that *Minerve* enjoyed greater harmony between officers and men than between the men themselves.[15]

Moreover it was a pattern in which punishments tended to diminish with continuity of service. In *Minerve* between 1796 and 1801 the number of punishments fell by 43 per cent per annum. Cockburn was particular by nature and probably no less so in recording punishments, the decline in which reinforces a view that the longer crews served together under the same captain the more they adapted to the standards he demanded. For the crew of *Minerve*, in which the average number of punishments declined from nearly six a month in 1796–97 to four in 1800, and to little more than three in 1801, relations would seem to have become increasingly harmonious.

This of course overlooks stresses, problems and breaks from the sea that naturally affected short-term patterns of punishment. There were seven calendar months in *Meleager*, and eighteen in *Minerve* in which the number of punishments fell away to nothing. These periods invariably coincided with spells in port, even though these were often for only a few days. Six consecutive months in 1799 passed without a single punishment, undoubtedly due to the

---

Minerve, L. C. Cockburn Papers, containers 2–3. In many cases punishments were awarded for two offences; for numerical purposes, the first-mentioned offence has been taken as the principal one and counted; the second one has not been counted.

14   These figures presume that drunkenness was punished as an offence against the whole shipboard community.

15   This balance was even more marked in *Meleager*. Of ninety punishments for offences recorded in lieutenants logs for *Meleager*, twenty-nine (32 per cent) were for drunkenness; nineteen (21 per cent) for fighting, quarrelling and theft; thirty-three (37 per cent) for neglect of duty and/or disobedience; one (1 per cent) for mutiny. NMM, ADM/L/M/145.

relief from work at sea by a succession of brief breaks in Leghorn, Palermo, Port Mahon, Gibraltar and the Tagus. On the other hand, a significant increase in offences against authority was registered over the winter of 1797–98, before *Minerve* refitted at Portsmouth, coinciding with the mutinies in the fleet and at the end of long commission. Likewise, on a smaller scale at the end of the Revolutionary War, after anchoring at Spithead, punishments for neglect of duty escalated with the necessity to get the vessel round to Deptford to be stripped and paid off.

Of course it would be wrong to generalise about the attitude of the whole crew from the nature of offences committed by a few. Elsewhere, on the Leeward Islands command, during the Revolutionary War, only 9 per cent of all seamen were flogged; on some vessels far fewer than that proportion were punished, while in others up to 18 per cent suffered.[16] In *Minerve* certain men seem to have courted punishment. Within two months of taking command, Cockburn punished Theodosius Lawson three times: for disobedience of orders and 'aggravating insolence', for mutiny and for quarrelling. But regular individual offenders were uncommon, and then for crimes which seem unlikely to have been common to most men: those, for example, like 'uncleanness', 'indecent familiarity' with some Portuguese boys, striking or drawing upon a superior officer. Such offenders probably possessed a predisposition to these crimes. This was also perhaps the case with thieves, who were particularly heavily punished, receiving up to two hundred lashes compared to the half to two dozen for fighting or quarrelling. But then these last offences were no doubt group activities where men were drawn in, sometimes drunk, carried by the spirit of the moment.[17]

If only a small proportion of the total crew was subject to punishment, it was a greater proportion that benefited from the attention of the ship's officers to the physical needs of the crew. Cockburn himself also attended to the financial and future interests of individuals. It was a form of paternalism that created a network of relationships that involved the captain through messmates, fathers and sons, with the whole crew. This created a critical fourth factor making for stability.

Care for a crew's physical well-being is not well documented. Logs record the opening of casks of pork, inevitably several pieces short and sometimes inedible. However, records for an earlier period show the proportion of victuals that were condemned was small (less than 1 per cent of all but one item – stockfish), against which must be set a total food allowance that was as varied and nutritious as contemporary techniques of preservation and knowledge of dietary necessities permitted.[18] In addition to provisions supplied by the Victualling Board, at the request of the surgeon Cockburn authorised

16 J. D. Byrn, *Crime and Punishment in the Royal Navy: Discipline on the Leeward Islands Station, 1784–1812* (Aldershot, 1989), pp. 108, 114.

17 Ibid., p. 147.

18 Admittedly the records are for four decades earlier; nevertheless, in the absence of evidence to the contrary, it is probably just to assume that standards of victualling did not decline. S. F. Gradish, *The Manning of the British Navy during the Seven Years War* (London, 1980), p. 144; see also Rodger, *The Wooden World* (Glasgow, 1990), pp. 82–5.

the purchase of 'necessaries' that included onions and fruit.[19] Lemons were purchased in large quantities while the fleet occupied the Mediterranean, so that *Minerve* suffered no significant incidence of scurvy until serving on the Atlantic coast of Spain and Portugal in October 1799. Then Cockburn again took the advice of the surgeon and went into the Tagus to procure lemons and fresh provisions, these being 'absolutely necessary to check this disorder in its infancy'.[20]

Provisions for physical welfare also included slop clothing and bedding. Allowances were made at discretion, any excess in value beyond deductions from wages being chargeable to the captain.[21] Stocks of stores were bought in bulk. In May 1799 Cockburn purchased three hundred pairs of shoes for the crew of *Minerve*, drawing a bill on the Navy Board in payment. He also attended to the needs of the marines or soldiers serving on board.[22]

Attention to the financial concerns of seamen was more onerous than might initially be expected. The main official tasks were the routine precise completion and submission of muster and pay books, along with alphabets, sick, dead and remove tickets, remittance slips and allotment accounts. Five copies of the pay books were necessary until May 1800, when the number was reduced to three owing to captains' 'multiplicity of business'. Most of the abstracting and copying was performed by subordinates and the captain's clerk, but the captain oversaw and took responsibility for the whole.

In addition to this official responsibility in matters of pay, Cockburn was regarded by the crew as their advocate for claims that arose from service in previous ships. The task of representing individuals or small numbers of men evidently proceeded from informal, personal approaches or notes to the captain. Thus, much of his administrative correspondence included requests for payments of bounty and back pay, some requests being revived up to three years after they were first made, owing to the intervention of service away from England.[23]

These appeals called for interest and confidence in the cases of seamen: for example, in the claims of ten men from two ships which had been lost (by foundering or capture) after they had left the vessels. On the return to England in April 1798, appeals were made to the master of the merchant ship *Weymouth* who still owed one seaman wages, and to a shipping company at Dartmouth by whom two men were due pay from the masters of two different ships. One of the men had lost the note of wages due; Cockburn nonetheless

19   Cockburn to the Victualling Board, 3 June 1796, 6 April 1801; *Minerve*'s surgeon to Cockburn, 14 December 1796, 27 June 1797, L. C. Cockburn Papers, containers, 9, 13.

20   Nelson to Sir John Jervis, 30 May 1796, Sir N. H. Nicolas, ed., *The Dispatches and Letters of Vice Admiral Lord Viscount Nelson*, VII (7 volumes, London, 1844–6), p. lxxv; log of *Minerve*, October 1799, L. C. Cockburn Papers, container 3.

21   See an Admiralty order of 30 May 1798 reiterating an order-in-council of 28 May concerning the equipment of destitute pressed men, L. C. Cockburn Papers, container 13.

22   Cockburn to the Navy Board, 18 May 1799, and to Lieutenant General O'Hara, 28 October 1797, L. C. Cockburn Papers, container 9.

23   See, for example, requests on behalf of men who had served in *Tarleton* prior to *Minerve* in letters to the Navy Board, 5 October 1798 and 17 December 1801, L. C. Cockburn Papers, container 9.

requested their remission 'if you find by the accounts of the said ship his state-ment is just'.[24]

This interest in individuals' financial concerns was intended to remove anxi-eties or grievances and to promote contentment with life on board. It was not confined to a particular ship or time but was part of a natural relationship with the crew.[25] In some ways it complemented the extra effort the crew itself occasionally exerted on behalf of Cockburn. His appreciation emerges in the cases of individuals: that of John Brady, for example, who acted as surgeon's second mate in *Minerve* until 1798. He was of great use to the surgeon through his 'assiduity and attention, ... although he did not feel himself equal to pass the necessary examination to retain the situation'. Cockburn was therefore anxious he be paid at the appropriate rate for the time he filled his temporary situation.[26]

Ensuring men received their just deserts for their good deeds as well as their bad worked to the natural advantage of both Cockburn and the men involved. Thus, after two years' service as acting warrant officers in *Minerve*, Robert Galway and Robert Taylor, who had both come from *Meleager*, were the sub-ject of Cockburn's request in September 1798 to have their warrants confirmed as master sailmaker and caulker.[27] Patrick Mooney, the acting master at arms, was included in this request. Richard Hobbs, acting boatswain in *Meleager* and in *Minerve* since 1795, and John Henley, acting cook, were the subjects of other requests.[28] These were always accompanied by commendations of conduct and sometimes by reference to supporting attributes. For example, on the death of John Henley, James Gregory was recommended to replace him, not only because he had acted in turn as yeoman of the sheets, boatswain and then been wounded, but because he had a family in the service 'out of which we have now in this ship a most active good seaman'.[29]

Men who were no longer fit for service were recommended for Greenwich Hospital. John Thompson, late boatswain of *Meleager*, whose health had failed and who had to return to England to convalesce, was recommended on

24 Cockburn to the Navy Board, 15 July 1798; to the Master of *Weymouth*, 28 April 1798; to Messrs Noble, Penson and Sons, 28 April 1798; and to John Bedingfield, Navy Pay Office, 22 October 1798, L. C. Cockburn Papers, container 9.
25 A later example of his representation of seamen was Cockburn's letter to Francis Freeling, the Secretary of the Post Office in London, 7 November 1806, in which he re-ported the despatch of eight pounds by a seaman through the Post Office at Plymouth to his mother who had been unable to obtain the money: 'I have therefore thought it right to forward her letter to you, fully convinced you will take such steps as will be most likely to procure these poor people redress and enable them to recover their money'. L. C. Cockburn Papers, container 9.
26 Cockburn to Navy Board, 5 October 1798, L. C. Cockburn Papers, container 9.
27 Robert Galway, aged twenty-six in 1796, had transferred to *Minerve* as an able seaman and served as a master's mate before becoming Master Sailmaker, TNA, ADM36/13135.
28 Cockburn to Navy Board, 9 July, 20 September 1798; and to Lord Keith, 21 August 1800, L. C. Cockburn Papers, container 9.
29 Cockburn to Navy Board, 11 July 1798, 20 August 1800, L. C. Cockburn Papers. The son was William Gregory, aged about nineteen. Another son may have been Jonathan Gregory who served as a midshipman in *Meleager*, May 1793 to May 1794.

his recovery for an equal or larger ship on account of his activity, sobriety and long hard services.[30] Even for men Cockburn did not know, regulations were followed fairly. In spite of a shortage of men, foreigners without settlement in England and apprentices who had received no slops were regularly discharged on failing to volunteer.

Strict compliance 'with the forms of the service', consideration for the future welfare of deserving men, confirmations of promotion where due, attention to financial concerns, provisions for the health and physical welfare of the crew, together created a caring environment in which disaffection did not flourish. This was even more the case in a crew largely composed of experienced men, the core of which had served together continuously for some years, and was managed by warrant and petty officers selected for their competence. This is not to speak of commissioned officers like Cockburn and Hardy who were beginning to make reputations for themselves, both for their seamanship and their capacity for making prize money.

Under such a regime, mutiny and the lesser offence of contempt occurred infrequently. In *Minerve* in the five and a half years between August 1796 and February 1802 there were only fifteen punishments for contempt, insolence or impertinence; and fourteen for mutiny, mutinous expressions or language, countenancing the same or making a mutinous assembly. That is, twenty-nine punishments in sixty-seven months, or less than one punishment for insubordinate language or behaviour every two months. This infrequency (over half of which was for the lesser offence of contempt) suggests that mutiny generally constituted an outburst of frustration directed at hard taskmasters. Under operational conditions, instances of such frustration, about three a year, do not seem abnormal.

Nevertheless the frequency of punishments for mutiny did wax and wane with contemporary events. Nine of the punishments were concentrated in the period June 1797 to March 1798 – an increase in frequency to almost one a month – which were certainly associated with the mutinies in the fleet at Spithead and the Nore, the vibrations from which were communicated to the crew of *Minerve* by the arrival at Madeira on 23 June 1797 of the frigate *Thames*. In his letter to Nelson, Cockburn failed to mention the flogging for mutiny on 24 June (the day after uniting with *Thames*) of a seaman who, after punishment, was discharged on shore; nor that four days later for mutiny and breaking leave on shore; nor that of 10 July for 'making mutinous assembly'.[31] Thereafter, relations on board *Minerve* were unavoidably affected by knowledge of the mutinies in home waters. Even so, the punishment of sympathetic feeling was undeniably light. On the voyage home, on 1 March 1798, six seamen accused of mutiny received but six or a dozen lashes each.

However, in England the mutinies in the fleet had deeply affected naval society, both high and low. In September 1798 at Portsmouth Cockburn appealed to the commander-in-chief to request the Admiralty for a court martial on a

---

30 Cockburn to Vice Admiral Sir W. Hotham, 31 September 1795; to J. Gymm, 9 November 1797; and to Sir P. Parker, 6 August 1798, L. C. Cockburn Papers, container 9.

31 These offences were punished with thirty-six, thirty-two and twenty-four lashes respectively. Log for *Minerve*, L. C. Cockburn Papers, container 2.

seaman, William Nugent, for 'having declared himself to be a United Irishman with many other improper expressions' and then riotously opposing the acting master at arms who attempted to put him in irons.[32] Affairs in Ireland were closely associated in people's minds with events in the fleet. Cockburn himself was not immune from the fears of rebellion bringing chaos to society and the war effort in England.[33]

It was a fear he expressed in the weight of punishments he awarded on his return to sea. In June 1799 he awarded two heavy summary punishments for mutiny: one of five dozen lashes, the other of seven dozen for 'countenancing the same'. Perhaps the weight of these sentences had the desired effect, for these were the last and only punishments recorded for anything smacking of mutiny during a voyage in *Minerve* which kept Cockburn and his crew together for another thirty-two months.

This remarkable mutiny-free period, contrasted with the increase in insubordination after June 1797, tends to suggest to me that mutiny on *Minerve*, when not a spontaneous product of frustration, was an attitude adopted with news of the happenings at Spithead and the Nore. As such, it was never a serious threat to the stability of the ship, and remained a marginal influence even in the ten months after June 1797. It remained marginal, and effectively disappeared after June 1799, because the greater part of the crew and the officers headed by Cockburn felt bound in relationships principally aimed at promoting their mutual welfare. It was a situation which most seamen would probably have acknowledged as one that could have been far worse, and not much better, in any other ship.

Moreover this attitude seems to have been promoted by the energy their captain put into managing his crew. He, after all, was responsible for the selection of many of the warrant and petty officers who managed the seamen. Later Cockburn was depicted as a flogging captain.[34] It was a régime he did not deny. But, as he pointed out, it is necessary to distinguish between what was common practice before 'the age of reform' and what was expected after it.[35]

So, in examining the mutinies of 1797, we too should not fail to recognise the change in attitudes that later presented the Spithead and Nore mutinies as potentially revolutionary occurrences. In focusing on the political character of those events, the many paternalistic practices and welfare provisions, common to all ships in the Royal Navy, have a tendency to be ignored. So too does the fact that many ships, especially those on foreign stations, remained unaffected by events in home waters, or, like *Minerve*, were only mildly affected. Any

---

32   Cockburn to Sir P. Parker, 20 September 1798. L. C. Cockburn Papers, container 9.

33   He followed events in Ireland closely while on leave in 1798, writing to Nelson on 1 June, 'The news from Ireland today is something better but in general I think there reigns a complete chaos of confusion.' BL, Add. MS. 34,907, fols 3–5.

34   T. C. Hansard, *The Parliamentary Debates … from 1803* 2nd series, XIII (1825), column 1098.

35   In *Ariel* in 1788 Cockburn had witnessed a seaman forced to run the gauntlet for theft, a form of punishment abolished in 1806. The practice of 'starting' was also forbidden by Admiralty order in 1809. Log of *Ariel*, 30 June 1788, L. C. Cockburn Papers, container 1; see also P. Kemp, *The British Sailor* (London, 1970), pp. 185–6.

reappraisal of the Spithead and Nore mutinies should take into consideration this stability elsewhere, and balance the revolutionary potential of the mutinies against the forces in the navy that made for cohesion and unity.

In particular, it should look at how the management of seamen and their expectations had diverged, not only because of a decline in the quality of management by subordinate officers, the import of uncommitted men and the fluidity of crewing, but because men now had aspirations of their own about improving their lot. These considerations might be addressed by looking at other ships and their management before and following the mutinies, and they might help to explain why, when concessions and examples had been made following the mutinies, the wounds inflicted appear to have healed relatively quickly and why the Royal Navy became, if anything, more of a force to be reckoned with after 1797 than it had been before.

7

The 1797 Mutinies in the Channel Fleet:
A Foreign-Inspired Revolutionary Movement?

Ann Veronica Coats

> The Ships at Spithead for a whole week in a perfect state of mutiny – the Men commanding their Officers, and a Parliament consisting of Delegates from each Ship of the Line, sitting all that time on board the Queen Charlotte, and issuing Orders to his Majesty's Fleet.[1]

George III, his government and the Board of Admiralty were horrified by this threat to naval discipline, expressed here by the Duke of Clarence to Nelson on 30 April 1797. The potential threat to the security of Britain while the French and Batavian fleets were preparing for invasion was a publicly expressed fear, but the breakdown in discipline was regarded as a far more serious risk by the British establishment, whose intelligence system had led them to expect *no* immediate invasion of Britain or Ireland.[2]

This chapter will examine the extent of revolutionary inspiration for the 1797 mutinies in the Channel Fleet. Was it a rebellion inspired by American, Irish or French revolutionary ideas, part of a plot to overturn the government, oust Pitt's ministry and substitute an opposition ministry, or impose a republic on French or American lines?

Many writers, from Pitt onwards, have portrayed the 1797 mutinies as overt proof of foreign-inspired revolutionary activity in Britain in the 1790s. He asserted that the 'whole affair was of that colour and description which proved it to be not of native growth'.[3] Historians have seen them as a response to the most reactionary and repressive British government of the eighteenth century and to political influences from American, French, Irish and Painite republi-

---

1   Duke of Clarence to Horatio Nelson, 30 April 1797, in N. H. Nicolas, ed., *The Dispatches and Letters of Vice Admiral Lord Viscount Nelson*, II (London, 1845), p. 387.

2   For reports of enemy preparations in France and Holland from January 1797, see TNA, ADM1/3974, ADM1/6033, ADM1/4172, ADM1/107.

3   W. Pitt, 'The Mutiny at the Nore', *Orations of the French War to the Peace of Amiens* (London, n.d.), p. 233.

7a.   7b.

7a. Local Trade Token obverse reads 'MAY THE FRENCH EVER KNOW HOWE TO RULE THE MAIN', with a portrait of Lord Howe, one of the most successful British admirals of the late 1700s. It commemorates the execution of the French royal family by the revolutionaries.

Copyright Portsmouth City Museum & Records Service, reproduced by kind permission of Portsmouth City Museum & Records Service.

7b. Local Trade Token reverse reads 'MUR^D BY THE FACTIOUS. LOUIS XVI JAN.21 M:ANTOINETTE OCT.16 1793'. It typifies a defiant British reaction to the increased terror of the French Revolution whereby the government feared its spread to Britain and the Royal Navy signified the most effective rejoinder.

Copyright Portsmouth City Museum & Records Service, reproduced by kind permission of Portsmouth City Museum & Records Service.

canism.[4] 'I am a republican' was a sentiment uttered by aristocratic and gentry reformers.[5] The address to the nation from the mutineers at the Nore stated: 'the – Age of Reason has at Length Arrived, We had Long been Endeavouring to find ourselvs Men – We Now find Ourselvs So – We will be Treated as Such –'[6]

Marianne Elliott, in *Partners in Revolution*, provided a defined French and Irish revolutionary context. She traced the forces which were driving Irish reformers, republicans and Catholics to form secret societies as Defenders or United Irishmen (or both), and to look towards France to provide political and military support:

4 See J. Ehrman, *The Younger Pitt: The Consuming Struggle* (London, 1996), pp. 303–16; M. Elliott, *Partners in Revolution* (London, 1982), p. 136; R. Wells, *Insurrection: The British Experience, 1795–1803* (Gloucester, 1983), pp. 89–92.

5 Quoted in Wells, *Insurrection*, pp. 68–9.

6 TNA, ADM1/5125, quoted by Gill, *The Naval Mutinies of 1797* (Manchester, 1913), p. 301.

The alliance of a secret catholic movement, which did envisage a reversal of the land settlement, with an advanced republican leadership and a hostile French government poised to assist their joint attack on the established order terrified the protestant nation and was responsible for the brutal repression which helped to provoke the 1798 rebellion.[7]

She has shown that the United Irishmen, originally part of the Protestant Ascendancy, were not social, but political reformers, a class similar to the English aristocratic opposition (in the case of Lord Edward Fitzgerald, closely related to them).[8] They sought a French alliance because they feared that unleashing the 'catholic lower classes' would endanger their own property.[9]

Elliott itemised a remarkable confluence of events, with the 1797 mutinies signposting the 1798 French and Irish insurrection.[10] The United Irish, closely linked with the Defenders, had become a military as well as a political organisation at the end of 1796.[11] For them, the French invasion at Bantry Bay in December 1796 was a catastrophe, caused by conflicting aims within the French military leadership, shortage of supplies, need for secrecy and the distrust of his colleagues by General Hoche, the French commander. It left his dispersed captains without the necessary instructions to go to Ulster, and the Irish unprepared.[12] Far from disheartening the Irish, however, this attempt encouraged them to prepare for another French fleet, and their membership tripled by early spring 1797.[13] This growth was undermined, however, by the failings of their internal security, which was

> too lax in that they did not prevent the Society from becoming too riddled
> with spies who kept the government well informed about every aspect of

7 Elliott, *Partners in Revolution*, p. xvii. There is no space here for a comprehensive Irish historiography, but much has been written since 1997. See Thomas Bartlett, *et al.*, eds, *1798: A Bicentenary Perspective* (Dublin, 2003). Defenders were a Catholic secret society who supported the Irish Rebellion of 1798.

8 He was a nephew of the Duke of Richmond and first cousin of Charles James Fox. Liam Chambers, 'Fitzgerald, Lord Edward', *ODNB* (2004). See A. G. Olson, *The Radical Duke* (Oxford, 1961), pp. 102–5; T. Pakenham, *The Year of Liberty* (London, 1969), pp. 235, 236. For comments on the leadership also see J. L. McCracken, 'The United Irishmen' in T. D. Williams, ed., *Secret Societies of Ireland* (Dublin, 1973), p. 66; T. Bartlett and K. Jeffery, eds, *A Military History of Ireland* (Cambridge, 1996), pp. 277, 278, 307, 310.

9 Elliott, *Partners in Revolution*, pp. xvii, 25, 99, 100.

10 Ibid., pp. 101, 134.

11 Ibid., pp. 108–9.

12 Ibid., pp. 109–16.

13 Ibid., pp. 121–3. Elliott states that only two communications were received by the United Irish executive from agents abroad in 1797: from Tone in May, and Teeling in July. Ibid., p. 159, but Edward Cooke, Under Secretary to the Civil Department, reported a letter from Lewins to Charles Greville, Under Secretary of State in the Home Department, 20 May 1797. TNA, ADM1/4172. See note 18. According to Pakenham, *The Year of Liberty*, pp. 33, 77, Cooke was the most experienced of the Viceroy's civil servants, in charge of intelligence and usually sided with the Protestant extremists.

its activity, and too rigid in that the men of second rank did not know the
leaders or what their plans were.[14]

Their communications with United Irish agents on the continent were
minimal. On 19 May 1797 the Monaghan militia destroyed *Northern Star*
presses which provided the only accurate source of continental information
in Ireland.[15] Communications between Ireland and the leaders abroad were
based on optimism and misinformation. United Irish agent Edward Lewins
had requested between twenty thousand and twenty-five thousand troops and
eighty thousand stand of arms, artillery and officers from Charles Reinhard
and the French Directory, to arrive by May 1797; Ulster rebels prepared to
receive them.[16] Wolfe Tone, Lord Edward Fitzgerald and Arthur O'Connor
had already represented to Reinhard 'the ease with which a French fleet could
reach and land in Ireland, the mutinous disposition of the large Irish element
in the British navy and overwhelming support in Ireland for a rising'.[17]

However, the Irish government in Dublin Castle was fully aware on 14 April
1797, 'from various accounts, and from the great activity of the United Irishmen
which they have lately shewn, and their numerous and daring outrages, that the
French are very shortly expected'.[18] On 20 May the Castle reported:

> Some Letter has been lately read in Societies here, as coming from ... M[r]
> Lewins an Attorney of this Town ..., in which he talked of the certainty of
> the French making an attempt on Ireland very soon. By the Rumours which
> run through the Societies, it appears that the French Fleet is expected off
> the Coast by the 26th Instant.[19]

The British government was also aware, from the constant flow of intelligence
reports from ships and continental agents, of the chronic state of French warships, flat-bottom boats, seamen, soldiers, dockyard workers, supplies and
finances which would make this event impossible.[20]

Elliott characterised the spasmodic nature of French support for Irish demands, always subordinated to their own military aims and political priorities.
France had no spare capacity to provide what the Irish needed: trained soldiers
and ships. Letters from Philippe D'Auvergne, Prince de Bouillon, British naval
officer and agent in Jersey, from March to May 1797 reported slow improvements to the French fleet 'owing to the great confusion that prevails in every
Departement and the extreme penury of means' and 'the great dependence
for the present Campaign' on the Spanish fleet.[21] He described desertions by
seamen, shortages of provisions and stores:

---

14 McCracken, 'The United Irishmen', p. 67.
15 Elliott, *Partners in Revolution*, pp. 128, 161.
16 Ibid., pp. 130–2.
17 Ibid., p. 101.
18 TNA, ADM1/4172. Edward Cooke to Greville, 20 May 1797.
19 Ibid.
20 From January 1797, TNA, ADM1/3974, ADM1/6033, ADM1/4172, ADM1/107.
21 TNA, ADM1/4172, 28 April 1797, D'Auvergne, Prince de Bouillon.

An attempt was made a few nights since by the workmen of [Brest] Harbour, to repeat what has lately happened in Toulon, that cost the Maritime Agent the famous Groignard, his Life, and exposed that of the Commandant of the Place; several Placards were stuck up, inviting the Soldiers to imitate the Toulonese, and do themselves justice of Sané the Maritime Agent here, stating their non payments, and their delapidations of the prizes as a proper motive.[22]

The French did not appreciate, because of extensive security in Britain, Ireland and France and distrust and lack of communication between United Irishmen, that by 1797 Irish Protestants and Catholics were engaged in a civil war. Colonel William Tate's *chouannerie* expedition which landed in Wales 22–23 February 1797 represented the utmost available in French ships, manpower and supplies that could be spared from other theatres of war.[23] By April 1797 it was too late to support the Irish against the British.[24] Despite this however, the French hoped to win over Irish sailors within the fleet in 1798. Eustache Bruix, Minister of the Marine, employed United Irish agent William Duckett to contact them. Thousands of printed addresses aimed at the 'mutinous tendency' within the armed forces were distributed to British crews in neutral European ports.[25]

Gill, Elliott and Wells have attached great importance to external political forces influencing the seamen. Gill's conclusion was that

> the Mutinies resulted from the fusion of two movements, the one economic and the other political; ... On their economic side they present an early example of a remarkably well organised and successful strike. And in their political aspect thay mark the climax of the revolutionary movement in this country.[26]

He believed 'the idea of mutiny was introduced into the fleet by men of a seditious character, who worked deliberately to spread the dissaffection among their fellow seamen.'[27] Elliott attributed the political cause to 'products of the Quota Acts of 1795 and 1796', which sent 'a different kind of recruit into the navy, usually younger, better educated, less inured to the traditional rigours of naval life, and unprepared to accept unreasonable manifestations of authority.'[28] Wells also deduced that the Quota men were responsible for the

---

22 Ibid., 19, 22 March 1797. D'Auvergne was referring to the capture of Toulon by the British in 1793. W. Laird Clowes, *The Royal Navy*, IV (London, 1997), p. 210; M. A. Thiers, *Histoire de la Révolution Française*, V (Paris, 1850), pp. 246–54; M. Crook, *Toulon in War and Revolution* (Manchester, 1991), chapters 6 and 7. Antoine Groignard was a notable French naval architect and engineer. *Ibid.*, p. 13.

23 Elliott, *Partners in Revolution*, pp. 116–8; *The Times*, 23 February–3 March 1797; TNA, ADM1/4172.

24 Elliott, *Partners in Revolution*, chapter 5.

25 Ibid., p. 218.

26 Gill, *Naval Mutinies*, p. 358.

27 Ibid., p. 313.

28 Elliott, *Partners in Revolution*, p. 136.

mutiny, arguing that the mutineers' literacy, their 'organisations, their elections, delegations, ship's committees, and central committees, reflect perfectly those of the popular democratic societies'. He insisted that 'political initiatives were made to the mutinous seamen' and repeated a stereotype: that the

> 'real British seaman was usually a simple soul, obstinately conservative, ill-educated', too unsophisticated to even conceive the organisation which was to be responsible for their initial triumphs over the Admiralty.[29]

These interpretations fail to acknowledge long-existing negotiating practices within the navy, which 'invariably followed a set of time-honoured unwritten rules which limited their mutiny to a formal demonstration of token disobedience, quite without violence.'[30] They denigrated the acquired skills of the seamen who *did* organise this labour dispute, with *no* assistance from outside and without alerting officers beforehand.[31] A more positive characterisation was made by J. S. Clarke, chaplain on *Impétueux* at the time of the mutiny:

> They are eminently characterised by a never-failing love of their Country; by humanity towards their fellow-creatures; by moderation in victory: by a noble disdain of the severe hardships of their profession, and an elevated sense of its glories.[32]

However, Wells contradicted himself by quoting a statement from Admiral Gardner that the seamen *were* literate: 'The Public Newspapers are read by almost everybody in the fleet.'[33]

The seamen were uniting for a common purpose, not withdrawing their labour.[34] Their own rules clearly said that 'the greatest attention to be paid to the Orders of the Officers' and that anyone 'neglecting their Duty shall be severely Punished'. What they refused was 'to lift an anchor to Proceed from this Port untill the Desire of the fleet is satisfyed'.[35] In other words, a clever

---

29   Wells, *Insurrection*, pp. 84, 98, 101. For other views, see C. Lloyd, *The British Seaman* (London, 1968), pp. 230–9; P. Kemp, *The British Sailor* (London, 1970), pp. 164–5; C. N. Parkinson, *Portsmouth Point: The Navy in Fiction* (London, 1948), pp. 60–71; D. Hannay, *Ships and Men* (London, 1910), pp. 1–15; M. Rediker, *Between the Devil and the Deep Blue Sea* (Cambridge, 1987), pp. 146–9.

30   N. A. M. Rodger, 'The Inner Life of the Navy, 1750–1800: Change or Decay?', *Guerres et paix 1660–1815* (Vincennes, 1987), pp. 172–3; Ehrman, *Younger Pitt: The Consuming Struggle*, p. 23.

31   See Earl Spencer to Jervis, 4 May 1797, J. S. Tucker, ed., *Memoirs of Earl St Vincent*, I (London, 1844), p. 320; Lady Spencer to William Windham, 20 April 1797, in Earl of Rosebery, ed., *The Windham Papers*, I (London, 1913), p. 48.

32   *Naval Chronicle*, III (Jan–June 1803), pp. 275–6.

33   Wells, *Insurrection*, p. 96. For a discussion on seamen's literacy, see A. Kennedy and D. Ellison, eds, *Pressganged* (Royston, 1984), pp. 64–5.

34   *OED*.

35   TNA, ADM1/5125, 16 April 1797, Papers from *Queen Charlotte*. Also ADM1/107, *Ramillies*, 7 May 1797; Seamen to Bridport, 23 April 1797.

avoidance of the incriminating clauses of the Articles of War and a unity behind a concrete slogan.

All the seamen's methods of organisation – red flags, oaths, delegates,
committees – can be traced to merchant seamen's disputes of the eighteenth
century or earlier.[36] Many assertions about their rights come, not only from
Thomas Paine's *Rights of Man*, but also from their seventeenth-century
democratic inheritance: the Commonwealth republican navy, collectivism of
the Diggers and Levellers in the New Model Army, and the 1688 bloodless
revolution.[37] From the 1770s the county associations, the Revolution Society,
the Society for Constitutional Information, the Whig Club and other political
reform societies articulated and celebrated their radical heritage.[38] At Daniel
Holt's trial for publishing seditious libel in 1793, barrister Thomas Erskine
cited constitutional freedoms of Englishmen established by the 1689 political
settlement.[39] The Radical Thomas Spence advocated common ownership of
land and government based on 'powers delegated from below'.[40] He also advocated electing captains and officers on ships and lauded the example of the
Spithead mutiny: 'as they accomplished their mutinies without bloodshed, so
may Landsmen be assured, if unanimous, of accomplishing their deliverance
in the same harmless manner.'[41]

36 See Coats, Chapter 2, 'The Delegates: A Radical Tradition'; N. A. M. Rodger, *The Safeguard of the Sea* (London, 1997), pp. 401, 403; Rediker, *Devil and the Deep Blue Sea*, p. 97–103, 109–15, 127, 166, 244, 263, 266, 298; T. R. Knox, 'Thomas Spence: The Trumpet of Jubilee', *Past and Present*, 76 (1977), pp. 43–4. For implications of the red flag, see J. B. Deane, *The Life of Richard Deane* (London, 1870), p. 191; T. Wilson, *Flags at Sea* (Greenwich, 1986), pp. 46, 61, 77, 79, 108; R. B. Rose, 'Red Flag over Liverpool: 1775 – A Liverpool Sailors' Strike in the Eighteenth Century', in B. Blick, ed., *Rebels against the Old Order* (Ohio, 1994), p. 69; *True Briton*, 27 May 1797, 2 June 1797; *The Times*, 1 June 1797; T. Barrow, 'The Greenlanders at Shields 1760–1830: A Labour Elite', *North East Labour History*, 24 (1990); N. McCord and D. Brewster, 'Some Labour Troubles of the 1790s in North East England', *International Review of Social History*, XIII (1968). I am very grateful to Tony Barrow for sending these last two articles and to R. Barrie Rose for sending his article.
37 A 'form of government in which the sovereign power resides in the people, and is exer-cised either directly by them or by others elected by them'. *OED*. Rodger, *Safeguard of the Sea*, p. 322, 404; J. B. Deane, *The Life of Richard Deane* (London, 1870), p. 103; Rediker, *Devil and the Deep Blue Sea*, p. 262; F. K. Donnelly, 'The Levellers and Early Nineteenth Century Radicalism', *Bulletin for the Social Study of Labour History*, 49 (1984), pp. 24–8; C. Chenevix Trench, *Portrait of a Patriot* (London, 1962), pp. 117–18; B. Capp, *Cromwell's Navy* (Oxford, 1992), pp. 2, 4, 35, 44–5, 118–9, 396, 400–1; H. N. Brailsford, *The Levellers and the English Revolution*, ed. C. Hill (Nottingham, 1976), p. 216. See the discussion in Coats, Chapter 2, 'The Delegates: A Radical Tradition'.
38 Pertaining to a change in a fundamental principle, reform. *OED*. A. Goodwin, *The Friends of Liberty* (London, 1979), p. 21 and *passim*.
39 See A. V. Beedell, 'John Reeves's Prosecution for Seditious Libel, 1795–6: A Study in Political Cynicism', *The Historical Journal*, 36, 4 (1993), pp. 805–7; K. Wilson, 'Inventing Revolution: 1688 and Eighteenth-Century Popular Politics', *Journal of British Studies*, 28, 4 (October 1989), pp. 349–86.
40 T. R. Knox, 'Thomas Spence: The Trumpet of Jubilee', *Past and Present*, 76 (1977), pp. 89, 90.
41 G. I. Gallop, ed., *Pigs' Meat* (London, 1982), p.77; T. R. Knox, 'Thomas Spence: The

The London Corresponding Society was established in 1792 to promote electoral reform, citing franchise restrictions since 1429.[42] It proclaimed peaceful and non-violent methods, resolving that:

> This Society do express their <u>Abhorrence</u> of Tumult and Violence, and that, as they aim at Reform, not Anarchy, Reason, Firmness, and Unanimity are the only Arms they themselves will employ, or persuade their fellow-Citizens to exert, against the <u>Abuse of Power</u>.[43]

Despite this declaration, the government cynically interpreted constitutional criticism as treason: a conspiracy to depose the King, imported from French Jacobin clubs.[44] 'The life of the prince [is] so interwoven with the constitution of the state that an attempt to destroy the one is justly held to be a rebellious conspiracy against the other.'[45] The Committee of Secrecy, conflating the proceedings of the LCS and Society for Constitutional Information, which 'tend to the subversion of the established Constitution', reported in May 1794 that since the outbreak of war with France the SCI had continued its 'attachment to the cause of the French Revolution' and was planning to call an English Convention, which would 'assume to itself all the functions and powers of a national Legislature'.[46] Icons of the Stuart restoration were still being celebrated by the establishment. The day Thomas Hardy, the LCS secretary, was taken to the Tower was 'the 29th of May the Anniversary of the Restoration which ought now <u>to be blotted out</u> as a day of rejoycing.'[47] To curtail LCS activities he was tried in October 1794 for treason.

The ministerial case rested on implicating Hardy with arming societies.[48] He was acquitted on 5 November 1794 because the Crown failed to prove this, despite extensive evidence from Home Office spies that individual members had contemplated an armed uprising to depose the King, telling soldiers that 'by their oath they were to fight for their king and country, but when the king and country were at variance, they had a right to fight on which side they pleased'.[49] His defence also claimed that he was following the plan and the methods advocated by the Duke of Richmond's 1780 reform bill.[50] Two weeks later Horne Tooke succeeded in calling as a witness at his trial 'Pitt, who re-

Trumpet of Jubilee', *Past and Present*, 76 (1977), p. 97.

42 M. Thale, *Correspondence of the LCS* (Cambridge, 1983), pp. 12, 13.

43 Ibid., p. 10.

44 Ibid., p. 232; Beedell, 'John Reeves's Prosecution', p. 812. First Report from the Committee of Secrecy of the House of Commons respecting seditious practices, 16 May 1794, in A. Aspinall and E. A. Smith, eds, *English Historical Documents 1783–1832*, XI (London, 1959), pp. 316–19; Goodwin, *Friends of Liberty*, 27.

45 Quoted by Thale, *Correspondence of the LCS*, p. 232.

46 Aspinall and Smith, *English Historical Documents*, XI, pp. 316–8.

47 Thale, *Correspondence of the LCS*, pp. 157–8. 29 May was Charles II's birthday and the date he entered London at the start of his rule. It was celebrated as Oak Apple Day to recall his escape after the Battle of Worcester in 1651, when he hid in the Boscobel Oak.

48 Ibid., p. 232.

49 Ibid., pp. 157, 320.

50 A. G. Olson, *The Radical Duke* (Oxford, 1961), p. 62.

luctantly admitted supporting reform meetings in the 1780s'.[51] Horne Tooke was also acquitted.[52]

In 1795 the LCS addressed a remonstrance to the King against the bills to prevent 'Treasonable and Seditious Practices' and 'Seditious Meetings and Assemblies', recalling:

> When the treacherous duplicity, and intolerable tyranny of the House of STUART had roused the long-enduring patience of the British People, the expulsion of one restored into their hands the primitive right of chusing another, as their Chief of many Magistrates.[53]

The remonstrance linked the Hanoverian monarchy to the revolution settlement: 'The preservation of the rights, reconfirmed at the Revolution, then became part of the obligations of George I.'[54] Their petition to the House of Commons urged: 'Consider the compact between the government and the people and the dreadful consequences of violating it.'[55] An advertisement listing places where the petition could be signed declared:

> Theologists must no longer choose the Doctrines they may believe, nor the Founts in which they would worship; to differ from the Religion extablished by Law, will be called a Rebellion against the State; and we may expect to see an Inquisition established, to persecute every Denomination of Dissenters.[56]

A proclamation against the 'two bills' coincided with the annual dinner, held by the Revolution Society on 5 November since 1789, to celebrate William, Prince of Orange's landing in 1688 and the fall of the Bastille in 1789. The government did not feel undermined by aristocrats dining on a discourse, but was threatened by artisans organising to 'Reform Parliamentary Representation'.[57] When the Duke of Richmond introduced a parliamentary reform bill in 1780 the King had complained, 'The Duke of Richmond is subverting the whole constitution', but the Duke was not tried for treason.[58]

51 Thale, *Correspondence of the LCS*, p. 234; J. Money, 'Birmingham and the West Midlands, 1760–1793: Politics and Regional Identity in the English Provinces in the later Eighteenth Century', *Midland History*, I (Spring 1971), p. 10. John Horne Tooke (1736–1812) was a political reformer and lawyer, arrested for high treason with Thomas Hardy and John Thelwall and tried 17–22 November 1794. He was defended by Sir Vicary Gibbs.
52 Thale, *Correspondence of the LCS*, p. 234.
53 36 Geo. III, c.7 and 36 Geo. III, c.8. Aspinall and Smith, *English Historical Documents*, XI, pp. 319–22. Known as the 'two acts', or the 'gagging acts', they restricted meetings and publications. The LCS was blamed for an attack on George III on 29 October 1795 and the government tried to find proof that it was treasonable. Thale, *Correspondence of the LCS*, pp. 319, 326; Goodwin, *Friends of Liberty*, p. 28; Thale, *Correspondence of the LCS*, p. 316.
54 Ibid., p. 316.
55 Ibid., p. 324.
56 Ibid., p. 325.
57 A. Wharam, *The Treason Trials* (Leicester, 1992), p. 13; Goodwin, *Friends of Liberty*, p. 25; Thale, *Correspondence of the LCS*, p. 12.
58 Olson, *Radical Duke*, pp. 51, 48.

The dilemma of the Whig government was that they could not deny the revolution of 1688 as their source of power: 'Not even Burke ever quite repudiated Locke and the right of resistance.'[59] In the parliamentary debate on the petitions against the two bills, Pitt resorted to sophistry, accusing the opposition of establishing doctrines which arose from 'extraordinary circumstances' as 'established maxims'; then reiterating them himself:

> because our ancestors had recourse to resistance to overpower a King, who aimed at the overthrow of the national religion, who attempted to govern without parliaments altogether; who was in fact, against all law; and who violated the constitution of the country.[60]

He succeeded in swaying Parliament to approve the two bills, because of MPs' 'fear of losing what is got for the protection of which a strong executive government and strong laws and a large military force are in their estimation considered solely adequate'.[61]

Yes, British seamen, the largest, most cosmopolitan labour force in Britain, absorbed ideas from Foxite reformists, Corresponding Societies, United Irishmen, and American and French republicanism. These ideas were grafted on to their native traditions, but the government reacted to the most obvious cause. In 1791 Walpole 'understandably expressed alarm when "vast numbers of Paine's pamphlet were distributed both to regiments and ships"'.[62] On 1 April 1797 John King, Under-Secretary of State at the Home Office, transmitted the assurance to Evan Nepean, Secretary to the Admiralty, that the 'the Outlawry ag[t.] Thomas Paine was complet[d.] in Nov[r.] 1793 and is still in force'.[63] After the Nore mutiny, on the same day as Parker's court martial concluded, a bookseller was found guilty of publishing Thomas Paine's *The Age of Reason*.[64] The judge, commenting that people had been taking notes during the trial,

> hoped that no part of this shocking detail would be published. No man who had the least regard for decency, or who paid the smallest attention to his own interest, would endeavour to disseminate among the Public, doctrines which no serious Christian could hear.[65]

The LCS had a branch in Portsmouth, and delegate John Binns had visited Portsmouth in February 1796. But the society was, from an 'Informant's' evidence, not responsible for any prior input to the mutiny:

> when the accounts of the mutiny on board the Fleet at Portsmouth came

---

59 Beedell, 'John Reeves's Prosecution', pp. 805–6.
60 Quoted Ibid., p. 816.
61 Lambton to Grey, April 1796, quoted Ibid., p. 821. See Olson, *Radical Duke*, p. 56.
62 J. Keane, *Tom Paine A Political Life* (London, 1995), p. 307.
63 TNA, ADM1/4172, 1 April 1797.
64 *The Times*, 26 June 1797.
65 Ibid.

to London, the Society expressd. the greatest Satisfaction & actually sent
delegates, namely Dr. Watson & John Bone down to Portsmouth to confer
with the leading Mutineers[.][66]

The Spithead delegates' role in collective organisation and responsibility
was a pragmatic response to the traditional Admiralty practice of punishing
ringleaders and pardoning the rest.[67] It was also a tactic of eighteenth-century
trade unions, and used by the General Chamber of Manufacturers of Great
Britain, opposing Pitt's Irish Commercial Treaty in 1785.[68] The delegates were
aware of the political context, the strategic dimensions and the weaknesses
of Pitt's government. They knew how to present their case to the Admiralty,
Parliament and the public, and support it with appropriate information. Their
argument was that their wages had not been increased since Charles II's reign,

> a time when the necessaries of life and slops of every denomination was at
> least 30 per cent cheaper than the present time which enabled seamen and
> marines to provide better for their Families than we can now do[.][69]

This claim is more than substantiated by Patrick O'Brien's economic indices
which begin in 1660.[70] By 1797 grain prices had risen from 118 to 173, animal
products from 105 to 212, vegetables (beginning 1684), from 113 to 150, with
the composite agricultural index rising from 111 to 186. The composite industrial index rose from 92 to 116 in the same period.[71] Inflation in the second
half of the eighteenth century had significantly reduced the seamen's wages.[72]
Philip Patton confirmed in 1795 that, compared with merchant seamen's pay,
'all those Men who have been compelled to serve their Country this War, have
been likewise obliged to relinquish nearly half the profits of their labour'.[73]

For the Admiralty, alarmed by the practice of both democratic and revolutionary societies swearing oaths (an act was swiftly passed forbidding this),

---

66   At the end of May. Thale, *Correspondence of the LCS*, pp. 427, 397.
67   'A person sent or deputed to act for or represent another or others; one entrusted with
authority or power to be exercised on behalf of those by whom he is appointed'. *OED*;
G. Rudé, *Wilkes and Liberty* (London, 1983), pp. 94–5. For a different use of 'delegate' in
Dutch Boards of Admiralty, see J. R. Powell and E. K. Timings, eds, *Documents Relating
to the Civil War 1642–1648* (London, 1963), pp. 265–6; C. T. Atkinson, ed., *First Dutch
War*, V (London, 1905), pp. 191, 199, 203, 219, 243, 247. Also see J. Barrow, ed., *Life of
Earl Howe* (London, 1838), p. 302; Lloyd, *Health of Seamen*, pp. 238–9; BL, Place Papers,
IXXIV, Add. MS. 35,143; Thale, *Correspondence of the LCS*, pp. 12, 426.
68   Money, 'Birmingham and the West Midlands', pp. 5–7.
69   TNA, ADM1/5125, February 1797. Their wages had not been raised since 1 January
1653, as an 'encouragement' for 'mariners, to induce them to come in cheerfully and
speedily to the service.' *CSPD*, 1652–53, p. 42. Charles II had repeated the terms. TNA,
ADM178/133, 'Mutiny in the Royal Navy', I, p. 10.
70   P. O'Brien, 'Agriculture and the Home Market for British Industry, 1660–1820',
Economic History Review, 100 (1985), pp. 773–800. 1720–44 = 100 (p. 790).
71   O'Brien, 'Agriculture and the Home Market for British Industry', pp. 787–98.
72   Rodger, 'Inner life of the Navy', p. 174
73   NMM, WYN/109/7/14, fol. 5.

the most seditious article agreed by the mutineers was the sixth.[74] 'Every Seaman and Marine' was to take 'an oath of Fiddelity not onely to ourselves but to the Fleet in General'. Every man 'swore by his maker that the Cause we have Undertaken we Persevere in till acomplished'. Messages reporting that the oath had been taken were sent by *Nymphe*, *Duke* and *Defiance*. *Nymphe*'s crew swore:

> We hereby agree upon Oath to stand true to the fleet, and not comply by any means Untill such Redress is fineally settled Respecting the Greavences of Perticular ships, and likewise that his Majesty's Pardon is granted to the Satisfaction of the fleet[.][75]

Spithead oaths served to protect the seamen and bond them to a common cause. By comparison, the *Pompée* oath, 'to ever stand true till Death in promoting the cause of Freedom with Equity, while any Probability [of] furthering its progress remain', was forced on seamen because they did not subscribe to this more nebulous issue.[76] The Admiralty and the government confounded the taking of oaths with sedition and godlessness.[77] When Daniel O'Connell renounced his freemasonry in 1837 he described his revulsion at taking oaths which epitomised this attitude:

> the profane taking in vain the awful name of the Deity, in the wanton and multiplied taking of Oaths – of Oaths administered on the book of God either in mockery or derision or with a solemnity which renders the taking of them, without any adequate motive, only the more criminal.[78]

Aaron Graham and Daniel Williams, magistrates sent to find evidence of sedition at the Nore,

> had various opportunities of remarking that the sailors in general had a very serious sense of the obligation imposed on them by an oath (even when administered as in the case of this mutiny) and are therefore of opinion that the attesting of seamen as well as soldiers would be attended with beneficial effects.[79]

The actual function of these oaths was, in merchant, naval and early trade union practices, to bind the mutineers together for protection in a life-threatening situation. They did not invoke treason or revolution. The more nebulous

---

74   37 Geo. III c.123, J. Ehrman, *The Younger Pitt: The Consuming Struggle* (London, 1996), p. 29.

75   TNA, ADM1/5125.

76   TNA, ADM1/5339, *Pompée* court martial, 20–23 June 1797, evidence of Surgeon Josiah Packwood.

77   See discussion of the role of secret societies and oaths in Williams, *Secret Societies of Ireland*, pp. 1–12, 15, 16, 20, 38, 41, 49–50, 62, 64, 68–70.

78   T. de Vere White, 'The Freemasons', *Secret Societies of Ireland*, p. 50.

79   TNA, HO42/41, Sheerness, 24 June 1797.

oath sworn during *Pompée*'s mutiny in June 1797 was nonetheless similar in concept.[80]

Some historians believed that United Irishmen instigated the Spithead mutiny, flagged by ministerial agencies such as the Commons Secrecy Committee.[81] Elliott considered that United Irish oaths were administered at Spithead, but the oaths sworn there were unlike the Defenderist and United English oaths she quotes.[82] The United English oath, which overtly included an intention to overthrow the government, was quite different:

> I swear ... to obey ... the Committee of United Englishmen and Irishmen then sitting in England and Ireland and Scotland, and to assist with arms, as far as it is in my power, to establish a republican Government in this country, and others, and to assist the French on their landing to free this country. So help me God.[83]

As was the Defenders' oath:

> To the National Convention – to quell all nations – to dethrone all Kings, and plant the Tree of Liberty in our Irish land – whilst the French Defenders will protect our cause, and the Irish Defenders pull down the British laws.[84]

Seamen's oaths were not offensive but defensive: they functioned to protect each other and to maintain unity until their aims were achieved, because they knew from experience that individually they would be picked out and punished.[85]

As for the threat from United Irishmen within the fleet, they were not perceived as such by the British government until 1797.[86] The prospect had been expressed in Wolfe Tone's address, probably written in 1796, and highlighted in Admiral Philip Patton's 'Observations on Naval Mutiny', presented to Earl Spencer in 1795.[87] Tone, Lord Edward Fitzgerald and Arthur O'Connor believed Irish seamen in the British fleet numbered eighty thousand (about two-thirds of the navy), and their actions in taking over the fleet would vitally aid invasion by disabling the British navy.[88] In 1796 Wolfe Tone had called upon the Irish in the navy to seize their vessels, hoist the Irish flag and steer them

---

80   TNA, ADM1/5339, *Pompée* court martial, 20–23 June 1797, evidence of Surgeon Josiah Packwood.

81   Elliott, *Partners in Revolution*, 137; Wells, *Insurrection*, pp. 81–2, 84; Gill, *Naval Mutinies*, pp. 313, 329.

82   Elliott, *Partners in Revolution*, p. 143.

83   Quoted in Elliott, *Partners in Revolution*, p. 149.

84   Ibid., p. 42.

85   See individual ship mutinies on *Raisonable*, 1783, *Culloden*, 1794 and *Terrible*, 1795.

86   See Secretary at War William Windham to Lord Grenville, 17 May 1798, *The Windham Papers*, II, p. 83.

87   Tone's Address is printed in Gill, *Naval Mutinies*, pp. 331–2. NMM, WYN/109/7/14.

88   Gill, *Naval Mutinies*, p. 330; Elliott, *Partners in Revolution*, pp. 101, 136, 138, 155–6, 218; Goodwin, *Friends of Liberty*, p. 410.

to Ireland.[89] (Gill considers the proportion of Irish seamen in 1797 to have been an eighth: 11,500 sailors and 4,000 marines).[90] Most damningly, Tone was unaware that Spithead mutiny was taking place until 29 April 1797. In August he wrote bitterly:

> Five weeks, I believe six weeks, the English fleet was paralysed by the mutinies at Portsmouth, Plymouth, and the Nore. The sea was open, and nothing to prevent both the Dutch and French fleets to put to sea. Well, nothing was ready: that precious opportunity, which we can never expect to return, was lost.[91]

In fact, Irish on Spithead ships composed on average about a quarter of the crews, and like the majority, were long-established members.[92] Numbers of Irish among the Spithead delegates was an even smaller proportion, four out of thirty-three.[93]

Patton had deduced the risks of a future general mutiny from his observation of the events at Spithead in 1783, when

> not only the most threatening symptoms of general Mutiny took place during service, but that actual possession was taken of the Command of many capital Ships. ... It is true this was not done with any intention of acting against their Country; but if Seamen know that they can combine and take possession of the Ships for one purpose, they must see that they can do it for another. A greater degree of discontent is only wanting to induce them to deliver the Ships to the Enemy.[94]

He emphasised 'the violent manner by which Seamen are supplied to the Navy during hostilities' and asked 'what custom can reconcile so violent a measure to those who are to suffer under it, and what necessity can persuade Seamen that they are to bear increasing hardships and oppression, of which they find they can clear themselves'?[95] Patton's anxiety was substantiated by a petition from *Shannon* dated 16 June 1796, which complained that the Captain was

> one of the most Barbarous and one of the most unhuman Officers That Eaver a Seet of unfortunect ... English men Eaver had the Disagreable

---

89 *Life of Wolfe Tone*, pp. ii, 326–8, reproduced in Gill, *Naval Mutinies*, pp. 331–2. 'In Tone's *Memoirs* it is included among papers written in 1796, but it is not dated.' (p. 331)

90 Gill, *Naval Mutinies*, pp. 329–30; Lewis, *Social History of the Navy*, pp. 73–8; M. Elliott, *Wolfe Tone* (London, 1989), pp. 261, 265.

91 Wolfe Tone, *Life*, pp. ii, 427, quoted in Gill, p. 337

92 Figure based on the muster books of the leading ships at Spithead. Jamieson discusses Irish seamen on the mutinying *Queen* in March–April 1783. 'Twenty-eight per cent were Irish ... yet *Queen* does not seem to have been especially undisciplined.' A. G. Jamieson, 'Tyranny of the Lash? Punishment in the Royal Navy during the American War, 1776–1783', *The Northern Mariner/Le Marin du nord*, IX: 1 (January 1999), p. 59.

93 See Coats, Chapter 2, 'The Delegates: A Radical Tradition'.

94 NMM, WYN/109/7/14, fols 3–4.

95 NMM, WYN/109/7/14, fols 4–5.

Misfortune of Being with, wich treatment And Bad useages Is Anufe to
make the Sparites of the English men to Rise, and Steer The Ship Into An
Enimies Port[.][96]

Patton had warned Earl Spencer in 1795:

the Seamen who seize upon the Ships, not only deliver themselves into the
hands of the Enemy, but they also deliver to them machines of great value,
which cannot be replaced in many years, provided with Arms, Ammunition
and Provisions, which can at once be transferred to another State, and instantly used against their Country.[97]

Wolfe Tone almost echoed these words in his address:

Suppose you profit of this favourable moment to do what is but your duty
as good Irishmen, that you seize upon the English vessels and bring them
into your own harbours. ... every vessel so brought into port shall be sold
for its full value, both ship and cargo, and the price faithfully paid to you
... And as the vessels will be directly put into commission again, under the
Irish flag, those brave seamen who wish to serve their country and to make
their fortunes at the expense of the common enemy, will, of course, have
the first promotion.[98]

Patton highlighted the recently changed international situation:

The Thirteen Provinces of America have opened an Asylum for the discontented as they may remain with safety on their shores or be employed
in their Ships without danger of discovery ... Even France presents itself
under a new aspect to Seamen, it expects to be called a Land of liberty.[99]

As did Tone:

Ireland is now at war with England in defence of her liberties: France is the
ally of Ireland, and England is the common enemy of both nations. You are
aboard the British navy. You will probably be called upon immediately to
turn your arms against your native land ... You are no longer the subjects
of the King of England; you are at the same time a great majority of those
who man his fleet, in the proportion of at least two to one. What is there
to hinder you from immediately seizing on every vessel wherein you sail,
man-of-war, Indiaman or merchantman, hoisting the Irish flag and steering
into the ports of Ireland?[100]

---

96 TNA, ADM1/5125.
97 NMM, WYN/109/7/14, fols 1–2.
98 Gill, *Naval Mutinies*, p. 332.
99 NMM, WYN/109/7/14, fols 6–7.
100 Gill, *Naval Mutinies*, pp. 331–2.

Wolfe Tone's address at his trial proclaimed his enduring mission:

> Upon all occasions have I endeavoured to subvert and destroy the connec-
> tion which subsists between Great Britain and Ireland, convinced as I am
> that such a connection is totally inimical to its Prosperity, and its Liberty
> and its Happiness.[101]

Once the government recognised the risk of importing potential revolutionaries into the fleet, they investigated the indiscriminate posting of suspected United Irishmen and Defenders, officially under the Insurrection Act
of 1796, but commonly practised since 1793.[102] The heightened political and
social unrest in Ireland provided a cause to which Irish seamen and marines
related and perpetuated traditional ties between the Irish minority and their
co-revolutionaries, the French.[103] Many Irish seamen were no more willing to
be in the navy than their English counterparts, having been impressed, sent
from minor courts, or having volunteered through economic necessity.

In June 1797 Phillip Cosby at Dublin Castle requested guidance from the
Admiralty 'whether such … United Irishmen … as may be found healthy or
fit to serve in the fleet may be sent'. He reported that one hundred and fifty
Irishmen had been sent in the previous two years, 'Exclusive of some sent on
board the Men of War that occasionally called in but I believe these were but
few'.[104] A few days later Cosby reported to the Admiralty:

> I have wrote to the Commanding Officer of the Marines, to request that he
> will cause the Non Commissioned Officers to be more attentive and par-
> ticular to the Men they raise as many of them are very troublesome when
> we receive them in the Tenders, and are of a complection that cannot be
> very desirable by some of the Corps they are sent to, some of them having
> been so audacious as to wear the Badge of the Society of United Irishmen,
> which we often correct.[105]

The Irish were valued as a fighting resource in the armed forces and the navy
needed them, even though they feared their suspect allegiance slightly more
than any generic group of seamen.[106] The Irish endured the same 'hardships
of confinement, and the operation of a severe martial law, added to low pay'
as English seamen, but bore the additional knowledge that their country was

---

101 BL, Add. MS. 38,355, fol. 21, 1798.
102 Elliott, *Partners in Revolution*, pp. 98, 138; Wells, *Insurrection*, pp. 81, 82. Since the
sixteenth century it had been customary to send convicted rebels to the fleet. See *CSPD*,
1655, pp. x, 249, 253, Penruddock uprising.
103 See Pakenham, *Year of Liberty*.
104 TNA, ADM1/579, Phillip Cosby to Evan Nepean, Admiralty Secretary, 7 June 1797.
105 Ibid., 18 June 1797, Phillip Cosby to Evan Nepean.
106 See TNA, PRO/30/8/51, Duke of Norfolk to Pitt, 12 January 1760; PRO/30/8/54,
Duke of Bedford to Pitt, 11 February 1760; T Bartlett, 'Defence, Counter-insurgency and
Rebellion: Ireland, 1793–1803', in Bartlett and Jeffery, *Military History of Ireland*, pp. 248,
257.

more repressively ruled than England.[107] Jervis gave a revealing order at Cadiz in 1797, when he was facing reverberating mutinies in the Mediterranean Fleet, concerning the marines, the men on whom he relied to enforce discipline: 'I exhorted [the Captains of Marines] to … prevent conversation being carried on in Irish.'[108] Marines were intentionally employed as agents of authority and physically separated the men from the officers, but shared conditions with the seamen. Although marines obeyed Vice Admiral Colpoys's orders to shoot seamen on *London* on 7 May 1797, they then threw down their weapons. Otherwise they participated in the Spithead mutiny, were included in the seamen's later demands and submitted their own petitions to Earl Howe. They were also riotous on a transport ship on 12 May 1797.[109] However, the Irish were only the largest of many alien nationalities within the Royal Navy, many unwilling to be serving under the British flag.[110] Line-of-battle ships held six to nine hundred men in cramped, unpleasant conditions.[111] Since the war of American independence, opportunity to go ashore was reduced by the introduction of copper sheathing, which kept hulls clean for longer.[112] Implementation of discipline and levels of punishment varied widely from ship to ship, but many petitions attest to individual brutalities which were difficult for the men to prove.[113]

Defining the Irish element within the fleet is as desirable as defining the numbers of Quota men, given the government's belated concern with United Irish infiltration, and some historians' convictions that the Irish were fomenters of revolution and insurrection.[114] Numbers of Irish-born on the leading ships and among the delegates at Spithead can be researched from the muster books, which normally noted the seaman's place of birth. A survey of Irish-born on the muster books of fifteen out of seventeen leading ships at Spithead gives an average of 25.7 per cent of the ships' companies (there was no data for two ships). The lowest was *Mars*, with 14.9 per cent, and the highest *Monarch*, with 72.1 per cent. This, incidentally, disproves the statement that *Mars* was '"manned

107   NMM, WYN/109/7/14, fol. 14. See Pakenham, *Year of Liberty*, *passim*; Bartlett, 'Counter-insurgency and Rebellion', pp. 260, 270–1.

108   James, *Old Oak*, pp. 104–5; H. Murtagh, 'Irish Soldiers Abroad, 1600–1800', in Bartlett and Jeffery, *Military History of Ireland*, p. 314.

109   See *Point of Honour*, by G. Cruikshank, NMM. D. Hannay states it represents an incident at the Spithead mutiny; J. S. Tucker, *The Memoirs of Earl S. Vincent*, I (2 vols, London, 1844), pp. 297, 335, 340; W. James, *Old Oak: The Life of John Jervis* (London, 1950), pp. 104–5, 129. Tucker, *Memoirs of Earl St Vincent*, I, p. 329. TNA, ADM1/5125; ADM1/3773, 12 May 1797.

110   TNA, ADM36, muster books.

111   Rodger, *The Wooden World*, pp. 60–8.

112   R. J. B. Knight, 'The Introduction of Copper Sheathing into the Royal Navy, 1779–1786', *Mariner's Mirror*, 59, 3 (1973), pp. 303, 307.

113   TNA, ADM1/5125. See Chapter 5, Orth, 'Voices from the Lower Deck: Petitions on the Conduct of Naval Officers during the 1797 Mutinies'; Chapter 6, Morriss, 'Crew Management and Mutiny: The Case of *Minerve*, 1796–1802'. Chapter 14, Slope, 'Discipline, Desertion and Death: HMS *Trent* 1796–1803'; Chapter 16, Neale, 'The Influence of 1797 upon the *Nereide* Mutiny of 1809'.

114   Elliott, *Partners in Revolution*, 138; Wells, *Insurrection*, p. 82.

principally by Irishmen"'.[115] *Monarch* was not one of the original Spithead ships, but 'came out of [Portsmouth] Harbour' on 16 April.[116] All the survey proves is that origins of individual ships' companies varied, depending primarily upon the original commissioning port, how many of the ship's company had been turned over from another ship, how many had joined because of a particular captain and how many had been joined since its commission. It certainly does not prove a correlation between proportions of Irish-born and revolutionary activity. The wide variations between ships (from 14.9 to 72.1 per cent) proves that they were not the subjective factor in the organisation of the Spithead mutiny.[117] Their proportion among the delegates was even less: 12 per cent.[118]

It would be surprising if Irishmen were not found to be active in the 1797 mutinies, given their population estimated at half that of the UK.[119] But Wolfe Tone's poor communications with the French Directory and leaders in Ireland; his optimistic exaggeration of numbers of Irish in the fleet; his lack of foreknowledge of the Spithead and Nore mutinies and his isolation at the Texel are conclusive proof of the absence of direct involvement by the exiled United Irish leadership. Undoubtedly there were United Irishmen in the fleet in 1797, given previous indiscriminate and deliberately punitive recruitment in Ireland, but not all Irish were revolutionaries and they were not capable of instigating a mutiny in the navy.[120] However, a contemporary poem from HMS *London* registered a sympathetic chord:

> The Genius of <u>Ireland</u> came in with her Harp,
> She saluted fair Freedom with Tears:
> They all mann'd the Yards to welcome her o'er
> And ev'ry Ship gave her three Cheers.[121]

For the government, the pursuit of political reform among the working

115 Wells, *Insurrection*, p. 101.
116 TNA, ADM1/5125.
117 TNA, ADM36, muster books.
118 Manwaring and Dobrée, *Floating Republic*, pp. 262–3. Among the miscellaneous papers on naval matters 1778–1829 of Rear Admiral Sir Charles Morice Pole is a return of Irish seamen and marines in his squadron in the Channel Fleet (his flagship 1797–1800 being *Royal George*) thought to have been compiled at Bridport's request. Comprising thirty-three vessels, headed by *Royal George*, are totalled 2,101 seamen and 646 marines, of whom 475 seamen and 137 marines were 'Supposed Evil disposed' (54 and 3 respectively on his flagship). NMM, Rear Admiral Sir Charles Morice Pole, 'Return of Irish Seamen and Marines in the Squadron', c.1797, Miscellaneous papers on naval matters 1778–1829, WYN/109/3. I am indebted to P. Crimmin for this information.
119 Census Act 1800 (41 Geo. III c.15). See 'Introduction, Analysis and Interpretation', note 6.
120 Tucker, *The Memoirs of Earl St Vincent*, I, pp. 321, 338, 339. See Pakenham, *Year of Liberty*.
121 Elliott, *Partners in Revolution*, pp. 98, 138; TNA, ADM1/579, Phillip Cosby to Nepean, 7 June 1797, 18 June 1797; 'Lines Composed on Board His Majesty's Ship LONDON', owned by John Pounds, loaned to Portsmouth City Museum for the Spithead Mutiny Exhibition, 1997.

Table 7.1. Irish Seamen as a Percentage of Ships' Companies from Muster Books of leading Ships in the Spithead Mutiny, April–May 1797

Ship	Muster books ADM/	Muster book dates	Sea victualling date	Rate	Complement	Ship's Co.	Other nationalities	Irish	Irish % SC
Terrible	36/11634	May–Dec 1796	27 Nov 1796	3rd	590	439	117	69	15.7
Royal George	36/11704	Jan–Oct 1797	1 June 1796 FB	1st	841	689	154	108	15.7
Glory	36/11715	March–Nov 1797	1 Oct 1796 FB	2nd	738	584	106	110	18.8
Queen Charlotte	36/11724	Jan 1796–April 1797	2 Jan 1796	1st	837	647	119	no data	
Monarch	36/11752	Jan–Dec 1797	1 July 1794	3rd	590	344	87	248	72.1
Marlborough	36/11759	Jan–June 1797	1 July 1796 FB	3rd	570	482	94	116	24.1
London	36/11769	Nov 1796–May 1797	1 Aug 1796 FB	2nd	738	575	127	127	22.1
Ramillies	36/11865	Feb 1793–April 1797	1 April 1796	3rd	590	467	93	no data	
Royal Sovereign	36/11978	June 1796–April 1797	17 June 1796	1st	839	669	146	124	18.5
Mars	36/12233	Feb–April 1797	1 July 1796 FB	3rd	640	521	90	78	14.9
Duke	36/12345	March–April 1798	Aug 1796	2nd	738	606	113	195	32.2
Pompée	36/12482	Sept 1796–June 1797	1 July 1796 2nd pay	3rd	718	586	116	90	15.3
Impétueux	36/12824	July 1797–Feb 1798	5 Oct 1796	3rd	670	518	102	97	18.7
Minotaur	36/12830	Apr 1797–Mar 1798	1 Sept 1796	3rd	640	525	125	120	22.9
Nymphe	36/13164	May 1796–Aug 1797	17 May 1796	5th	254	206	45	71	34.5
Defence	36/14344	April–May 1797	1 Oct 1796 FB	3rd	590	406	100	129	31.8
Robust	36/14794	March–Oct 1797	3 Feb 1793	3rd	590	468	98	131	28

Average of Irish percentages: 25.7

classes, and even more threateningly, among the armed forces, was the context which informed its treatment of mutiny: 'From the moment that men cease to respect, it leads them to cease to obey, and tends to riot and tumult throughout every part of the kingdom.'[122] The conventional naval view was expressed by Captain Kempenfeldt in 1779:

> One grand object of the admiralty should be to restore a strict, orderly discipline in the fleet. ... Captains should not be absent from their ships, nor lay on shore when at Spithead.[123]
>
> Without discipline is well planned and strictly supported, a military corps or a ship's crew are no better than a disorderly mob; it is a well-formed discipline that gives force, preserves order, obedience and cleanliness, and causes alertness and dispatch in the execution of business.[124]

But discipline and the command structure of the Channel Fleet had deteriorated.[125] The expanded wartime influx of inexperienced captains and lieutenants, rather than the unproven influence of Quota men, is a more likely cause of the discipline crisis of the 1790s. Prize money and leave were of more importance to many officers than care for the men, and created an unbridgeable gulf.[126] Jervis's view of the Channel Fleet was 'You cannot conceive how

---

122 Judgement at trials for seditious libel in Edinburgh, January to March 1793, T. B. and T. J. Howell, *A Complete Collection of State Trials*, XXIII, 1793–94 (London, 1809–28), p. 1019.
123 Captain Kempenfeldt to Charles Middleton, 19 September 1779, in J. K. Laughton, ed., *Letters of Lord Barham*, I (London, 1906), p. 299.
124 Ibid., 28 December 1779[?], pp. 304–5.
125 R. Saxby, 'Lord Bridport and the Spithead Mutiny', *Mariner's Mirror*, 79, 2 (May 1993), p. 170; A. Price, *The Eyes of the Fleet* (London, 1992), pp. 68, 70.
126 BL, Add. MS. 35,197, 17 April 1797; TNA, ADM1/107, Bridport to Spencer, 15 April 1797 and numerous officers' requests for leave, January to April 1797; Gill, *Naval Mutinies*, p. 81; Barrow, *Life of Earl Howe*, pp. 415–7; Admiralty Library, National Museum of the Royal Navy, J. J. Fresselique, *Sermon for the Late Victory 1794* (Gosport, 1794), p. 4; Rodger, 'The Inner Life of the Navy', p. 173; Chapter 5, Orth, 'Voices from the Lower

---

Notes to Table 7.1
1. Source: The National Archive, Royal Navy muster books of leading ships at Spithead, plus *Nymphe* and *Monarch*, whose ships' companies also appointed delegates. The muster books of *Queen Charlotte* and *Ramillies* did not note the place of birth.
2. Numbers have been taken from the second week of April 1797 where possible, representing the situation at the beginning of the mutiny.
3. 'Irish' were counted as men whose place of birth was in Ireland.
4. 'FB' indicates that this muster book was a continuation of a former muster book, with the same ship's company.
5. Irish have been counted as a percentage of the 'Ship's Company Borne'. 'Others' is the total of 'Volunteers', 'Boys', 'Marines' and 'Supernumararies Borne for Wages', as Irish within these categories could not consistently be identified.
6. 'No data' indicates the place of birth is not noted in the muster book.

few men are qualified to command ships of the line.'[127] Edmund Burke's view was that

> among all the parts of this fatal measure of the Mission of my Lord Howe has been by far the most mischievous. Had a great naval commander been sent down – Gravem pietate et meritus virum quem – to awe the seditious into obedience, it would have been the best thing that could have been thought of; but to send the first name in the Navy, and who had been but lately a Cabinet Minister and First Lord of the Admiralty, at upwards of 70 years of Age, to hunt amongst mutineers for grievances, to take the Law from Joice, a seditious clubist of Belfast, and to remove by his orders some of the principal Officers of the Navy, puts an end to all hopes forever. Such mischief need not to have been attended with such degradation. There is an amnesty for rebellion, but none for Officers who do their duty. They, and they only, are punished and degraded. The Mutineers now choose their own Officers, or have at least a Negative on them, and all officers who go to sea are apprised of the tenures by which they hold, and must, in future, comport themselves, not as Naval commanders; but as Candidates at an election.[128]

That is why the Admiralty, compelled by considerations of national security and financial instability, made concessions at Spithead, but would not consider negotiating with the mutineers at the Nore.

Opposition Whig Richard Brinsley Sheridan expressed the partisan answer to this chapter's question:

> I will not say that there have been no instances of sedition; but I will affirm even that the evidence of these appears in so questionable a shape as ought to excite your suspicion. It is supported by a system of spies and informers, a system which has been carried to a greater extent under the present administration than in any former period in the history of the country. ... [T]he Government which avails itself of such support does not exist for the happiness of her people. It is a system which is calculated to engender suspicion, and to beget hostility; it not only destroys all confidence between man and man, but between the governors and the governed; where it does not find sedition, it creates it.[129]

Deck: Petitions on the Conduct of Naval Officers during the 1797 Mutinies'; Chapter 14, Slope, 'Discipline, Desertion and Death: HMS *Trent* 1796–1803'; Chapter 16, Neale, 'The Influence of 1797 upon the *Nereide* Mutiny of 1809'. The surgeon on *Pompée* was described as 'a butcher of men', James, *Old Oak*, p. 154; N. A. M. Rodger, 'Jolly Tars Were our Men?' in *Mutiny on the Bounty 1789–1989* (Greenwich, 1989), p. 16; Rodger, 'Inner Life of the Navy, p. 173. See Rodger, *Safeguard of the Sea*, pp. 300–3, for closer ties in an earlier era.

127 James, *Old Oak*, p. 149. See Capp, *Cromwell's Navy*, p. 400.

128 Edmund Burke to Secretary at War William Windham, 17 May 1797, Earl of Rosebery ed., *The Windham Papers*, II (London, 1913), pp. 54–5.

129 F. O'Toole, *A Traitor's Kiss* (London, 1997), p. 301.

The seamen of the Channel Fleet were *not* inspired by foreigners and were *not* revolutionary in their aims.[130] They *did* become revolutionary in their methods, in the eighteenth-century sense of returning to previous working procedures, but remained loyal to their country.[131] They were not conspiring to overthrow the state, but to reclaim a traditional role on their ships.[132] Historians have missed the truly revolutionary aspect of the mutinies by swallowing Pitt's propaganda, disseminated through his organs of misinformation – the newspapers. *The Times*, quoting *King Lear*, blamed France as the source of revolutionary ideas, because the British government, terrified that the Royal Navy could mirror the French navy and become an agent of revolution, would not publicly acknowledge that this country was riven by social and political divisions:[133]

> From France there comes a power
> Into this scatter'd kingdom, who already,
> Wise in our negligence, have secret feet
> In some of our best Ports, and are at point
> To shew their open Banner.[134]

Lady Hester Stanhope, Pitt's niece, on the other hand, wrote:

> Mr. Pitt used to say that Tom Paine was quite in the right, but then he would add, "What was I to do? ... It would be very well, to be sure, if every body had sense enough to act as they ought; but as things are, ... we should have a bloody revolution".[135]

---

130 *OED.* For changes in the meaning of revolution in the eighteenth century, see S. Prickett, *England and the French Revolution* (London, 1989).

131 See the discussions of loyalism in M. Elliott, 'The "Despard Conspiracy" Reconsidered', *Past and Present*, 75 (May 1977), p. 53 and A. Booth, 'Reform, Repression and Revolution: Radicalism and Loyalism in the North-West of England, 1789–1803' (Ph.D. thesis, University of Lancaster, 1979).

132 Deane, *Richard Deane*, p. 626; Rodger, *Safeguard of the Sea*, p. 405; Rodger, 'Mutiny or Subversion?'

133 From January 1789 to 1799 the editor of *The Times*, John Walter, received a subsidy of £300 a year from the Treasury to 'continue his general support of Government, and, in particular, to publish articles sent from the Treasury'. Aspinall, *Politics and the Press*, pp. 74–5.

134 *The Times*, May 23 1797, quoting Lear III, p. 1.

135 Quoted in Ehrman, *Younger Pitt: The Consuming Struggle*, p. 311. See Ehrman's comment on Hester Stanhope.

8

The Nore Mutiny: Introduction

Philip MacDougall

The mutiny associated with the Nore anchorage has always been more controversial than the preceding events which took place at Spithead. In part, this has resulted from a failure of some authorities to understand the motives that underpinned the events. Perhaps one of the most absurd offerings came from the pen of A. Temple Patterson in one of the earliest 'Portsmouth Papers'. Admittedly, he was chiefly concerned with the parochial affairs of that particular naval town, but this was no excuse for castigating the mutiny on the east side of the country as nothing more than a desire to compete with the Channel Fleet. According to Temple Patterson, the seamen of North Kent would look foolish if they brought their mutiny to an end almost as soon as it had begun, by accepting the same terms. Not to be outdone by their Spithead

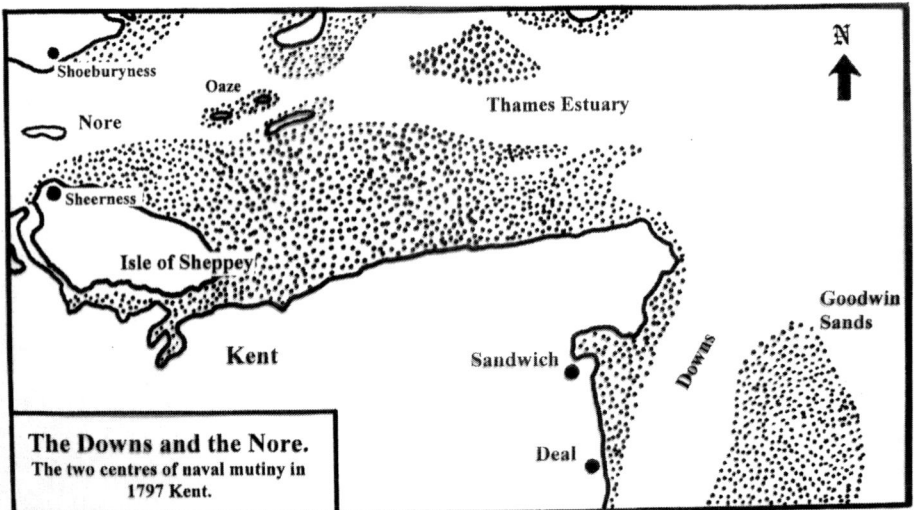

8. The Downs and the Nore. Two centres of naval mutiny in 1797 Kent showing the channels between the sandbanks which limited the manoeuvrability of both mutineers and merchant shipping and the significance of the government's removal of the buoys marking safe routes. It shows the risks to the Nore ships of both running aground on the sandbanks and being fired upon from Sheerness Fort.
Copyright Philip MacDougall.

comrades, he argues, they devised a list of additional demands, of which shore leave, a fairer distribution of prize money, and indemnity for former deserters who had returned to the service under false names were the chief.[1]

Something much more powerful must have motivated the seamen involved in the Nore mutiny. While I see my first contribution to this section, 'The East Coast Mutinies', as an introduction to the events that took place, I include a possible motivating factor that could have prompted the seamen in their decision to remain in mutiny once the news of the Channel Fleet's return to duties had been received. After all, it must be recognised that those at the Nore, during the first few weeks of that mutiny, consisted of fewer than three thousand seamen. As such, they were taking an incredible risk. The Channel Fleet, on the other hand, during the period of their mutiny and as already demonstrated in this volume, had security in numbers. This was not so with the seamen at the Nore anchorage where they could so easily have been overwhelmed by superior forces as represented by Curtis's squadron, the Channel Fleet or Duncan's North Sea Squadron. As I have tried to show in that chapter, the seamen at the Nore appear to have had no such fears, possibly convinced that support from these same elements of the navy was on the horizon. Given that, during the opening weeks of the Nore mutiny, contact had only been made with the Channel Fleet, then it is from here that such support must have been considered most likely.

Another issue that has served to add controversy to the Nore mutiny is that of its political content. Was it, to borrow the words of E. P. Thompson, a movement of 'revolutionary portent' or a 'parochial affair of ship's biscuits and arrears of pay'?[2] It is a question that has interested observers of the mutiny for the past two hundred years. The government under Prime Minister Pitt feared that those who wished to undermine the state had orchestrated the mutinies of 1797. For this reason, three magistrates were despatched to North Kent to discover evidence, which would 'tend to shew any connection or communication between them and the proceedings of the Corresponding Societies or of any other person or persons either at home or abroad tending to endanger the state'.[3]

It is this particular issue that Christopher Doorne addresses in Chapter 11: 'A Floating Republic? Conspiracy Theory and the Nore Mutiny of 1797'. I would not necessarily agree with his assertion that it is correct to refer to historians such as Thompson and Wells as 'conspiracy theorists' simply because they assign an important role to those who espoused radical, revolutionary or democratic ideas. This aside however, Christopher has produced an excellent synthesis that correctly highlights the involvement of those with political associations. The political content of the mutiny is something upon which I also dwell in Chapter 15 '"We went out with Admiral Duncan, we came back without him": Mutiny and the North Sea Squadron'. While this paper is primarily an examination of the North Sea Squadron's contribution to events taking place at the Great Nore anchorage, it does so through the eyes of the

---

1   A. Temple Patterson, *The Naval Mutiny at Spithead* (1978), 15.
2   E. P. Thompson, *The Making of the English Working Class* (1978), 184.
3   TNA PC1/38, 27 June 1797, fol. 40.

seamen on board those ships. Using the rarely used letters written by the seamen themselves, but subsequently intercepted by the government, they reveal the feelings and aspirations of those involved. In particular, a number of these letters were sent upon the immediate arrival of the squadron at the anchorage, with a further set of letters also quoted (for the purpose of providing a broader perspective) and which emanate from the friends and relatives of these same seamen.

A third controversial issue that surrounds the Nore mutiny is that of the reasons for its eventual failure. This issue is addressed in a number of chapters, including those by Ann Coats and Christopher Doorne. Between them they list a number of reasons for its failure to survive beyond mid-June, Doorne asserting it to be the 'mutineer's unwillingness to continue' while Coats draws attention to the Nore seamen being restricted in their ability to communicate with the public at large. In Chapter 10, 'Reporting the Mutinies in the Provincial Press', I concentrate upon the role of county-based newspapers, contrasting the sympathetic or neutral treatment of the Spithead mutiny to be found in the Hampshire press with the increasingly unsympathetic reporting of the Nore mutiny by the Kentish and East Anglian press. A major factor in this process was the passing of new legislation 'restraining Intercourse with the Crews of His Majesty's Ships, now in a State of Mutiny and Rebellion'. By effectively denying the seamen access to the public, the government ensured the success of its propaganda campaign, likening events occurring on board ships at the Nore to revolutionary France at the height of the Terror.

The subject of Ann Coats's chapter 'Launched into Eternity: Admiralty Retribution *or* the Restoration of Discipline?' is that of the Admiralty's need to restore discipline once the mutinies had been brought to an end. Coats concentrates partly on the actual punishment as represented by the paper's title, but also considers the various means used at Spithead to bring about a return to discipline among the seamen of the Channel Fleet. The failure of those efforts however, led, in her own words, to Richard Parker serving as a scapegoat, 'executed to expiate the establishment's impotence at Spithead'.

The actual use of the death penalty at the Nore, although a harsh measure, was not excessive in terms of what could have been the outcome. In the event, only twenty-eight seamen were executed, a surprisingly small number when compared with several of the single-ship mutinies which occurred over the next few years. In fact, as Jonathan Neale shows in his chapter on the *Nereide* mutiny of 1809, the Admiralty, for restitution of authority, depended as much upon mercy as it did cruelty. With regard to *Nereide*, a 'cruel' example was set with the sentencing to death of ten seamen; this subsequently tempered by the pardoning of all but one. However, in discussing the *Nereide* mutiny, Neale does not simply draw parallels with the events of 1797. He goes on to demonstrate that a change of attitude was beginning to permeate the fleet, a possible result of those earlier mutinies. As he points out, the captains of this later period were the midshipmen and lieutenants of 1797 who had seen the mutinies at first hand. From remarks that they made in later memoirs, they appear to have believed 'that the men had been justified in many of their grievances but too forward in their method'. Furthermore, as Neale further indicates, they had witnessed the power of the ships' people. As such, they did not wish to ignite a similar occurrence through a misjudged or over-harsh response to grievances that might now be brought before them.

Brian Lavery echoes this change in attitude in Chapter 12, 'Lower Deck Life in the Revolutionary and Napoleonic Wars'. He shows that a more liberal attitude existed in the fleet during the post-1797 period, although he does not necessarily attribute this to the mutinies. However, the main thrust of Lavery's paper is an examination of the increasing number of regulations that were affecting seamen by the end of the eighteenth century and how these may have contributed to the outbreak of mutiny in 1797. It was the subsequent amelioration of this stricter discipline that also helped make mutiny less likely during the following century.

Nick Slope in Chapter 14, 'Discipline, Desertion and Death: HMS *Trent* 1796–1803', through the use of a computer-generated database, provides new insight into the question of man management on board a naval warship of the period. *Trent*, the vessel chosen for this study, was one of the few vessels of Admiral Duncan's North Sea Squadron to remain on duty following the mass desertion of ships, which took place at the end of May 1797. While Slope accepts the possibility of inaccuracy through captains failing to complete logbooks accurately, the database provides an unrivalled examination of how more formal methods of discipline were used in practice.

Of *Trent*'s various captains during the periods of Slope's study, one is of particular interest. This is Edward Hamilton who held the post from November 1800 until his court martial for 'gross cruelty' in January 1802. This was the same Hamilton who, as captain of *Surprise*, had been responsible for cutting out the former British frigate *Hermione*, this particular vessel having been handed over to the Spanish as a result of one of the most bloodthirsty mutinies in naval history. More relevant though, was the cruel reputation that Hamilton had already acquired at that time, many seamen holding the belief that his excesses were greater than those of Pigot, *Hermione*'s deposed and murdered captain. That the crew of *Surprise* had to endure the hardships of this particular officer is in sharp contrast to those on board *Trent*, for it was they who were successful in bringing about his court martial.

Maybe, indeed, events on board *Trent* help to confirm the conclusions drawn by Jonathan Neale. That the crew of *Surprise*, in 1797, appear to have been unable to remove the much-hated Hamilton, while those on board *Trent*, just five years later, were able to call upon higher authorities to come to their aid, was doubtless a result of changing attitude. If, as Neale suggests, this was a result of the mutinies, then those seamen at both Spithead and the Nore achieved much of which they could be proud. Almost certainly, the harder line taken by those at the Nore was as much a contributory factor as the more conciliatory attitude shown by those at Spithead. While one proved how it was possible to negotiate with the 'lower deck', the other showed that there were serious issues over and beyond that of a simple pay increase and the removal of a few despised officers.

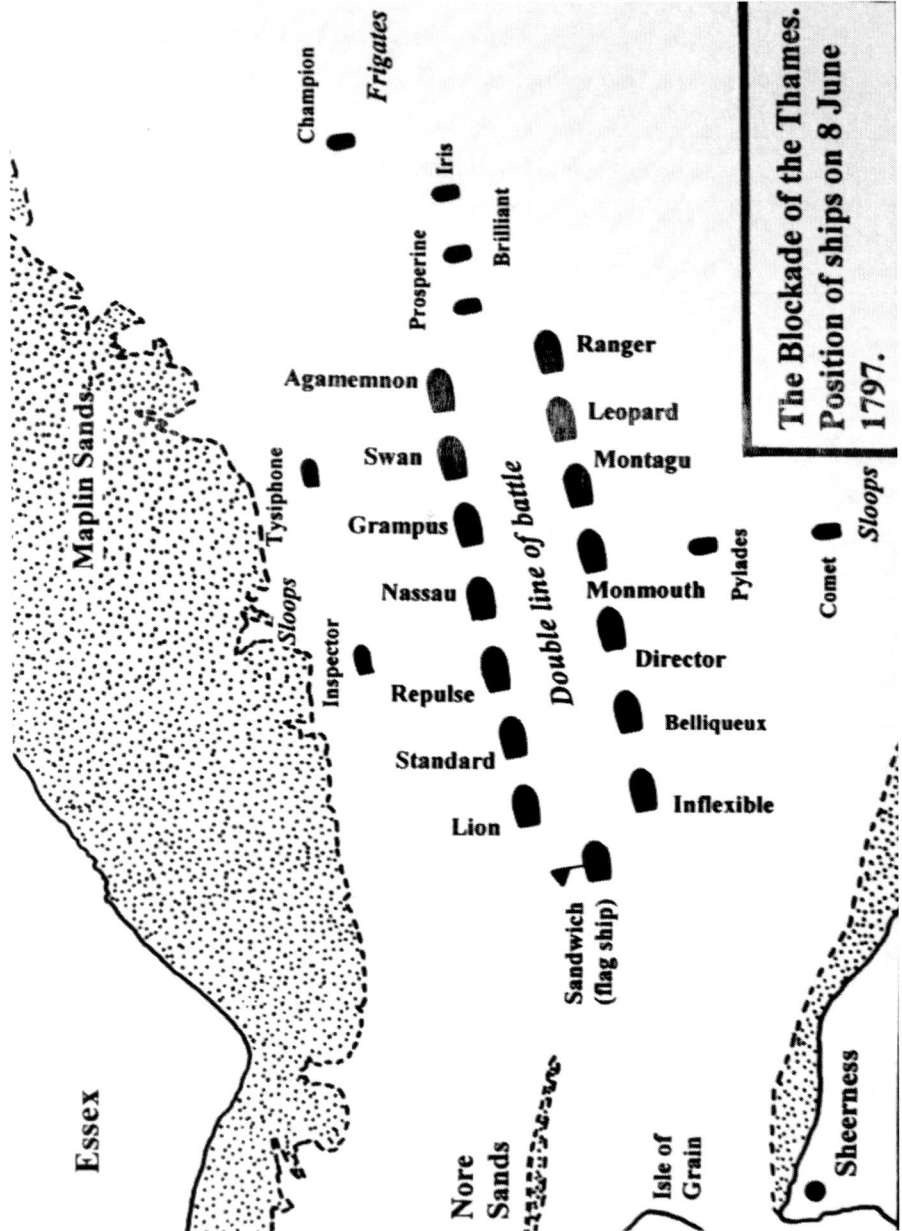

The Blockade of the Thames.
Position of ships on 8 June 1797.

Essex

Maplin Sands

Nore Sands

Isle of Grain

Sheerness

Frigates

Champion

Iris

Brilliant

Prosperine

Ranger

Agamemnon

Leopard

Swan

Montagu

Tysiphone

Grampus

Sloops

Nassau

Monmouth

Pylades

Inspector

Repulse

Director

Comet

Standard

Belliqueux

Sloops

Lion

Inflexible

Sandwich
(flag ship)

Double line of battle

9

The East Coast Mutinies: May–June 1797

Philip MacDougall

With celebrant seamen and admirals jostling shoulder to shoulder in the streets of Portsmouth, the national crisis would appear to have ended. A reluctant government having begrudgingly conceded three of the demands that had been placed before them, the mutinous seamen of the Channel Fleet and Plymouth Squadron had returned to duty. And why should they do anything else? They had received an increase in pay, improved victualling arrangements and the removal of some of the least popular officers.

But not everything was as it seemed to be. In various ill-lit alehouses or in the secluded corners of cramped gun decks many continued to weave the web of intrigue. Gathering in small groups, messmates continued to be harangued by their more vocal brethren. On such occasions they were reminded of the demands that had not been granted. Despite his efforts at conciliation, Admiral 'Black Dick' Howe had not given a thought to the issue of shore leave, better treatment of the sick and wounded, nor to a range of separate grievances that had been prepared by most of the ships assembled in the Spithead anchorage.

Into this cauldron of unease and scepticism stepped four seamen who had arrived post-haste from North Kent. Bewildered by what they saw and heard, none of the group could believe that the seamen of the Channel Fleet were returning to duty. As delegates who had been appointed to represent crews on board naval warships anchored in the Thames and Medway, these four seamen had been sent to Portsmouth to glean accurate and up-to-date news of the state of affairs. Furthermore, it had been intended that the seamen whom these delegates represented were to have acted in unison with those of the Channel Fleet. But the four delegates, Charles McCarthy, Matthew Hollister, Thomas Atkinson and Edward Hines could not understand what was taking place. The mutiny on board the ships of the Channel Fleet appeared to

Left: 9. The blockade of the Thames. Position of Nore ships on 8 June 1797 after the government removed the navigational buoys in the Thames. This ensured that none of the vessels in mutiny could escape to other ports. Between the Nore Sands and the North Foreland at the mouth of the Thames are a number of treacherous sand banks. Even with the navigational buoys in place, these sands present a considerable danger. Unmarked, there existed an extremely high risk of one of the larger warships running aground.

be over. Yet, as they soon realised, the seamen here were far from content. Everywhere they walked, they heard nothing but bitterness and the continual reiteration of long-held grievances.

For Admiral Howe, the arrival of the four delegates was seen as a useful propaganda tool. He insisted that none of them, although technically deserters, should be arrested. Instead, they would be allowed to return to North Kent. In doing so, he assumed they would take with them news of a happy and contented work force. As close as the ageing Admiral had become to the once mutinous seamen, he was deaf to their continued complaints. He heard only what he wanted to hear. As far as he was concerned, everything was resolved and all were happy with the outcome. As for McCarthy, Atkinson, Hines and Hollister, they were hearing something very different. Not only were mutterings of discontent still to be heard but there was talk of further mutiny. In particular, some of those on board the more militant ships, *Pompée, Mars* and *Prince*, were giving vent to some incredible ideas.[1] If the fleet once again combined, then the ultimate might be achieved. Pitt, hell bent upon continued war with France, might be forced to sue for peace. In such a situation, there could be no further grievances to be redressed as ships would be paid off and their crews return to a more natural state of existence.

Of the four delegates from the Nore, only McCarthy and Hollister had sufficient determination to make an immediate return to North Kent. Indeed, Hinds was not to trek that road at all, taking advantage of his sudden freedom to desert. As for Atkinson, he was to remain in Portsmouth a further week, imbibing both great quantities of liquor and the atmosphere of a town outwardly in celebration. That he returned at all was only the result of fellow seamen from Portsmouth clubbing together and raising a sufficient sum to cover his return fare. In their somewhat more speedy return, both McCarthy and Hollister briefly sojourned in London. Here they met with others who were also unhappy with the collapse of the Spithead mutiny. For the most part, these were political activists, members of the London Corresponding Society. They indicated that, among fellow workingmen of the metropolis, there was much support for the seamen's cause. There were even hopes that the mutiny could be made more political, more directed towards the cause of peace.

Arriving at the Nore on the evening of 19 May, both McCarthy and Hollister presented a very different picture of events at Spithead than the one 'Black Dick' had expected. They told not of celebration but of discontent and despair. Angrily they informed the committee that had sent them of the many unresolved issues and of how seamen on board some ships were planning to continue the mutiny. Furthermore, so they reminded the amazed audience, the seamen at the Nore were being offered even less. While they might be sharing in a pay increase and general improvements in victualling arrangements, they were not to be given the opportunity of removing some of their most unpopular officers.

Perhaps the academic world will castigate these opening statements as mere

---

1 Even while Howe was on his celebratory tour of the Fleet, those on board *Prince*, the flagship of Admiral Curtis, had refused to fly the Union Jack, this an indication of their disapproval of the agreed settlement.

flights of fantasy. After all, the actual experience of the seamen delegates who went to Portsmouth is not recorded in any detail.[2] But it is hard to believe that all of the seamen with whom they met were entirely happy with the outcome of the dispute. Most certainly a discontented element existed, some of this group coming to the fore only a few weeks later. They were the seamen of *Mars* and *Pompée*, desperate enough to ferment further mutiny. It had, of course, been their hope to involve more ships, these single-ship mutinies intended to spread to the entire Channel Fleet. Maybe, and I would not see this as a complete flight of fantasy, these plans were revealed to McCarthy and Hollister. As for their later discussions in London with members of certain political organisations, this too was well within the range of possibility. McCarthy, who is generally supposed to have been a member of the United Irishmen, had many contacts in London.[3] During the period between their arrival in London and the departure of the Sheerness coach that following morning, the two seamen had ample opportunity of meeting with others and discussing developments that had taken place at Portsmouth.[4]

The real point however, is that the two returning delegates must have brought with them news of earth-shattering significance. Why else would the seamen of the Nore have continued in what outwardly appeared as such a hopeless situation? Whereas the Channel Fleet mutiny had involved some eighty ships and nearly thirty thousand men, that at the Nore was comparatively insignificant. At its outset there were but three capital ships and no more than 3,500 seamen.[5] Surrounded by hostile forces such a comparatively insignificant force of seamen stood not a chance against the force of arms that the government could bring against them. Apart from the fire power of the Army, there was always the possibility of an overwhelming force of naval warships being brought against them, these drawn from the Channel Fleet or other vessels waiting to

2   The only available account is one supplied by Thomas Atkinson. However, he was only present with the two returning delegates while they were in Portsmouth. See TNA, ADM1/3685, 17 June 1797, Testimony of Atkinson.

3   Evidence of McCarthy's politics may be discerned from the minutes relating to McCarthy's court martial. See TNA, ADM1/5486. According to Atkinson in his subsequent account of what had taken place at Portsmouth, McCarthy had contacts in London including friends who lived in Well Place Square. See TNA, ADM1/3685, 17 June 1797. In addition a certain John Carter, an innkeeper of Leman Street, London, confirmed that McCarthy had Irish political contacts in London, meeting with him at Carter's inn during McCarthy's brief stopover in London while making the journey to Portsmouth. At that time, McCarthy also met with another possible activist, an attorney who is simply named as Fitzgerald. See TNA, ADM1/3685, 16 June 1797.

4   McCarthy is undoubtedly one of the most enigmatic figures of the mutiny. At his own court martial he indicated a falling out with the leaders of the mutiny and that they had ostracised him by sending him to *Pylades*. However, this makes little sense as he was sent to that vessel to take command. Subsequently, his influence on the crew of that ship appears to have prevented her from joining *Clyde* and *San Fiorenzo* when they departed the 'Floating Republic' on 31 May.

5   The three capital ships were *Sandwich* (90), *Director* (64) and *Inflexible* (64). In addition, there were eight other vessels involved initially: *Grampus* (storeship), *Swan* (16), *Champion* (24), *San Fiorenzo* (38), *Clyde* (38), *Iris* (32), *Espion* (38), *Niger* (32) and *Firm* (24).

be commissioned. But the seamen of the Nore must have realised that this was
unlikely. If McCarthy and Hollister had brought news of continued discontent at Spithead, then those at the Nore would fully have expected their own
mutiny to be quickly reinforced.

Of other suggestions put forward for the continuance of seaman at the Nore
to disobey orders these, at the very least, are often fatuous to the extreme. For
A. Temple Patterson, the mutiny at the Nore was motivated by nothing more
than a desire to compete with the Channel Fleet:

> For the men at the Nore were ill-led, and though their grievances were re-
> ally the same as those of the Channel Fleet, they would look foolish if
> they brought their mutiny to an end almost as soon as it had begun, by
> accepting the same terms. Not to be outdone by their Spithead comrades,
> therefore, they devised a list of additional demands, of which shore leave, a
> fairer distribution of prize money, and indemnity for former deserters who
> had returned to the service under false names were the chief.[6]

Even if such were true, it hardly explains why eleven ships of the North
Sea Squadron should mutiny some three weeks after the Spithead mutiny had
ended. If those elements of the North Sea Squadron in the Thames were only
refusing to climb down because of a fear of looking foolish, then those on
board ships at Yarmouth would never have joined them, having at this time no
need to be saved from any such 'foolishness'.

More recently, Anthony G. Brown has also sought to explain why the Nore
mutiny 'dragged on for a month after the resolution of the Spithead dispute'
by suggesting that the elected delegates 'could see no safe way out'.[7] However,
this brings with it an immediate imponderable. If the Nore mutiny had been
brought to an end in mid-May, then it is unlikely that the delegates at the Nore
would have suffered any real punishment. Indeed, it was the prolonging of the
mutiny that actually endangered the leadership.

In the meantime though, during the absence of the four delegates, the seamen at the Nore had rapidly organised themselves. The mutiny was declared
on 12 May. On board the 90-gun *Sandwich* the crew had publicly signalled
their intentions by venting three loud cheers and raising a red flag on the main
mast. The other vessels in the Medway and Thames anchorages quickly replied, hoisting their own red flags while their crews also cheered loudly, making it clear that all were unwilling to obey their officers. The level of organisation must have been immense. Over the previous few days, various ships had
already elected committees, with secret meetings held on board the two key
ships, *Sandwich* and *Inflexible*. In many ways, these two ships were rivals.
Sandwich was the most obvious vessel to lead the mutiny. As Vice Admiral
Buckner's flagship, this vessel had a certain standing in the river. All were accustomed to taking instruction from this vessel and for this reason it became

6   A. Temple Patterson, *The Naval Mutiny at Spithead 1797*. Portsmouth Paper, 5
(Portsmouth, 1968), p. 15.
7   Anthony G. Brown, 'The Nore Mutiny – Sedition or Ships' Biscuits? A Reappraisal',
Mariner's Mirror, 92, 1 (February 2006), pp. 60–74.

the Parliament ship where meetings of the elected delegates were held. On the other hand, *Inflexible* offered something else. She was the powerhouse behind the mutiny and there is evidence that those on board other ships frequently deferred to the wishes of those on board *Inflexible*.[8] Furthermore, her crew had a militancy that was later to shock those on board the smaller ships of the anchorage. When any vessel appeared to lower the red flag, frequently they were confronted by the guns of *Inflexible*. On more than one occasion, these guns were used in anger. When *Clyde*, *San Fiorenzo*, *Leopard* and *Repulse* slipped their cables to escape the mutiny, they found themselves having to run the gauntlet of *Inflexible*'s guns.

Having, during the second week of May, declared themselves to be in mutiny, each of the ships' committees immediately sent two delegates to a meeting convened on board the Parliament ship. Future directions were discussed and a preliminary set of regulations drawn up and sent to each ship:

1. Unanimity the only means of gaining the end in view.

2. Strict discipline to be maintained. No private liquor allowed.

3. Respect to superior officers. Duty to be carried on as before.

4. An early communication with all delegates, to bring about a speedy remedy.

5. No master or pilot to go ashore.

6. All unsuitable officers to be sent ashore, as at Spithead.[9]

At that time however, the seamen at the Nore felt themselves to be merely in support of those at Spithead. In other words, they were taking their lead entirely from the Channel Fleet. It was for this reason that McCarthy, Hollister, Atkinson and Hines were despatched to Portsmouth on the following day. Furthermore, only one major development appears to have taken place during the absence of these delegates, this being the election of Richard Parker to serve as President. A newly recruited Quota man who had only been mustered on board *Sandwich* since March, he might appear to have been a rather surprising choice for this illustrious position. Parker himself was probably as much surprised as anyone, subsequently indicating his thoughts as to why his messmates should have elevated him to this position:

> The following day [13 May] I thought the conduct of the Ships Company was too violent, as they talked of hanging People & doing things which appeared to me to be against the interest of the Country. I consulted with Simms the Carpenter's Mate, who agreed with me in opinion that the proceedings were too violent, & that it appeared to be necessary for

---

8 TNA, ADM1/727. *Inflexible* papers. This collection of papers, removed from *Inflexible* once the mutiny had been brought to an end, show that the elected committees of various ships were frequently in correspondence with *Inflexible*'s elected committee, often taking instructions from this ship rather than from the central committee which sat on board *Sandwich*.

9 TNA, ADM1/727. *Repulse* Papers No.2.

a Person of a cool temper to have the regulating the Business; and Simms
observed that he thought it a pity, as the business had taken place, that I
was not amongst them to endeavour to keep down the Spirit that seemed
to be raising in the Fleet. The next day [14 May] a select Number of the
Ship's Company, Gregory, Patman, Hughes, Hockless, Davies, with several
others whose names I do not recollect, received me into their Society in the
Starboard Bay, which was hung round with Hammocks. In the course of
that, or the next day it was proposed that I should take the Chair; which I
did, with a view of serving my country; knowing the temper of Seamen to
be Such, that when raised they know not where to stop; and at the hazard
of my life I have frequently stop'd that sort of spirit.[10]

Throughout the following weeks, Parker carried out his duties with a degree
of commitment that, in other circumstances, would not have shamed many
senior statesmen of the age. In particular he strove, with great difficulty, to
hold together the disparate elements of mutiny. Furthermore, his aims were
entirely directed to that of achieving an acceptable compromise that would
quickly have the seamen returning to duty. While the great mass of seamen
probably supported him, he was frequently to clash with a small but powerful
group of militants that dominated a number of the ship committees. At his
court martial, he much lamented the influence of *Inflexible* upon the general
direction of the mutiny.[11]

Upon the return of McCarthy and Hollister from Portsmouth, events began
to take on a dramatic change of direction. Instead of taking their lead from
the Channel Fleet, the seamen at the Nore were now clearly in the van and
awaiting the centre and rear columns to rejoin them. The first independent
broadside fired by the ships at the Nore came on 20 May, the day immediately following the return of the two delegates from Portsmouth. On that day,
Admiral Buckner was requested to return to his own flagship where he was
confronted by Richard Parker. Treating the admiral as an equal, the elected
president of the seamen handed him a carefully worded document that set
down eight articles of grievance:

> Article 1. That every indulgence granted to the Fleet at Portsmouth,
> be granted to His Majesty's subjects serving in the Fleet at the Nore, and
> places adjacent.
> Article 2. That every man, upon a ship coming into harbour, shall have lib-
> erty (a certain number at a time, so as not to injure the ship's duty) to go and
> see their friends and families; a convenient time to be allowed to each man.
> Article 3. That all ships before they go to sea shall be paid all arrears of
> wages down to six months, according to the old rules.
> Article 4. That no officer that has been turned out of any of His
> Majesty's ships shall be employed in the same ship again, without consent
> of the ship's company.

10 BL, MS. G197. Declaration of Richard Parker, executed 30 June 1797.
11 For an analysis of the character of Richard Parker see P. MacDougall, 'The Vilification
of Richard Parker', *The Journal of Kent History*, 44 (March 1997), pp. 6–7.

Article 5. That when any of His Majesty's ships shall be paid, that may have been sometime in commission, if there are any pressed men on board, that may not be in the regular course of payment, they shall receive two months advance to furnish them with necessities.

Article 6. That an indemnification be made any man who have run, and may now be in His Majesty's naval service, and that they shall not be liable to be taken up as deserters.

Article 7. That a more equal distribution be made of prize money to the crews of His Majesty's ships and vessels of war.

Article 8. That the Articles of War, as now enforced, require various alterations, several of which to be expunged there from; and if more moderate ones were held forth to seamen in general, it would be the means of taking off that terror and prejudice against His Majesty's service, on that account too frequently imbibed by seamen from entering voluntarily into the service.[12]

Buckner was told that only upon a promise to redress all these grievances would the assembled crews of the Nore return to duty. The Admiral, unable to provide an answer, had the eight articles immediately communicated to the Board of Admiralty in London. Here, without undue ceremony, and at the following day's Board meeting, they were rejected out of hand.[13] Two days later, a further request of the seaman, that the Board should travel to Sheerness and meet with the seamen, was also rejected.[14]

Initially, as with Earl Howe, those who made up the Board of Admiralty had expected the mutiny at the Nore to collapse upon the Spithead settlement being communicated to its organisers. For this reason the government, together with the media, had seen the events taking place on the east side of the county to be of little significance. Yet the continuance of this mass disobedience meant that attitudes had shortly to be redefined. In place of ignoring it, some sort of action had to be taken. Under no circumstances though, would this include the making of concessions. As far as the government and Admiralty were concerned, this would simply make matters worse. If seamen, whenever they mutinied *en masse*, were encouraged to return to duty by concession to their wishes, then large-scale fleet mutinies would simply become common practice. To avoid such a future, the Nore mutiny had to be quelled by some form of decisive government action. In particular, thought was given to the possibility of using other warships to quash the mutiny. On 26 May William Bligh, who had been temporarily relieved of his command of the 64-gun *Director*, was sent to Yarmouth where the North Sea Squadron lay at anchor. He carried a secret despatch, the contents of which were outlined in the Board minutes:

Their Lordships have in consequence directed Captain Bligh, who has been an eye witness to all the transactions, to proceed to Yarmouth for

---

12 TNA, ADM3/137, 20 May 1797.
13 TNA, ADM3/137, 21 May 1797.
14 Ibid., 24 May 1787.

the purpose of communicating confidently the particulars thereof, and learning from you whether, in the event of being reduced to the necessity of resorting to extremities, you have reason to think that the crews of the ships of your squadron can be depended upon should they be called upon for the purpose of reducing the crews of the ships in the Nore to a state of submission.[15]

The Board of Admiralty was convinced that seamen under the command of Admiral Duncan would willingly act as strike breakers. Although shortly to learn otherwise, they had been directed in their thinking by Duncan himself. On no less than three occasions he had affirmed that those crews who served under his command were 'perfectly satisfied and quiet'.[16] In many respects it was an absurd statement to have made. Already he knew otherwise. On 31 April Duncan himself had become directly involved in suppressing signs of trouble that had broken out on board his own flagship, the 70-gun *Venerable*. On that occasion seamen on board had challenged his authority with three orchestrated cheers; these, in turn, taken up by seamen on board *Adamant*. The matter had also been reported to the Admiralty, Duncan indicating that he had tried to uncover the cause of the disturbance. According to Duncan,

> Soon after I ordered all hands to be sent aft on the quarterdeck, and the five men to be brought from the poop, I then interrogated them upon their conduct;– they had nothing to say for themselves, but that as their friends at Spithead had done so, they thought not harm and wished to know when their increased Pay and Provisions was to commence.[17]

In considering the secret despatch delivered personally into his hands by Captain Bligh, Duncan appears to have been less optimistic as to the loyalty of those under his command. Although he did not completely reject the idea of using ships of his squadron to suppress the mutiny, he felt that it was a dangerous road to follow:

> Your two letters of the 21st and 22nd was [sic] yesterday received with the last requiring some delicacy to answer, the Fleet here continue to behave well and I am sure will refuse no common service. At the same time to ask them who have most in order to chastise those at the Nore, would in my opinion subject them to a disagreeable jealousy from all other parts of the fleet who engaged in this unhappy business. But for all this I don't shrink from the business if it cannot be otherwise be got the better of[.][18]

On 27 May, Duncan gave the order to sail, intending to continue the blockade of the Texel. It was his belief that, once at sea, all signs of discontent would be eliminated. However, quite the reverse occurred, with crews on board the

15   TNA, ADM3/137, 26 May 1797.
16   TNA ADM1/524, 10, 11, 15 May 1797.
17   Ibid., 1 May 1797.
18   Ibid., 23 May 1797.

majority of ships choosing to place themselves under the authority of newly established elected committees. Following a brief return to Yarmouth, the ships of the North Sea Fleet, under the command of these committees, proceeded to remove themselves to the Great Nore anchorage.

At the Nore, in the meantime, the mutiny was on the brink of collapse. Members of the Board of Admiralty, having visited Sheerness, made it absolutely clear that there would be no further concessions. Furthermore, upon their departure, a new tougher line was signalled, food supplies were no longer permitted to those ships in a continued state of mutiny while military reinforcements were brought into the area. The fort at Sheerness was strengthened and mortar batteries were erected on the Isle of Grain, while troops mounted regular patrols along the coastline.[19] It was this new outward display of aggression that ensured a consequent decline in morale on the part of the seamen. On board those ships less favourable to the cause an open debate ensued. Might it now be the time to admit their loyalty and make a run for Sheerness Harbour? If they did, the guns of the powerful 64-gun *Inflexible* would certainly threaten them. On the other hand, once they entered the Medway, they would quickly find themselves under the protection of the numerous batteries that looked down from the fort at Sheerness. The crews of two 38-gun frigates, *Clyde* and *San Fiorenzo*, decided that the chance was worth taking. On the evening of 31 May, both ships quietly slipped their cables and began to drift with the tide. With little difficulty, *Clyde* successfully navigated her way into the harbour. As for *San Fiorenzo*, matters were not quite so straightforward. Misjudging the time, she was caught by a fresh westerly wind that took her straight through the middle of the fleet. Running a gauntlet of musket fire and grapeshot, she eventually emerged with considerable damage to her rigging. However, her seagoing qualities were little affected, the vessel able to continue a passage that eventually took her into the English Channel and from there she proceeded to Portsmouth.

The escape of these two frigates might well have proved to have been the beginning of a steady trickle of desertion. Yet it was not. Only a few hours later Duncan's fleet began to arrive. Indeed, *San Fiorenzo*, on her way to Portsmouth, came within hailing distance of that first group of ships sailing under the order of their elected committees. That these ships did not force *San Fiorenzo* to return was due to the prescience of her captain, Harry Neale. In detaching his vessel from those anchored at the Nore, he had retained the red flag at the mast head. As his small frigate passed the towering two-deckers of the North Sea Fleet, *San Fiorenzo* was mistaken as a vessel still in mutiny. To confirm such thoughts, Neale ordered his men to cheer the passing ships.[20]

Upon the arrival of such massive reinforcements, the seamen at the Nore were once again able to take the initiative. Rather than standing firm and simply awaiting events, it was now possible to take a pro-active role. On 2 June the fleet moved to a new mid-river position, the intention being to implement a

---

19 *Kentish Chronicle*, 2 June 1797, 4d; C. Cunningham, *A Narrative of the Occurrences that Took Place during the Mutiny at the Nore* (Chatham, 1829), p. 21.

20 C. Gill, *The Naval Mutinies of 1797* (Manchester, 1913), p.130; C. Cunningham, *Narrative of the Occurrences*, p. 6.

blockade of the Thames. All ships bound for London were to be stopped, with those carrying non-perishables ordered to remain.[21] However, the initiative, even putting aside the short-lived blockade, did not long remain with the seamen. The government, aware that a major reason for the success of the seamen at Spithead had been that of public support, introduced an important item of legislation. Passed by Parliament on 5 June, it became a felony to either communicate with or be on board a warship named as being in a state of mutiny.[22] This made it virtually impossible for seamen of the Nore to publicise their version of events. From now on, the only accounts available to the press would either be based on hearsay or ministry-produced carefully massaged accounts. A more careful analysis of the role of the press during the period is to be found elsewhere in this volume.[23]

A further important government initiative taken during this period was the removal of all navigational buoys from the Thames estuary. This ensured that none of the vessels in mutiny could escape to other ports. Between the Nore Sands and the North Foreland at the mouth of the Thames are a number of treacherous sand banks. Even with the navigational buoys in place, these sands present a considerable danger. Unmarked, there existed an extremely high risk of one of the larger warships running aground. For the government, the object of this move was to prevent the ships in mutiny making a run for a foreign port. At the time, the Admiralty was uncertain as to how the seamen would react at their refusal to negotiate, fearing that some crews might decide to take their ships into an enemy port. As for the seamen themselves, such a possibility was certainly raised, with the crews of each ship voting on a range of alternative destinations. Although the possibility of sailing into a French port was included, other destinations included Scotland, Ireland and the Americas.[24] On 9 June a signal to sail was made on *Sandwich* but not a single ship weighed anchor.[25] Although the seamen resented the attitude of the government, the majority appear to have retained a high degree of loyalty to the state. On the other hand, given the undoubted problems of navigating the Thames, it does not seem improbable that many rejected the sailing orders for fear of risking their own safety. Even if a vessel running aground remained undamaged, the leading delegates on each ship would find escape from the clutches of a vengeful government that much more difficult to achieve.

With the government once again firmly in the driving seat, the end of the mutiny was only a matter of time. Isolated from their supporters on land, gradually being starved into submission and unwilling or unable to sail elsewhere, the future looked bleak. Furthermore, with no word of a supporting mutiny from the Channel Fleet, an increasing number of seamen began to recognise that surrender was the only available avenue open. On some ships fighting was to break out as those who favoured a continuance of the situation clashed with

---

21   TNA, ADM1/737, C359.

22   37 Geo. III, 70; Gill, *Naval Mutinies*, p. 206.

23   See MacDougall, Chapter 10, 'Reporting the Mutinies in the Provincial Press'.

24   Cunningham, *Narrative of the Occurrences*, p. 90; Gill, *Naval Mutinies of 1797*, pp. 226–7.

25   Gill, *Naval Mutinies*, p. 227.

those who were now less certain. Such a division occurred on board *Leopard*, the first of the North Sea ships to break with the mutiny. According to the *Kentish Chronicle*, there was a hard-fought battle to recover the ship,

> The boatswain it seems, in concert with some others, was about to cut the cable at the Nore, when a fellow ran up to him with a cocked pistol, and swore he would blow his brains out. The boatswain's mate, who was standing nearby, immediately knocked the fellow down and seized his pistol. He then called out with a loud voice, 'All you that are for the King go aft, and you that are for the mutiny go forwards, and we'll fight it out fairly.' The crew immediately divided and a very severe conflict ensued, in the course of which several were wounded on each side. At length the loyal party got the better, and twenty-five of the most violent mutineers were 'laid in irons'.[26]

Repulse soon followed *Leopard*. The crew had once been 'impressed with the most sensible feelings of gratitude' towards the central committee sitting on board *Sandwich* and were 'determined not to be influenced by the artful insinuation of [their] oppressors'.[27] But now there was a majority for surrender. Despite advice from the pilot, an attempt was made to reach the safety of Sheerness Harbour. Owing to an ebbing tide and the unmarked channels, the vessel ran aground on the Nore sand bank. Still within range of the fleet, a number of ships opened fire on her. But it would appear those firing these guns had little heart for the task in hand, most firing deliberately wide. Clearly, if an enemy ship had been stranded in that position, she would never have survived. As for *Repulse*, she eventually drifted free and, upon reaching Sheerness, reported only one crew member injured.

Leopard and *Repulse* having surrendered, a heated discussion broke out on board numerous other ships. From time to time one vessel or another would lower the red and replace it with a blue flag. As fighting and discussion continued, the red flag might once again appear.

> By every account it appears that the sailors are extremely disunited, and it is to be feared that dreadful scenes of slaughter have taken place on board particular ships. In the *Isis* they fought twice on Saturday; in the first battle the Blue (or Loyal) Party had the advantage; in the second the Bloody (Mutineer) Party, had the conquest, and a midshipman and five seamen were killed – a woman shot the midshipman through the head.[28]

Eventually, over the next few days, all of the ships of the Nore Fleet were to surrender. By 15 June only two vessels were still holding out, *Director* and *Inflexible*. However, even the crews on board these two ships eventually realised the hopelessness of the situation with those two vessels surrendering later that same day.[29]

---

26 *Kentish Chronicle*, 16 June 1797, 4d
27 TNA, ADM1/727 *Repulse* Papers No. 5.
28 *Norfolk Chronicle*, 17 June 1797, 1b.
29 TNA, ADM1/737, C380, 15 June 1797.

The retribution that followed was certainly harsh, but lacked the extremes of severity so often associated with this age of cruelty. Of four hundred seamen detained for punishment, the majority were eventually pardoned. As for the remainder, fifty-two were condemned to death (of whom twenty-nine were eventually hanged) while a further twenty-nine were imprisoned and nine flogged. Given the severity of punishments meted out to seamen involved in several single-ship mutinies that continued to occur throughout the period of the French Revolution and Napoleonic Wars, such a level of punishment must be seen as comparatively lenient.[30]

Somewhat more worrying however, was the haphazard and unfair nature with which this justice was dispensed. To begin with, the selection of those to be punished was nothing less than a lottery. Officers on board each vessel were ordered to submit the names of 'the ten most guilty men' on board their particular ships. Inevitably, this meant that crews on board the most active ships were appearing to face punishment to the same level of harshness as those on the least active ships. Nor did this lack of fairness stop here as the likelihood of actual punishment also depended on the timing of the court martial. Those crews who faced an early court martial were punished much more severely than those appearing before the later courts martial. Furthermore, a large number of seamen still awaiting trial in October 1797 were simply released, given an amnesty as a result of Duncan's victory at Camperdown.

Finally, there was the unfairness of procedure as adopted by the courts responsible for those accused of mutiny. At the head of these courts were admirals whose legal training was non-existent. In addition, the actual verdict would be dependent upon the decision of various naval captains who were far from unbiased. While none of them were directly involved, in having had ships taken from them, they were, nevertheless, well versed in the events that had taken place. For this reason it would be most unusual if these individuals had not already arrived at a verdict before ever seeing some of the seamen brought before them. Indeed, as officers on board other naval warships, they had a vested interest in ensuring that those who were in the slightest way tainted with mutiny should be condemned and punished. Furthermore, the various courts overlooked a variety of glaring absurdities in order to arrive at a guilty verdict. None of the accused, for instance, was allowed legal counsel or access to trial transcripts when preparing their defence. In addition, the clear confusion between two mutineers, Thomas McCann and Charles McCarthy, both Irish and of similar build and complexion, led to both being condemned for a crime that only one of them could have committed. Similarly, the most damning evidence against Richard Parker, the first of the mutineers to be tried and condemned, related to an accusation that he had personally commanded one of the guns fired by *Monmouth* upon the grounded *Repulse*. As shown by defence witness Matthew Hollister, he could not possibly have been on board

---

30   In 1798 *Defence* alone saw the execution of nineteen seamen as a result of mutiny. Similar numbers at the Nore, under the pretext of retribution, might well have been executed from among the most active on board vessels such as *Director*, *Inflexible*, *Sandwich*, *Montagu* and other ships at the forefront of the East Coast mutinies.

Monmouth at that point in time. Nevertheless, it was a point that those sitting in judgement on Parker chose to ignore.[31]

Undoubtedly the seamen of the Nore were treated badly. They asked for nothing that was unreasonable. Shore leave, regular payment of wages and better treatment for the sick was nothing less than their natural right. The only crime of which they were guilty was that of having to press their demands in a fashion that the establishment considered to be unlawful. Unfortunately, this same establishment failed to provide them with an alternative road by which to express their grievances. If the men wished to protest, they had little alternative but to strike. Other methods of indicating discontent, such as the petition, as shown by events at Spithead, were too easily ignored. Furthermore, those writing or signing such petitions left themselves open to later victimisation.[32] More recent historians, who have been inclined to castigate the mutiny at the Nore as a product of a few misdirected leaders, remove themselves from the frustrations of the men who served upon the lower deck.[33]

---

31 TNA, ADM1/5486. Trials of Richard Parker; McCann and McCarthy.

32 On board *Defiance* in 1795 a dispute over refused shore leave led to the seaman petition writer, John Graham, being flogged round the fleet. Further details of the *Defiance* dispute will be found in Jonathan Neale's *The Cutlass and the Lash* (1985), pp. 119–152.

33 James Dugan, *The Great Mutiny* (London, 1966), pp. 198–200, L. Gutteridge, *Mutiny: A History of Naval Insurrection* (Annapolis, 1992), p. 64. Gutteridge appears to take the view that Parker was 'somewhat mad' and drove the seamen forward by way of 'incoherent' oratory and a 'recklessness that bordered on insanity'.

10. Richard Parker, President of the Committee of Delegates for the Redress of Grievances. Whether this is an accurate depiction of Parker is debatable, but is one of several widely distributed portraits that were circulated during the period of the Nore mutiny. This particular one appeared in a pamphlet of June 1797 that detailed the proceeding of his court martial: 'The Whole Trial and Defence of Richard Parker President of the Delegates for Mutiny &c on board the Sandwich, and others of His Majesty's Ships, at the Nore in May 1797.'

Copyright Philip MacDougall.

10

Reporting the Mutinies in the Provincial Press

Philip MacDougall

The naval mutinies of 1797 placed a select number of provincial newspapers at the very forefront of one of the greatest news stories to hit a maritime nation while at war. With hostile invasion fleets seemingly ready to leave the port of Brest and the Texel, the ordinary seamen of the British navy suddenly refused to obey their officers. In one swift move, the nation's first line of defence had been removed.

To report the passing events of the various naval mutinies, the provincial press of the eighteenth century relied primarily upon a series of local correspondents. For the most part, these were readers of those same newspapers who had shown a willingness to provide a brief written account of local events. Normally, these correspondents were submitting news of somewhat less importance. As often as not, those living near naval ports were providing information on the arrival and departure of warships, changes in dockyard procedure and the promotion and movement of various officers. At other times however, they were reduced to the more mundane, sending in reports of local marriages or sudden and unexpected deaths. However, the important point to remember is that none of these correspondents were professional journalists, simply amateurs who were sending in their impressions of particular events. Given a situation in which a random group of self-selected individuals were sending in material that was frequently a product of their own impressions, it is hardly surprising that error, partiality or confusion was often the result. Consider two reports from the Great Nore anchorage, which appeared in the 16 May edition of the *Kentish Gazette*. They both refer to events that took place on 12 May, the day on which seamen at the Nore began their refusal to obey orders. While both are seemingly accurate, taken individually and out of context they had the potential to mislead. The first is a general account:

> I am sorry to write you, that His Majesty's ships in this port have caught the mutiness [*sic*] infection; it first discovered itself a few days since, on board the Inflexible, of 74-guns, in the Medway; but by the conciliatory exertions of the officers was subdued. On Friday it broke out on the Sandwich, the Ness guard ship when the crew insisted upon two Lieutenants, who had been the most vigilant, being sett ashore ... which was complied with, in hopes of preventing further commotion; but we feel it will not have the desired effect.[1]

---

1 *Kentish Gazette*, 16 May 1797, p. 4d. This letter dated 13 May and referred to the

The second, clearly written by a different correspondent, made absolutely no reference to the dispute having already broken out. Instead, the writer dwelt upon a change in command on board the 20-gun warship *Tisiphone*. While those on board this particular vessel had already committed their support, the correspondent dwells uncompromisingly on a crew's undying loyalty to their commanding officer:

> Yesterday Captain James Wallis, who has lately had command of the Tisiphone in the North Seas, and now promoted to a Post-Captain in the navy, was succeeded in the command of that ship by Captain Honeyman. Captain Wallis's natural urbanity of manners enabled him to command discipline in his ship, without ruling with a rod of iron; and the whole crew were sensible to this, that on his quitting the ship, they all went up to him, and expressed their concern in losing him.
>
> This affectionate attention of the officers and men were highly pleasing to Capt. Wallis, who, in return, thanked them for their expressions of regard to him, as well as for their good conduct while under his command, and exhorted them as the brave defenders of their country, to pursue the same line of conduct towards his successor, which they, una voce promised to do; and when Capt. Wallis and his baggage were in the boat, leaving the ship, the men, as the last token of their regard for him, mann'd ship, and with three times three, bid adieu to him.[2]

There was also a tendency for county newspapers, when relying upon the submission of these correspondents, to print unfounded rumours as fact. At a time when Valentine Joyce was on board *Queen Charlotte*, flagship of the Channel Fleet, the *Kentish Gazette* felt able to report,

> We hear that Joyce, one of the Delegates from Portsmouth, passed through Milton [Sittingbourne] early on Thursday morning, in a post-chaise and four, proceeding in great haste to Sheerness.[3]

Despite such inherent difficulties in using provincial newspapers of the period, they still have considerable value as an historical source. Through the process of collating and printing material previously submitted by readers, these newspapers served as a funnel through which the views of their readers might be expressed. Furthermore, given that these correspondents were likely to be established members of the social stratum within which they operated, it is not unreasonable to assume that the views expressed (either explicitly or implicitly within their news reports) also reflected that of their social peers. As a result, the provincial press provides an unrivalled insight into how members of the provincial middle class viewed the mutinies, their received submissions detailing reactions to any new initiatives either on the part of the seamen or government.

---

situation as seen by this correspondent on 12 May.

2   Ibid., this letter headed: 'Extract of a letter from Sheerness, dated May 13'.

3   *Kentish Gazette*, 26 May 1797, p. 4c.

The use of material submitted by corresponding readers of the provincial press was of inestimable value to the printer. Individuals such as Joseph Groves of the *Kentish Chronicle* and James Linden of the *Hampshire Chronicle* were entirely responsible for every stage of the production process. Having a background in printing, the newspapers they produced were primarily seen as a venture that would help ensure the economic viability of their printing offices. They were not, in their own right, crusading journalists inspired with a desire to change the world. Indeed, due to the oppressive workload that was associated with the production of a newspaper on a hand press, there was little time for the inclusion of original material that emanated from the news office itself. Lack of time also meant that such items, as submitted to the office, were rarely verified. A further point is that the provincial newspaper carried only a limited amount of local news. A far greater proportion of the paper was taken up with advertising, together with additional unedited material drawn directly from one or other of a dozen or so London newspapers to which the newspaper printer specifically subscribed.[4] In turn, London papers were also dependent upon the provincial press for important news stories that took place outside the metropolis. As with the county papers, printers of many of the London newspapers also directly copied items from a range of provincial newspapers to which they also subscribed. For this reason, the provincial press might be considered as having a greater degree of national importance than is often realised. In reporting major events, such as the mutinies of 1797, items initially found in a Kent or Hampshire paper might, through reproduction in the London press, eventually appear in a range of other provincial newspapers.[5]

---

4   The inclusion of unaltered material from a London newspaper was then seen as an acceptable process. A large proportion of the reading public were unable to acquire newspapers printed in London, finding it easier and less expensive to acquire newspapers that had been produced in one of the larger county towns. Furthermore, the purchaser of one of these county papers would have the satisfaction of seeing a selection of news stories drawn from not just one London paper, but of several. Fairly typical, in this respect, was the *Portsmouth Gazette* which, in its first edition, declared that readers would be 'furnished with the substance of the LONDON GAZETTE ... together with every material article contained in the different London papers ... brought by express'. See *Portsmouth Gazette*, 8 July 1793, p. 1a.

5   A careful reading of provincial newspapers during the period of the mutinies shows that a range frequently reproduced items that had their origins in one or other of the newspapers published closest to where the mutinies were taking place. One example is a letter from a Sheerness correspondent which was originally submitted and reproduced by both the *Kentish Gazette* and *Kentish Chronicle*. It was a general description of the disposition of the Nore fleet and began, 'in order to concentrate the scene of operation, and to render their [the seamen at the Nore] plans more effectual, the seamen have compelled all ships which lie at Sheerness to drop down to the Great Nore'. First appearing in the two Kentish newspapers in their 30 May edition, it subsequently appeared in the *Dublin News Letter* (3 June), *Belfast News Letter* (3 June) and *Newcastle Chronicle* (3 June). Similarly, a number of items which appeared in the *Kentish Gazette* of 2 June, including one that began, 'this afternoon four sailors' and reproduced elsewhere in this paper, appeared in the *Dublin News Letter* of 6 June. Generally, provincial newspapers with items datelined Rochester or Portsmouth were items that had first appeared in either a Hampshire or Kentish newspaper. However, some provincial papers, although far from the centre of where events were taking

It was the county newspapers of Hampshire, the *Portsmouth Gazette* and *Hampshire Chronicle*, that found themselves geographically closest to the initial outbreak of discontent that occurred on Easter Sunday 1797.[6] Adopting an unemotional and matter-of-fact style, the *Chronicle* provided its readers with a brief outline of the events that accompanied the seamen's action:

> For some days a spirit of discontent had manifested itself throughout the fleet at Spithead and anonymous letters had been addressed to the superior officers there, and to the Board of Admiralty, stating the hardships the seamen suffered from the smallness of their pay. At length, this dissatisfaction showed itself in a more open manner, by petitions signed by the large body of seamen of the fleet, having been presented to Lord Bridport, Sir Alan Gardner, the Port Admiral, and other officers of rank, at Portsmouth.[7]

After outlining the content of these petitions, it was stated that unless the demands were complied with, the seamen had indicated their refusal to weigh anchor, unless it should appear that 'an enemy's fleet is on the coast, or a convoy for merchant ships shall be required.'[8] Despite such threats, both the *Chronicle* and *Gazette* were convinced that matters would soon be resolved. Following its own account of the mutiny, the *Gazette* simply declared, 'here the matter at present rests, and we trust it will be speedily and finally adjusted'.[9]

Underpinning this belief was a general understanding that the seamen were entirely reasonable in their demands. Perhaps, indeed, the attitude of the Hampshire press might have been summed up by the content of a letter printed in the *Gazette* on 24 April. It came in the form of a note of advice addressed to senior officers of the navy and written by 'a naval officer':

> The seamen are intrusted to your care as children to a parent – View them with a parental eye, and remember the only difference between you and them is education – They neither want for good sense, or Affection for their King and Country; and as to yourselves, how often have they, by their gallant conduct and obedience, caused your names to be recorded in the glorious Annals of our naval history?[10]

---

place, did provide some original material. This sometimes came from merchant sea captains and other members of a ship's crew who had passed through the Nore on their way to a home port. Thus, the *Dublin News Letter* carried a brief report, in its 10 June edition, from 'a person just arrived from Margate and who in coming up river, was detained and examined on board of the Sandwich'. He correctly reported that preparations were made for the burning of an effigy of Prime Minister Pitt.

6   The *Hampshire Chronicle* was first established in Southampton in 1772. The newspaper was later removed to Winchester (for ease of distribution) where it has remained ever since. The *Portsmouth Gazette*, first published in July 1793, was a Portsmouth-based paper owned by the printer W. Donaldson.

7   *Hampshire Chronicle*, 22 April 1797, p. 4e.

8   Ibid.

9   *Portsmouth Gazette*, 24 April 1797, p. 3b.

10   Ibid.

That readers of the two Hampshire papers might judge for themselves the reasonableness of the demands, both printed a selection of material that emanated directly from the seamen. In particular, the *Chronicle* and *Gazette* carried the full wording of a petition submitted to the Admiralty on 18 April. The subsequent attempt by the Admiralty to ignore some of these demands resulted in both the *Gazette* and *Chronicle* printing the seamen's response, 'that until the Flour in port be removed, the vegetables and pensions augmented, the Grievances of private ships be redressed, an Act passed, and His Majesty's gracious pardon for the Fleet now lying at Spithead be granted, that the Fleet will not lift an Anchor; and this is the total and final Answer'.[11]

The attitude and behaviour of the seamen during the general course of the dispute was greatly commended. Throughout, it was recognised that they acted with considerable dignity and self-control. According to the *Hampshire Chronicle*, the seamen at Spithead

> carried on the strictest and most systematic discipline, and the captains of the forecastle had the command: sobriety was not only strongly enjoined, but intoxication or riot was punished in the most exemplary way[.][12]

Even during the confinement of Admiral Colpoys on board his own flag-ship, the *Chronicle* felt able to state: 'the crew of the London behaved with utmost respect to Admiral Colpoys during his confinement, and repeatedly told him, that they had no intention of hurting him.'[13]

Furthermore, these same newspapers were determined to protect the seamen from a number of false accusations that began to appear in some of the London newspapers. In the *Gazette* of 15 May it was reported,

> We are sorry the accounts of the second discontent amongst the seamen of St. Helens, should have been so grossly misrepresented in several of the London news-papers – In some, this may have arisen from misinformation; but in others we fear willful and wicked perversion[.][14]

For this same reason, a letter signed by the 'seamen of the Mars', stated,

> We, the Ship's Company of His Majesty's Ship Mars, have seen in the Star and other London Papers, extracts of their Correspondents with the Fleet, dated the 12th instant, asserting the Mars to be the only dissatisfied ship in the Fleet, which information we politely contradict. Our intention was to behave how the Fleet did, nor have we any other intention, being fully convinced of our grievances being redressed.[15]

---

11 Ibid., 24 April 1797, p. 3b, c.
12 *Hampshire Chronicle*, 22 April 1797, p. 4e. This particular report, which does not appear to have originated in the *Hampshire Chronicle*, was widely circulated, also appearing in the 23 April edition of the *Norfolk Chronicle*.
13 *Hampshire Chronicle*, 13 May 1797, p. 4c.
14 *Portsmouth Gazette*, 15 May 1797, p. 2d.
15 *Portsmouth Gazette*, 15 May 1797, p. 3b.

Some weeks later the *Gazette* also carried a letter written by Valentine Joyce and designed to correct further errors of the London press,

> I beg leave to say, that in the Sun of the 11th instant, the Editor is pleased to mention my name jointly with a suppositious one of Evans, and to describe me as a Tobacconist of Belfast in Ireland who, for seditious harangues, had been shipped on board a tender by Lord Carhampton.
>
> The above statement is totally erroneous – I am now twenty-eight years old and have been seventeen years in His Majesty's Navy – am a seaman, who, from his soul, wishes well to his King and Country, and whose conduct, I flatter myself, has and will free his character from the effects of malice and misrepresentation.[16]

As for the fighting that broke out on board *London* at the outset of the second Spithead mutiny, this might well have caused the Hampshire press to lose faith with the seamen.[17] However, they chose to report the affair without apportioning blame. According to the *Gazette*,

> Between three and four o'clock in the afternoon of that day [7 May], a boat from each ship, with the Delegates, came up to Spithead, went on board the Marlborough, and ordered her to go down to St. Helens the next morning – They then made for the London, on board which ship Admiral Colpoys's flag was flying. The Admiral was determined to resist their coming on board – and the Delegates persisted in the attempt, orders were given by the Admiral to the Marines to fire, who (with the officers) were armed. This they refused; when the officers fired, and wounded several seamen: The men then fired on the officers, and Lt. Sims of the Marines, with a midshipmen, was also wounded and these gentlemen, with four sailors, were sent to the Royal Hospital at Haslar.[18]

As to the eventual ending of the Spithead mutiny, the Hampshire press was clearly pleased by the outcome. Furthermore, it provided an opportunity of further underlining the general attitude of the seamen, indicating that the Channel Fleet had always remained fundamentally loyal to the Crown. Using a larger than normal press type, it joyously declared,

> that the whole of the fleet was PERFECTLY SATISFIED, and wanted only an opportunity of meeting the Enemies of Old England, to convince their country that they were not the Tools of Foreign agents, but that still Britannia rules the Waves.[19]

---

16 *Portsmouth Gazette*, 10 July 1797, p. 4d. See also the *Sun*, 18 and 20 April, 1797. It is interesting to note that the letter printed in the *Gazette* was originally written on 15 May. The explanation given by the newspaper was that the letter 'would have appeared before, but accidentally was mislaid'.

17 The incident on board *London* is more fully detailed elsewhere in this volume. See London, Chapter 3, 'What Really Happened On Board HMS *London*?'

18 *Portsmouth Gazette*, 15 May 1797, p. 2d.

19 Ibid., 15 May 1797, p. 3a.

To begin with, reports in some of the Kentish and East Anglian newspapers, in regard to those mutinies which took place on the eastern side of the country, were as favourable to the seamen as the Hampshire press had been to the earlier mutinies. Two of the newspapers in Kent, the *Kentish Gazette* and *Maidstone Journal*, carried reports which demonstrated that those involved were behaving in a controlled and orderly fashion. On 18 May, the *Maidstone Journal* reported,

> The mutiny at first took place on board the Sandwich guard-ship; and when the Officers called all hands to clear haws, the men ran up the rigging and gave three cheers. They afterwards consulted together, and instantly ordered Mr Justice, the First Lieutenant, another Lieutenant, and two Master's Mates to leave the ship. Delegates were then appointed, who proceeded to the ship next the Sandwich, called all hands, and such Officers as were disliked by the crew, were ordered on shore.[20]

The *Kentish Gazette* of 26 May affirmed the high degree of orderliness: 'The Delegates of the fleet are very desirous to keep good order on shore, and inflict severe punishment on those men who act improperly.'[21]

These reports, which appeared within the first few weeks of the outbreak of mutiny, contrast sharply with those reports that had already appeared in the *Kentish Chronicle*.[22] From the outset, this particular newspaper was showing itself to be much less favourable to the seaman at the Nore. On 19 May, for instance, it prefaced an account of the seamen allegedly threatening to hang Stephen Saffery, one of the surgeons for the sick and wounded at Sheerness, with the remark that 'the mutiny among the seamen at Sheerness has been carried to such extremes as must make every peaceful bosom shudder'.[23] However, both the *Gazette* and *Journal* were soon to be producing items that were equally unfavourable. Fairly typical is this report that appeared in the *Kentish Gazette* on 6 June: 'A report has been circulated, that Capt. Lock, of the Inspector, has been tried, and condemned to death, for having punished some men on board his ship in Yarmouth Roads.'[24] The fact of violence and

---

20 *Maidstone Journal*, 18 May 1797, p. 1a. Extract of a letter from Chatham, May 16. This same news item subsequently appeared in the *Kentish Chronicle* (19 May) and the *Ipswich Journal* (20 May). An examination of other provincial papers would probably show this item to be widely dispersed. Established in 1768, the *Maidstone Journal* was the most recent of three Kentish newspapers. It fulfilled the need for a paper on the western side of the county. In its first edition (January 1768) it declared its support for the ideas of Addison, Swift and Pope while opposing the Whigs which it castigated as 'the hydra party': a reference to this political grouping's confused leadership.

21 *Kentish Gazette*, 26 May 1797, p. 4c. The *Kentish Gazette* was a Canterbury-based newspaper that had been established in 1768 by two local printers and booksellers, Simmons and Kirkby. In 1797 it was still in the hands of its original proprietors.

22 As with the *Kentish Gazette*, the *Kentish Chronicle* had been established in 1768. Based in Canterbury, but with a circulation throughout the county, it had been acquired by Joseph Groves, a bookseller, in 1788.

23 *Kentish Chronicle*, 19 May 1797, p. 4d.

24 *Kentish Gazette*, 6 June 1797, p. 4b.

terror being used to ensure support among the seamen had been a point alluded to by the *Kentish Chronicle* just a few days earlier:

> Every inducement is held out to the ships of the Nore, to desert the muti-
> nous confederacy there; and it is with great satisfaction that I have to state,
> that a disposition to that effect is very prevalent at this moment in the
> greater part of the ships there; but their sailors are restrained by the terrors
> by which a few violent and seditious persons among them have contrived to
> inspire; and the Sandwich, which is the fountain head of the mutiny, keeps
> most of the ships in awe.[25]

It was further suggested that this tendency to violence was also directed towards the officers, with the *Kentish Gazette* reporting that 'acts of violence
committed upon some of the officers is almost too shocking for narration'.[26]
However, such reports were not confirmed by the subsequent courts martial. In addition, the Kentish papers also made frequent references to the
influence of unnamed outsiders who, it was suggested, were responsible for
encouraging the actions of the mutineers. According to the *Kentish Gazette*,
'It is the general opinion here [Sheerness] that the seamen are set on by
higher powers; sums of money having been sent to them, to encourage them
in their dangerous proceedings'.[27] This notion was repeated by the *Kentish
Chronicle* in its edition of the same date: 'The Delegates have received sums
of money from persons on shore, but no one knows from whom the money
came originally.'[28]

In their reporting of events at the Nore, the county press of Hampshire was
no less hostile. Even as early as 20 May, the *Hampshire Chronicle* wrote off
the seamen at the Nore, referring 'to the mutiny at Sheerness being carried
to a dreadful extreme'.[29] As for the *Portsmouth Gazette*, this emphasised the
extent of public fear: 'The public attention is wholly engrossed by the state of
the mutiny at the NORE. A greater degree of anxiety scarcely ever prevailed
on any subject.'[30]

In general, the provincial press of East Anglia, the *Ipswich Journal* and
Norfolk Chronicle, were equally hostile to the mutinies.[31] However, the re-

25 *Kentish Chronicle*, 2 June 1797, p. 4c.
26 *Kentish Gazette*, 6 June, 1797, p. 4d
27 *Kentish Gazette*, 2 June 1797, p. 4c.
28 *Kentish Chronicle*, 2 June 1797, p. 4c.
29 *Hampshire Chronicle*, 26 May 1797, p. 4c.
30 *Portsmouth Gazette*, 5 June 1797, p. 3b.
31 The *Ipswich Journal* was distributed throughout East Anglia (including Yarmouth).
First published in 1720, it was, by 1797, under the ownership of Shave and Jackson. Unlike
many provincial papers, it had no sympathy for the seamen, be they in mutiny at Spithead
or the Nore. In particular, it expressed concern that, during the mutiny at Spithead, 'all discipline was superseded in the Fleet' and that the men 'in defiance' of authority had assumed
'the power of commanding those whom it was their bounden duty to obey'. See *Ipswich
Journal*, 29 April 1797. The *Norfolk Chronicle* was a much more radical paper than its
East Anglian rival, showing considerable sympathy towards the seamen. It was printed by
Crouse, Stevenson and Matchett from their printing office in Norwich.

ports of the mutiny, as they appeared in the *Norfolk Chronicle*, were much more favourable to the seamen than those of any other newspaper. In its edition of 10 June it was one of the few papers that quoted, in full, the petition presented to Admiral Buckner on 20 May.[32] Furthermore, its treatment of the outbreak of the mutiny in the North Sea Fleet, while expressing alarm, was not singularly unsympathetic to the seamen and their cause. Following the return of the *Lion*, *Standard* and *Belliqueux* to Yarmouth Roads, the *Norfolk Chronicle* reported that,

> An Officer, whom the delegates confided in, was then sent ashore to the Mayor, begging the inhabitants not to be alarmed, that they would take care the town should be perfectly safe, that they should fire in honour of the day [the anniversary of the Stuart Restoration, 29 May], and hope it would give no alarm: this they did in perfect order, lowering their flags at the time of firing, and then immediately hoisting them again. In the afternoon 12 delegates came ashore, after having struck their flags; merely as they afterwards stated, of quietening the inhabitants; they waited on the mayor, to whom they behaved well, and appeared, from what I heard, to be shrewd, but moderate well behaved men[.][33]

The second of the two East Anglian newspapers, the *Ipswich Journal*, shared no sympathy with the seamen and adopted the same hostile line as taken from the outset by the *Kentish Chronicle*. Indeed, it went somewhat further, not only accusing seamen of violence towards those who did not support the mutiny, but also to that of their officers: 'A few days ago the sailors of the Albion took their boatswain, and carrying him from ship to ship, treated him with a great deal of cruelty, in order to terrify officers of the same description.'[34]

Continuing to dwell upon the theme of violence, the *Ipswich Journal* also carried a highly inaccurate and unfavourable report on 10 June, this one purporting to show how violence was directed towards those who disobeyed the general orders of the fleet:

> Four seamen have been hung at Sheerness by order of the delegates. The crime for which they suffered was remaining on shore 4 hours longer than their leave. It is added that not a man of the ships to which the poor fellows belonged, could be prevailed upon to run them up to the yardarm; the delegates in consequence performed the execution themselves; the bodies were thrown into the sea.[35]

Both the *Ipswich Journal* and *Norfolk Chronicle* however, expressed considerable concern at the setting up of the commercial blockade of the Thames. The *Journal* contented itself with mere description:

---

32 *Norfolk Chronicle*, 9 June 1797, p. 1a.
33 Ibid., 9 June 1797, p. 2e. Extract of a letter from Yarmouth, 1 June 1797.
34 *Ipswich Journal*, 27 May 1797, p. 2e.
35 *Ipswich Journal*, 10 June, 1797, p. 4c.

Sunday some of the rebel ships altered their position, the better to block up the chops of the channel. They have detained several colliers and other vessels, which have come in their way; and even the Margate hoys are constantly brought to and searched by the mutineers. On Saturday a small brig from London to Chatham, laden with porter, cheese and butter, was fired at several times by them, but she escaped to Sheerness without having received any injury. All communication between the town and the mutineers is completely cut off. On Friday, when His Majesty's proclamation was sent to the mutineers, they informed the person on board the cutter, which went off with it, that they would have nothing to do with them. Several of the Malden and other hoys, from the ports of Essex, were brought to at the Nore, and stripped of their valuable cargo of flour, consigned to the London market.[36]

The *Chronicle*, on the other hand, while retaining its less hostile attitude towards the mutiny, still wished to voice its concerns:

The sailors we fear, are by no means aware of the immense injury they have done bating all other considerations, to the commerce of their country – Within a very short period prizes to the amount of more than Three Millions Sterling have been carried into Nantes only! This could never have happened had our fleets been cruizing and employed upon their duty as usual.[37]

Despite the less critical viewpoint taken by the *Norfolk Chronicle*, the provincial press closest to the various centres of mutiny were generally much more hostile to the seamen of the Nore during this later period than they had been towards those who had mutinied at Spithead. The reasons for this are not difficult to discern. The government, having conceded to the main demands of the seamen at Spithead had no intentions of making any further concessions. In strengthening his position when dealing with the seamen of the Nore, Prime Minister William Pitt had become aware of an increasing need to muzzle the press. Recognising that a major factor in the success of the Spithead seamen was the ability to influence opinion through the press, the government began instituting a number of measures that would undermine the position of those involved in these subsequent disputes.

First of the new measures to be introduced was the establishment of a military watch along the Kent and Essex shoreline, intended to hinder communication between the seamen and the outside world. In particular, strangers found on the Isle of Sheppey were held for questioning and arrested if they could not give a satisfactory reason for their presence in the area. Those considered not under suspicion were simply returned to the mainland. According to the *Norfolk Chronicle*, 'At Gravesend and Rochester likewise troops of cavalry are stationed, and parties are certainly on duty on the roads between those places, to stop all sailors and suspected persons'.[38]

36 Ibid., p. 4d.
37 *Norfolk Chronicle*, 3 June 1797, p. 2a. This item also appeared in the *Ipswich Journal*, 3 June 1797, p. 2d.
38 *Norfolk Chronicle*, 3 June 1797, p. 2a. This item also appeared in the *Ipswich Journal*,

However, none of this could have had an impact upon the resident correspondents who were providing news for the Kentish press. Less fortunate though, were the London newspapers whose own correspondents were not always so well placed. The London *Evening Post* carried this report from a correspondent, who was forced to view the situation from Brompton Hill, some twelve miles from where the fleet was anchored:

> We perceive this day, through glasses from Brompton Hill, the red flags still flying on board ships at the Nore; at the same time there was an union flag on each top gallant mast of the Sandwich, on the occasion of it being His Majesty's Birth-day; each of the other ships had a similar flag; from which circumstance it would appear as if the mutineers did not wish to be considered as having entirely withdrawn their allegiance from their Sovereign.[39]

This military cordon was extremely effective. Not only did it prevent non-residents gaining access to the Isle of Sheppey but it also restricted the general movement of seamen. At Rochester, for instance, the bridge was guarded by a troop of soldiers who were ordered to apprehend anyone who gave the appearance of being a seaman. Among those who were prevented from using the bridge because of the presence of these soldiers were four delegates from *Overyssel* and *Beaulieu*, two ships which had mutinied in the Downs. Following that mutiny, these delegates had been despatched to London with a petition addressed to the Admiralty. In common with the seamen of the Nore, this petition addressed such issues as the removal of unpopular officers and less frequent use of the 'cat'.[40] The *Kentish Chronicle*, while not indicating the reason for these delegates being unable to reach London, did carry a brief

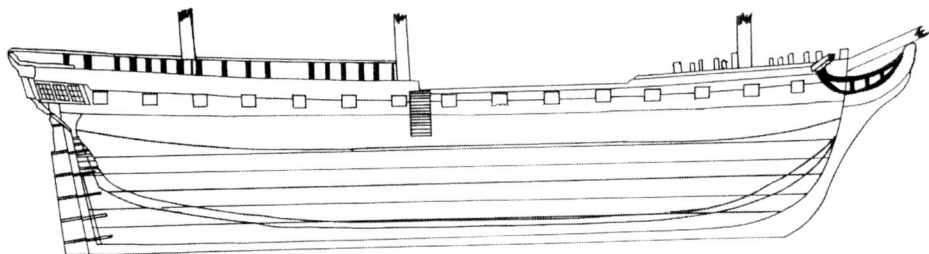

11. The fifth-rate frigate *Beaulieu*, 1809. At the time of the mutinies she served as a guard ship in the Downs. Although it may have been intended that this vessel might be used by the Admiralty to help quell the mutiny at the Nore, the crew of *Beaulieu* was one of several vessels', in areas away from the Nore, who chose to give their support to the Nore delegates. A drawing based on the ship's lines.
Copyright Philip MacDougall.

---

3 June 1797, 2d.

39 *London Evening Post*, 3–6 June 1797, p. 1c. Actually the anniversary of the Stuart Restoration, 29 May 1660.

40 Ibid. This same report was also reproduced, unacknowledged, two days later in the *Sun*, 5 June 1797, p. 3d.

report: 'Rochester, May 31. This afternoon four sailors in a post-chaise and four, arrived here from Deal, and immediately proceeded for Sheerness.'[41]

As far as the government was concerned, the use of military patrols was a simple stopgap. It was, after all, neither illegal for strangers to visit the Isle of Sheppey nor for newspapers to carry reports favourable to the seamen at the Nore. For this reason, a new piece of legislation voted by Parliament on 5 June and passing through the remaining stages on the following day, made it illegal for persons on shore to communicate with seamen on board any ship deemed to be in mutiny. The penalty for those infringing this new law was death without benefit of clergy. On the following day an order-in-council was issued which, in accordance with the Act, announced that all ships named by the Lords of the Admiralty as mutinous would forthwith become subject to the prohibition and penalties of the Act. Twenty ships were immediately named, with only Admiral Buckner allowed to make contact with them.[42]

The importance of these two items of legislation cannot be underestimated. A major factor at Spithead had been the ease with which the seamen had made contact with the press. On occasions, both the *Hampshire Chronicle* and *Portsmouth Gazette* had carried items written by seamen and specifically aimed at inclusion within those newspapers. For the seamen of the Nore, no such access to the press now existed. That they had intended making such contact cannot be denied. Among documents subsequently discovered on *Repulse*, one of the ships that joined the mutiny from Yarmouth, was a direct appeal to those on shore. In first laying out a list of demands, it was indicated that the government response to the petition was a new law that declared them to be mutineers and in which 'we are denounced':

> we are mutinous, we are even proclaimed so – We are denounced, all good subjects are told to use their endeavours to quell and punish us, and desire on pain of sharing our (crime) not to have any communication with, or give any assistance – they even proclaim us as traitors & proclaim whom as traitors? Why, the very men who have always come forward to suppress treason & the Enemys of this country ascribe treason and treachery to a British seaman – Good God, what a thought. A thought that never entered the breast of a British tar. They have even, brothers, inhuman to relate, re-fused to receive our sick into the Hospital previously established to receive them & sent them back to perish on board the ships as it is impossible that they can get the necessary nourishment and attendance which their situation require they have likewise told us that we must receive those tyrannical officers again. The very idea of which we cannot bear.[43]

Despite this draconian legislation it was still not impossible for newspapers to carry reports favourable to the seamen. To ensure, however, that the

---

41 *Kentish Chronicle*, 2 June 1797, p. 4d. This same sentence, identically worded, also appeared in the *Dublin News Letter* of 6 June 1797.
42 33 Geo.III, 70.
43 TNA ADM1/727, 12 June 1797, no. 20.

government's point of view took prominence, a ministerial campaign was initiated. This was directed towards convincing the public that the demands of the seamen were both unreasonable and unrealistic. Almost certainly, the single greatest success of this propaganda campaign was the Board of Admiralty's visit to Sheerness on 28–9 May. According to General Sir Charles Grey, commander of the military garrison at Sheerness, the mutiny on first being declared had met with popular acclaim within the town of Sheerness.[44] However, the failure of the visiting Board to reach a negotiated settlement resulted in Grey declaring that upon 'the very morning' of the Board's departure, 'the irritation of the whole was so complete against the mutineers, that I am convinced they would have hung every man that came on shore, had they had their will'.[45]

The *Kentish Gazette*, for its part, had certainly put considerable faith in the Board's visit:

> The Admiralty Board arrived here this morning [28 May], and there is every prospect of the unhappy difference in the Fleet being adjusted; an event most sincerely to be wished; as every hour produced some more serious cause for alarm.[46]

As for the progress of discussions, the *Gazette* and *Chronicle* carried an identical report. Clearly the same correspondent had written to both newspapers:

> A Board of Admiralty set out for Sheerness on Saturday evening, to endeavour to quell the alarming spirit of mutiny, which has raged in that quarter for some time past, and has every day increased in violence. At seven o'clock, Earl Spencer, Admiral Young, Lord Arden and Mr Marsden, left the Admiralty, and at twelve the same night a messenger followed, with His Majesty's proclamations, offering his most gracious pardon to such men, as having been seduced from their duty, should return to it. It must be the ardent hope of every friend to his country, that these measures may be successful, for the proceedings of our Sailors are disgraceful to the British character, and ruinous to the nation.[47]

None of the newspapers was aware of the true reasons as to why the talks failed. Instead, correspondents were influenced by the government's own interpretation of events, leading to this declaration which appeared in the *Kentish Gazette* of 2 June:

44 At the time Sir Charles Grey was a national hero, his name associated with recent military successes in the West Indies. Later acquiring the title 1st Earl Grey, he was the father of the Whig politician Charles Grey who became Prime Minister in 1830.
45 TNA ADM1/4172, 25 June 1797. Observations of recent mutinies, General Grey to Henry Dundas.
46 *Kentish Gazette*, 30 May 1797, p. 4b.
47 *Kentish Chronicle*, 30 May, 3b; *Kentish Gazette*, 30 May, p. 4b.

I was in great hopes to have said that the communication between the Lords of the Admiralty and the Delegates of the fleet would have terminated happily, and to the restoration of good order; but dreadful to say, their Lordships went from hence on Monday night [29 May], without adjusting the business.[48]

The resultant change in attitude of those living in Sheerness, as already indicated by Grey, was clearly recorded by the county press. In addition, the *Kentish Gazette* of 2 June, concentrated attention upon the fears now entertained that open hostility would result in considerable destruction of local property:

To picture the horror and anxiety of the inhabitants here would require much time, and perhaps offend the feelings of a generous public too much, suffice it to say, it is to be hoped that the liberal and honest sentiments of the British seamen will ever spurn at the incendaries [*sic*] that may endeavour to divide them from the interests of the public.[49]

Furthermore, the *Kentish Chronicle* carried a report from Rochester: 'This place [Rochester] is crowded with people from Sheerness, who fled from thence with their families and property, from apprehension of the excesses of the Seamen.'[50]

At about this time also, the Kentish and East Anglian press began to notice that the seamen at the Nore had acquired Richard Parker as their elected leader. Rather than see him as someone with whom the Admiralty might negotiate, Parker was rapidly vilified as an unstable political extremist. The first references to Parker came in the Kentish newspapers dated 2 June, with the *Gazette* and *Chronicle* reprinting the same letter, albeit with minor alterations, that they had both received from a correspondent in Sheerness:

The two Delegates who were yesterday on shore, have been sent away to their respective ships, with positive directions not to come back any more. One of these is a very desperate fellow, of the name of Parker, whom the report of the day supposes to have been sent to sea in consequence of the commission of crimes.[51]

The following week both papers claimed Parker as 'the Robespierre of the Delegates ... The system of terror is so effectual, that no two men dare to be seen consulting together.'[52] The belief that Parker used violence to control the seaman was also expressed by the *Kentish Gazette* of 16 June:

48 *Kentish Gazette*, 2 June 1797, p. 2c.
49 Ibid., 2 June 1797, p. 2b.
50 *Kentish Chronicle*, 2 June 1797, p. 4d.
51 *Kentish Gazette*, 2 June 1797, p. 4c; *Kentish Chronicle*, 2 June 1797, 3d. Although this account is taken from the *Gazette*, that in the *Chronicle* was not dissimilar, with the phrase that described Parker 'as a very desperate fellow' appearing in both newspapers.
52 *Kentish Gazette*, 9 June 1797, 4c; *Kentish Chronicle*, 9 June 1797, p. 3d.

The manners and behaviour of this fellow [Parker] are represented as the most vulgar and ferocious imaginable. He exercises the most savage tyranny on board the Sandwich, and calls himself the Admiral: nothing but terror and mutual suspicion prevent the crew from shaking off his yoke.[53]

On 10 June 1797 the *Norfolk Chronicle* reported further on the methods used by Parker to control the seamen:

Parker, one of the delegates of the Sandwich, calls himself Admiral, and Davies another delegate of that ship is appointed by the Committee, regular captain of the Sandwich, and acts accordingly. Many of the principle are mates of merchantmen, lately impressed into the service.[54]

The *Kentish Chronicle*, on the other hand, reserved most of its comments on Parker until the mutiny had finally ended. In a lengthy report it was indicated that Parker and other leading delegates had deliberately withheld important information from the seamen. Among this was part of the King's Proclamation offering a pardon:

Parker and the principle rebels had in the first instance, on receiving the proclamation, gone on board each ship of the fleet, and read just as much of it as served their purpose, leaving out that part of it that promised pardon to those who should return to their duty within a certain time.[55]

While the provincial press served as an effective organ for the dissemination of middle-class opinion, those drawn from the lower strata of society were less well placed. Admittedly, during the naval mutinies at Spithead the voice of the lower deck had been given access to the provincial and national press, but the space accorded to sentiments expressed by the seamen was still limited in comparison. Instead, those of the lower deck, throughout the period of the mutinies, were heavily dependent upon other means to express their point of view. At both Spithead and the Nore there is evidence of the use of handbills while the corresponding societies also disseminated supportive printed material.[56] However, unlike the middle class, those involved in the mutinies, when disseminating their viewpoint, were much more dependent upon personal media: letter writing and word of mouth.

Unlike the newspaper medium, personal media, by its very nature, is considerably more difficult for the historian to access: the spoken word rarely goes beyond living memory while letters are frequently destroyed. Surprisingly

53 *Kentish Gazette*, 16 June 1797, p. 4a.
54 *Norfolk Chronicle*, 10 June 1797, p. 1b.
55 *Kentish Chronicle*, 20 June 1797, p. 3d.
56 Philip MacDougall, 'The English Reign of Terror' in *John Gale Jones: A Political Tour through Rochester, Chatham, Maidstone, Gravesend &c* (1997 edn). For evidence of the use of handbills see TNA, PC1/38/122, 29a; while for a general discussion on the role of the corresponding societies see Roger Wells, *Insurrection: The British Experience, 1795–1803* (Gloucester, 1983).

though, in the case of the fleet disturbances of 1797, a fairly extensive range of personal evidence has survived. Primarily, these come in the form of letters written either to the seamen by their families and friends or by the former in reply. In fact, these are letters that never arrived, confiscated in transit by government agents in the relentless campaign of isolating the seamen of the Nore.[57]

In reading these letters, it is clear that the seamen retained widespread support throughout the period of the mutinies, a fact that is not apparent from a reading of the provincial press. Thomas West, a seaman on board *Isis* off Sheerness, would have been informed by his parents that 'the lower class of people in general wish the Sailors good Success' while Hardwick Richardson on board *Inflexible* would have learnt from a correspondent in Leith that 'people of all ranks in the country support greatly the regular and manly conduct of the gallant seamen of the Nore'.[58] In fact, many of those who corresponded with the seamen at the Nore made a point of rejecting what was appearing in the newspapers. It is unlikely that they were regular subscribers to such papers, choosing to acquire or share a copy because of family or fraternal connections with those involved. Although, equally, they may have been regular attenders at a tavern where such papers were set aside for perusal. Whatever the circumstance in which they gleaned information from these newspapers, their written comments show the clear emergence of a culture which both suspected press accuracy while being aware of an inherent bias.

Most forthright in his condemnation of newspapers was Patrick Robertson in a letter to his son William, who was serving on board *Brilliant* at the Nore: 'assertions and contradictions fill up every newspaper that a man can of veracity (to be right) must cease reading and repeating against what he hears'.[59] Another who found the newspapers to be less than believable was Agnes Maitland. Writing to Hardwick Richardson, she wrote: 'I understand by what is in the public papers that some of your situations as individuals has been very dangerous, but you have perfectly relieved me from perplexity.'[60]

As for word of mouth, there is further evidence of entrenched nationwide support for the Nore mutineers. On board *Lancaster*, a 64-gun warship lying in Long Reach, the cheers they received from passengers on board a passing tilt boat must have heartened the crew, who were supporting their colleagues at the Nore. This was the normal means of working-class conveyance between London and Gravesend. It must however, be added that not all those on board were in agreement with this expression of support, for the cheers 'so enraged the other passengers, that a general battle ensued'.[61] Elsewhere, word of mouth took the form of seamen addressing meetings and receiving the support of those in attendance. A meeting certainly appears to have been organised by

---

57 Letters leaving the Fleet at the Nore fell primarily into the hands of the Admiralty, while those addressed to the Fleet were confiscated by the Home Office. A transcribed selection of extracts from some of these letters may be found in TNA, HO42/212 and PC1/38/122.

58 TNA, HO42/212, 5 June 1797, quoted in Wells, *Insurrection* (1983), p. 89.

59 TNA, HO42/212, 25 June 1797.

60 Ibid., 6 June 1797.

61 Wells, *Insurrection* (1983), p. 89.

one of the corresponding societies, with Samuel Smart, a seaman on board *Grampus*, addressing the audience.[62] It is also possible that other delegates of the fleet in mutiny attended similar meetings. Most certainly members of the London Corresponding Society in White Cross received Thomas Jephson, formerly a shoemaker from Belfast, but at that time a seaman on board *Sandwich*. Here, he was presented with a bundle of newspapers, which he was to take to his shipmates.[63]

As with those passengers on board the Gravesend-bound tilt boat, society was far more divided over the activities of the seaman at the Nore than a reading of the provincial newspapers might suggest. Even among the middle classes, opinion was not entirely directed against the seamen. It has already been demonstrated that the *Norfolk Chronicle* was less antagonistic towards the events played out at the Nore.[64] Much more informative however, is a comment which appeared in the *Portsmouth Gazette* of 5 June:

> The people are divided between those who are friendly to coercion and those who would grant to the seamen all that they demand. Ministerial Men are chiefly of the former party, and to coerce is currently the present system.[65]

As for the working classes, while seeming more committed to the seaman at the Nore, such support was far from universal. Samuel Pritchett, in writing to his brother on board *Serapis*, felt able to state that 'the proceedings at the Nore … are condemned by every body' and that 'the general opinion of people' is to hold the mutiny in abhorrence.[66] In another letter, Charlotte Osbaldeston wrote to James Gregory of the *Montagu*, that the dispute at the Nore 'must ever disgrace the name of an Englishman'.[67]

In helping foster such viewpoints, the provincial press may well have played an important role. While some working-class families rejected newspaper accounts, others must have been alarmed by the events of the Nore and the dangers that their friends and relatives appeared to be facing. Thus a number of letters offer clear advice, the recipients being told to distance themselves so as to avoid future retribution. Such was the advice given to William Green in a letter he received from his parents: 'We hope that with the blessings of God you will all return to your duty and not be led away for to come to an untimely end. Pray be careful what you say and keep your mind to yourself.'[68]

These concerns, as the preamble to this advice showed, was a result of

---

62 TNA, ADM1/5340, *Grampus* court martial, 32.

63 TNA, PC1/38/122, 29a.

64 In addition, a small selection of more distant provincial newspapers showed similar sympathies to that held by the *Norfolk Chronicle*. These included both the *Dublin News Letter* and the *Newcastle Chronicle*.

65 *Portsmouth Journal*, 5 June 1797, p. 3b.

66 Re-quoted from Wells, *Insurrection* (1983), p. 89.

67 TNA, HO42/212, 27 June 1797.

68 TNA, HO 42/212, 3 Jun 1797. William Green was a seaman on board *Montagu*.

having learnt 'from the newspapers that you are all in disobedience'.[69] As for the previously quoted Charlotte Osbaldeston, she was another who had gained her information from the newspapers, choosing to write to James Gregory upon her discovery in 'the public papers' that he was an active participant in the mutiny.[70] This report, regardless of which newspaper Charlotte Osbaldeston had read, would have been based on a news report that originally appeared in various Kentish newspapers between 19 and 23 June. These indicated that one of the seamen being prosecuted was, indeed, named Gregory. Charlotte Osbaldeston was wrong in assuming it was James Gregory of the *Montagu*, for no James Gregory on this vessel was either apprehended or later court-martialled.[71]

Thus, the provincial newspapers would appear to have held a pivotal position in the dissemination of news during the period of the 1797 naval mutinies. Despite the inaccuracies and contradictions that were contained within these papers, they remain of considerable value in furthering an understanding of the mutinies. However, in making full use of the information they contain, it must be understood that both their regular subscribers and corresponding readers were primarily drawn from among the ranks of the middle classes. This however, does not in any way diminish their value. It merely shows that these papers, in common with any other source, have to be treated with considerable care. Understood as an organ for the dissemination of views held by the middle classes living outside the metropolis, then they are of inestimable value. Taken further, and used as a means of demonstrating nationwide attitudes, then they are clearly flawed. As shown by the brief digression into the attitudes of the working classes, society was not completely as one.

---

69 Ibid.

70 Ibid., 24 Jun 1797.

71 TNA, ADM1/5340, 17 June. This gives the names of all those on board *Montagu* who were considered to have been participants in the mutiny.

11

A Floating Republic?
Conspiracy Theory and the Nore Mutiny of 1797

Christopher Doorne

The 'conspiracy theory' view of history is as popular today as it has ever been. It should, therefore, come as no surprise that it is often used to explain the causes of the great naval mutinies at Spithead and the Nore from April to June 1797 and the motives of the mutineers themselves. This is particularly so in the case of the Nore. E. P. Thompson, for example, wrote that:

> It is foolish to argue that, because the majority of the sailors had few clear political notions, this was a parochial affair of ship's biscuits and arrears of pay, and not a revolutionary movement. This is to mistake the nature of popular revolutionary crises, which arose from exactly this kind of conjunction between the grievances of the majority and the aspirations articulated by the politically conscious minority.[1]

I am not denying some radical or even revolutionary involvement in the events at the Nore in May and June 1797. Given the social, political and military circumstances of the time, it would have been very surprising if radical elements, both in the mutinous ships themselves and on shore, had not taken advantage of such a golden opportunity to influence events.

There was certainly social and political unrest in Britain and Ireland. This included an increasing sense of war-weariness and a desire for political reform among some of the middle and working classes. This manifested itself in the formation of various radical organisations, such as the corresponding societies.[2] These had their greatest support in London and in growing industrial towns such as Manchester and Sheffield. Although their membership included a sprinkling of militants, the most overtly revolutionary groups were the 'United' societies: the United Scotsmen, United Englishmen, United Britons, and the United Irishmen. The latter, founded in 1791 and led by the Protestant Wolfe Tone, was the first to be established, and was the best-organised United group. Growing anti-British republicanism, fuelled by the spread of French-style revolutionary ideas among both Catholics and Protestants, added to the long-standing Catholic resentment of the

---

1 E. P. Thompson, *The Making of the English Working Class* (Harmondsworth, 1968), p. 184.
2 See M. Thale, *Correspondence of the LCS* (Cambridge, 1983).

Protestant Ascendancy. It found champions in the United Irishmen.[3] The government viewed the situation with growing alarm. This was the period of Pitt's so-called 'Reign of Terror', which included such repressive measures as the suspension of habeas corpus 1794–95 and the passing of the Treasonable Practices and Seditious Meetings Acts in 1795.

There were also problems in the navy. Before the outbreak of the Spithead mutiny, seamen's pay had not been increased since the reign of Charles II. This and other grievances, such as the lack of shore leave and fresh vegetables when in harbour, and the 'fourteen-ounce pound', formed the basis of the mutineers' demands. Pay was the most important issue. The government's capitulation on this point set a potentially dangerous precedent. After the mutiny, discipline on many ships of the Channel Fleet became lax or virtually broke down altogether. Evidence for this can be found in the correspondence of the Commander-in-Chief of the Mediterranean Fleet, Lord St Vincent, who was disgusted by the behaviour of many seamen serving in the ships sent to reinforce him from the Channel.[4]

Both before and after Spithead, however, the navy's greatest problem was a shortage of manpower. This was due to its increased wartime size, casualties, disease, normal wastage and desertion. Brian Lavery has estimated that some 42,000 men deserted between 1793 and 1802, from a peak of about 150,000 officers and men.[5] When, by 1795 the impressment of merchant seamen and offering of bounties to volunteers failed to solve the problem, the government passed the Quota Acts, whereby counties and ports were required to supply a set number of men for the navy.[6]

Any political conspiracy at the Nore in 1797 would have come from the radical and revolutionary societies. This view was shared, to some extent, by the government itself. As soon as the mutiny began to collapse, two London magistrates, Aaron Graham and Daniel Williams, were sent to investigate the causes of the outbreak and the motivation of its participants.[7]

Graham had carried out a similar investigation at Portsmouth in the aftermath of Spithead. Both his methods, including the effective kidnapping of Valentine Joyce's family after Spithead, and his findings have been criticised. Roger Wells has dismissed the latter as a 'whitewash'. Wells considers that, as a member of the ruling class, Graham was completely out of touch with the motives of the mutineers. But this view is far too simplistic. In fact, Graham's investigations at Portsmouth were hindered by the non-cooperation of the civic authorities, headed by the mayor, John Carter, a

3   See N. A. M. Rodger, 'Mutiny or Subversion? Spithead and the Nore' in Thomas Bartlett, *et al.*, eds, *1798: A Bicentenary Perspective* (Dublin, 2003), pp. 556, 559–63.
4   O. A. Sherrard, *A Life of Lord St Vincent* (London, 1933), pp.120–3; W. James, *Old Oak: The Life of John Jervis* (London, 1950), pp. 113–7.
5   Brian Lavery, *Nelson's Navy: The Ships, Men and Organisation 1793–1815* (London, 1989), p. 143.
6   Ibid., pp. 120, 124, 129; An Act for procuring a Supply of Men, 35 Geo. III, c.9, 1795; Rodger, 'Mutiny or Subversion?', pp. 555–61; N. A. M. Rodger, *Command of the Ocean* (London, 2004), pp. 443–4, 448–50, 724, 801.
7   TNA, HO42/41, Report on the Nore Mutiny by Aaron Graham and Daniel Williams to the Duke of Portland, 24 June 1797.

man of somewhat radical views whose relations with the naval authorities were often strained.[8]

Graham was not sent to 'hush things up', but to seek out any alleged radical political activists, whom the authorities believed were the secret instigators of the mutiny. Given this last point, it can be seen that their investigation, far from being an official 'cover-up', was an indication of the authorities' belief in the role of conspiracy in the mutiny.

The magistrates submitted their written report to the Home Secretary, the Duke of Portland, on 24 June 1797. Their findings were by no means as clear-cut as historians such as Wells and Thompson have suggested. Although believing there was no provable connection between the mutineers and 'any private person or any society on shore', Graham also stated that he had proof that:

> several whose mischievous dispositions would lead them to the farthest corner of the kingdom in hopes of continuing a disturbance once begun have been in company with the delegates on shore, and have also (some of them) visited the ships at the Nore, and using inflammatory language endeavoured to spirit on the sailors to a continuance of the mutiny without, however, daring to offer anything like a plan for the disposal of the fleet or to do more than insinuate that they were belonging to clubs or societies whose members wished well to the cause.[9]

But Graham and Williams then went on to assure Portland that nobody was ever regularly deputed from these societies and:

> Neither do they [Graham and Williams] believe that any club or society in the kingdom or any of those persons who may have found means of introducing themselves to the delegates have in the smallest degree been able to influence the proceedings of the mutineers, whose conduct from the beginning seems to have been of a wild and extravagant nature not reducible to any sort of form or order and therefore capable of no other mischief than was to be apprehended from a want of the fleet to serve against the enemy.[10]

However, towards the end of their report the magistrates commented with some alarm on the 'systematic appearance which the delegates and sub-committees on board different ships conducted the business of the mutiny', and they warned that it was

> a matter of very serious consideration and should not be lost sight of by government; for there can be no doubt that the force [of the mutiny] was increased and kept much longer together with than it could possibly have

---

8   Roger Wells, *Insurrection: The British Experience, 1795–1803* (Gloucester, 1983), pp. 92–6.
9   TNA, HO42/41, Report on the Nore Mutiny by Aaron Graham and Daniel Williams to the Duke of Portland, 24 June 1797.
10   Ibid.

been without such a system being adopted and which was in the end more likely than anything else to have brought about a connection between the Fleet and some of the corresponding societies.[11]

Graham and Williams were saying that there appeared be no direct evidence that the mutiny at the Nore was primarily or even largely the work of radical or revolutionary groups. No such organisation had taken control of events or greatly influenced them once the mutiny had broken out. But they were not complacent. Although radical societies did not start or greatly influence the mutiny, individual members of such groups almost certainly came into contact with some of the mutineers.

The main source for conspiracies would have been contact with radical organisations on shore, either in the dockyards or in such towns as Sheerness and Chatham, and an influx of politically motivated recruits. The latter came into the service either by the established recruiting methods of volunteering or impressment or by the new Quota Acts. The magistrates' report shows that there was at least some contact between the mutineers and the corresponding societies on shore. There had been an active society in Chatham in 1795 and 1796, although it had been disbanded by the time of the 1797 mutinies.[12] Radical literature was certainly circulating among the Nore mutineers themselves during the outbreak. The way in which the mutineers were organised, with elected delegates serving on ships' committees, from which delegates served on a central committee, might also be evidence of contacts with the corresponding societies, though irrefutable proof is lacking.

But by the end of 1796, most groups were in decline. This was partly because of the repressive government legislation, but they also appear to have been running out of steam, their more revolutionary elements deserting to the various United groups. In *Stress and Stability in Late Eighteenth-Century Britain*, Ian Christie demonstrated that many corresponding society members were somewhat lukewarm in their support of the mutinies. The decline of the corresponding societies explains why Graham and Williams reported that contact between them and the Nore mutineers was at best sporadic.[13]

At first sight, a more fertile field of enquiry is the possible influx of agitators into the navy, particularly through the Quota Acts. No less a person than the future Admiral Cuthbert Collingwood, then a captain, wrote that both the Spithead and Nore mutinies were the fault of

What they call Billy Pitt's men, the county volunteers, your ruined politicians, who having drank ale enough to drown the nation, talked nonsense enough to mad it, your Constitution and Corresponding Society men, Finding politics and faction too rare a diet to fat on, took the county bounty and embarked with their budget of politics and the education of

11 Ibid.
12 Philip MacDougall, 'The English Reign of Terror' in *John Gale Jones: A Political Tour through Rochester, Chatham &c* (Rochester, 1997), p. ix.
13 Ian Christie, *Stress and Stability in Late Eighteenth-Century Britain: Reflections on the British Avoidance of Revolution* (Oxford, 1984).

a Sunday's school into the ships, where they disseminated their nonsense and mischief.[14]

In other words, the Quota Acts of 1795 had infected the navy with politically undesirable elements. In Collingwood's opinion it was only a matter of time before something like the mutinies of 1797 occurred.

In 1797 the authorities were looking for new or additional factors to explain what, to them, appeared to be a sudden and frightening outbreak of discontent among Britain's first line of defence, the Channel and North Sea Fleets. The Quota men provided plausible scapegoats. High-ranking officers like Collingwood found it convenient to blame the mutiny on such 'troublesome newcomers'.[15]

It is difficult to say how many Quota men were involved in the mutinies at the Nore and in Duncan's North Sea Fleet in May 1797. By far the commonest type of recruit shown on the relevant muster lists is that of 'volunteer'. But most 'prest' men were given the opportunity to enter as 'volunteers', which enabled them to receive a volunteer's bounty. Similarly, many Quota men were technically volunteers, who also received a bounty on entering the service. Men can only positively be identified as Quota men if the word 'Quota' appears next to their names on the muster lists. Only forty-three of approximately four hundred-and-fifty men arrested for mutiny at the Nore can be identified in this way.

It is possible to make a very rough estimate of the number of Quota men involved, however, by including men who joined their respective ships and who had not been turned over from other vessels from June 1795, two months after the Quota Acts were passed. If such 'possibles' are added, the total rises from forty-three to nearly one hundred, but this last figure is pure conjecture. The fact that, according to the court-martial evidence, the mutiny started on the receiving ship *Sandwich*, suggests that Quota men took a leading part in the incident, although only two of those subsequently arrested can firmly be identified as such. One of the two identifiable Quota men on the *Sandwich* was the mutiny's titular leader, Richard Parker, although he had also been a midshipman at the beginning of the war.[16]

Some magistrates saw the Quota Acts as an opportunity to rid their localities of 'undesirable elements'. Although there is a dearth of firm evidence, it is reasonable to assume that there were political agitators among the vagrants and petty offenders who helped to fill local quotas. But the number of such offenders was very small and their influence has been exaggerated.[17] Most of

---

14   Edward Hughes, ed., *The Private Correspondence of Admiral Lord Collingwood* (NRS vol. 98, London, 1957), p. 85.

15   See Anthony Brown, 'The Nore Mutiny – Sedition or Ships' Biscuits? A Reappraisal', *Mariner's Mirror*, 92, 1 (2006), pp. 60–74.

16   He was court-martialled and reduced for misbehaviour on 12 December 1793. He was discharged from the navy as insane in 1794. See TNA ADM12, Volumes 58 and 62, Section 28.3.

17   See Clive Emsley, *North Riding Naval Recruits: The Quota Acts and the Quota Men 1795–1797* (North Yorkshire County Records, 1978), p. 8.

them were merchant seamen or labourers, with the same standard of literacy and education as existing crew members. The influx of such 'new blood' might have given extra encouragement to ships' companies to mutiny over pay and conditions. But this should be seen only as a contributory factor.[18]

Irish recruits deserve a special mention. In Ireland, radical and revolutionary agitation was combined with long-standing Roman Catholic resentment, which exploded into full-scale rebellion in the spring and summer of 1798. Manwaring and Dobrée have estimated that Irishmen comprised at least one-twelfth of the Royal Navy's manpower between 1793 and the end of 1796.[19] The spread of sedition in the armed forces was an important part of Irish republican strategy at the time. This is shown by the arrest of more than sixty Irish sailors and marines in the summer of 1798 for planning mutinies on four of the Channel Fleet's battleships, 74-gun *Captain* and *Defiance*, 80-gun *Caesar* and 98-gun *Glory*.[20]

These later events raise inevitably the question of whether Irish radicals took a leading part in the mutiny at the Nore. In this connection, a letter written by an Irish Whig MP, Sir Edward Newenham to Earl Spencer on 28 April from his sick bed is of particular interest:

> during my illness two friends of Mine from the Neighbourhood of Belfast came to see me and gave me the following Information.
>
> That both on the Late and former Tryals they conversed with Several of the *United Rebels*, who were sentenced to be put on Board Ship, & that their Common Declarations were, that they would be of more Service to *the Cause* on Board a Man of War, than they could be at present on Land, for they would immediately form Clubbs, & Swear every Man to be true to each other. They mean to begin Quietly until they found themselves Strong; I can rely on the Veracity of my Information.
>
> I submit to you Lordship that no more of these Rebells Should be Sent on Board the Fleet, for one of them would poison 700 Men[.][21]

From this evidence it is clear that some United Irishmen had already started to find their way into the navy in the spring of 1797, perhaps through the Quota Acts. But there is insufficient evidence to ascertain whether they were an important element in the mutiny itself. There were certainly Irishmen among those arrested after the event. Some eighty-nine or nearly a fifth of the men arrested for participating in the Nore mutiny were Irish. But not every Irish sailor was a potential rebel.

The case of one Irish sailor, Thomas Jephson, has been cited by Roger Wells, in *Insurrection: The British Experience, 1795–1803*, as evidence of

---

18 Ibid., p. 13

19 G. E. Manwaring and Bonamy Dobrée, *Mutiny: The Floating Republic* (London, 1987), p. 101. See Rodger, 'Mutiny or Subversion?' pp. 556, 561–3; Rodger, *Command of the Ocean*, p. 498.

20 See James Dugan, *The Great Mutiny* (London, 1966), pp. 427–31.

21 BL, Althorp Papers, G196, Letter from Sir Edward Newenham to Earl Spencer, 28 April 1797.

Irish radical participation in the mutiny. At his trial the most damning testimony against Jephson was that of Thomas Phipps Hewson, a supernumerary in *Sandwich*. On one occasion during the mutiny, when Lord Northesk had come on board, Jephson had apparently refused to play 'God Save the King' (besides his normal duties, Jephson also played in the ship's band), saying that it was 'an old stale tune and I care nothing about kings or queens. Bad luck to the whole of them.' Hewson also said the Jephson had very enthusiastically supported the mutiny from the beginning, calling it a 'glorious thing and that he would be damned if ever it would end till the head was off King George and Billy Pitt'. The most important part of Hewson's testimony, however, concerned an occasion when Jephson showed a paper to some of his shipmates:

> which he said was an address from the people of Ulster in Ireland to the people of England specifying their grievances and demanding the dismissal of his majesty's ministers. He said he thought the people of England were not possessed with so good a spirit as the people of Ireland to demand a redress of their grievances. He said something of a society that he belonged to in London where a member of the society threw down a note for 10,000 pounds. I believe he mentioned the name of the Duke of Bedford and that the note was made use of for the purpose of buying 10,000 arms.[22]

Thomas Bailey Watson, another supernumerary in the *Sandwich*, confirmed the story. Watson added that Jephson had also said that 'the Duke of Bedford had sixty thousand men ready and ten thousand stand of arms deposited in a house at the back of his own'. On another occasion, when there was talk of sailing away from the Nore, Hewson said the Jephson had suggested that Ireland 'was a very proper place for the fleet to be supplied with fresh water and provisions and any other necessaries they might want'.[23]

This testimony indicates that Jephson was strongly against both the King and the government and that he at least sympathised with groups such as the United Irishmen, which may have been the society he is reported to have belonged to in London. Given his apparently outspoken revolutionary intent, however, it is surprising that he was sentenced to receive two hundred lashes rather than to be hanged for mutiny, sedition or even treason. One of the reasons for his lighter sentence appears to have been the unreliability of Hewson's testimony. For example, at one point Hewson implied that the person who allegedly threw down the note for £10,000 was the Duke of Bedford himself, which he later changed to 'a member of the society'.[24]

Secondly, Hewson's testimony differs from that of some of his shipmates regarding the importance of Jephson's role in the mutiny itself. Hewson stated that he saw Jephson frequently going into the cabin where the committee met, implying that Jephson was a member of that body. But Watson denied that

---

22 TNA, ADM1/5486, Volume XXIV, Minutes of the court martial of Thomas Jephson, 27 July 1797, evidence of Thomas Phipps Hewson, fols 5–7.
23 Ibid.
24 Ibid., fols 5–7.

Jephson had ever served on the committee. Watson agreed that Jephson had refused to play the national anthem and that he disapproved of Pitt and the government, but Watson also said that Jephson had never spoken against the officers. The other witnesses also produced conflicting accounts of Jephson's importance as a mutineer and of his conduct.

On the court-martial evidence all that can be said for certain is that Thomas Jephson was an outspoken critic of the government and probably the King as well, but it is impossible to say whether or not he played an important part in the mutiny. What is certain is that he was prone to exaggeration and even to telling outright lies. For example, his alleged comments about the Duke of Bedford's revolutionary activities were pure fantasy. It is true that Bedford was a close associate of Charles James Fox, a supporter of reform, opposed to the war and a prominent critic of the Pitt administration. However, he was no violent revolutionary. Indeed, in the winter of 1797–98 he even made a voluntary contribution of £100,000 to the war effort. This was definitely not the behaviour of a committed Jacobin.[25]

The example of the Duke of Bedford also shows that there is a danger of confusing radicals with revolutionaries at this time. Only a small minority of the government's critics can be classed as 'revolutionaries' or 'Jacobins'. At the time of the naval mutinies actual revolutionaries were more likely to have been found in the developing 'United' societies, rather than the declining corresponding societies, most of whose members, although they might have been against the war, were in favour of peaceful reform rather than violent revolution. In short, a radical was not necessarily a revolutionary or a traitor.

Whether Jephson was a United Irishman or not is impossible to say. Had there been irrefutable proof of his membership, he would most certainly have been hanged instead of flogged. What can be said is that he was definitely not part of the supposed plot to contaminate the navy with Irish revolutionaries of which Sir Edward Newenham had apparently been informed. Neither was he a Quota man. The muster books for the *Sandwich* clearly state that he had joined the ship on 1 April 1793, more than two years before the Quota Acts were passed and some four years before Newenham's letter to Spencer.

From the tone and content of this letter, the alleged Irish plot seems to have still been in its early stages in the spring of 1797. If this is so, then the outbreak of the Spithead and Nore mutinies must have taken any United Irish supporters in the navy completely by surprise. Admittedly, this view is based on circumstantial evidence, but so is the opposing view.

The evidence comes from two main sources. The first and most persuasive is to be found in the mutinous plots in the Channel Fleet during the spring and summer of 1798. On each of the four battleships affected, the plans and procedures were virtually identical. First the leaders recruited as many of their fellow Irishmen to the cause as they could. Secondly they made them swear a solemn oath of loyalty to 'the Cause'. Thirdly, they planned to seize the ship from the officers, killing them and any of the crew who opposed them. Fourthly, they intended to sail the ship to an enemy port or to Ireland, where they would be sold to the enemy or destroyed. It is interesting that each plot

25   See A. G. Olson, *The Radical Duke* (Oxford, 1961), pp. 20, 26, 126, 138, 177.

was betrayed by one or more of its members, which indicates that support among some of the Irish was somewhat lukewarm.

These plots were revealed before their implementation. They were elaborate and carefully organised, which indicates that they had been in preparation for many months, and perhaps had their beginnings in the events of the previous year. They share some characteristics with the mutinies of 1797, particularly the swearing of oaths. But in the main, they were very different. In 1797 there was no serious violence used against the officers. Those who were not sent on shore were treated with at least some degree of respect. In 1798 the murder of officers was an integral part of the plan. At the Nore the proposal to sail to a continental port was a desperate act of last resort, which was neither approved by a majority of the men, nor was it acted upon. In 1798 it was the mutineers' main purpose. Finally the plots of 1798 were an exclusively Irish affair. Few, if any, English sailors were involved.

The second source comes from the activities of the Irish rebels themselves. Following the abortive French landing at Bantry Bay at the end of 1796, the Irish republicans made plans for a major rising. These were only nearing completion in the early spring of 1798. It would not, therefore, have served any useful purpose to instigate large-scale mutinous activity almost a year before the rebellion was due to break out. Unlike the mutinies of 1797, the abortive mutinous plots of 1798 were planned to coincide with the main rebellion in Ireland itself.

Based on this admittedly circumstantial evidence, it appears that, although United Irishmen might have been involved in the 1797 mutinies to some extent, the outbreaks took them by surprise, in that they broke out before they had had time to begin planning their own mutinous actions. The most which can be said is that once the mutinies began, particularly that at the Nore, some of the Irish radicals in the fleet tried to take advantage of the situation. Their influence might well explain Parker's threat to sail the mutinous ships to a continental port about a week before the mutiny came to an end. However, it was probably also a desperate last-minute bluff to disguise the depressing reality that morale among the mutineers was falling and the mutiny was on the point of collapse.

It should also be remembered that not every Irish sailor was an actual or potential revolutionary. This was the case in 1798, when Irish sailors themselves revealed the mutinous plots in the Channel Fleet to their officers. It must also have been so in 1797.

At this point, it is well to consider the general attitudes of the mutineers. Both Graham and Williams were at pains to warn the government of the potential danger of sedition in the navy's home-based squadrons, while at the same time endeavouring to avoid a panic or 'witch-hunt' by looking for alternative explanations for apparently revolutionary actions. For example, the blocking of the Thames by the Nore mutineers might have seemed like an act of rebellion. However, Graham and Williams were of the opinion that it was merely an act of retaliation following the authorities' stopping supplies of fresh provisions reaching the mutinous ships on 30 May 1797.[26]

---

26 TNA, HO42/41, Report on the Nore Mutiny by Aaron Graham and Daniel Williams

Parker and other mutineers publicly denied that they were acting in a traitorous manner. Some of these pronouncements must have been intended to gain public sympathy and support. Nevertheless, one document, received by Evan Nepean on 7 June and intended for public consumption, reveals something of the frustrations and attitudes of the mutineers:

The public prints teem with falsehood and misrepresentations, to induce you to believe things as far from our design as the conduct of those at the helm of state is from honesty and good decorum. Shall we who have endured the toils of a long and disgraceful war bear the tackles of tyranny and oppression, which vile pampered knaves wallowing in the lap of luxury choose to load us with? Shall we who in the midst of tempests and war of elements, undaunted climb the unsteady bondage and totter on the topmasts in dreadful nights suffer ourselves to be treated worst than the filthiest dregs of London streets? Shall we who in the battles sanguinary rage, confound, terrify and subdue the proudest foe, guard your coasts from invasion, your children from slaughter and your lands from pillage be the footballs, shuttlecocks and merry Andrews of a set of tyrants who derive from us alone, their honours, titles and fortunes. No – the Age of Reason is at Length arrived, we have been endeavouring to find ourselves men. We now find ourselves so. We will be treated as such. Far from our very ideas to subvert the Government of our beloved country we have the highest opinion of our beloved sovereign and have to hope that none of the measures taken to deprive us of our Common Rights have been instigated by him. You cannot, countrymen, have the smallest idea of the slavery under which we have for many years laboured. Rome – that has had the shame to acknowledge her Neroes and Caligulas, how many such like characters might we not mention in the British Fleet, men without the least tincture of humanity, without the faintest spark of virtue, education or abilities exercising the most wanton acts of cruelty over those whom misfortunes or patriotic zeal may have placed in their power – basking in the sun of prosperity, whilst we, need we report who we are? Labour under every disagreement and affliction which African slaves cannot endure. The British seaman has justly been compared to the Lion, gentle, generous and humane. No one would certainly wish to provoke such an animal. We have laboured either to oblige our sovereign or you – we are obliged to wish to think of ourselves – for there are many – most of us in the Fleet – who have been prisoners ever since the war commenced without receiving a single farthing. Have we not a right to complain? Let His Majesty but order us to be paid, and the little grievance we demand to be redressed, we shall enter with alacrity upon any employment, for the safety of our country. But until that be accomplished we are determined to stop all commerce and intercept all provisions whatsoever for our own subsistence. The military have had their pay augmented to insult us as well as to enslave you. Do not be appalled, we will adopt the much abused motto on a certain garter (Dieu et mon droit) and defy all attempts to deceive us. We do not wish to adopt

to the Duke of Portland, 24 June 1797.

the plan of a neighbouring nation however it may be suggested. But we will sell ourselves dearly to maintain what we have demanded, we have already discovered some of the tricks of Government in supplying our enemies – a few days will probably lead us to something more.[27]

The tone and style of the document give somewhat conflicting messages, being a combination of threats and reassurances. But the vehemence of the attacks on the authorities other than the King is striking. There is the centuries-old 'evil counsellors' theme of earlier revolts. There is also a suspiciously revolutionary stress on their 'Common Rights' and the 'Age of Reason', which suggests radical influences at work, perhaps even a limited knowledge of the works of Tom Paine. The apparently seditious tone of the document is reinforced by the ominous threat of 'something more' at the end, which implies that further action might be taken if the dispute was not resolved to the sailors' satisfaction.

Closer examination, however, also shows that there were divisions within the mutineers' ranks. For example, emphatic professions of loyalty to King and country temper the attacks upon the tyranny of unnamed officers. The mutineers explain the necessity of blockading the Thames, 'the ends justifying the means', but (not surprisingly) they also stress that they have no intention of starting a French-style revolution in England. This constant contradiction shows that the finished document is very much a compromise statement, which combines the views of moderates and radicals; of those who merely demanded a redress of grievances over pay and conditions and those who perhaps had more political motives. But it should also be remembered that the document was written during the last week or so of the mutiny, when divisions within the sailors' ranks were widening, and the more inflammatory passages might be evidence of frustration as well as seditious forces at work, particularly as its authors still insist the revolution is out of the question, given their duty as 'defenders of the realm'.

Some of the material found on board *Repulse* after the mutiny is of an apparently radical nature, but very little can be interpreted as being wholly revolutionary in content. Most of it conveys a less overtly seditious message. Rather the impression is one of impatience and frustration at the lack of response from the authorities to the redress of what the men saw as their legitimate grievances. An example of this was in a note written at the end of a song, and on the same page by one Henry Long:

> For the Lords Commissioners of the Board [of] the Admiralty.
>   Dam my Eyes if I understand your lingo or Long Proclamations,
> but in short give us our dues at once and no more of it, till we go
> in Search of the Rascals the Enemyes of our Country.[28]

The mood expressed here is one of anger and frustration with the government, but also loyalty to King and country, and even an impatience to have the

---

27 TNA, ADM1/5125, Address by the representatives of the mutineers at the Nore, 7 June 1797.
28 TNA, ADM1/727, Section 370d, Papers found on board *Repulse*, 12 June 1797, no. 29.

whole business settled, so as to be able to set sail again and fight Britain's real enemies. In short, the men were fed up with their lot.

One does not need to resort to conspiracy theory in order to explain the causes and course of the Nore mutiny. There are several less spectacular explanations. When taken together, I believe they paint a more realistic picture of the situation.

The mutiny broke out while the situation at Spithead was still unresolved. In effect, the men at the Nore were involved in a 'sympathy strike' in support of their brethren in the Channel. The continuation of the Nore mutiny is not really surprising. The mutineers' victory at Spithead served to encourage their colleagues at the Nore to hold out for further concessions. Conrad Gill has pointed out that the mutiny's leaders delayed telling the men about the passing of the Seamen's Act, presumably for this reason.

My second point, in a sense, lends some credence to Collingwood's opinion that the mutiny was primarily the work of disaffected Quota men. The presence of political agitators in their ranks was almost certainly a contributory factor. However, there was also a more mundane element. It is frequently forgotten that Quota men differed from the usual kind of recruit in one very important respect: the overwhelming majority of them were from non-seafaring backgrounds. The 'prest' men who augmented the small number of professional peacetime seamen on the outbreak of war, were generally merchant seamen of some description. Some had already been 'prest' into naval service during the American War of Independence. Such individuals were at least partly accustomed to the hardships and disciplines of shipboard life. The discipline exercised by many masters of merchant ships was hardly less harsh than that of the majority of Royal Navy captains. Most Quota men were, however, entirely unfamiliar with the realities and discipline of naval life. Many were virtual conscripts; all were effectively 'civilians in uniform' rather than sailors.

The ships based at the Nore formed a sort of reserve squadron and a second line of seaborne defence for London and south-east England. The squadron was also a source of reinforcements for Duncan's North Sea Fleet. As largely a second-line force, it inevitably contained more raw recruits than such front-line squadrons as those of Duncan, the ships patrolling the Downs and Admiral Lord Bridport's Channel Fleet.

The outbreak of mutiny at the Nore should not really come as much of a surprise. Faced with the unfamiliar hardships and stern discipline of naval life, it was probable that sooner or later, the 'civilians in uniform' might take some sort of action to register their disquiet. The fact that the mutiny began on the overcrowded *Sandwich*, which was crammed with newly raised Quota men, lends further credence to this explanation. So too, does the somewhat haphazard way in which the mutiny was organised in its early days. Indeed, had the mutinous vessels not been reinforced by Duncan's squadron at the end of May, it is likely that the outbreak would have collapsed.

The arrival of Duncan's squadron transformed the nature of the mutiny to some extent. Here was a front-line force, containing a high proportion of experienced seamen. It was also one with long-standing grievances, particularly over pay arrears. Thus, in both its composition and its grievances, it closely resembled Bridport's Channel Fleet before the Spithead mutiny. The motivation of Duncan's men was more likely to have been to take advantage of the authorities' climb-down after Spithead by wringing more concessions out of them. From the courts martial minutes it appears that, as at Spithead, the sailors on Duncan's ships treated their officers with a good deal of respect throughout the mutiny. Among the ships of the Nore, however, the men's behaviour towards their officers was more mixed. For example, when, shortly after the mutiny began, Admiral Buckner came to the *Sandwich* and spoke with Parker, the latter's attitude was an odd mixture of insolence, defiance and deference. That of his shipmates was equally ambiguous, some refusing to take off their hats in Buckner's presence.

So far I have stressed the role of the *Sandwich* in the outbreak of the mutiny. But the 64-gun *Inflexible* deserves special mention. It certainly played an important role in continuing the mutiny. From early on, despite outward appearances, most of the real power and impetus behind the mutiny came from this ship rather than the *Sandwich*. At his trial, Parker stated that the idea of hoisting the red flag had come from *Inflexible*, although the first acts of mutiny occurred in the *Sandwich*. Of course, Parker might have been trying to shift the blame from himself, but other events prove that *Inflexible* was very much the mutiny's 'power house'. Any ship's company which showed signs of wavering in its support of the mutiny would suffer intimidation by *Inflexible*.

Despite this ship's prominent role, all its forty-one men arrested for participating in the mutiny were pardoned, but not one of the twenty-five arrested in *Sandwich* were pardoned. Indeed, fifteen were executed, including Parker himself. But this is not the whole story. On 15 June, the day before the last of the mutinous ships surrendered, a dozen sailors left *Inflexible* and rowed to Faversham. Seizing a sloop, the *Good Intent*, they escaped to Calais.

Five of the twelve were Irish, which again raises the question of the participation of the Irish radical and revolutionary groups. If such individuals were anywhere in May and June 1797, it was in *Inflexible*. The circumstantial evidence of their presence is, I think, pretty convincing. But the important question is not whether there were radicals in *Inflexible*, or indeed on any of the mutinous ships at the Nore, but how influential they were and how important a role they played in the mutiny.

Any answer to these questions must be based on one's personal interpretation of the evidence. First, there is the organisation of the mutineers, delegates and committees. This had much in common with the organisation of the corresponding societies, but most of the latter's supporters were reformists rather than revolutionaries. In any case, once the mutiny had started, the men had to organise themselves in some manner, so the adoption of a radical society's organisation does not mean the wholehearted adoption of its principles. Besides, as Manwaring and Dobrée have pointed out, the organisation at the Nore was by no means as efficient at the Nore as that of Spithead, and shortly before Duncan's ships joined it, the mutiny was showing signs of disintegration. Yet this fact seems to contradict the theory that the Nore mutiny was primarily the work of radicals and revolutionaries. Had it been so, one might expect that the organisation would have been tight and efficient from the beginning.

Secondly, there is the mutiny's outbreak and continuation. *Inflexible*'s role appears to have developed after the initial outbreak, which occurred in *Sandwich* and was itself a somewhat haphazard affair. It is likely therefore that any radical influence on events came after the mutiny had broken out, hence the importance of *Inflexible* in the continuance of the affair.

Radical and revolutionary involvement can only have been limited, however. The most important evidence to support this conclusion is that none of the ships involved ever sailed to the continent. Parker's threat to take the fleet to sea on 9 June was almost certainly a last desperate attempt to present a façade of united resolve. In reality, the mutiny was in a state of terminal decline, ending a week later.

There was little to prevent any of the mutinous ships from sailing to France or the Netherlands. Duncan's blockade of the Low Countries had been reduced to a mere two ships of the line. Although they had officially returned to duty, the men of the Channel Fleet could not yet be relied upon. Their victory over the authorities at Spithead had created an atmosphere of indiscipline in the fleet as a whole, which was to continue for some months. In any case, it was too far away to prevent the mutinous ships from putting to sea. Much has been made of the authorities' removal of the buoys and beacon lights from the Thames estuary. This made any escape very difficult and hazardous, but by no means impossible, particularly to experienced sailors, of whom there were many in Duncan's ships. Had the Nore mutiny been the work of determined revolutionaries some escape attempt would have been made. Even in *Inflexible* the spirit was far from willing. Additionally the blockade of the port of London imposed by the mutineers was a somewhat lukewarm affair.

In the event, the mutiny at the Nore collapsed of its own accord. Although concerted intimidatory measures undertaken by the authorities contributed to its failure, the most important factor was the mutineers' unwillingness to continue. By the middle of June it was clear that the government would make no further concessions beyond those made at Spithead. The only remaining courses open to the mutineers were either capitulation or the doubtful and dangerous option of more militant, perhaps even violent action. This last alternative was clearly not to the taste of most of the men. It is true that some radical literature found its way into the fleet. In addition there must have been several mutineers who were radicals or even revolutionaries, many of which must have been present in *Inflexible*.

Beyond the veiled threats and obvious frustrations, there was, both in the mutineers' dealings with one another and with the authorities, a definite feeling of loyalty to their service and to their country. It was a loyalty that was reiterated throughout the mutiny. It was the loyalty of the majority which prompted many of the militants to flee to the continent shortly before the mutiny collapsed. It has been estimated that between two and three hundred men escaped from the Nore to the continent during the last days of the mutiny. This is a high figure; but even assuming that every man was committed to the radical or revolutionary cause (which was probably not the case), this figure represents only a very small fraction of those involved in the mutiny.

Although it would be foolish to deny the involvement of radicals and revolutionaries in the Nore mutiny, I believe that such 'conspiracy theorists' as E. P. Thompson and Roger Wells have overestimated their power and influence. A comparison between events at the Nore in 1797 and the plots by Irish revolutionaries in the Channel Fleet the following year reveal many differences between the two. Besides the obviously violent intentions of the latter, which were absent from the Nore, the most striking difference is the relative absence of any active conspiratorial element in the months before the actual outbreak, compared with the months of preparation and plotting in 1798. After all, the one thing that is needed for a 'conspiracy theory' to be plausible is a conspiracy.

12

Lower-Deck Life in the Revolutionary and Napoleonic Wars

Brian Lavery

No one disagreed that the life of the eighteenth-century seaman was filled with danger and discomfort. Dr Thomas Trotter wrote of 'the unparalleled hardships to which seamen are exposed from the nature of their employment. Toil and danger are their constant attendants. They suffer privations to which all other men are strangers.' They had 'unfailing fortitude' and 'matchless patience'. Perhaps the actual amount of work was not as much as some believe; another naval surgeon wrote:

> While employed in the ports of those regions [i.e. the coasts of Great Britain], more particularly those termed their own, or even in those of the European allies of Great Britain, they are liberally supplied with diet at once nutritive and invigorating, consisting of a due admixture of well-chosen articles from the animal and vegetable kingdoms ... It will also be admitted that during even their longest cruises on these stations, unless some unforseen exigency has occurred requiring a great share of exertion and some degree of sacrifice on the part of the sailor, his duty is not only light but his allowance as above is profuse in quantity and of an excellent quality.[1]

But separation from family, very limited shore leave, overcrowding below decks and many other hardships made the seaman's life hard nevertheless. In a world in which life was very cheap in any case, a seaman had to begin his career at the age of eleven or twelve in order to become 'inured to the hardships of a sea life'. To the outsider, it seems surprising that the seamen did not have a general mutiny much earlier than they did.

What had changed in the late 1790s? This chapter will focus on the internal factors in shipboard life. It is not intended to deny that outside factors, such as radicalism ashore, the vast expansion of the fleet and the influx of thousands of non-seamen, had some effect. But it is equally important to see what had changed in the narrow, claustrophobic world of the lower decks to make mutiny inevitable.

It should be remembered that it is always dangerous to generalise about service in the navy at this time. Officers and seamen underwent no common training course, so ideas about how a ship should be run were varied. A ship

---

1 B. Lavery, ed., *Shipboard Life and Organisation* (NRS, vol. 138, London, 1998), p. 530.

might spend years away from the supervision of an admiral, so that the captain had complete control. Service in a small ship was very different from that in a large one, and the type of protest available to the men varied – small ships were much more prone to the 'revolutionary' type of mutiny in which the officers were overthrown, as in *Bounty* and *Hermione*. Sailors were not uniformed or drilled in the modern sense and under the cover of naval discipline, still retained some vestiges of personal liberty.

Regulation

By the 1790s, life on board many ships had become increasingly regulated. One senses that in the past, captains had been perfectly happy if the crew turned up for duty without being completely incapacitated by drink and if the desertion rate was not too high. But in the second half of the eighteenth century, this began to change. Admiral St Vincent was the best-known example of an admiral who interfered in the running of his ships, but his case is not entirely relevant here – he tended to regulate the officers more than the men, and his greatest unpopularity was on the quarterdeck.

The earliest known attempt to regulate life on board ship, beyond the *Naval Instructions* issued by the Admiralty, took place in 1755, when, as commander of the Downs Squadron, Admiral Thomas Smith issued a set of orders that regulated the officers and crews of the ships under his command.[2]

In the first place, he ordered that the system of 'divisions' be adopted by his ships (discussed later in this chapter). Secondly, he gave orders for training with the great guns and in sail handling; in prevention of fire and how to fight it; and for the midshipmen to inspect below decks to prevent drunkenness and disorder. He ended with the rather liberal injunction that the midshipmen were

> not to interrupt the men in mirth and good fellowship while they keep within the bounds of moderation; the intention of it being to prevent excessive drinking, which is not only a crime in itself but draws men into others which when sober they would most abhor.

The navy reached a kind of watershed during this period. Larger ships such as 74s and frigates were built in considerable numbers from 1755 onwards, and larger ships needed much more regulation. In 1730 there were only 60 ships with crews of more than four hundred men in the fleet. By 1762 there were 134 such ships, and the number had increased to 177 by 1803. The figures for ships with more than six hundred men are even more dramatic – 7 in 1730, 65 in 1762 and 132 in 1803.[3]

The service of the ships had also changed. They were far more likely to spend time on overseas stations, reliant on the primitive and often distant

2 Hodges and Hughes, eds, *Select Naval Documents* (2nd edn, London, 1936), pp. 147–50.
3 Charles Derrick, *Memoirs of the Rise and Progress of the Royal Navy* (London, 1806), pp. 132, 148, 219.

facilities of the overseas bases.[4] Even in home waters, the policy of continuous blockade of Brest was introduced in 1759, and it was precisely in these circumstances that Howe issued standing orders for *Magnanime* – the first known captain's orders.[5] With much longer periods at sea, captains had to pay more systematic attention to the health, cleanliness, discipline and morale of their crews.

By the 1750s the problems of running large ships were becoming apparent. The ship's company was divided up into messes, watches, parts of ship, gun crews at quarters, but none of these brought any regular contact with the officers. In the case of watches, for example, the seamen might only be in two watches, with the officers in three or four, in which case an individual officer would only work with the same group of seamen occasionally. Officers

> were dealing with an undifferentiated mass of persons, few of whom they knew as individuals. ... Except in small ships with stable companies (itself something of a contradiction) officers could not hope to know even their men's names.[6]

The answer was the system of 'divisions', by which each of the lieutenants had a party of men under him for welfare and administrative purposes, in order to increase contact between officers and men. Howe's orders of 1776 gave a fairly concise account of the system:

> The petty officers and seamen of the ships companies are to be formed into two or three divisions, according to the complements and classes of ship, and subdivided into squads with a midshipman appointed to each, who are respectively to be responsible for the good order and discipline of the men entrusted to their care.[7]

Over the next four decades it became increasingly common for captains to produce regulations on how their ships should be run. The motives were varied. For Charles Middleton (later Lord Barham), religion and order were inextricably mixed. He kept his ship's company 'as regular as any private family'. He was convinced that with proper leadership from captains and chaplains the crews 'would be amongst the foremost of the lower classes of people in examples of piety and good conduct'. But he conceded that 'a great part' of the 'regularity' of his ship was 'owing to good discipline and not the effect of religion'.[8] Middleton was aware that he could not go too far in propagating his beliefs:

4　For fleet distribution in the 1790s and 1800s, see Lavery, *Nelson's Navy* (London, 1989), pp. 245–51.
5　Lavery, *Shipboard Life and Organisation*, pp. 82–7.
6　N. A. M. Rodger, *The Wooden World. An Anatomy of the Georgian Navy* (London, 1986), p. 216.
7　W. G. Perrin, ed., *The Keith Papers*, I (NRS vol. LXII, London, 1927), p. 30.
8　J. K. Laughton, ed., *The Barham Papers*, I (NRS vol. XXXII, London, 1906), pp. 165–6.

By the naval instructions, divine service is to be performed morning and evening, on board of every King's ship, according to the liturgy of the Church of England. ... I was sixteen years in the sea service before I became a captain, and never, during that time heard prayers or divine service performed aboard of ship. ... As soon as I became a captain I began reading prayers myself to the ship's company of a Sunday, and also a sermon. ... I did not indeed venture to carry it further than Sundays ... and I should only have acquired the name of methodist or enthusiast if I attempted it.[9]

Captain Edward Riou was equally moderate in his religion. Despite his 'deep sense of every Christian obligation', his orders for the frigate *Amazon* in 1799 demanded only that 'Should no chaplain belong to the ship, the Sabbath day nevertheless will be attended to as much as possible'. Very different was James Gambier (1756–1833). According to one of his subordinates,

Our captain in all his arrangements evinced a determination to enforce his religious principles on board the ship under his command. He had prayers in his cabin twice a day, morning and evening. I was obliged to attend every morning with the other younger mids, he in person superintending.

He enforced the rule that 'none but married women' should be allowed to visit the men on board ship. Swearing was forbidden, and any seaman found guilty of it was forced to wear a wooden collar with two thirty-two-pound shot attached, until it was banned after one seaman became seriously ill as a result of wearing it. His men were not allowed to visit other ships on Sunday, and the captain became known throughout the fleet as 'preaching Jemmy'.[10]

For Lord Howe, regularity throughout the fleet was perhaps a more important motive. In 1758, as a commodore, he was the first to issue a printed signal book for the ships under his command, and this desire to regularise naval signals, as well as tactics, remained with him all his life. His interference made him unpopular with his officers, but he became known as the 'sailor's friend', because of his concern for their welfare. Sir Charles Knowles came from the same tradition, and he too published signal and order books, which he put forward as a model for other ships.[11] He too was a great innovator. Sir Home Popham also produced an order book and he produced the signal book that allowed words to be spelled out for the first time.

But the most important reason for regulating the crew was the need to maintain their health. This was clearly implicit in the division system, and is reinforced by the tone and emphasis of virtually all order books which have

---

9 J. K. Laughton, ed., *The Barham Papers*, II (NRS vol. XXXVIII, London, 1910), p. 163.
10 M. A. Lewis, ed., *Dillon's Narrative*, I (NRS vol. XCIII, London, 1953), pp. 96, 97, 100, 104. This is not to deny the influence of religion in individual cases and in certain ships over a range of periods. See, for example, Thomas Lurting, *The Fighting Sailor Turn'd Peaceable Christian* (London, 1710), reproduced in Charles Vipont, *Blow the Man Down* (London, 1939); Richard Blake, *Evangelicals in the Royal Navy, Blue Lights and Psalm Singers* (Woodbridge, 2008); H. D. Capper, *Aft from the Hawse Hole* (London, 1927).
11 NMM, HOL/77.

come to light. The importance of this was supported by Sir Gilbert Blane, the
Physician of the Fleet under Rodney in 1780.

> I hardly ever knew a ship's company become sickly which was well regu-
> lated in point of cleanliness and dryness. It is the custom in some ships to
> divide the crew into squads or divisions under the inspection of respective
> officers, who make a weekly review of their persons and clothing. ... This
> ought to be an indispensable duty in ships of two or three decks.[12]

To many historians, all this concern for order, health and discipline was
highly laudable.[13] But to the seaman it often seemed like an assault on his few
liberties. In the past, officers had hardly cared what seamen did as long as they
turned out for duty when needed. But from the 1780s onwards, the seaman
found his own space greatly reduced. Washing was done outside his normal
working hours, without any provision for soap or even fresh water. When he
was obliged to supply himself with a minimum quantity of clothing, this was
bought from the purser's monopoly in the slop chest and paid for out of the
man's own, very limited earnings. When officers decreed that he was to walk
the deck rather than sleep during quiet times on watch, the seaman did not
necessarily agree that the intentions were good. Admiral Patton was aware
that the seamen were forced to spend their own money on clothing and that
they resented any regulation:

> an idea has always prevailed among seamen that the service of their coun-
> try does not confine them with regard to the mode of their dress, according
> to the custom in armies, and it is by them deemed injustice to deprive sea-
> men of the disposal of their own money farther than necessity requires.[14]

Captain A. J. Griffiths made a similar point.

> Much dissatisfaction does arise from a too constant interference with
> them, from the attempt to keep them fidgeting about trifles and works of
> supererogation, all with a view to employ their minds. This seems a want
> of knowledge of human nature. Such perpetual fiddle faddle and interfer-
> ence only disgusts.[15]

Commander G. P. Monke believed in 1806 that it was the inconsistency of
regulation which caused the trouble.

> It has been found necessary by almost every captain or commander to
> adopt various other rules and regulations for the maintenance of good or-
> der and discipline on board of the ship or vessel under his command; and

---

12 C. Lloyd, ed., *The Health of Seamen* (NRS vol. CVII, London, 1965), p. 168.
13 For example M. Lewis, *A Social History of the Navy* (London, 1960), p. 273; C. Lloyd,
The British Seaman (London, 1968), p. 234.
14 Lavery, *Shipboard Life and Organisation*, p. 628.
15 Ibid., p. 357.

as these regulations are introduced or abolished according to his sole whim or caprice, it may be conceived what inconsistency or confusion must, in the progress or time, have arisen from such a contrariety of opinions on certain points of discipline. ... If an impartial enquiry was made into the origin of the frequent scenes of insubordination and mutiny which, during the last 25 years have distracted and convulsed the British Navy, it would be found that they have chiefly arisen from discontent which has, with few exceptions, been generated by the mutability of the system of discipline too often introduced by different commanders in different ships ... continually subject to be revoked or differently interpreted according to the will or caprice of the commander.[16]

But Monke was applying to the Admiralty for a job collating captains' orders. Admiral Phillip Patton, on the other hand, was against a single system of discipline.

One ship is necessarily totally separated and unconnected with any other ship; that it is impossible to bring the real state of the internal discipline under the review of any superior officer not embarked in that ship; that naval service removes ships to such a distance as puts them beyond all control of any power whatever; that ships, which are of great value and immense importance, may be with ease transferred, with all their tackle and ammunition, from one state to another.[17]

Cleanliness

Cleanliness of ship, clothes and person was at the root of much of this regulation. Cleaning of the ship was an issue in the 1790s, as for example in a petition from *Blanche* in 1795;

In the first place, we are employed from morning to two or three of clock in the afternoon washing and scrubbing the decks, and every day our chest and bags is ordered on deck, and not down till night; nor ourselves neither even so particular as to wash the decks with fresh water, and if we get wet at any time and hang or spread our clothes to dry, our captain throws them overboard.[18]

In 1796 the issue of washing was the cause of a protest in the depot ship *Gladiator* at Portsmouth. The men were ordered to take their dinner on deck while the lower deck was drying but refused to eat it. The first two called out were tried for 'endeavouring to make a mutinous assembly' but the court martial decided it was not an offence.[19]

---

16 TNA, ADM1/2152, Captains' In-letters, M.
17 Lavery, *Shipboard Life and Organisation*, p. 623.
18 Ibid., p. 423.
19 John D. Byrn, ed., *Naval Courts Martial 1793–1815* (NRS vol. 155, London, 2009),

This issue is not mentioned in petitions of the 1800s, perhaps because captains themselves reacted against excessive washing. Up to about 1800, it was an article of faith that the washing of decks was good for keeping the ship clean, and the men employed. St Vincent went as far as to recommend that 'the decks and sides of the ships of the fleet be washed every evening as well as morning during the summer months'.[20] In 1801 Admiral Keith was of the opinion that 'the custom of washing the decks of ships of war in all climates in every temperature of the air, and on stated days, let the weather be what it may' had become 'universally prevalent to the destruction of the health and lives of valuable men'. He rescinded the orders issued by St Vincent, and ordered that the lower deck be washed not more than once in fourteen days.[21]

This trend was repeated in the orders of other officers. On board *Mars* in 1804 the lower deck was to be washed once or twice a week, and swept clean on other days.[22] In Popham's orders of the same year, between decks were to be washed twice a week 'if the weather will permit it'.[23] In *Hyperion* in 1811, the decks were to be swept after every meal, but not washed.[24] This was probably on the advice of surgeons, for those of *Theseus*, *Ethalion* and *Ariadne*, for example, were keen to keep the men dry and Michael Jefferson of *Vanguard* seems satisfied that the lower deck was washed only twice a week.[25]

In 1795–97 the seamen of *Reunion* and *Proserpine* had difficulties with cleaning their clothes and persons, though it was not the fact of cleaning which was at issue, but the inadequate means available to do it and the punishments for failing to comply. In *Reunion* in 1795 the men wrote,

> Captain B also obliges us to wash our linen twice a week in salt water, and put two shirts on every week, and if they do not look as clean as if they was washed in fresh water he stops the person's grog for three or four days. Which has the misfortune to displease him in the above and if our hair is not tied to please him he orders it to be cut off. [26]

From *Proserpine* in 1797,

> in regard of mustering clothes clean is our next complaint and a small quantity of a gallon water once per fortnight to complete the same. If not clean, stoppage of grog or other punishment would ensue.[27]

If such petitions do not occur after 1800, it is perhaps because seamen got more

---

pp. 420–7.
20 Lavery, *Shipboard Life and Organisation*, p. 210.
21 Christopher Lloyd, ed., *The Keith Papers*, II (NRS vol. XC, London, 1950), pp. 412–3.
22 R. O. Bellasis, ed., 'The Trafalgar Order Book of HMS *Mars*', *Mariner's Mirror*, 22 (1936), p. 91.
23 TNA, ADM1/58, Letters from C-in-C, Cape of Good Hope, 9.
24 H. G. Thursfield, ed., *Five Naval Journals* (NRS vol. XCI, London, 1951), p. 332.
25 Lavery, *Shipboard Life and Organisation*, pp. 524–7, 536.
26 Ibid., p. 424.
27 Ibid., p. 426.

used to the need for cleanliness, or officers provided more fresh water or soap for doing it. Even in 1811 however, Philip Patton was aware of the need for a captain to 'explain himself on this matter publicly, showing the necessity of orderly cleanliness'. He discounted this obsession with the appearance of seamen:

> It is not to be expected that the vanity of personal appearance by which armies are in some measure managed can have any sensible effect in regulating the companies of ships. Seamen cannot be made the objects of an admiring crowd and are, from their previous education and changes of situation from merchants' to the King's service, and from their country's to the service of trade, incapable of being modelled so as to imbibe military ideas. Or, if these ideas could be introduced, it is impossible they should prevail without destroying the enthusiasm of seamen, who must always be less exposed to danger from the enemy than from the inconstancy of the atmosphere and the instability of the ocean. This want of security and state of uncertainty seem to render seamen in a great measure incapable of the order and uniformity of land forces; and the services in many respects quite dissimilar.[28]

Admiral Patton was aware of the problem, because thirty years earlier he had dealt with a mutiny of the crew when he was in temporary command of *Prince George* in 1779. The seamen were already discontented at being ordered to leave port to patrol in the Western Approaches and a revolt flared up on 16 January when the captain ordered the men to bring their hammocks up on deck, as the lower and middle gunports had been closed for several days due to bad weather and the decks needed to be aired. The men refused and threatened death to the boatswain who was sent below to order them. Patton called the men on deck and explained why the order was necessary but he added 'that this explanation was not necessary, because it was sufficient for them that such were his orders'. He called the officers to the quarterdeck and in the hearing of the men instructed them to take parties of men below according to the hammock list and order each individually to bring his hammock on deck. Eventually it was done and the leader of the mutiny was soon identified and punished. Quite typically, the mutiny was barely mentioned in the ship's logs.

Level of Work

Traditionally, naval seamen had been arranged in two watches when at sea. Apart from a minority of 'idlers', craftsmen and servants who were excused watches, the ship's company was divided into two halves and one was on duty at any given moment, day and night. Since a watch lasted for four hours, the majority of men never had more than four hours' continuous sleep at sea and often that occurred only one night in two.

Partly because fleets were spending longer times at sea, a three-watch system was introduced in many ships, entirely on the initiative of the captain. Inspection reports from St Vincent's fleet in 1797 show that six ships out of

28 Ibid., pp. 623–4.

eleven mentioned were at three watches.[29] Furthermore *Vanguard* used the three-watch system during the Nile campaign in the following year.[30]

But after 1800, there seems to have been some reaction by captains against the three-watch system. On taking command of the *Otter* sloop in 1809, Captain Willoughby found the men in three watches, which he regarded as part of a general slovenliness. 'Agreeably to the general line of discipline and arrangement I placed the men at watch and watch, obliged them to two changes of linen in the week and to keep their berths and the ship in general clean and wholesome.'[31] Captain John Davie, whose book on ship organisation was first published in 1804, provides strong arguments for arranging the ship's company in three watches rather than two. In this he was probably at odds with much of the Navy, for most other documents of the period assume two watches and his arguments are rather defensive:

> As there are various opinions respecting the propriety of a ship's company being at three watches … An insufficient number of men cannot be offered as an objection in large ships, and I think not with propriety in small ones. A large frigate, that has not more men in her watch at two watches than a 64 has at three, with deeper courses and every other sail in proportion, frequently excels her in the smartness of her manoeuvres, whilst with such an inferior complement she is at three watches and the 64 at two. This circumstance, strange in principle and dangerous in its tendency, may be attributed to many causes, but the most prevailing ones are;
>
> That captains, prejudiced in favour of old customs, cannot divest themselves of the idea that their ships would not be safe with less than half the ship's company upon deck.
>
> And again, it is a very predominant opinion that a ship's crew, being at three watches, acquire a habit of laziness which disqualifies them for active pursuits when required, and that by inaction a restlessness of disposition is created, which degenerates either into gambling or a spirit for politics, two of the most baneful tendencies of a ship's company.[32]

In a two-watch system, it is clear that the men were not expected to be at work for all of the time when on watch. In *Amazon*, at two watches, the officer of the watch was expected to keep the watch 'awake and in motion', but they were allowed to relax and indeed entertainment such as fiddling was positively encouraged.[33] For Davie in his three-watch system, the men could be kept walking the deck all the time during their watches if required in order to prevent illness, because they were well enough rested at other times.

> I am confident the medical part of the service will give their sanction, as in a single point of view, it holds out an inestimable advantage against

---

29   Ibid., p. 247.
30   Ibid., p. 527.
31   TNA, ADM1/5392, Court Martial Papers, February 1809.
32   Lavery, *Shipboard Life and Organisation*, p. 271.
33   Ibid., p. 124.

catching cold, because all the watch will then be enabled, and should be required, to walk the deck, which will prevent them from lying down on the damp deck or in wet places; a practice that does more injury to the constitution of seamen than at the moment can be imagined; and which, when a ship's company is at two watches, it is scarcely possible to prevent.[34]

In a sense then, the three-watch system did not alleviate the hardships of the seaman. He was often expected to be fully alert during his watch in the latter system, while two watches often allowed him an informal rest. However there is no sign that seamen complained about the three-watch system and captains often regarded it as a reward for an efficient crew.

> Fixing a ship's company at three watches should be done after the ship has been some time in commission and at sea, that it may be considered as an indulgence; and that, if from sickness, desertion or other cause of being short of complement it be necessary to reduce them to two watches again, it should not be considered as a hardship.[35]

Changing Messes

The Royal Navy seaman had very few liberties. He could not decide whether to be in the navy or not, which ship to be on, how long his service was to last or his duties on board. His greatest privilege, jealously guarded, was the right to choose his own companions for the hours of day, especially mealtimes, when he was off duty and able to relax. Yet there are signs that even this moderate right was under attack during the years of mutiny. As Captain Griffiths wrote,

> Till within these few years, the privilege the seamen and marines had of changing their messes the first of the month if they thought fit was their Magna Carta and I confess I am inclined to attach much benefit to it. The original interference therewith I trace to the complaints of the pursers and the little squabbles about double days and single days where there was an odd man. To obviate this it became common to order all messes to be even numbers, and afterwards they were in many ships obliged to be not less than four or more than eight. In some others the number was decided by the size of the berths, each being one mess. Some little probable advantage might be gained by these arrangements, but as the pursuit of man is to obtain the largest possible portion of happiness his situation is capable of affording and as there are infinite varieties of opinion wherein it consists, mine is that few things are more annoying than an unpleasant or quarrelsome messmate. Few but have experienced this in their passage through a midshipmen's berth, or a wardroom mess.[36]

34 Ibid., pp. 271–2.
35 Ibid., p. 272.
36 Ibid., p. 355

There is very little data on the messes aboard a ship, but certainly there were more messes than one would expect. It is often assumed that each mess was allotted a single table, but this was not the case on a ship of the line. According to Captain Griffiths, 'While in command, my crew ever messed as they liked. The berth was allotted to the number it was calculated to hold and if one, two or three messes were in it, that rested with themselves.'[37] This was confirmed by Captain Basil Hall who wrote 'In a line of battleship the tables are larger [than those of a frigate] and two messes sit at the same table, one on each side.'[38] This explains how very small messes of as few as four, or variable numbers such as those allowed in some ships, might be viable. In *Victory* in 1797 there were 165 messes for a crew of about eight hundred – approximately five men in the average mess.[39]

Even so, it must have been difficult to accommodate all the men on a ship of the line. According to 'Jack Nastyface', who served on board a 74-gun ship in 1805, 'each mess ... generally consists of eight persons who berth in between two of the guns on the lower deck and where there is a board placed which swings with the rolling of the ship and answers for a table'.[40] If there were at most twenty-eight such places on board the ship, then only 224 men could have been accommodated, whereas at least five hundred would have been needed on a 74-gun ship. If we accept Hall's premise of two messes per table, then 408 men can be accommodated. If we then accept that further berths were placed along the centre line and perhaps yet more could be sited on the orlop on a ship of the line, as is suggested in a book by Daniel Ross, then we might be close to a figure of five hundred. Even so, sixteen men round a mess table between the guns might be considered as gross overcrowding, extreme even by the standards of a sailing warship.[41]

The problem was not solved by having the crew eat by watches, in either a frigate or a ship of the line, for in general both watches ate together. This is made clear by the recurring phrase in many captain's order books, 'The ship's company are never to be interrupted at their meals but on the most pressing occasions.' Riou elaborates on this: 'the commanding officer should be very punctual as to their hours of dinner and breakfast ... But with this time allowed it is expected they will, when the hands or watch is turned up, be ready to run up immediately'.[42] This is confirmed by Seaman Robert Wilson: 'If the duty of the ship is required to be executed at meal times, so that the hands, or the watch is disturbed, the time they may want of their allowed times is made

37 Ibid., p. 356
38 Basil Hall, *Fragments of Voyages and Travels* (London, 1860), p. 137.
39 Lavery, *Shipboard Life and Organisation*, p. 589.
40 William Robinson, *Jack Nastyface* (reprinted Annapolis, 1973), p. 33 His work is often questioned as being polemical and one-sided, but on the whole it seems reasonably accurate as an account of seamen's culture. See my comments in *Nelson's Fleet at Trafalgar*, Greenwich 2004, p. 112. Incidentally the name of 'Nastyface' was not peculiar to Robinson. According to Grose's *Dictionary of the Vulgar Tongue* of 1811 (reprinted Stroud, 2008), p. 113, 'Jack Nasty Face' was 'a sea term signifying a common sailor'.
41 Daniel Ross, *The Perpetual Berthing and Watch Bill Book* (London, 1797), reproduced in *Shipboard Life and Organisation*, pp. 257–62.
42 Lavery, *Shipboard Life and Organisation*, p. 151.

up to them when the duty is done.'[43] It is quite clear that the crew ate as a whole, apart from a few helmsmen, sentries and lookouts.

Lists of the men in their messes must have been kept by first lieutenants, but as far as I know none have survived. Analysis of such a document, compared with a muster book, would give fascinating information on the social life of the seaman.

Reactions to Petitions

The official reaction to seamen's petitions gives an important indicator of relations between officers and men. The legality of such petitions was doubtful, and sometimes the naval authorities attempted to suppress them. The *Eurydice* petition of 1796 seems relatively moderate in its complaints:

> we are to holystone the decks from 4 o'clock in the morning until 8, for if a man should rest he is kicked in the face and bleeds on the stone, and afterwards made to wash the stone from the blood and then reported to the captain and flocked [flogged?] for no provocation, unless by our lieutenant report to be conceive [*sic*] other grievous complaints which are too tedious to mention.
>
> Our captain is a very worthy commander, but Mr Colvile our First Lieutenant and Mr McCloud, master's mate, are beyond description, and so tyrannical that such officers are a disgrace to the service. We only request, as your lordships have remedied such grievances before now, we wish to have them either discharged from the ship or better usage for us on board another ship, as we have experienced the service this many years past, and willing to fight for King and country. We wish to have the same usage as other ships have done to us, so we require an answer from your lordships, and most compassionably require redress.[44]

In the atmosphere of the time, this led to a man called MacDonough being tried by court martial. He was a literate seamen, who had helped write letters for his messmates and kept the boatswain's accounts, but the court found no real evidence that he had written the petition.

Judging by several books which were published by officers in the years after 1805, much more liberal ideas had begun to prevail as the effects of the mutinies began to be reconciled with good order and discipline. After Trafalgar there are signs that the crisis was over and that a more benign discipline could return to the fleet. By 1811 Captain Griffiths was able to write that 'if such a spirit [of mutiny] did then continue to exist, it has long since subsided' and that 'If you reflect on the very heavy responsibility on seamen who come forward to accuse their officers and the prejudice which does actually exist against such complaints, you will perceive it requires no little conduct and stamina to do this in what we should consider a proper way'.[45]

---

43 Thursfield, *Five Naval Journals*, pp. 254.
44 Lavery, *Shipboard Life and Organisation*, p. 425.
45 Ibid., p. 357.

He went on,

> The Articles of War expressly direct, 'If any person shall find cause of complaint etc, he shall quietly make the same known.' Yet sometimes when the men come aft to complain they are sent away unsatisfied. This cannot be right. If men complain with reason they are entitled to redress. If they complain without, it appears to be our duty to show them the impropriety of their complaint by a due examination of it; and at all events as a less evil arises from their acting up to the Articles of War, and making their idle complaint known, than would were they to let it canker, and growl over it in secret below. They should be dismissed without harsh language; indeed of the two be rather encouraged than checked.
>
> The recollection of the disgraceful mutinies of 1797 and 1798 seemed to have made us so tenacious on the subject that we were too apt perhaps to resolve everything to a spirit of mutiny. This was probably a very natural consequence, but if such a spirit did then continue to exist, it has long since subsided. Time has produced its usual effect and at all events it is a feeling which should not be cherished or encouraged. If in the management of a ship's company after the attainment of all the essentials of discipline, activity, sobriety and obedience etc, they were more left to themselves, there would not be anything which bore even the semblance of it.[46]

Informal Punishments

Informal punishments inflicted by petty and warrant officers figured largely in seamen's complaints in the years around 1797. Attitudes to these changed through the years. In 1775, Charles Middleton was positively in favour of them. Lieutenants of divisions were to punish lesser crimes on their own authority, to prevent the need for excessive flogging. The master at arms was to punish any man found beating another, and was 'to carry a stick for this as well as the other purposes of his office'. Men who were 'careless about their clothes or dirty in their persons' were to be 'punished through the boatswain's mate by order of the midshipmen commanding them, as far as a few strokes'. Men who swore might be forced to wear a wooden collar, and those who got drunk were obliged to drink a pint of salt water.[47]

In 1786 Prince William was slightly in advance of his time when he ordered that 'No seaman, marine or other person in the ship is to be struck or otherways ill used on any pretence whatever by any officer or gentleman'.[48] When Captain Keats wrote the orders for *Superb* in 1803 he was barely tolerant of informal punishments. 'The boatswain and his mates conformable to the old custom of the service are to carry rattans, but they are to be used with discretion.'[49] By 1811 Captain Cumby of *Hyperion* was totally opposed: 'The

---

46 Ibid.
47 Laughton, *Barham, Papers*, I, p. 39–45.
48 Lavery, *Shipboard Life and Organisation*, p. 94.
49 David Norris, ed., 'Captain's Orders for HMS *Superb*', *Mariner's Mirror*, vol. VII,

highly improper practice of what is called starting the men, is most peremptorily forbidden; punishment shall only be inflicted by order of the Captain, to whom alone the Lords Commissioners of the Admiralty have thought proper to delegate that power.'[50] This may have reflected the general situation, because according to Captain Corbet of *Nereide*, 'an idea has crept in and is gaining head, that the punishment they call starting is not legal'. A court martial in 1809 reprimanded him for issuing his petty officers with sticks of an excessive size, but tacitly recognised its legality.[51]

The reduction in starting may have done something to reduce the day-to-day brutality of the seaman's life, but it also tended to raise the stakes for him – if punishment was only by order of the captain, it was likely to be more formal and severe. This was part of an era of slightly greater liberalism towards the ship's company, after the immediate effects of the mutinies had died down. There seems to have been a general humanisation of the navy after about 1805, with many small reforms such as the abolition of running the gauntlet and starting; and the regularisation of the position of the chaplain on board ship. This might be seen as a part of the long-term effects of the mutinies, after the immediate shocks had died down. Admiral Patton believed,

> Although seamen may have been regarded (by certain characters who have unfortunately had power and who were ignorant of their real dispositions) as a species of mankind deficient in the nicer feelings of humanity, whose attachments might be sacrificed, their friendships disregarded and even their healths ruined or destroyed upon the most frivolous occasions; yet they are very far from being inferior to other men, either in generous or in elevated sentiments. They are, like landmen, fully sensible of the eternal obligations and immutable effects of justice; they are open to the dictates of common sense and uncommonly alive to every generous and to every noble feeling. Nor will they ever fail to return the full measure of gratitude and affection that commander who treats them as rational beings, endued with the same faculties and perceptions which he himself possesses. The author of these pages, from a long course of experience in the management of seamen, can affirm that if they are governed with justice and candour they will not only show an affectionate attachment to superiors, but they will enter with pleasure into the views and second the intentions of the person who hath evidently pursued a line of conduct most favourable to the happiness of the whole, without deviating from a zealous discharge of his public duty.[52]

Captain Griffiths' chapter of 'Conduct to the ship's company' ranges over many issues and is perhaps the most humane and liberal of all the documents

---

p. 345.

50 Thursfield, *Five Naval Journals*, p. 333.

51 TNA, ADM1/5392, Court Martial Papers, February 1809.

52 Quoted from Philip Patton, *Strictures on Naval Discipline and the Conduct of a Ship of War, Intended to Produce a Uniformity of Opinion among Sea Officers* (NMM, c.1807), section VI, 43, in Lavery, Shipboard Life and Organisation, p.627.

which have emerged from the period. Perhaps this is because the bitterness caused by the great wave of mutinies culminating in 1797 had died down and officers such as Griffiths were able to consider ways to keep up morale for the future. As he commented,

> Seamen are nowadays a thinking set of people and a large portion of them possess no inconsiderable share of common sense, the most useful sense after all. They are capable certainly of judging when they are well treated, whether those in authority over them exercise it with mildness and a due attention to their comforts, and it is natural to suppose they sit lighter under the yoke of a man who they see knows and does his own duty.[53]

---

53 Lavery, *Shipboard Life and Organisation*, p. 355.

13

'Launched into Eternity'[1]
Admiralty Retribution *or* the Restoration of Discipline?

Ann Veronica Coats

The fatal morning is arrived – the signal of death already displayed – the assemblage of boats, manned and armed, surround the ship appointed for the execution. The crews of the respective ships are arranged on deck, to whom the commanding officer makes known the crime for which the culprit is condemned to suffer; and after hearing the articles of war distinctly read, they await with silent dread and expectation the awful moment. At length a gun is fired (the last signal to rouse attention), and at the same instant the unhappy victim is run up by the neck to the yard-arm – a dreadful spectacle, and an example to deter others from the commission of similar crimes.[2]

On 30 June 1797, Richard Parker, elected leader of the Nore mutiny, was launched into eternity from the yardarm of *Sandwich*, not only in a spirit of retribution, but also to achieve the restoration of discipline. Parker was the first scapegoat, and is reported to have uttered the customary words of a condemned man: 'I acknowledge the justice of the sentence under which I suffer; and I hope my death may be considered a sufficient atonement, without involving the fate of others.'[3]

His death was not sufficient, however. Fifty-one further scapegoats were sentenced to be hanged, and eight more to be flogged or imprisoned. Admiral Viscount Keith, sent to Sheerness by the Admiralty to counteract the mutiny, gave instructions after its conclusion that 'the ten most guilty men' were to

1   NMRN, 1993.453(2), 4 September 1797.
2   J. McArthur, *Principles and Practice of Naval and Military Courts-Martial*, II (London, 1813), p. 344.
3   W. J. Neale, *History of the Mutiny at Spithead and the Nore* (London, 1842), p. 362. For a discussion of the function of such speeches see J. A. Sharpe, '"Last Dying Speeches": Religion, Ideology and Public Execution in Seventeenth-Century England', *Past and Present*, 107 (May 1985), pp. 144–67 and L. B. Faller, *Turned to Account* (Cambridge, 1987). Such speeches were reported at the executions of *Pompée* and *Royal Sovereign* mutineers in June and September 1797, see note 82 below.

be arrested from each ship, regardless of their degree of involvement in the mutiny.[4] Three hundred and fifty-four were pardoned and the remaining prisoners were released after victory at Camperdown removed an invasion threat to Britain on 11 October 1797.[5]

Parker was originally charged with the civil crime of High Treason at Maidstone Jail on 15 June. Under civil law he would have been entitled to a trial by jury. With a defence barrister such as the Whig Thomas Erskine, Parker could conceivably have been acquitted, the outcome of Erskine's defence of London Corresponding Society members in 1794.[6] Admiral Keith, supporting Sir Charles Grey, commander of the Sheerness garrison, reported to Earl Spencer on 6 June that

> a printed Paper was yesterday circulated in the Fleet setting forth that M[r] Fox would be Minister in the course of a few days and that he and his friends approved of the seamen's conduct and would certainly grant them trial by Jury and a full redress of all their grievances[.][7]

Parker was therefore returned to naval custody, where his conviction was certain. As the Whig historian W. J. Neale emphasised:

> After the long series of most gross blunders that had disgraced Pitt's policy at the outbreak of the mutiny at Spithead, it would indeed have been a climax to his shame and confusion, had an English jury pitied the wrongs that drove their naval defenders into crime, and availed themselves of any doubtful point to acquit the ringleaders.[8]

---

4 Quoted in James Dugan, *The Great Mutiny* (London, 1966), p. 321. Officially, Vice Admiral Charles Buckner was commander-in-chief at Sheerness, but Gill condemns his early measures against the mutineers as 'altogether useless': C. Gill, *The Naval Mutinies of 1797* (Manchester, 1913), p. 133; Keith makes the hierarchical situation clear in his correspondence with Earl Spencer, British Library, Althorp Papers, G195, 2 June 1797. George Keith Elphinstone was created 1st Viscount Keith on 16 March 1797. D. Syrett and R. L. DiNardo, *Commissioned Sea Officers of the Royal Navy 1660–1815* (London, 1994), p. 252.
5 Gill, *Naval Mutinies*, pp. 251–2.
6 David Lemmings, 'Erskine, Thomas', *ODNB* (2004) www.oxforddnb.com ; A. Wharam, *Treason Trials* (London, 1992), 143–226; Neale, *History of the Mutiny*, pp. 309–321.
7 BL, Althorp Papers, G195, Keith to Spencer, 6 June 1797.
8 Neale, *History of the Mutiny*, p. 314.

Left: 12. *Mutiny at the Nore – Ill-treatment of Officers* by Colonel C. Field RMLI. The illustration was made for his history of the Royal Marine Corps, *Britain's Sea-Soldiers*, Volume 1, Lyceum Press, 1924. It represents a defiant attitude shown by the Nore mutineers towards their officers and the establishment and signifies officers' continuing fear of mutiny long after 1797. Effigies, not officers, were hanged at the Nore, although ships' boats were typically ordered to witness a hanging when a seaman was hanged following a court martial.

© Trustees of the Royal Marines Museum, reproduced with permission from the Trustees of the Royal Marines Museum.

While nominally second in command to Admiral Charles Buckner, Lord Keith 'practically, it would seem, relieved Buckner of his responsibility for suppressing the revolt'. As ships surrendered he collected for the courts evidential papers not already destroyed.[9]

Evan Nepean, Secretary to the Board of Admiralty, instructed Vice Admiral Sir Thomas Pasley, President of Richard Parker's court martial:

> You may prove almost anything you like against him, for he has been guilty of everything that's bad. Admiral Buckner will be a material evidence to state the proceedings which took place on his visit to the *Sandwich*, and which, indeed, of itself appears to be enough to dispose of a dozen scoundrels of Parker's description.[10]

Parker was court-martialled on *Neptune* moored in Long Reach on the River Medway, 22–26 June. Captain Mosse, prosecuting, charged Parker with 'Making and endeavouring to make mutinous assemblies on board Sandwich … on or about the 12th of May; disobeying the lawful orders of his superior officers, and treating his superior officers with disrespect'.[11] He sought to prove that Parker had led the mutiny and had ordered firing by *Monmouth* and *Director* on *Leopard* and *Repulse* on 9 June. Mosse established that Parker was President of the committee from 14 May, actively involved in decisions and punishments, and directed the firing, but failed to prove that he fired personally on the ships. Was he the real leader? The committee was established before he became involved, but his actions clearly shaped and prolonged the mutiny. Parker insisted that he only obeyed the delegates' commands, prevented more violence and was neither Jacobin nor traitor. After the trial Pasley wrote to Nepean:

> The conviction of this villain Parker must have been so very dear to you at the Admiralty that the place and time of his execution might have been previously settled. It would have been on such an occasion perhaps more exemplary, had the court assumed the power lodged in their own breast by the articles of war, and executed him the hour of conviction.[12]

Maintenance of discipline had always preoccupied the Admiralty, but this became more defined from the mid-eighteenth century through revisions of the Articles of War, as the navy and ships increased in size. It relied on the normal effectiveness of immediate punishments, reinforced by regular readings of the Articles of War and ultimately courts martial.[13] However, Captain

---

9   Gill, *Naval Mutinies*, pp. 194, 247.
10 Gill, *Naval Mutinies*, p. 247, citing TNA, ADM1/727.
11 *Portsmouth Gazette*, 26 June 1797.
12 Gill, *Naval Mutinies*, p. 248.
13 They were regularly noted in the muster books as being read to the ship's companies. See N. A. M. Rodger, *Articles of War* (Havant, 1982); N. A. M. Rodger, *The Wooden World: An Anatomy of the Georgian Navy* (Glasgow, 1990), chapter VI; B. Lavery, *Nelson's Navy* (London, 1989), parts V, VI, IX.

Philip Patton in 1795, after observing a general mutiny at Spithead in 1783, and Captain Thomas Pakenham in 1796, had clearly predicted the possibility of another general mutiny if petty officers and leading seamen were not better rewarded and their numbers increased on each ship.[14] Earl Spencer, First Lord of the Admiralty, chose to reject their advice for financial reasons and because it was not politically expedient to raise naval expenditure in Parliament when the navy debt already stood at £12 million.[15] Ironically, Pitt admitted to Spencer on 20 April: 'The amount of the expense is comparatively of no consequence.'[16]

Discipline depended upon that very class of petty officers and leading seamen identified by Patton and Pakenham as natural leaders of the men and articulators of their grievances: the class which actually led the mutiny at Spithead.[17] In 1946, recalling Castlereagh's 1813 statement on naval impressment of Americans, Richmond criticised 'the long neglect of successive British Parliaments to establish a just system of manning the navy, or rewarding seamen, of alleviating the hardships of service and the brutality of discipline'. He quoted the Earl of Galloway's suggestion that an effective remedy for desertion might be an 'increase in petty officers from the best among them, and by more liberal remuneration'.[18]

The fragility of officers' control over the men had been articulated in 1794, when Howe

> perceived a feeling of discontent to have recently crept into the minds of the seamen, and he does not scruple to lay the blame on the captains, who kept their men as prisoners on board, when they came to harbour, while they themselves spent a great part of their time on shore, leaving the command of their ships to subordinate officers.[19]

Reverend Fresselique's sermon celebrating the 'late victory', aimed to 'shew the effect of proper discipline and good order, which is the main spring of Action'.[20] He asked if 'this great purpose could have been effected had there been no regulations in force, and the ships company left to act at their own discretion?' He recommended 'a continuance of Friendship and Harmony

---

14 NMM, WYN/109/7/14, fols 5, 15–16, April 1795; BL, Althorp Papers, G187, Pakenham to Spencer, 11 December 1796. See Coats, Chapter 2, 'The Delegates: A Radical Tradition'. Captain Patton was promoted to Rear Admiral of the Blue, 1 June 1795: Syrett and DiNardo, *Commissioned Sea Officers of the Royal Navy*, 350. Woodes Rogers, *A Cruising Voyage round the World* (London, 1928), p. 4.

15 BL, Althorp Papers, G187, Spencer to Pakenham, 12 December 1796; G191, Spencer to the Duke of Bedford, 12 May 1797.

16 J. S. Corbett, ed., *The Private Papers of George, 2nd Earl Spencer, First Lord of the Admiralty 1794–1801*, II (London, 1914), p. 116, Pitt to Spencer, 20 April 1797.

17 G. E. Manwaring and B. Dobrée, *The Floating Republic* (London, 1935), p. 262–3; TNA, ADM36, Muster Books.

18 H. Richmond, *Statesmen and Sea Power* (Oxford, 1946), p. 347–9.

19 J. Barrow, *Life of Earl Howe* (London, 1838), p. 301.

20 NMRN, J. J. Fresselique, *Sermon for the Late Victory 1794* (Gosport, 1794), p. 4.

amongst ourselves, which hath, by uniting made us powerful'.[21] Revealing the 'almost unbridgeable gulf between upper and lower decks in the navy at this time',[22] he continued:

> I believe the late transaction has naturally strengthened the social bond by which we are united – I therefore only mean to guard against a possibility of anything like a difference of opinion happening, by a general system of accommodation pervading the whole ship's company.[23]

This 'difference of opinion', had, by the end of 1796, manifested itself as a concrete plan to achieve an improvement in the living and working conditions of the seamen. Effective leadership was the key to the maintenance of discipline, and the toast, 'May the Mediterranean discipline never be introduced into the Channel Fleet', given at Lord Bridport's table on *Royal George*, conveyed a view of Bridport's discipline as very different from that of St Vincent.[24] There was a lack of overall control in the administration of the Channel Fleet, and a lack of communication among the admirals at Portsmouth. To quote Richard Saxby:

> By 1796 it is fair to say that the Channel Fleet did not really have a commander in chief but was being administered by the Admiralty as a number of independent squadrons. This system broke down under the strain of Hoche's expedition to Ireland in December 1796.[25]

Conversely, the ships' companies of the Channel Fleet clearly did have good communications, meeting regularly at Spithead, Plymouth or Torbay. Lessons learnt by the seamen from the general mutiny at Spithead in 1783, and the individual mutinies on *Windsor Castle*, *Culloden* and *Terrible* in 1784, had taught them to unite against divisive Admiralty tactics.[26] Their demands arose from a material desire to correct a decline in their standard of living, as they had not had a pay rise in 144 years.[27] They also knew they were a scarce commodity in wartime who could expect higher pay in the merchant navy. Many experienced naval seamen had served in the merchant navy and knew that

---

21 NMRN, Fresselique, *Sermon*, pp. 11–2, 14.
22 R. Saxby, 'Lord Bridport and the Spithead Mutiny', *Mariner's Mirror*, 79, 2 (May 1993), 171. Also see N. A. M. Rodger, 'Jolly Tars Were Our Men?' in *Mutiny on the Bounty 1789–1989* (Greenwich, 1989), p. 16.
23 Fresselique, *Sermon*, p. 15.
24 James, *Old Oak*, p. 155.
25 R. Saxby, 'Lord Bridport and the Spithead Mutiny', p. 170. Also see J. Barrow, *Life of Earl Howe* (London, 1838) p. 303; TNA, ADM1/107, Bridport to Spencer, 13 April 1797; ADM1/1022 Parker to Nepean, 14 April 1797; ADM1/107, Bridport to Nepean, 15 April 1797; BL, Althorp Papers, G191, Bridport to Spencer, 15 April 1797.
26 See Coats, Chapter 2, 'The Delegates: A Radical Tradition'.
27 TNA, ADM1/107, ADM1/5125. The Act of Charles II was cited because that was the last occasion that Parliament had set the wage rates, but they were the same as the Act of 1 January 1653 (able seamen's wages raised from 19s to 24s a month; ordinary seamen's wages remained at 19s). *CSPD*, 1652–53, p. 43.

wartime wages were four times greater than those of the Royal Navy.[28] Even Earl Spencer acknowledged that 'the wages were undoubtedly too low in proportion to the times'.[29]

Demands increased through Admiralty insensitivity and miscalculation. The first demand, in December 1796, was for a pay rise. Bridport complained to Nepean in April 1797:

> I have been informed, that this plan was to have taken effect before the Fleet sailed from Spithead in Dec. last, and it is reported to me that Petitions were presented six months ago, for an increase in pay, of which I was totally ignorant, 'till I wrote my first letter on this subject.

Further demands made in the petitions to Admiralty and the House of Commons after the mutiny broke out concerned conditions and the amount of provisions issued. Resulting from a petition of 1776 the purser was allowed to deduct an eighth of the value of his stores to cover wastage, so seamen lost two ounces in the pound of dry goods and one pint per gallon of beer. Weights on board ships were only fourteen ounces.[30]

Representatives were chosen on 16 April from the sixteen largest warships and 'Impowered to act for the Ships Company'. They discussed issues with their respective ships' companies and took opinions back to the delegate's committee, which reached a final decision, for example on whether *Romney* and *Venus* should protect a merchant convoy.[31] Thus the delegates remained in touch with the seamen, and their experience and skills as leaders were able to guide them through Admiral Gardner's attempt to 'seperate our Interest' and Colpoys's attempt to prevent a meeting on board *London* on 7 May.[32]

From 16 April the delegates directed their propaganda campaign effectively, exploiting political divisions within the press to obtain wide and largely sympathetic coverage to attain popular support.[33] The petition sent to Charles James Fox (intercepted by the Post Office so it never reached him), stated that 'our pay does not bear a proportion above half of its Original Value' and was intended to increase their chances of success by expanding public awareness of their case. They

> Lay these our grievances before Honble. the House of Commons & we entertain not the least doubt but that, that Ever Generous house will grant

---

28 BL, Althorp Papers, G187, Pakenham to Spencer, 11 December 1796. P. Patton NMM, WYN/109/7/14, fol. 5, April 1795.

29 Spencer to Jervis, 4 May 1797, in J. S. Tucker, ed., *Memoirs of Earl St Vincent*, I (London, 1844), p. 320.

30 C. Lloyd, 'Victualling of the Fleet in the Eighteenth and Nineteenth Centuries', in J. Watt, E. J. Freeman, W. F. Bynum, eds, *Starving Sailors* (Greenwich, 1981), p. 11.

31 TNA, ADM1/5125, documents from *Queen Charlotte*; ADM1/1022, 16 April 1797, 17 April 1797; ADM3/136, fol. 412, 18 April 1797.

32 TNA, ADM1/5125 *Royal George*'s ship's company to Lord Bridport, their flag commander, 22 April 1797.

33 See the numerous articles drawn up during the mutiny by the ships' companies at Spithead and Plymouth, TNA, ADM1/5125, ADM1/811.

such relief to their oppressed & Faithful Servants as they may in their great Wisdom think most proper.[34]

Continuity and long association among the seamen of the Channel Fleet ensured their close coordination, commitment and unity, proved by a document from Plymouth: 'Our Resolutions are: An exact obedience + submission to the Captain of the Fore Castle, According to the plan laid down at Spithead.'[35]

The supportive mutiny at Plymouth was ready to start at 8a.m. on 26 April, as soon as *Porcupine* brought the news of the Admiralty's delay in agreeing to the petitions.[36] Its leaders were from the same petty-officer class as at Spithead and their articles were designed with the same aim: to maintain the self-discipline of the men.[37] The officers reported that the seamen were 'so bent on sending two or three men to Spithead from each ship that they could not be turned from their Purpose, but on the contrary, if absolutely refused, that they would clearly carry off the ships or proceed to some violence'. Any doubt of their intentions was removed by the seamen sending the women ashore. The captains were 'freed from the humiliating necessity of giving them leave' when 'two men from each ship in the Sound and Cawsand Bay, stiling themselves Delegates, had taken a boat and gone for Cawsand in order to hire a Vessel and proceed to Portsmouth'.[38] Sir Richard King, Commander-in-Chief, was dismayed that the men followed Spithead's example of sending unpopular officers ashore.[39]

The Admiralty's traditional methods of dealing with mutiny were manifestly unsuccessful at Spithead: 'let me know … particularly what Information you may have received, and whether any individuals are pointed out as leaders in the Business', wrote Spencer to Bridport on 14 April.[40] Bridport, more attuned to the mood of his men, recognised the complete impotence of these methods in countering the mutineers. He replied to Nepean the next day:

Their Lordships desire me to use every means in my power to restore the discipline of the Fleet, would to God I had influence sufficient for this important object which nothing in my opinion will be able to effect, but a compliance with their Petitions.[41]

And on the following day:

---

34 TNA, ADM1/107, 15 April 1797.
35 TNA, ADM1/811, n.d., but from filing, April 1797.
36 TNA, ADM1/811, Edmund Nepean, First Lieutenant, *Atlas*, 26 April 1797. Evan Nepean's son.
37 TNA, ADM1/811, 'a person having the appearance of a petty officer', Captain J. MacDougall, *Edgar,* to Orde, 26 April 1797; Articles sent from *Atlas* to *Edgar,* ibid.
38 TNA, ADM1/811, Orde to Nepean, 28 April 1797
39 TNA, ADM1/812, King to Nepean, 28 May 1797.
40 TNA, ADM3/136, Spencer to Bridport, 14 April 1797.
41 TNA, ADM1/107, Bridport to Nepean, 15 April 1797.

> With respect to using vigorous and effectual measures for getting the better of the crews of the Ships, at Spithead, their Lordships will see that it is impossible to be done or securing the Ringleaders[.][42]

Equally unsuccessful was the constantly reiterated request made by the Admiralty for Bridport to get the ships to sea, in order to separate them. The seamen refused to weigh anchor, recognising this as the key to their success.[43]

Whenever the Admiralty used traditional punitive measures at Spithead they failed. Admirals Colpoys, Pole and Gardner tried on 21 April 'by Persuasions threatings, and all other means in their Power to Perswade the delegates to agree to the Proposals', but 'the People was determined'.[44] It prompted the seamen to send news to the other fleets to gain their support.[45] *Porcupine* had already taken the news to Plymouth; on 22 April *Niger* conveyed it to the Nore.[46]

The Admiralty Order of 1 May was a further blunder which precipitated the incident on *London*, but was intended to remedy the faults revealed by the outbreak and prevent future mutinies. Believing that the dispute had been settled, the Admiralty Lords saw their primary task as the restoration of discipline. The document ordered that

> the strictest attention should be paid by all officers in His Majesty's Naval Service, not only to their own Conduct, but to the Conduct of those who may be under their Orders, the more effectually to insure a proper subordination and discipline, and to prevent as far as may be, all discontent among the Seamen.[47]

Commanders were also warned to

> see that the arms and Ammunition belonging to the marines, to be constantly kept in good order and fit for immediate Service, as well in Harbour as at Sea; and that they are in future to be careful to rate their Ships Companies according to the Merits of the men, in order that those who may not be deserving thereof, may not receive the Pay of Able, or Ordinary Seamen.[48]

This order, together with the lack of full provisions and correct weights as promised, prompted a fear amongst the seamen that the government would renege on the pay agreement and pardon.[49] The delegates at St Helen's, aware that the three ships remaining at Spithead felt isolated, determined to talk to

---

42 Ibid., 16 April 1797.
43 Saxby, 'Lord Bridport and the Spithead Mutiny', pp. 173–6.
44 TNA, ADM1/5125, documents from *Queen Charlotte*.
45 Gill, *Naval Mutinies*, p. 105.
46 TNA, ADM1/1022, P. Parker to Nepean, 18 April 1797, 22 April 1797.
47 TNA, ADM2/133, 1 May 1797, Admiralty Orders and Instructions.
48 Ibid.
49 See TNA, ADM1/5125, letter from *Ramillies*, 7 May 1797.

them. Colpoys failed in his attempt to confront the delegates and implement the order on *London* on 7 May, 'at a time when it was first determined to endeavour the mutineers to subordination'.[50] Instead, the delegates, pushed to the limit of their patience, 'finally determined not to receive any of the officers that have been turned on shore from the ships, and insist that no two of them shall ever be appointed to the same ship'.[51]

The Admiralty recognised that the seamen at Spithead and Plymouth were morally justified in their actions and held the sympathy of the nation. It acceded to most of their demands. The causes of their success were succinctly expressed by an officer in the Channel Fleet:

> I could say many things to extenuate their conduct, and I cannot but admire their moderation in so daring an exercise of illegal power, and their patriotism in having so studiously prevented our enemies from conceiving they can derive any advantage from it, by declaring that if their fleets appear at sea they are ready to follow them.[52]

Underlying this acceptance, however, was the recognition that the seamen had expanded normal channels of protest, negotiating directly with the Admiralty and the government after the initial fruitless approach to their commander-in-chief, Howe.[53] Even more seriously, they had ousted 113 officers, directly challenging the authority of the navy.[54] Criticism of Howe for conceding this point was parried by Admiral Young, a member of the Board of Admiralty: 'The ministers were so anxious to get the fleet to sea, that they directed it to be done, rather than protract the settlement of the business.'[55] Additionally, Howe was acting as the special representative of the King as he had finally retired by this date. The fear expressed one hundred years later was, however, that 'The men had tasted the pleasure of defying authority, which is, of itself, corrupting'.[56]

As soon as the Plymouth ships were satisfied (on 6 June) that the Spithead demands had been met, Sir Richard King reported that 'the different ships Crews here have returned to their Duty', adding that he 'never knew less disturbance in the Towns of Plymouth, Dock, and Stonehouse, when an equal number of Ships were in Port'.[57] King also reported that 'the People who had been Delegates here requested I would permit them to send by this Post [a

---

50   Letter from Lieutenant P. Bover, 14 May 1797, *Gentleman's Magazine*, XX (July 1843), p. 33.

51   Ibid.

52   Lieutenant Philip Beaver, 17 April 1797, in Moorhouse, E. H., ed., *Letters of the English Seamen: 1587–1808* (London, 1910), p. 181.

53   Despite many unsigned petitions to the Admiralty in TNA, ADM1/5125 and the precedent for seamen to petition set in 1654. H. W. Hodges, E. A. Hughes, eds, *Select Naval Documents* (London, 1936), pp. 67–8.

54   TNA, ADM1/4172, May 1797. See J. Ehrman's discussion in *The Younger Pitt: The Consuming Struggle* (London, 1996), p. 23, n. 3.

55   Barrow, *Life of Earl Howe*, p. 339.

56   *Saturday Review*, 13 June 1891.

57   TNA, ADM1/812, King to Nepean, 6 June 1797.

letter] directed to the Captain of the Forecastle of the *Sandwich* at the Nore'.[58]
This letter wished

> to know your Grievances that makes you still dissatisfied, as we have had
> every Grievance settled here with us, and that we can further assure you,
> that the Grand Fleet is at Sea, and in greater Spirits than they ever were,
> and we, as your Brothers, expect that you will be satisfied with the same
> Terms we are.[59]

The methods of self-discipline and organisation practised at Spithead and
Plymouth provided a model of a successful trade dispute, capitalising on the
contemporary political and strategic vulnerability of Britain. The majority
of seamen in the Channel Fleet recognised that they had achieved all that was
possible at the time, given their innate loyalty, constantly articulated in their
public statements.[60]

On Monday 15 May, Portsmouth, Southsea and Gosport celebrated, with
crowded beaches. Delegates arrived at the Sally Port and marched to the governor's house for discussions. They then returned to the fleet with Lord and Lady
Howe, the Governor Sir William, and Lady Pitt, and officers to *Royal George*
at St Helen's, where Lord Howe read out the amended royal pardon. Three
cheers were given, mutinous symbols were removed, and the royal standard
flown. A tour of Sir Roger Curtis's ships followed. Howe returned to a '*feu
de joye*', from the North Gloucester, West Kent and South Devon militia, was
carried to the governor's house on the delegates' shoulders, amid celebrations
said to have been the largest ever witnessed in Portsmouth.[61]

The 'difference of opinion' seen by Fresselique in 1794 had manifested itself
at Spithead in 1797, but the amicable ending of the Spithead mutiny did not
mean an end to the discontent. *Pompée*'s mutiny, 2–4 June 1797, showed what
could have happened at Spithead and Plymouth (and mirrored what happened
at the Nore) if a minority had pushed forward demands which the Admiralty
were not prepared to concede.[62] At the end of May 1797 government agent
Aaron Graham, noting the 'melancholy appearance' of naval officers, suggested positively that they might 'recover their consequence' and aid reconciliation and restoration of discipline:

> There is one thing which the [men] have never much insisted upon but
> which if granted as a boon (in the end it will – and perhaps be claimed as

58   Ibid.
59   NMRN, 1988.500(295), Delegates on *Cambridge*, Hamoaze to Nore, 6 June 1797.
60   E.g. 'Address from the Seamen at Spithead to their Brethren at the Nore', 4 June 1797.
NMRN, 1988.500(294).
61   The largest previous celebrations were said to be those following 1 June 1794, described
in Barrow, *Life of Earl Howe*, pp. 235, 260; *The Times*, 17 May 1797.
62   TNA, ADM1/5339, *Pompée* court martial, evidence of Martin Welsh.

a right) would tend much to the purposes of a prompt reconciliation – it is more a reasonable Distribution of Prize Money.

This was by many of the ships brought forward and will no doubt on the return of the Channel fleet be made a question of.

To forestall demands for equal distribution of prize money he urged: 'let the Captains anticipate the design of the men by voluntarily soliciting His Majesty to take from them and give to the Ships Company – one of their Three Eighths'.[63] Gill deduced more pessimistically 'that the more violent party among the seamen merely feigned satisfaction with Lord Howe's proposals, and yielded because they saw that it was expedient to do so'. He concluded: 'Any hope that may have been entertained of further success must have been crushed by the failure of the Nore mutiny.'[64]

The Spithead and Plymouth mutinies, even when concluded, posed a most serious threat to naval discipline, and ultimately, to the strategic safety of the country. George III was 'sorry to find the spirit of mutiny in the fleet has extended to every quarter of the globe, which certainly renders the putting the sentences of court martial into execution', and he entirely 'coincide[d] with Earl Spencer that any relaxation of punishment would be highly detrimental to the discipline of the navy'.[65] Earl Spencer clearly saw 'that the consequences of what has passed must necessarily be highly prejudicial to the future discipline of the Navy'.[66] Early Admiralty judgement was

> that the Mutiny at the Nore originated in the concessions which had been made to the fleet at Spithead [and the leaders] took advantage of this impression, and not only pointed out new Demands to the Seamen, but invited them to ... concert what Demands they might chuse to make.[67]

Forced by the Channel Fleet to make concessions to the whole navy, the government and Admiralty would not risk further erosion of their authority, and therefore refused to negotiate with the mutineers at the Nore, Cadiz, or later outbreaks in the Channel Fleet. On 27 May Earl Spencer promised George III that the Board would not 'add to the concessions already made'.[68] At Sheerness Spencer met the mutineers and Parker, 'always the spokesman', on the 29th, but refused to discuss 'other articles which they had since brought forward'. The mutineers 'instantly went away, without saying a word more'.[69] George III urged Earl Spencer that 'vigour with temper can alone restore discipline in the fleet'; Spencer had already left Sheerness,

---

63   Aaron Graham, 'Hints' BL, Add. MS. 37,877, Windham Papers, XXXVI, fols 72–73v.

64   Gill, *Naval Mutinies*, pp. 84–5.

65   George III's views of the mutinies on *Tromp* and *Haughty*. George III to Spencer, 6 January 1798, 11 June 1798, in Corbett, *Spencer Papers*, II, pp. 173–4.

66   Spencer to St Vincent, 4 May 1797, in Tucker, *Memoirs of Earl St Vincent*, I, pp. 320.

67   TNA, ADM3/137, Report on Nore Mutiny, May 1797.

68   Spencer to George III, 27 May 1797, in Corbett, *Spencer Papers*, II, p. 136.

69   Spencer to Nepean, 29 May 1797, printed in Gill, *Naval Mutinies*, p. 380.

having failed in our attempt to restore order and obedience, though I hope
we have placed everything in a train more likely to lead to a permanant restoration of it than any compromise or accommodation could have done.[70]

Meanwhile, garrison commander Sir Charles Grey was prepared 'to take the
most vigorous means of defence that this situation will afford', the Order to
take up the buoys was made on 6 June, and Pitt suggested laying a chain and
boom across the River Thames between Tilbury and Gravesend to prevent
the ships at the Nore and Sheerness reaching those moored at Long Reach.[71]
Keith suggested sending fireships into the mutinous ships, 'fitted with Rosin,
Tar, Reeds'.[72] As direct action was limited by a shortage of boats and men, he
proposed a volunteer taskforce raised for a month from the revenue service,
East India Company, Thames watermen, and merchant seamen. With these
'we should be enabled with a mixture of what we now have to get a Good
force against the Insurgents'.[73] A Captain Dixon personally offered to rid 'the
country of so great a traitor as the delegate Parker', as his 'destruction …
might tend to restore the remainder to obedience', if Spencer could get him on
to *Sandwich*.[74] Spencer diplomatically rejected the offer.

As well as military actions, the full force of the establishment was brought
into force to isolate the mutineers. The Royal Proclamation, 31 May,
commanded

all Our loving Subjects whatsoever not to give any Aid, Comfort, Assistance
or Encouragement whatsoever to any Person or Persons concerned in any
such mutinous and treasonable Proceedings, as they will answer the same
at their Peril.[75]

On 7 June London merchants at the Royal Exchange resolved to raise sub-
scriptions for

detecting and bringing to public justice such lurking Traitors as may have
excited and fomented the present Mutiny at the Nore, and of affording
additional Encouragement to such well-disposed persons as may, by early
and vigorous exertions, contribute to its suppression.[76]

Finally, 'An Act for more effectually restraining Intercourse with the Crews
of certain of His Majesty's Ships, now in a State of Mutiny and Rebellion,
and for the more effective suppression of such Mutiny and Rebellion', warned

---

70 George III to Spencer, 30 May 1797, in Corbett, *Spencer Papers*, II, p. 144; Spencer to
Nepean, 29 May 1797, Gill, *Naval Mutinies*, p. 382.
71 Gill, *Naval Mutinies*, pp. 380–3; Pitt to Spencer, 7 June 1797, in Corbett, *Spencer
Papers*, II, pp. 149–50.
72 BL, Althorp Papers, G195, Keith to Spencer, 2 June 1797.
73 Ibid., 8 June 1797.
74 Dixon to Spencer, 9 June 1797, Corbett, *Spencer Papers*, II, pp. 151–2.
75 *London Gazette*, 3 June 1797.
76 NMRN, 1988.500 (297), 6 June 1797.

'all His Majesty's faithful Subjects to abstain from all Communication or Intercourse with all the crews of the said Ships'.[77] Lord Keith discussed the lack of unity on board the ships with Spencer: 'There is every reason to think that the Proclamations sent hence has [sic] never got farther than the <u>Delegates</u> but have been destroyed by them.'[78] They planned to divide the moderates from the delegates by sending on board 'by the Bumboat men' newspapers containing the Proclamation: 'The Newspapers we can send off without suspicion and do it every day.'[79] Admiral Duncan informed him that *Serapis* and *Standard* 'are extremely moderate saying they have no grievance and only want to be paid – a communication with those ships might induce them to run up to Gravesend'.[80] As the 'conversation in the disaffected Fleet is that they intend going to Cork or Belfast where they will be received with open Arms', and violence on board increased, Keith suggested 'an offer of pardon to such as would return to their duty, certain Delegates and ringleaders excepted, might merit consideration, and a large reward for seizing or surrendering any of the excepted'.[81] These suggestions were not taken up because ships were starting to leave the mutiny.

The penalties which Spithead delegates averted were paid by the Nore mutineers. Only because the Spithead mutineers were united, kept open channels of communication, remained true to their aims, and supported each other, did they escape the awful consequences enacted at the Nore and other isolated mutinies. Those who paid this price recognised their role as scapegoats and components of the disciplinary process, shown in this address from Thomas Preston and William Lee, *Royal Sovereign*, September 1797.

Shipmates and Brethren
    We who this morning are doomed to bid adieu to this World, think it our duty before we are launched into the Gulph of Eternity, fully to acknowledge to you, that we have received a fair Trial for the Crimes which we have committed, and have merited the Punishment which we are about to suffer. – But as dying Men, and Christians, we now most earnestly entreat you, to beware of that Rock on which we have foundered. We are now fully convinced of the necessity of obeying those, who are set in Authority over us, and of living content in the situation in Life, in which it has pleased God to place us. Having received assurances, as our last request, that those who have been so unfortunate as to have been connected with us in our late Crimes, will not for the same be brought to Punishment; we now look forward with Pleasure to the moment of our Fate, in a full and joyfull Expectation of partaking in those Joys, which in Heaven are prepared for Penitent Sinners.[82]

77 *London Gazette Extraordinary*, 7 June 1797. The Acts passed on 6 June 1797 against the mutineers were 37 Geo. III c.70 and c.71. Ehrman, *The Younger Pitt: The Consuming Struggle*, p. 29, fn. 1.
78 BL, Althorp Papers, G195, Keith to Spencer, 3 June 1797.
79 Ibid., 3 June 1797, 6 June 1797.
80 Ibid., 6 June 1797.
81 Ibid., 5, 6, 7 June 1797.
82 NMRN, 1993.453(2), 4 September 1797. See the discussion in the secondary sources, cited in note 3 above.

The abuses which led to the mutiny, and their political context, inspired Herman Melville in 1891 to celebrate the justice of the seamen's cause, represented by the death of Billy Budd as the apotheosis of innocence.[83]

> Now, as elsewhere hinted, it was something caught from the Revolutionary Spirit that at Spithead emboldened the man-of-war's men to rise against real abuses, long-standing ones, and afterwards at the Nore to make inordinate and aggressive demands – successful resistance to which was confirmed only when the ringleaders were hung for an admonitory spectacle to the anchored fleet.[84]

But the horror felt by the Admiralty reverberated into the twentieth century, when the Invergordon mutineers repeated many of the actions of the Spithead mutineers.[85] Colonel Field's drawing of a man hanging from the yardarm was an image of dread for naval officers one hundred years later, but the only deaths were among the mutineers.

The Nore mutiny failed to achieve its extended aims because the government and Admiralty had learnt the lessons from Spithead, which had disseminated its grievances widely and gained public approval. At the Nore they prevented the seamen from appealing to public opinion.[86] They withheld their mail, divided them and starved them out.[87] Individual outbreaks in the Channel Fleet, the Mediterranean Fleet at Cadiz, in the West Indies and South Africa failed because individual mutinies succumbed invariably to the Royal Navy's traditional retribution.[88] Evan Nepean, warning Admiral St Vincent that some of the ships involved in the planning of the Spithead mutiny were joining his fleet at Cadiz, urged him to 'take the most vigorous and effectual measures for counteracting any attempt ... to excite a spirit of mutiny'.[89] St Vincent vigorously countered mutinies on no less than nineteen ships during 1797 and 1798.[90] He directed a 'prompt execution' on *Marlborough*, 'to stop the contagion of so large an importation of sedition and mutiny at one time' and gave orders to fire into her if her crew resisted the hanging.[91] The sentence on the mutineers of *St George*

---

83 H. Melville, *Billy Budd, Sailor* (London, 1995), p. 80.

84 Ibid., pp. 7–8.

85 Was it a consequence of Invergordon that TNA, ADM178/133, 'Mutiny in the Royal Navy', I, was written in 1933 to prepare officers against mutiny (p. 3), and that distribution of Volume II was delayed until after World War II?

86 Gill, *Naval Mutinies*, pp. 200–1.

87 BL, Althorp Papers, G195, Keith to Spencer, 2 June 1797; W. Marsden to Nepean, 29 May 1797, Spencer to Nepean, 29 May 1797; Gill, *Naval Mutinies*, pp. 214, 220–1, 381, 383.

88 Gill, *Naval Mutinies*, pp. 252–3; W. James, *Old Oak* (London, 1950), pp. 113–29; Tucker, *Memoirs of Earl St Vincent*, I, pp. 300–25; E. P. Brenton, *Life and Correspondence of John Earl of St Vincent*, I (London, 1838), chapter XIII; J. K. Laughton, ed., 'Letters of William Cathcart', *Naval Miscellany*, I (London, 1901), p. 268.

89 Nepean to St Vincent, 2 May 1797, in Tucker, *Memoirs of Earl St Vincent*, I, p. 318.

90 J. S. Tucker, ed., *Memoirs of Earl St Vincent*, I (London, 1844), pp. 300–43; Brenton, *Life and Correspondence of John Earl St Vincent*, I, chapter XIII; James, *Old Oak*, pp. 113–29.

91 St Vincent to Nepean, 30 May 1797, in Tucker, *Memoirs of Earl St Vincent*, I, pp. 337, 306.

was controversially carried out the day after their court martial, a Sunday, but approved by Nelson: 'We know not what might have been hatched by a Sunday's grog; now your discipline is safe.'[92] St Vincent's remedy for restoring discipline was by 'carrying on the most active desultory war against the port and town of Cadiz, to divert the animal from these damnable doctrines which letters from England have produced.'[93] From 1800, as commander-in-chief, he applied the same remedy to the Channel Fleet, by ordering closer blockades of Brest so that the men were at sea longer, fully occupied and less able to concoct mutiny.[94]

At the Crown and Anchor in London on 18 May 1797 the toast raised by the Society for Constitutional Information was 'The Wooden Walls of Great Britain and when the Country gives may it forgive'.[95] This reflected the feelings of reformers, but not the King:

> The offence of which Richard Parker has been convicted is of so heinous and dangerous a nature that I can scarcely suppose there can be any legal objection, after confirming the sentence for his being hanged, to order his body to be hung in chains on the most conspicuous land in sight of the ships at the Nore. Earl Spencer has therefore very properly directed the legality of hanging the body in chains to be enquired into, and if it can be done is to order it to be effected.
> George R.[96]

Pasley, writing on the same day, also wished Parker to be 'hung in chains in some conspicuous place as an example.' However, the Board of Admiralty feared this would provoke a fresh uprising.[97]

Parker's wife Ann, who was not allowed to visit him, watched from a small boat before he was hanged from *Sandwich*'s yardarm on the morning of 30 June.[98] Mosse reported he died 'decent & steady'.[99] He was immediately interred in the 'new burying ground' at Sheerness. Ann was not permitted to remove his body, to bury him 'like a gentleman, as he had been bred'.[100] She

92 Nelson to Sir Robert Calder, 9 July 1797, in Tucker, *Memoirs of Earl St Vincent*, I, pp. 327, 328.
93 St Vincent to Nepean, 4 May 1797, in Tucker, *Memoirs of Earl St Vincent*, I, p. 325; James, *Old Oak*, p. 154.
94 James, *Old Oak*, p. 146.
95 *Belfast News Letter*, 29 May 1797. Six hundred and thirty-two reformers dined at the Crown and Anchor on 14 July 1790 to celebrate the first anniversary of the Fall of the Bastille. The Revolution Society held its annual dinner there on 4 November 1791, when Dr Price's toast was 'The Parliament of Britain; May it become a National Assembly'. Throughout the 1790s it was the meeting place of the Society for Constitutional Information, Wharam, *Treason Trials*, pp. 14, 17–8, 26, 27, 42.
96 George III to Spencer, 27 June 1797, in Corbett, *Spencer Papers*, II, pp. 159–60.
97 Gill, *Naval Mutinies*, p. 248.
98 BL, G14560, Richard Parker, 'An Impartial and Authentic Account of the Life of Richard Parker', p. 19.
99 TNA, ADM1/728.
100 BL, Parker, 'Impartial Account', p. 20; P. Burke, *Celebrated Naval and Military Trials* (London, 1866), pp. 258–60.

secretly retrieved his coffin, however, and took it to Rochester, then to the Hoop and Horseshoe, Little Tower Hill, London. Crowds gathered to see him and his head and shoulders were sketched. Magistrates feared riots and ordered his burial in St Mary Matfelon's vault, Whitechapel, on 4 July.[101]

Richard Parker was truly a scapegoat, for he was executed to expiate the establishment's impotence at Spithead. The restoration of discipline relied upon the seamen not only accepting 'military subordination and legal obedience' but also respecting the justice of the rules imposed upon them.[102] The Admiralty was unable to exact retribution at Spithead because of the unanimity and self-discipline of the seamen. Concessions were made to the seamen to correct an imbalance of discipline caused by the 'disobedience of the Officers'.[103] As Spencer recognised: 'We have had a very severe lesson in this business, and I trust all the officers in the Fleet will feel the Effect of it'.[104] Officially Parker was executed in retribution for actions carried out in his name at the Nore. In reality he was ritually sacrificed on a day of atonement for 'the unanimity of the nation at large – an unanimity not in support of administration, but in support of the constitution itself, and of all those laws by which it was guarded'.[105]

101 BL, Parker, 'Impartial Account', pp. 20–2.
102 See TNA, ADM1/107, February–March 1797, where numerous requests made by officers for leave were granted; Adam Duncan and Robert Wilson on officers' discipline quoted in Lavery, *Nelson's Navy*, p. 217; Gill, *Naval Mutinies*, pp. 278–9; Woodes Rogers, *A Cruising Voyage Round the World* (London, 1928), p. 33; Bridport's and St Vincent's contrasting views of discipline: James, *Old Oak. The Life of John Jervis*, p. 155.
103 TNA, ADM1/5125, Delegates to Howe, 13 May 1797.
104 BL, Althorp Papers, G191, Spencer to the Board of Admiralty, 6 May 1797.
105 E. Rhys, ed., *Orations on the French War by William Pitt* (London, n.d.), p. 229.

Discipline, Desertion and Death:
HMS *Trent*, 1796–1803

Nick Slope

Perhaps the most prevalent public image of the Royal Navy of the French Wars is of the shipboard flogging of sailors.[1] Naval discipline and in particular the practice of flogging is subject to much historical controversy. Views on the subject of flogging range from the use of the lash as a brutal and brutalising imposition of authority over oppressed and impressed sailors to flogging as a minor imposition on men who would prefer to receive instant retribution for their offences rather than suffer trial and incarceration at some future date.[2]

Works by J. D. Byrn Jr, *Crime and Punishment in the Royal Navy* and *Naval Court Martials 1793–1815*, look at Royal Navy discipline in the social context of the times, as well as applying a systematic approach to the subject.[3] Byrn's thesis is that naval discipline conformed in most respects to how law and order was conducted on land in contemporary society:

> Simply stated, the methods used to maintain harmony in the king's fleet were similar to those of the eighteenth-century English system of criminal justice … In short, the precepts of the unreformed system of criminal justice were applied at sea wherever feasible.[4]

In his analysis Byrn examined all the extant court-martial records for the period and station in question, as well as other contemporary naval records including ship's muster books. This chapter attempts to take Byrn's work forward by concentrating on how discipline was used to manage a ship's company on a day-to-day basis.

In order to gain valid and reliable quantitative data that could be statistically analysed in the field of Royal Navy social history, a systematic study of a naval frigate of the French war period has been undertaken utilising information technology. The overall aim of this study has been to adopt a 'case study' approach to naval history in the hope that findings from the case can indicate

---

1   The period of the Revolutionary and Napoleonic Wars, 1793–1815.
2   J. Masefield, *Sea Life in Nelson's Time* (3rd edn, London, 1971), pp. 71–6 and D. Pope, *Life in Nelson's Navy* (London, 1981), pp. 211–230.
3   J. D. Byrn, *Crime and Punishment in the Royal Navy: Discipline on the Leeward Islands Station 1784–1812* (Aldershot, 1989) and *Naval Courts Martial 1793–1815* (London, 2009).
4   Byrn, *Crime and Punishment*, p. 5.

further areas of study, test how effectively information technology can be applied to the social history of the Royal Navy and to provide quantitative as well as qualitative social information concerning the lower deck of the Royal Navy in the French wars.

HMS *Trent* was a 36-gun fir-built frigate commissioned in 1796 that saw active service until 1803.[5] The ship had a fixed Admiralty complement of 264 'men and boys' but the realities of wartime meant that it normally averaged around 247.[6] *Trent* commenced her commission as part of Duncan's North Sea Fleet, served twice in the West Indies, and was, on a number of occasions, part of the Channel Fleet. In 1803 she became a hospital ship, a receiving ship in 1818 and was finally broken up in 1823. The information below relates only to *Trent*'s active service: 1796–1803, a period of just over seven years.[7]

During *Trent*'s service as part of the North Sea Fleet commanded by Admiral Duncan she became involved in the Nore mutiny. On 22 May 1797 the crew mutinied and refused to up anchor and leave their moorings.[8] Admiral Duncan had his flagship *Venerable* taken alongside, the gunports opened and the guns run out. *Trent*'s crew then wisely unmoored. News then reached Duncan that the enemy Dutch fleet was preparing to sail. However, contrary winds prevented Duncan from setting sail with the fleet until 29 May. As he sailed out of the Thames estuary, one by one his ships mutinied and turned back to join the main mutiny at the Nore or to return to their moorings at Yarmouth. By the time that Duncan reached the mouth of the Texel he had with him only two line-of-battle ships (*Venerable* and *Adamant*), two frigates (*Trent* and *Circe*) and some unrated vessels. In order to convince the Dutch that he had his whole fleet with him, Duncan ordered *Trent* and *Circe* to patrol the Texel and send out signals to a non-existent British fleet. The ruse proved successful and the Dutch fleet remained in harbour.[9] *Trent* stayed at sea and took no further part in the Nore mutinies.

Data taken from the muster books and captain's log books of *Trent*'s period of active service were put on to a Microsoft Access database.[10] The records of over eleven hundred individual crew members, marines, volunteers and boys constituting around twenty thousand data entries were input. The tables set up in the database can now be interrogated in order to produce, within certain

---

5   D. Lyon, *The Sailing Navy List: All the Ships of the Royal Navy – Built, Purchased and Captured, 1688–1855* (London 1993), p. 123 and R. Winfield, *British Warships in the Age of Sail: 1714–1792, Design, Construction, Careers and Fates* (Barnsley, 2007), p. 148.

6   N. Slope, 'Serving in Nelson's Navy: A Social History of Three Amazon Class Frigates Utilising Database Technology, 1795–1811' (Ph.D. thesis, Thames Valley University, 2006), p. 62. A. G. Jamieson refers to N. Slope's MA methodology and uses a similar process in 'Tyranny of the Lash? Punishment in the Royal Navy during the American War, 1776–1783', *The Northern Mariner/Le Marin du nord*, IX: 1 (January 1999), pp. 53–66.

7   Slope, 'Serving in Nelson's Navy', pp. 41–4.

8   TNA, ADM3/137.

9   G. E. Manwaring and B. Dobrée, *The Floating Republic* (London, 1935), pp. 171–9.

10   All the muster books are located at TNA: ADM36/13253; ADM36/15226; ADM36/15227; ADM36/15228; ADM36/15229; ADM36/15230. All the captain's logs are located at TNA: ADM51/1167; ADM51/4510; ADM51/1305; ADM51/1429; ADM51/1352; ADM51/1397; ADM51/1439.

parameters, statistically valid and reliable evidence concerning social aspects of *Trent*'s crew.[11]

Ships' captains had a real problem over how they kept discipline on board a Royal Navy ship of the period. Sailors were not drilled into obedience like their army counterparts. A sailor's role was much more that of an artisan than a fighter. Clearly sailors were called upon to fight, but fighting was very rare. The records of *Trent* reveal that of the 952 seamen that served on her during her seven-year commission, eighty-one (9 per cent) were recorded as having been 'discharged dead' from her muster books. Of these eighty-one, only six seamen were recorded as having been killed by enemy action as opposed to, for instance, accidental drowning that accounted for seven seamen's deaths. Therefore a sailor serving on board *Trent* had around a 0.6 per cent chance of being killed by the enemy. Unlike soldiers, a seaman's profession was in demand outside the military sphere and how easy it was to desert a king's ship is all too evident from *Trent*'s muster books, which record a desertion rate of 27 per cent of seamen. Unlike soldiers and marines, sailors were not drilled or regimented except in the most general of ways. For example, although the captain's logs regularly record the 'exercising of the great guns' (approximately once every two weeks) there is only one mention of practice live firing in the entire seven-year period of *Trent*'s commission.[12] Furthermore Royal Navy ships of the period had a much lower ratio of commissioned officers to men than the Army. For example, a typical British infantry battalion that consisted of about eight hundred men would have around thirty-six commissioned officers, a ratio of around twenty-two to one.[13] A first rate ship of the line would carry a similar number of men but with just nine commissioned officers, a ratio of around eighty-nine to one.[14]

Compared with the merchant marine, Royal Navy ships carried large crews. Rodger states in *The Wooden World* that merchant crews varied from one sailor per ten ship tons to one per twenty ship tons, depending on trade and station.[15] In comparison, *Trent* carried one man per 3.7 tons. Larger ships carried even more men per ton: in *Victory*'s case, for example, it was one man per 2.5 tons.[16] Even allowing for specialists such as marines that would not normally be carried by merchant ships, the difference is significant. The extra men on board Royal Navy ships were required for fighting the ship: firing the great guns and carronades, small arms, boarding and boat work. But, as noted above, the amount of fighting that a ship's crew would normally be called on to undertake was very small indeed. Therefore for the greater part of a ship's commission, compared

---

11   For a discussion on the use of databases in historical research see: C. Harvey and J. Press, *Databases in Historical Research: Theory, Methods and Applications* (London, 1996), pp. 5–9.

12   TNA, ADM51/1167, 25 April 1797: 'fired 6 – 18pdrs and 6 – 32pdrs shotted at a mark'.

13   S. Reid, *Redcoat Officer 1740–1815* (London, 2002), p. 16.

14   B. Lavery, *Nelson's Navy: The Ships, Men and Organisation 1793–1815* (London, 1989), p. 9.

15   N. A. M. Rodger, *The Wooden World: An Anatomy of the Georgian Navy* (Glasgow, 1986), pp. 40–1.

16   Lyon, *The Sailing Navy List*, p. 62: 2,162 tons with a crew of 850.

to the merchant marine, a king's ship would have a significant number of off-duty hands. If the overcrowded conditions of the lower deck are added to a large number of off-duty men that are supplied with considerable daily amounts of alcohol the potential for disciplinary problems are clear. It is little wonder that men were regularly holystoning the decks and painting the ship in order, no doubt to give them something to do.

Therefore we have a situation in which large numbers of men, concentrated together, plied with alcohol and with time on their hands, had to be managed by few commissioned officers. One of the major management tools available to ships' officers was punishment. Punishment in the Royal Navy was regulated by the amended Articles of War of 1749.[17] The Articles set down contain thirty-six ordinances. Byrn divides the ordinances into four broad categories of offence against: religion and morality, King and government, individual rights and finally purely naval infractions.[18] That the Articles were widely regarded as the naval code of law can be demonstrated by the fact that they were regularly read out by ships' captains to ships' crews and this was then recorded in the captain's log. Some of the thirty-six ordinances listed mandatory penalties whilst the others allowed discretionary sentences to be passed. However, in the case of floggings Admiralty instructions required that captains should not administer more than twelve lashes per man without recourse to a court martial and that such floggings should be recorded.[19] These instructions gave captains real problems. If a captain believed that a sailor or marine deserved more than the statutory twelve lashes or that the Articles invoked in a particular case a mandatory sentence then he was obliged to apply for a court martial. In order to avoid the trouble of convening a court martial 'an unwieldy and unpredictable instrument', the instruction to limit floggings to twelve lashes was widely ignored.[20] Some captains seem to have paid lip service to Admiralty instructions by charging men with more than one offence in order to 'legitimise' more than twelve lashes. For example marine private John Hay of *Trent* was given twenty-four lashes on 29 October 1796 for 'stabbing his messmate and contempt'.[21]

One of the major difficulties when looking at discipline in the Royal Navy of the French War period is the nature of the evidence. Captains did not always fill in their log books consistently. For example they might leave out the name of the offender, number of lashes and/or offence and it is likely that some captains did not record all the floggings that had actually taken place. It was unusual for captains to record punishments other than floggings and yet it is known that casual violence against the men was commonplace, such as the practice of 'starting' the men with a rope's end or rattan cane.[22] Other less formalised punishments were rarely recorded.

17   Admiralty, *The Articles of War of 1749 as amended by 19 Geo.III c.17*. For a full set of the Articles see Byrn, *Crime and Punishment*, Appendix A, pp. 203–10.
18   Byrn, *Crime and Punishment*, p. 12.
19   Admiralty, *Admiralty, Regulations and Instructions Relating to His Majesty's Service at Sea* (1787).
20   Rodger, *The Wooden World*, p. 222.
21   TNA, ADM51/1167.
22   Lavery, *Nelson's Navy*, pp. 216–20.

The court martial of Captain Sir Edward Hamilton can demonstrate this.[23] Hamilton was captain of *Trent* from 1 November 1800 to 21 January 1802 and during this period inflicted a total of twenty-nine recorded floggings on the crew. At Hamilton's subsequent court martial for 'gross cruelty' it transpired that he had had the gunner and a gun crew lashed to the rigging in inclement weather as a punishment but this is not recorded in the *Trent*'s log book. It is interesting to note that Hamilton's use of the lash was not considered by either the prosecution or defence as evidence worth bringing before the court. In a personal memoir Admiral G. V. Jackson, who served as a midshipman under Hamilton on board the *Trent*, records that 'as each day passed, so did I conceive new terrors of this man. A more uncompromising disciplinarian did not exist, or one less scrupulous in exacting the due fulfilment of his orders, whatever they were ... the "cat" was incessantly at work' and that although the ship was 'in excellent order' this was 'at no small sacrifice of humanity'.[24]

Therefore any study of discipline as a shipboard management tool must be largely confined to what individual captains have chosen to record in their log books and this must be accepted as a limited and incomplete picture. Despite the caveats above, systematic study of ships' records can give some insight into how discipline affected shipboard life and how it was viewed by officers and men. The data given below is the result of interrogating the tables set up in the *Trent* database.

Table 14.1 below shows the basic data taken from the various captains' logs and muster books of *Trent* and gives an overall view of the number of recorded floggings of seamen and marines. A total of 952 seamen (the category of 'Volunteers and Boys' is not included in this number) and 158 marines served during *Trent*'s commission of just over seven years (2575 days). During this period there were a total of 219 recorded floggings: 160 seamen and 59 marines flogged. However, of the 219 recorded floggings, the number of lashes awarded for each flogging were only recorded in 168 cases. This leaves fifty-one floggings (thirty-seven seamen and fourteen marines) in which the number of lashes inflicted were not recorded. By dividing the total number of lashes inflicted (3177) by the number of floggings where the lashes were recorded (168), gives us an average number of lashes inflicted per flogging of nineteen. The validity of this calculation can be demonstrated by the fact that both seaman and marine averages, when calculated separately, give us the same average figure of nineteen lashes per flogging. By multiplying the number of floggings without recorded lashes (fifty-one) by the calculated average of 19 lashes we end up with a figure of 219 recorded floggings against a notional total of 4,146 lashes. When the number of floggings and the number of lashes inflicted are set against the time period of *Trent*'s commission we come up with an average of 1.6 lashes per day inflicted with a flogging occurring on average every twelve days. Clearly these are notional figures but it does allow us to set up benchmarks by which we can judge individual ship's captains.

23   TNA, ADM1/5360.
24   G. V. Jackson, *The Perilous Adventures of a Naval Officer 1801–1812* (London, 1927), pp. 4–12.

Table 14.1 Flogging Statistics on HMS *Trent*, 1796–1803

	Seamen	Marines	Total
Served	952 (86%)	158 (14%)	1110 (100%)
Recorded floggings	160 (73%)	59 (27%)	219 (100%)
Recorded lashes	2327 (73%)	850 (27%)	3177 (100%)
Floggings (lashes not recorded)	37	14	51
Average no. lashes per flogging	19	19	19
Multiplied by average lashes	703	266	969
Recorded lashes	2327	850	3177
Total	3030	1116	4146

Length of Trent's commission	2575 days (7 years)
Total lashes given	4146
Number of days per flogging	12
Average lashes per day	1.6

Perhaps the most interesting statistic to emerge from the above table is that although the marines only make up 14 per cent of the ship's complement they received 27 per cent of the recorded punishments. Perhaps this is due to the marines' role as 'ship's policemen'. It may have been thought that as a disciplinary force themselves, they had to suffer a tougher disciplinary regime in consequence. It is of course possible that the marines were a rowdier bunch than the seamen and brought a sterner regime on themselves as a consequence. Alternatively it may well be that the sample of marines is too small to be able to draw any firm conclusions at present.

Table 14.2 Recorded Offences on HMS *Trent*, 1796–1803

Offence	Number	Lashes per offence	Article ordinance no.
Absent without leave	1	36	16
Attempting to desert	8	19	16
Desertion	33	15	16
Fighting	11	14	23
Quarrelling	11	15	23
Mutinous behaviour	3	19	19
Insolence/contempt	15	18	19
Neglect of duty	72	16	36
Negligence	4	18	36
Uncleanliness	5	19	2
Drunkenness	46	17	2
Theft	12	19	30
Other/unspecified	15	19	

Table 14.2 attempts to demonstrate what was perceived as constituting an 'offence', how that offence related to the Royal Naval legal code; the Articles of War and how severely punished. The table has been constructed from log discipline entries for both seamen and marines that specified both an offence and the number of lashes awarded. Added to the table is the Articles of War Ordinance number that would apply to the offence recorded, as discussed above. Where a man is given more than one reason for a flogging the number of lashes awarded has been divided by the number of offences recorded. This results in a very crude and rather subjective measure of rating 'offences' but does give some broad indications of what was considered unacceptable behaviour, how that behaviour related to the Articles of War and how severely an offence was treated.

The most 'popular' offence appears to be 'neglect of duty' which is almost certainly a catchall expression for a number of perceived minor offences. However 'neglect of duty' also carries an apparently low level of punishment compared to other offences. 'Neglect of duty' is often associated with other offences in the log book such as 'insolence/contempt' and 'drunkenness' and may well be a device that a captain would use to legitimise an increase in punishment over and above the 'legal' level of twelve lashes; particularly when those offences are from different ordinances. Ordinance 36, which applies to 'neglect of duty', must have been very useful to captains and is worth quoting in full:

> 36. All other crimes not capital committed by any person or persons in the fleet, which are not mentioned in this act, or for which no punishment is hereby directed to be inflicted, shall be punished according to the laws and customs in such cases used at sea.

This ordinance gave a captain virtual *carte blanche* to punish a ship's crew as he saw fit. The ordinance does not specify what the 'laws and customs' of the sea are. It would be a brave seamen indeed who would ask for a court martial of a ship's captain for ordering a punishment that he considered was not a law or custom of the sea. It is clear from the above table that captains made full use of this open-ended ordinance and that ordinance 36 of the Articles of War enabled captains to have seamen flogged almost at will.

Being absent without leave attracts the heaviest punishment but it is difficult to draw any conclusions given the smallness of the sample. Surprisingly 'desertion' attracts a comparatively low level of punishment and yet in the Articles of War desertion (Ordinance 16) attracts a death penalty 'or such other punishment as the circumstances of the offence shall deserve'. One of *Trent*'s marines, Private William Conner, was court-martialled and sentenced to death on 28 February 1797 for desertion.[25] Conner deserted 'from duty' which appears to have been treated much more severely than if not. However, the Articles of War do not address the issue of on or off duty. The Articles do specify in ordinances 34 and 35 that offences by persons 'belonging to any of His Majesty's ships' committed 'on shore' whilst on 'active service' should be covered by the Articles.

Fighting and quarrelling are perhaps less common offences than would be

---

25   TNA, ADM1/5338.

expected given the conditions of life at sea in one of His Majesty's vessels, as discussed above. It is interesting to note that these offences do not appear to attract a heavy punishment. Likewise, 'mutinous behaviour' does not seem to attract particularly heavy punishment given the modern understanding of the word and must surely be of a minor nature to rate with 'insolence' and 'contempt'. It is unclear what exactly is meant by 'uncleanliness'; it may refer to general uncleanliness or is perhaps a euphemism for urinating or defecation in an improper place. Drunkenness is a fairly common offence, which is hardly surprising given the amounts of alcohol distributed to the crew. According to Admiralty *Regulations and Instructions* each crewman was entitled to either a gallon of beer, a pint of wine or half a pint of spirits per day.[26] Theft was considered a particularly odious offence by all the crew and offenders were flogged with a nastier version of the standard 'cat-of-nine-tails'.[27]

Table 14.3 looks at the relationship between the recorded floggings of seamen (marines are not included in this table as the size of the sample is very small) and those discharged dead.

Table 14.3 Discipline and Death on HMS *Trent*, 1796–1803 (Seamen only)

	Number of seamen	Percentage of total seamen	Percentage of flogged seamen
Discharged dead	81	9	-
Flogged	95	10	100
Flogged, later discharged dead	15	2	16
Served	952	100	-

On the face of it, the above table shows that a flogged man was significantly more likely to be discharged dead than a man who had not been flogged. All but one of those that had been flogged died of sickness, the other man, Samuel Finch, rated carpenter's crew, was reported 'drowned at Port Royal Jamaica'.[28] Closer inspection of the ship's muster and log books reveals that of the fifteen men who had been flogged and subsequently died, only two had died within three months of their flogging and another within six months and so it would seem that in the majority of cases we can assume that there is no direct relationship between death and flogging.

Table 14.4 compares the total numbers of seamen and marines that were recorded as having been 'Discharged Sick' as against the number of seamen and marines that were subjected to a flogging and were then subsequently discharged sick. Contemporary descriptions of floggings and modern perceptions of corporal punishment would lead us to believe that such physical punishment would produce an adverse health effect on the recipient.[29] Table 14.4 seeks to demonstrate whether that opinion can be supported by the evidence.

---

26 *Regulations and Instructions*, p. 283.
27 Lavery, *Nelson's Navy*, p. 218.
28 TNA, ADM36/15230; ADM51/1439.
29 Lavery, *Nelson's Navy*, p. 218.

Table 14.4 Discipline and Sickness on HMS *Trent*, 1796–1803

	Seamen	Marines	Total
Discharged sick	180 (19%)	50 (32%)	230 (21%)
Flogged	95 (75%)	32 (25%)	127 (100%)
Flogged, later discharged sick	19 (20%)	9 (28%)	28 (22%)
Served	952 (86%)	158 (14%)	1110 (100%)

The evidence shows that a 'normal' flogging, as opposed to a 'flogging round the Fleet' that could involve up to seven hundred lashes and could only be awarded by a court martial, did not materially affect a seaman's or marine's chance of being discharged sick from the ship. This would seem to indicate that flogging did not have an adverse long-term effect on a crewman's health.

Table 14.5 compares the number of seamen who were recorded as having deserted from the ship as against those seamen who had been flogged and then subsequently deserted. Marines are not included in this sample as the number of desertions were so low (three in total) that statistically this would not be valid.

Table 14.5 Discipline and Desertion on HMS *Trent*, 1796–1803 (Seamen only)

	Number of seamen	Percentage of total seamen	Percentage of flogged seamen
Deserted	253	27	-
Flogged	95	10	100
Flogged and deserted	17	2	18
Served	952	100	-

It would appear from Table 14.5 that flogging a seaman would not encourage him to desert. It is possible that the deterrent effect of flogging, much advocated by contemporary authority, worked better on those that had been flogged rather than on those who had not. Alternatively it is possible that shipboard flogging was accepted as a normal part of shipboard life and as such did not really enter the equation of whether a seaman decided to desert or not. It was the case that a seaman deserting his ship would be more likely to do so shortly after joining his ship and would therefore have less time on board in which to be flogged. As an example, of the 253 seaman that were recorded as having 'Run' the ship, 119 (47 per cent) deserted before they had completed six months' service on board *Trent*.

Table 14.6 compares the recorded nationality of *Trent*'s seamen against the flogging record. Marines are not included as their nationality was not normally recorded on the muster book. Seamen listed as 'Foreign' were those seamen who were listed as non-British. Those listed as 'unrecorded' are either warrant or commissioned officers whose origins were not normally recorded or crewmen whose place of origin was indecipherable.

It would appear from Table 14.6 that nationality was not a determining factor in whether a seaman was flogged or not. The statistics are slightly imbalanced in that a large number of the men whose nationality was unrecorded were commissioned or warrant officers who would not have been subjected to shipboard flogging. This imbalance would account for the marginally higher percentage chance of being flogged for other groups.

Table 14.6 Discipline and Nationality on HMS *Trent*, 1796–1803 (Seamen only)

Nationality	Served (number/percentage of total crew)	Flogged (recorded) (number/ percentage of men flogged)
English	390 (41%)	46 (48%)
Irish	202 (21%)	25 (26%)
Scottish	139 (15%)	11 (13%)
Foreign	75 (8%)	7 (7%)
Welsh	25 (3%)	3 (3%)
Unrecorded	121 (13%)	3 (3%)
Total crew	952 (100%)	95 (100%)

Table 14.7 lists the recorded method of the recruitment of seamen set against the flogging record. In the table below 'Turned Over' refers to those men who have come from another ship. 'Returned Sick' refers to those seamen who have been discharged sick from *Trent* and who have returned to the ship on their recovery. 'Turned Over (returned sick)' refers to those seamen who have come from other ships via sick quarters. 'Boys' refers to those originally entered as 'Volunteers and Boys' but who were subsequently, on gaining the requisite age, put onto the crew muster record. Marines are not included in this table as their method of recruitment is not recorded in the muster books.

Table 14.7 Discipline and Recruitment on HMS *Trent*, 1796–1803 (Seamen only)

Recruitment	Served (number/ percentage of total crew)	Flogged (number/ percentage of men flogged)
Turned over	308 (32%)	32 (33%)
Volunteer	185 (19%)	21 (22%)
Turned over (returned sick)	113 (12%)	7 (7%)
Pressed	109 (11%)	18 (19%)
Returned sick	61 (6%)	6 (6%)
Quota Men	46 (5%)	2 (2%)
Boys	24 (3%)	2 (2%)
Others (officers/unrecorded etc.)	85 (9%)	7 (7%)
Total crew	952 (100%)	95 (100%)

For most seamen it would appear that the method of recruitment does not appear to be a determining factor in whether a man was flogged or not. In most cases, where there appears a significant variance between recruitment and the incidence of flogging the sample is quite small and it is therefore difficult to draw conclusions. However what is noteworthy is that those seamen recorded as 'Pressed' do seem to have a higher chance of being flogged. There is a major difficulty in the interpretation of those seamen recorded as having been 'Pressed' and those recorded as having 'Volunteered'. It is clear from the records that some pressed men were subsequently entered as having volunteered. It is probable that some pressed seamen were offered the opportunity to 'volunteer' and to then receive the five-pound bounty that volunteers were entitled to.[30] This can be demonstrated from *Trent*'s records. On 19 August 1796 the captain's log records that 'boats employed impressing men from the convoy, Recd [*sic*] 13 impressed men'.[31] However cross-referencing the muster book for the same period reveals that on the 19 August 1796 thirteen men were recorded as having 'Appeared' on board: seven men were entered as 'Pressed' and six men were entered as 'Volunteers' and as having been awarded the bounty due to volunteers.[32] It is interesting to note that of the seven 'Pressed' men, five were later discharged by orders of the port admiral.

The other statistic worthy of note is the low incident of the flogging of 'Quota men'. Only two of the forty-six Quota men that served were flogged. Of the two Quota men flogged, both were flogged only once, James Stewart receiving nine lashes for theft on 12 November 1798 and David Benny receiving twenty-four lashes on 4 April 1799 for 'disobedience and drunkenness'.[33] In both cases the men had been serving on board the *Trent* for some considerable time before the floggings took place, Stewart for nearly twenty-one months and Benny for two years and by that time Benny had been promoted to ship's corporal.[34]

Quota men were men recruited by local county and town authorities in order to meet the Quota Acts passed by Parliament in 1795.[35] The Quota Acts were an attempt by William Pitt's government to address the Royal Navy's manpower needs by forcing local government to provide a set 'quota' of men for sea service. There is no doubt that the Quota Acts resulted in making large numbers of men available for the Royal Navy (approximately ten thousand men from the county quota and twenty thousand from the seaport quota).[36] However, from a qualitative perspective we get a different reaction. It is clear that Quota men were generally unpopular with naval officers, some going so far as to blame them directly for the 1797 mutinies and this negative view has been followed by some historians. Admiral Collingwood claimed that they were in part responsible for the general mutinies of 1797.[37] The Quota men have been accused of having Jacobin sympathies and being the sweepings of the gaol and the gutter and 'outcasts from

30 Lavery, *Nelson's Navy*, p. 124.
31 TNA, ADM51/1167.
32 TNA, ADM36/13253.
33 TNA, ADM36/15226 and ADM36/15227.
34 A ship's corporal's main duty was to instruct the crew in the use of small arms. W. H. Smyth, *The Sailor's Word-Book: An Alphabetical Digest of Nautical Terms* (1867, reprinted Conway 1991) p. 215.
35 The first was 35 Geo. III c.5 and the second was 35 Geo. III c.29.
36 P. Kemp *The British Sailor: A Social History of the Lower Deck* (London, 1970), p. 163. He gives the exact figures as: County Quota 9,764 men and Seaport Quota 20,354 men.
37 Quoted, Lavery, *Nelson's Navy*, p. 128.

society'. Kemp claims that the Quota Acts gave local justices the opportunity to empty the jails of convicted felons and that 'they [Quota men] were largely responsible for the increased incidence of flogging during the period of the two wars with France'.[38] Kindleberger follows this view and states that the Quota Acts '...rapidly degenerated into clearing out the jails, delivering tramps, idlers, poachers, beggars, minor thieves and pickpockets'.[39] Perhaps the most virulent critic of the Quota men is Lewis whose pen, dipped in venom, castigates them as 'miserable specimens' and '...gaolbirds, ne'er-do-wells and puny starvelings ... social misfits and outcasts ... riffraff of the new town slums', calls their introduction into the navy an 'infection' and concludes that 'Sufficient bodies were forthcoming but, full and by, they were the wrong bodies'.[40] However evidence produced by Emsley does not seem to support this view and other historians are more measured in their view of Quota men.[41] Bromley calls the castigation of Quota men a 'fashionable denigration' and 'the Quota Acts of 1795–6 – anathema to naval officers (and to historians who follow their opinions)'.[42]

Examination of *Trent*'s records and further research on comparable frigates does not support the view that Quota men made poor and troublesome sailors. It would appear from the shipboard evidence that Quota men, although suffering higher rates of sickness and death through sickness, deserted less, were flogged less and developed into competent sailors.[43] Until more research has been carried out on local county and seaport records as well as tracing Quota men's subsequent naval service it is difficult to assess where the truth lies.

Table 14.8 Discipline and Quality on entry into HMS *Trent* (Seamen only)

Quality	Served (number/percentage of total crew)	Flogged (number/percentage of men flogged)
Able seamen	389 (41%)	44 (46%)
Ordinary seamen	220 (23%)	23 (24%)
Landsmen	207 (22%)	21 (22%)
Midshipmen	37 (4%)	1 (1%)
Others (idlers/unrecorded etc.)	49 (5%)	6 (6%)
Officers	50 (5%)	0 (0%)
Total crew	952 (100%)	95 (100%)

38 P. Kemp, *The British Sailor: A Social History of the Lower Deck*, (London, 1970), p. 164.

39 C. P. Kindleberger, *Mariners and Markets* (London, 1992), p. 18.

40 M. Lewis, *A Social History of the Navy 1793–1815* (London, 1960), pp. 116–27. Lewis quotes seamen and officers in support of his view but it does seem that the large bounties that Quota men were reputed to get were the main cause of other sailors' resentments.

41 C. Emsley, *North Riding Naval Recruits: The Quota Acts and the Quota Men 1795–1797* (North Yorkshire County Council, 1978), pp. 11–13.

42 J. S. Bromley, ed., *The Manning of the Royal Navy: Selected Public Pamphlets 1693–1873* (NRS vol. 119, London, 1976) p. xlii and J. S. Bromley, 'The British Navy and its Seamen: Notes for an Unwritten History' in P. Adam, ed., *Seamen in Society* (London, 1980), II, p. 34.

43 See Slope, 'Serving in Nelson's Navy', Chapter 3, pp. 81–194.

Table 14.8 compares the flogging record of seamen against the recorded quality or rating of seamen on their entry into *Trent*. It demonstrates that a seaman's quality on entry into *Trent* did not affect statistically his chances of being flogged as all categories were within 5 per cent of each other.

Table 14.9 compares recorded floggings against recorded promotions and demotions of seamen.[44] This table looks at only initial promotions/demotions of seamen and initial floggings. This is because the number of seamen who were flogged more than once and promoted and/or demoted more than once is too small to be statistically valid.

Table 14.9 Discipline and Promotion on HMS *Trent*, 1796–1803 (Seamen only)

	Served (number/ percentage of total crew)	Flogged
Crew	952 (100%)	95 (10% of total crew)
Promoted	220 (23%)	28 (13% of those promoted)
Demoted	78 (8%)	13 (17% of those demoted)
Crew members flogged before promotion		10 (36% of those flogged and promoted)
Crew members flogged after promotion		18 (64% of those flogged and promoted)
Crew members flogged before demotion		4 (31% of those flogged and demoted)
Crew members flogged after demotion		9 (69% of those flogged and demoted)

Table 14.9 demonstrates that whether a seaman was flogged or not appears to have some effect on his chances of promotion although a percentage difference of 3 per cent is very small. Are we possibly seeing that the men that get into trouble are the lively ones and as a consequence are more likely to get promoted?[45] Although there are more seaman flogged following their promotion this can be explained by the fact that many seamen were promoted relatively quickly and would therefore have not had the time to incur the wrath of the captain. This is also true of seamen who were demoted.

44 The notions of 'promotion' and 'demotion' are not always applicable to shipboard rating of the period. For the purposes of this paper 'promotion' is taken as a sailor's move up the competence ladder. Either 'landsman' to 'ordinary seaman' or 'able seaman, 'ordinary seaman' to 'able seaman' or any of the above to petty officer or specialist. 'Demotion' is taken to be the reverse.
45 See Slope, 'Serving in Nelson's Navy', p. 291

There is only one case of a seaman, William Bowen, who was demoted within a few days of being flogged. All other demotions occurred over one month following a seaman's flogging. The inescapable conclusion is that flogging and a seaman's chances of promotion do not appear to be significantly linked.

Table 14.10 considers the relationship between recorded floggings and individual captains of *Trent*. There is a slight discrepancy between the figures given below and those given in Table 14.1 on the amount of floggings and the number of lashes awarded (Table 14.1: 219 floggings/4146 lashes and Table 14.10: 215 floggings/4067 lashes). This discrepancy is due to a period of just over eleven weeks between the death 'on board' of Captain Bagot and the commissioning onto the ship of Captain Otway. During this period a number of floggings were carried out, presumably on the orders of the First Lieutenant.

Table 14.10 Discipline and Captains on HMS *Trent*, 1796–1803

Captain (service in days)	Floggings ordered	Lashes	Daily average
Bowater (476)	31	582	1.2
Bagot (364)	22	395	1.1
Otway (766)	88	1708	2.2
Hamilton (441)	68	1256	2.9
Brisbane (94)	5	102	0.9
Haton (434)	1	24	0.1
Total (2575)	215	4067	1.6

The above table shows a startling difference between the flogging records of individual captains. This ranges from the severest use of the lash by Captain Sir Edward Hamilton to the mild regime of Captain James Haton, who had only one man flogged in over a year's command of *Trent*. The man flogged was a marine: Private James Gibson was given twenty-four lashes for 'Sleeping whilst on watch'.[46] It is not really surprising that Hamilton appears as the severest captain to command *Trent*, given his subsequent court martial for cruelty. However Captain Otway is not far behind him in his use of the lash.

R. Morriss claims that longevity of service between captain and crew saw a diminishing of shipboard floggings as the men got familiar with their captain's standards. He states that the continuity of service between the crew of HMS *Minerve* and the ship's captain Sir George Cockburn in the period 1796 to 1801 led to an annual reduction of the number of floggings of 43 per cent and that 'the decline reinforces a view that the longer crews served together under the same captain the more they adapted to the standards he demanded'.[47]

Captain Bowater does not seem to conform to Morriss's pattern of

---

46 TNA, ADM51/1439. Gibson was clearly a difficult case. He had previously been flogged for 'drunkenness' (January 1802), 'disobedience of orders' (May 1801), 'neglect of duty' (April 1801) and 'disobedience of orders' (November 1800).

47 R. Morriss, *Cockburn and the British Navy in Transition: Admiral Sir George Cockburn 1772–1853* (Exeter 1997).

floggings. In the first four months of his captaincy there are only two floggings recorded and this was during the time of the recruitment of the ship's
company. During the next five months a total of twenty-one floggings are
recorded. Seven of these took place in the month of September 1796 when
a number of seamen were caught trying to desert; two were flogged for
'attempting to desert' and one for 'enticing' others to desert. Another seven
men were flogged in December 1797, four of these for 'quarrelling'. Over
the next seven months eight men are recorded as having been flogged, five
of these in the month of March 1798. Two were flogged for 'theft', two for
'neglect of duty' and one for drunkenness. It would seem in Bowater's case
that floggings peaked to deal with specific incidents of what was considered unacceptable behaviour rather than tailing off as the crew got used
to his ways. However Bowater did not command the *Trent* for as long as
Cockburn did the *Minerve*.

The same can be said of Bowater's replacement, Captain Bagot, who served
a year in command of the *Trent* until his sudden death in Port Royal, Jamaica
on 12 June 1798. With the exception of two months, there was at least one flogging a month during his tenure as captain. There were three 'peak' months of
flogging activity, two in the middle of his command period and one just before
his death. In January 1798 four men were flogged, three of these for 'neglect
of duty', two of which were punished on the same day. The following month
another three men were flogged once again for neglect of duty. Four men were
flogged in May 1798 all for 'attempting to desert'. There was no tailing off of
floggings, just a regular procession of defaulters punctuated by small groups
of men being collectively punished to deal with particular incidents.

During Captain Otway's twenty-seven-month period as captain of the *Trent*
eighty-eight floggings were recorded. The pattern of the punishments seems
more to support Morriss' view of a tailing off of punishments as a crew got
used to the ways of their captain but not as markedly as in his example. In
the first half of Otway's command a total of fifty-two (60 per cent) floggings
were recorded and thirty-six (41 per cent) in the second half. This represents a
monthly total of four floggings a month in his first year of command and three
in his second. Once again we see collective punishments for the same offence.
For instance, in February 1800 there were eight recorded floggings. Four were
for 'drunkenness and quarrelling' and four for 'insolence and disobedience of
orders'. Each group of punishments was carried out on the same day and this
makes it likely that the groups of offences were related.

Captain Hamilton only served onboard *Trent* for one year and Captain
Brisbane for three months, not long enough for our purposes, and although
Captain Haton was in command for nearly eighteen months he had only one
man flogged during that whole period. Therefore there is limited evidence to
support Morriss's view but it would need further study on ship's captains and
crew that served for periods of several years together in order to examine the
question in more detail.

So what does the above tell us about the use of flogging in the Royal Navy
of the French War period in general and of the use of flogging as a shipboard
management tool onboard *Trent* during its active service of just over seven

years? In analysing the records of *Trent* a number of factors must be borne in mind. Firstly, how typical was *Trent*? There is no evidence to suggest that she was untypical but that alone does not allow us to say that she was. Secondly there is the nature of the evidence. As discussed above, captain's log entries were idiosyncratic and often incomplete but the muster book entries were normally consistent and, with a few exceptions, as accurate as could be expected for the time. Therefore the conclusions drawn from the evidence could be generally said to be a reasonable if incomplete picture of the use of flogging in the Royal Navy of our period that needs to be supported by further studies in this area. As to *Trent* itself, the findings are likely to be as near to the truth as we are able to get, given that the record of every man that served as a crew member has been put on to the database and that all the evidence used has been of a primary nature. The records of *Trent* have given us a very general picture of what was considered an offence in the Royal Navy of the period and how severely it was treated.

As regards shipboard life, it would appear that flogging the men did not seem to have a detrimental effect on their health. Flogged men were less likely to desert from the ship than non-flogged men but this discrepancy can be explained away by the fact that most men that deserted the ship did so shortly after joining and in consequence would have had little time in which to have been flogged. Alternatively the flogging itself could have had a deterrent effect on the recipient and this can be demonstrated by the fact that, as far as the evidence allows us to tell, of ninety-five (10 per cent of the crew) named seamen flogged only seventeen (18 per cent of those flogged or 2 per cent of the crew) were flogged more than once.[48] This would indicate either that there were few regular offenders and that being flogged was largely down to chance, or that the flogging itself acted as a deterrent to the recipient.

The background of seamen would appear to have made little or no difference to their chance of being flogged. Nationality, quality on entry or how a man was recruited would not seem to have been major factors in a seaman's chances of being flogged. In this the captains could be said to have been even-handed. However the one factor that made it much more likely whether or not a man was to be flogged was if he was a marine rather than a seaman. A marine was twice as likely to be flogged as a seaman was: 10 per cent of seamen were flogged as opposed to 20 per cent of the marines. It would also appear that having been flogged did not harm a seaman's chance of promotion.

Perhaps one of the most important factors to emerge from this analysis concerns the much maligned Quota men to whom much of the blame for the naval mutinies of 1797 has been laid. If the ship's records are to be believed it would appear that these men, far from being poor sailors and gutter sweepings, contributed much to the Royal Navy of the period.

In general it would appear that flogging was seen by both officers and men to be a normal, if not brutal, part of everyday shipboard life. This can be supported by the fact that the abolition of flogging was not put forward as a demand from the mutineers of the Spithead and the Nore in 1797; in fact

---

48   This is the conclusion that Byrn comes to: Byrn, *Crime and Punishment in the Royal Navy*, p. 74.

they continued its use when they were in control of the fleets but restricted the number of lashes to twelve.

The one real variable was the captain. It would appear from *Trent*'s evidence that individual captain's views on shipboard management were the major single determinant in the use of the lash. This can be demonstrated by looking at Captains Brisbane and Haton's eighteen-month period of command in which there was one flogging approximately every three months and comparing this to the thirty-nine months under Captains Otway and Hamilton when there was an average of one flogging per week. There is also some evidence, limited by the relatively short periods of captaincy on board the *Trent*, that a ship's company would get used to their captain's standards over a long period of command by him and that this would reduce the number of floggings inflicted on them.

Given all the above evidence it would appear that the major determining factors as to whether a crew member was going to be flogged or not were if they were a marine rather than a seaman and what sort of captain the ship possessed at any given time. The choice of being a marine or a seaman was largely an individual one, the choice of captain was the luck of the draw.

'We went out with Admiral Duncan, we came back without him': Mutiny and the North Sea Squadron

Philip MacDougall

For the North Sea Squadron under Admiral Duncan, the year 1797 was a time of seemingly irreconcilable contrasts. During the early summer of that year the North Sea Squadron, which he had commanded for the past two years, was taken from him. Not because of his transfer elsewhere, but through the emergence of elected shipboard committees that assumed power in their own right. These committees, which represented an indeterminate proportion of the seamen of Duncan's fleet, after consultation among themselves, de-cided upon sailing the squadron into the Thames. Here, at the Great Nore anchorage, they joined other vessels in mutiny, some of these also part of Duncan's squadron.[1] Admiral Duncan, for his part, remained off the Texel, continuing to blockade an enemy invasion fleet, with no more than two bat-tleships (*Venerable* and *Adamant*) and two frigates (*Circe* and *Trent*). Within four weeks, however, Duncan had regained total control of his squadron. Furthermore, on 11 October of that same year, he not only led this once dis-loyal fleet into battle, but also gained a massive naval victory over a superior force of Dutch warships.

These are powerful and extreme contrasts. In one part of the year virtu-ally an entire squadron had not only rejected their admiral but had shown contempt for authority by sailing, on their own volition, to an alternative port. Yet, in complete contrast, and towards the end of that year, these same seamen were prepared to sacrifice life and limb in a viciously fought naval engage-ment. The purpose of this paper is to examine this dramatic turnaround of events, placing emphasis on the underlying causes of this extensive rejection of naval authority. Was it, to borrow the words of E. P. Thompson, a move-ment of 'revolutionary portent' or a 'parochial affair of ship's biscuits and arrears of pay'?[2] It is a question that has interested observers of the mutiny for

---

1 Ships belonging to the North Sea Squadron and already in mutiny were *Inflexible* and *Director*. The crews of these two ships had joined the mutiny on 12 May. At that time, seamen on ships at the Nore had simply been supporting the Spithead mutiny, the seamen of the Channel Fleet having demanded an increase in pay.

2 E. P. Thompson, *The Making of the English Working Class* (Harmondsworth, 1978), p. 184.

13. Admiral Duncan from a contemporary print, of unknown provenance, in the author's collection. However, it does resemble the Wedgwood medallion drawn by John De Vaere of 1798. Undoubtedly a popular naval commander, Duncan found himself in the strange position of having virtually an entire fleet taken from him by mutiny. This was in the summer of 1797, yet only a few months later this same fleet, under Duncan's command, proved itself entirely loyal when fighting the Dutch at Camperdown.

Copyright Philip MacDougall.

the past two hundred years. The government under Prime Minister Pitt feared that those who wished to undermine the state had orchestrated the mutinies of 1797. For this reason the magistrates Aaron Graham, Henry Litchfield and Daniel Williams were despatched to North Kent to discover evidence that would 'tend to shew any connection or communication between them and the proceedings of the corresponding societies or of any other person or persons either at home or abroad tending to endanger the state'.[3] The conclusion, as drawn by these magistrates was mixed. Aaron Graham (who had previously been sent on a similar mission to Portsmouth following the ending of the Spithead mutinies) together with Daniel Williams devoted much of their time to the examination of prisoners awaiting trial. Over a ten-day period, they interviewed a number of desperate and frightened men who would have been on their guard as to what they were prepared to admit. The outcome, as expressed in a letter to the Duke of Portland, and written by Graham in the third person, was a confident assertion that,

> Mr. Graham and Mr. Williams beg leave to assure his Grace [Portland] that they have unremittingly endeavoured to trace if there was any connexion or correspondence carried on between the mutineers and any private person or society on shore, and they think they may with the greatest safety pronounce that no such connexion or correspondence ever did exist.

However, in a somewhat contradictory statement, Graham and Williams immediately added:

> They do not however mean to say that wicked and designing men have not been among the mutineers; on the contrary, they have proof sufficient to found a belief upon that several whose mischievous dispositions would lead them to the furtherest corner of the kingdom in hopes of continuing a disturbance once begun have been in company with the delegates on shore, and have also (some of them) visited the ships at the Nore, and by using inflammatory language endeavoured to spirit on the sailors to a continuance of the mutiny without however daring to offer anything like a plan for the disposal of the fleet or to do more than insinuate that they were belonging to clubs and societies whose members wished well to the cause.[4]

A third magistrate, Henry Litchfield, as well as attending the court martial of Richard Parker, the elected President of 'the floating republic' at the Nore, 'examined the books and most of the papers belonging to the Committee of Delegates which were found on board the Sandwich'.[5] From these, he found no reason to

3 TNA, PC1/38, 27 June 1797, fol. 40. For further information on the possible involvement of local Corresponding Societies, see P. MacDougall, 'The English Reign of Terror' *John Gale Jones: A Political Tour through Rochester, Chatham, Maidstone, Gravesend &c* (1997 reprint).

4 TNA, HO41/42, 20 June 1797.

5 TNA, PC1/38, 27 June 1797. H. C. Litchfield to John King, Under Secretary, Home Office. The term 'floating republic' was one coined by contemporary British newspapers.

believe that the mutiny originated in anything other than a desire to bring about improvements in shipboard conditions. However, he further asserted, from the 'different expressions' to be found in the papers he examined that there was

> very little reason to doubt that an attempt has been made to convert the mutiny into an engine of disaffection to the Government of the Country, but upon the whole it appears to me that the Success and progress of the attempt have been very considerable.[6]

In 1913 Conrad Gill, who has provided one of the finest accounts of the mutinies so far produced, clearly indicated his belief in there being a political dimension to the mutinies. In his introduction to a later, broader analysis, Gill says of the seamen of the North Sea Squadron that, at the time of their sailing to the Nore, a diversity of opinion existed within their ranks:

> Some possibly welcomed the opportunity of mutiny on political grounds; some lawless persons might be glad simply to break loose from authority. These two classes would include the prime movers of the mutiny. Other seamen, a majority on some ships, were opposed to the enterprise ... Probably the greater part of the seamen had only the vaguest idea of their purpose in joining the mutiny. They would be a 'centre' party, acting on no definite principle, but spurred on by the novelty of the event, urged by the example of zealous mutineers, and conscious in a general way that they were upholding with some heroism the cause of the British seamen, and supporting the praiseworthy efforts of their brethren at the Nore.[7]

To those who 'welcomed the opportunity of mutiny on political grounds' Gill ascribes an important role in both fermenting and continuing the dispute:

> the influence of the revolutionary doctrines, penetrating through the whole fleet, and stirring the imagination of the seamen, although it left the loyalty of most of them unshaken, was one of the most important causes of the Mutinies.[8]

Manwaring and Dobrée, writing in 1935, are less forthright than either the magistrates of 1797 or Gill in 1913, but appear to accept that there may have been a political ingredient within the fleet, but were reluctant to consider it to be of any real importance:

> The Government of the day was extremely anxious to put the trouble down to subversive foreign influence instead of its real cause. Some of the men were, no doubt, animated by political ideas, but how far it is difficult to say. ... There were, of course, libertarian and revolutionary ideas in the air; the American War of Independence, the French Revolution, the troubles

6 Ibid.
7 Conrad Gill, *The Naval Mutinies of 1797* (Manchester, 1913), p. 178.
8 Ibid., p. 347.

in Ireland, not to mention such idealists as Thomas Paine in England; had spread them abroad: the notion had been borne that men had rights. To say that many of the mutineers were imbued with a sense of such doctrines is one thing, but to say that any of these men had any effect on the course of events, or in any way directed the Delegates, is altogether another.[9]

However, in contrast to such views there are some who have rejected any form of political content to the mutiny. Gutteridge, in a 1992 history of naval mutinies, provides a brief analysis of one of the final petitions of the seamen at the Nore. In doing so, he completely dismisses its startlingly radical over-tones as nothing more than novel sentiment:

> Two days later [5 June], in the great cabin of the Sandwich, the central committee, with Parker at the head of the table, drafted a petition to the King. This contained a list of grievances, some soft soap for His Majesty – 'We have the highest opinion of our Most Gracious Sovereign' – and some startlingly novel sentiments: 'Liberty – the pride and boast of a Briton, has always been denied us. The Age of Reason has at last evolved'.[10]

Furthermore, he makes nothing of the threat to carry the fleet to revolution-ary France, one of the options the delegates had under consideration when they submitted this particular petition. Instead, Gutteridge merely states,

> The petition concluded with an ultimatum. The mutineers would 'aston-ish their dear countrymen' with an unspecified action and withdraw 'as outlaws' to another country if no response came to their petition within fifty-four hours.[11]

A complete rejection of political motivation also comes from the naval his-torian Christopher Lloyd. In his account of the St Vincent and Camperdown battles, he gives some attention to the mutinies of that same year:

> It was supposed by many officers at the time, and it has been frequently suggested since, that this was not a mutiny but a revolution, that, as one officer wrote, 'the character of the present mutiny is perfectly French'. But there is no trace of Jacobinism in all the records of those dangerous months.[12]

Elsewhere, Lloyd is even more forthright: 'the fact is that the mutineers had no political aspirations whatever; they were simply strikers protesting against intolerable conditions'.[13]

---

9   G. E. Manwaring and B. Dobrée, *The Floating Republic* (London, 1935), pp. 248–9.
10   Leonard F. Gutteridge, *Mutiny: A History of Naval Insurrection* (Annapolis, 1992), p. 69.
11   Ibid.
12   Christopher Lloyd, *St Vincent and Camperdown* (London, 1963), p. 98.
13   Christopher Lloyd, *The British Seaman* (London, 1968), p. 183.

The problem though, is not so much whether there was a politically motivating force to the mutiny, but rather the extent of its influence upon the minds
of the seamen themselves. This is, perhaps, a point missed by Dugan in his
major study of the mutiny which appeared in 1966. He produces considerable
evidence of political involvement but fails to consider how this might have
affected the course of the mutiny. E. P. Thompson, on the other hand, chooses
to directly address this particular question. As a social historian, his intention
is to set the mutiny into the context of the times. In words that will already be
familiar, Thompson declared in 1963:

> It is foolish to argue that, because the majority of the sailors had few clear
> political notions, this was a parochial affair of ship's biscuits and arrears
> of pay, and not a revolutionary movement. This is to mistake the nature of
> popular revolutionary crises, which arise from exactly this kind of conjunc-
> tion between the grievances of the majority and the aspirations articulated
> by the politically conscious minority.[14]

This line of thinking was continued by Roger Wells:

> The involvement of democrats and revolutionaries in the mutinies cannot
> be denied in spite of disclaimers by mutineers themselves and by historians
> who for one reason or another persist in viewing the mutinies as purely
> naval affairs. These political initiatives not only revealed themselves during
> the mutinies, but their course and the history of the period immediately
> following cannot be properly understood without recognising the funda-
> mental importance of the political dimension.[15]

However, Wells is also careful to point out that he was not suggesting

> that the mutinies were caused by UI [United Irishmen] members, Defenders,
> British Democrats, or fluctuating alliances between all three groups. But we
> do assert that without their presence the course and nature of the mutinies
> would have been very different.[16]

In presenting this chapter, it is my intention to enter this debate by throwing
further light on the motivating factors that led to the seamen of the North Sea
Squadron acting in the way that they did. To this end, I wish to concentrate
upon their own words, these coming in a variety of forms. Most obvious are
the petitions submitted to the Admiralty. However, it cannot necessarily be accepted that these represented the views of all seamen, nor were they expressed
in ways that the majority might have found acceptable. A further source that
provides access to the words of the seamen are transcripts of the trials of those
seamen who were court-martialled. Again, care has to be taken. These transcripts do not necessarily provide the exact words used nor the precise mean-

---

14   Thompson, *Making of the English Working Class*, p. 184
15   Roger Wells, *Insurrection: The British Experience*, 1795–1803 (Gloucester, 1986), p. 99.
16   Ibid., p. 84.

ing that an individual seaman may have intended. Furthermore, there were restrictions on exactly the type of evidence the courts would permit. Primarily, they were interested in examining only acts of mutiny committed and were not interested in the factors that might have been responsible for either their cause or continuance. In being present at the court martial of Richard Parker, the magistrate Henry Litchfield confronted similar difficulties:

> In the course of the trial no circumstances were discoverable that furnished any information or assistance as to the object of my enquiry, the court martial directing their attention solely and very properly to the examination of acts of mutiny committed. Whereas my object was to ascertain the causes, which produced or continued the mutiny and the circumstances with which it was connected.[17]

A third and quite invaluable source is an extensive collection of letters written by seamen of the North Sea Squadron. They provide a unique insight into the views of some of the literate personnel who had, during the last day of May 1797, taken their ships to the Nore. While some of these individuals may have been leaders, most were not. Instead, they were the passive majority whose views ranged from total support to that of complete opposition. It is, of course, unusual that such a collection of letters survive. For this, we must be grateful to a state mechanism that chose to intercept all correspondence between the shore and naval vessels at the Nore. The seamen, themselves, certainly knew that letters going through official channels were being intercepted and attempted to use alternative methods for getting news to their families. As the intercepted letters demonstrate, these alternative methods did not always prove successful. Wills, a seaman on board *Leopard*, in a letter to his wife, stated that he had not sent his letter 'via the boatswain to be franked' but it was still intercepted. Similarly Day, on board *Sandwich*, hoped his letter would arrive, when he declared he was sending it 'by long boat by stealth'.[18] In using these letters the original spelling and syntax has been rigorously adhered to, this to avoid any loss of meaning or emphasis taken by each of the writers.

The first petition to emanate from a ship of Duncan's North Sea Squadron came from *Nassau*. This vessel was Sir Richard Onslow's flagship, Onslow being Duncan's second in command. The petition was dated 18 May and was not unconnected with events that had already taken place at the Nore. On 12 May the vessels anchored in the Thames and Medway estuaries had already thrown off the shackles of authority and by the date of *Nassau*'s petition, news of this event would have reached his squadron through reports carried in both the national and local provincial newspapers.[19] While those at the Nore, at this point in time, were simply expressing their support for the much more extensive dispute at Spithead, those on board *Nassau* were striking out in a very different direction.[20] They were concerned with the long-overdue payment of wages:

17   TNA, PC1/38, 27 June 1797.
18   TNA, PC1/38/122, 31 May 1797; HO42/212, 2 Jun 1797.
19   *Norfolk Chronicle*, 16 May 1797, p. 4a.
20   The demands made by the Channel Fleet at Spithead were as follows: Increase in wages;

The humble address of the aforesaid ship's company humbly sheweth that from a due sense of your honourable accustomed clemency and goodness have been fully assured that your main object has always been to remove as much as possible every inconvenience attending not only your own ship's company but all those under your command, therefore, actuated by the hope of obtaining redress from your honourable hands and through your influence we the aforesaid ship's company do most humbly beg leave to submit to your perusal a statement of the present grievances we labor under. Having had nineteen months wages due to the ship and being in general in want of almost every article of wearing apparel that may be conducive to make our lives comfortable in this situation of life, we flatter ourselves to think your honor will be kind enough to take the same into consideration and remedy the inconvenience by obtaining leave from the Board of Admiralty for the Commissioners to come to this port if it be not convenient to have the ship ordered to a King's port where she might be paid.[21]

This does not however, represent the North Sea Squadron's first show of discontent during this period. Some eighteen days earlier the seamen on board *Venerable*, Duncan's own flagship, had challenged his authority with three orchestrated cheers. These in turn had been taken up by seamen on board *Adamant*. The matter was reported to the Admiralty, Duncan indicating that he had tried to uncover the cause of the disturbance:

I immediately assembled the officers and ordered the marines under arms, being thus prepared, I went on the forecastle and demanded to know the cause of such improper conduct, to which they made no reply; but, five of them appearing more forward than the rest, I ordered aft on the poop, and directed the others to disperse, which they did. Soon after I ordered all hands to be sent aft on the quarterdeck, and the five men to be brought from the poop, I then interrogated them upon their conduct;– they had nothing to say for themselves, but that as their friends at Spithead had done so, they thought not harm and wished to know when their increased Pay and Provisions was to commence; having satisfied them on that head I pointed out the enormity of the crime of mutiny and pardoned the of-fenders and again established good order; I have the satisfaction to say they have behaved very properly since.[22]

Once again, the evidence must be treated carefully, those 'brought from the group' not wishing to implicate themselves too heavily. Furthermore, any more radical motivation would have been carefully concealed.

On board the 16-gun sloop *Inspector*, Hawkins and Watt have recently

provisions to be of sixteen ounces to the pound and of better quality; sufficient quantities of vegetables to be provisioned; that the sick be better attended to; more liberty on shore; pay of men wounded in action be continued; grievances of particular ships be redressed.
21 TNA, ADM1/524, 1 May 1797
22 Ibid., 26 May 1797.

uncovered other early signs of mutinous activities among the seamen of the North Sea Squadron. Some of these go back to the early part of May, but the most significant occurred on 24 May when Charles Lock, the ship's captain, supposedly uncovered evidence of a plot to take the ship to France. In a report submitted to the Admiralty, Lock wrote,

> Yesterday afternoon it was mentioned to me that a plan was in agitation for the purpose of taking off His Majesty's Sloop Inspector and that Thomas Potts, Thomas Staggs, Mathew Rush and William Valentine, Seamen belonging to her, had said was it not for His Majesty's ships Redoubt and Nonsuch, they would take the ship off.[23]

The reference to France appeared elsewhere in this report, together with a further reference to Thomas Potts, it being stated of him, that he had said 'he would stick a knife in any bugger that did not stick by them'.

That the entire North Sea Squadron was on the verge of mutiny became clear on 27 May. On that day, when the squadron was ordered to continue blockade duties off the Texel, two vessels were not among those that should have sailed. One of these, *Nassau*, had been instructed to remain at anchor, Duncan being aware that the crew were disaffected as a result of their not being paid for nineteen months.[24] It was his intention to order this vessel to Sheerness where the crew would be paid. However, he was in no position to issue this instruction until all vessels in that area had returned to duty. The second vessel which should have sailed was *Montagu*. Although ordered to sail, the crew had simply refused to weigh anchor. They indicated that they also wished to receive payments that were long overdue.[25]

Once at sea, Duncan believed the discontent so obviously felt throughout the squadron would soon be forgotten. Indeed, he even hoped that *Montagu* would join the rest of the squadron. For this purpose, once out of Yarmouth Roads, the fleet again lowered their anchors and awaited *Montagu*. It was a serious miscalculation. Instead of *Montagu* joining Duncan, the squadron joined *Montagu*. One by one, crews on board the various vessels voted to return to Yarmouth. By the end of the third day, the only ships still at sea were *Venerable*, *Adamant* and the frigates *Circe* and *Trent*.[26] As one seamen correspondent succinctly declared, 'we went out with Admiral Duncan, we came back without him'.[27]

From Yarmouth, the ships of the North Sea Squadron, under the command of their elected committees, proceeded to remove themselves to the Great

---

23   TNA, ADM1/2062, letter L259, fols 112–13, 25 May 1797. Re-quoted from Ann Hawkins and Helen Watt, '"Now is our time, the ship is our own, Huzza for the red flag": Mutiny on the *Inspector*, 1797', *Mariner's Mirror* 93, 2 (May 2007), p. 159.

24   Ibid., 27 May 1797.

25   Ibid.

26   Ibid., 27, 28, 29 May 1797. The frigate *Trent* is the subject of Nick Slope's Chapter 14, 'Discipline, Desertion and Death: HMS *Trent* 1796–1803'.

27   TNA, HO42/212, 31 May 1797. James Jones, a seaman, to Margaret Stroud of Sheerness.

Nore anchorage. Arriving on the morning of 1 June, the first contingent of
these ships, consisting of *Belliqueux* (64), *Lion* (64), *Repulse* (64), *Nassau*
(64), *Standard* (64) and *Inspector* (16) placed themselves under the command
of Richard Parker.[28] The situation at the Nore had been transformed.[29] Only
a few days earlier it looked as if the mutiny had run its course. Although
members of the Board of Admiralty had journeyed to Sheerness, they had
refused to meet with the seamen. Instead they declared that no concessions
would be made, although pardons would be given to all those who immediately returned to duty.[30] The consequent refusal of the seamen to accept these
terms resulted in the Board returning immediately to London.[31] As they left,
they ordered Vice Admiral Charles Buckner, Sheerness port admiral, to cease
supplying all ships in mutiny with food and other essential commodities.[32]
Not unnaturally, it was quickly deduced that it was the Admiralty's intention
to starve the seamen into submission.[33]

Upon the arrival of the first contingent of ships from Yarmouth, a meeting
of delegates took place on board the Medway flagship, *Sandwich*. Richard
Parker, who had been elected president some weeks earlier, took responsibility
for chairing the meeting. Joseph B. Devonish, a seaman on board *Belliqueux*,
gives one version of what happened in a letter to his wife:

> This day a general meeting of the Delegates from each ship, repair'd on
> board of the Sandwich where they have the Cabin as a Committee room,
> and have been told that they have come to a resolution that if they are not
> supplied as usual, they will draw the ships up against the fort & town of
> Sheerness, and blow it down, and proceed up the river and serve all the
> towns in the same manner. They have stopped 14 or 15 sail of transports
> that have some provisions of different kinds on board (and will) if they
> have not a satisfactory Answer from the Minister and Admiralty, stop the
> trade up the river, and suffer no kind of shipping to pass or repass.[34]

Devonish was referring primarily to a plan to blockade the Thames in order to put more pressure on the government to negotiate. This plan was put
into operation on 2 June, when the fleet moved into a mid-river position and

---

28 C. Cunningham, *A Narrative of the Occurrences that Took Place during the Mutiny at
the Nore* (Chatham, 1829), p. 53; Gill, *Naval Mutinies*, p. 177. Cunningham was an eyewitness to events, being captain of *Clyde*. It appears that *Montagu* sailed independently to the
Nore on the previous day and was the first of the North Sea Squadron to reach the Thames.
29 On the same day that ships of the North Sea Squadron began arriving at the Nore, the
seamen there also learnt of disaffection on board *Beaulieu* and *Overyssel*, the guardships
in the Downs. At about this time also, the crew of *Lancaster*, moored in Long Reach,
also mutinied. For additional information on the Downs mutiny, see P. MacDougall, 'The
Seamen Have Taken Command', *Bygone Kent*, 17, 12 (Dec 1996), pp. 711–18.
30 TNA, ADM3/137, 29 May 1797.
31 Ibid.
32 Ibid., 30 May 1797.
33 *Kentish Chronicle*, 2 June 1797, p. 4d; Cunningham, p. 21.
34 TNA, PC/38/122, fol. 64, 31 May 1797. Joseph B. Devonish, seaman on board Belliqueux
to his wife, Mrs Jane Devonish of 3 Little Bath Street, Cold Bathfields, Clerkenwell, London.

stopped all ships bound for London. Those carrying perishable items would be allowed to proceed onwards while those carrying non-perishables were to be ordered to anchor and remain. This proved extremely successful: about one hundred merchant ships, within the first few days of the blockade having been implemented, found themselves unable to reach London.[35] In many ways, though, the plan was too successful. The seamen were unable to find sufficient quantities of food to feed such large numbers of merchantmen, resulting in the blockade plan being abandoned only three days after it had begun.[36]

In addition, the meeting of delegates on 2 June also discussed and drew up a list of demands. These were specific to the North Sea Squadron and were in addition to a set of demands that had previously been given to Admiral Buckner on 20 May. On that occasion, the demands had included the payment of wages in arrears.[37] To these, however, the delegates from the newly arrived ships included an increase in the wages of marines and a more equitable distribution of prize money.[38] The demands, once neatly copied, were then taken ashore by Richard Parker in company with two delegates belonging to the squadron, William Wallace (*Standard*) and Samuel Widgery (*Nassau*). The account of the handing over of these demands to the Commissioner of the naval dockyard at Sheerness, Captain Hartwell, was subsequently written down in a letter that was signed by Parker, Wallace and Widgery:

> At 9pm messrs Parker, Widgery and Wallace proceeded on shore with the flagg of truce and deliver'd in the final determination of the North Sea Fleet to Commissioner Hartwell who informed us that it was out of his power to go to London with the Articles then produced. But if there had been no desire but what was demanded by the Fleet of the Nore he was ready to go off Express to the Lords of the Admiralty and Endeavour to get the same ratified to the whole – We delivered a demand of Anchors and Cables for HMS Repulse and were answer'd that none were to be admitted to be drawn from the yard without an Express order from the Lords of the Admiralty. We desired to be admitted to go and get Necessaries but were refused under the pretence that it was not propper at night to be granted.[39]

Having arrived at the Great Nore anchorage, many of those on board ships of the North Sea Squadron began posting letters to various friends and relatives. Some of these letters were written as soon as the vessels arrived at the Nore, others had already been written but not, as yet, posted. Doubtless, a few of these letters may have been successful in reaching their respective

35 TNA, ADM1/737, C359.

36 Gill, *Naval Mutinies*, p. 184. Christopher Doorne's Chapter 11, 'A Floating Republic? Conspiracy Theory and the Nore Mutiny of 1797', notes that magistrates Graham and Williams saw the blockade as retaliation for the government's stopping of supplies to the fleet.

37 TNA, ADM1/727, 20 May 1797. The full list of demands is set out in MacDougall, Chapter 9, 'The East Coast Mutinies: May–June 1797'.

38 TNA, ADM1/727, 12 June 1797, paper No. 25.

39 Ibid., No. 23.

destinations. However, approximately sixty did not, the Home Office having issued instructions to various local postmasters to intercept correspondence connected in any way with the seamen at the Nore anchorage. Using these letters, which have been preserved at the National Archive (Kew), it is possible to get a clearer understanding of the factors driving them forward. Already it has been noted that many seamen of Duncan's squadron were concerned about pay and conditions. Since the outbreak of war with France, the country had undergone a massive bout of inflation that had reduced a relatively low wage to a mere pittance. In 1796, both lieutenants and captains in the navy had received a considerable increase in their wages as had many other sectors of society including the army. This, most certainly, was why the men on board *Venerable* and *Adamant* had been so keen to support their brethren at Spithead. In addition though, the seamen of Duncan's squadron were faced with additional problems of excessive delays in payment of wages. Due to the urgencies of blockade duties, his ships seemed rarely in a position where crews could claim and receive wages. As such, several of Duncan's ships had remained unpaid for periods of a year or more. It was this delay in paying the seamen that had sparked the squadron into mutiny.

John Pickering, a seaman on board *Nassau*, had written a letter on 29 May while his vessel was at Yarmouth. Unable to post it at that port, he attempted to send it as soon as his vessel arrived at the Nore:

> We remain still in this harbour but the fleet are gone to sea under the command of Admiral Duncan and none remain behind but the Montagu and us as we absolutely refuse going to sea until we receive our wages and here we remain expecting daily to receive orders from the Board either to be paid here or otherwise to go to some King's port where we might be paid, but the ship's company are unanimously of the resolution never to weigh anchor until they receive the same, having now twenty months wages due and are in general in want almost of all necessaries in regard to wearing apparel.[40]

Seaman Durnford, who was an elected committee member on board *Nassau*, writing of the vessel's arrival at the Nore, also provided his parents with account of why the squadron had mutinied.

> We came round here to get paid, which I hope we shall soon – you need not answer this until you here from me again which will not be long as we are in a situation very curious to some. I wrote this to satisfy you that we came here true hearted.[41]

In a similar account, Thomas King, on that same day, informed his wife that the crew of *Nassau* were owed a total of £13,000 in unpaid wages.[42] On board other ships, the issue of wages was also considered to be of importance. An

---

40 TNA, PC1/38/122, fol. 1
41 TNA, PC1/38/122, fol. 64, 31 May 1797. Joseph B. Devonish to his wife.
42 Ibid., fol. 7.

anonymous seaman, possibly on board *Belliqueux*, wrote to Anne Broth of
North Shields,

> We sailed out from Yarmouth Roads on the 28th of last month with a very
> unsettled mind for we was in the course of pay so the ships company would
> not go to sea until they were paid, so we took the ship from the officers
> and took her to the Nore when we expected Admiral Duncan to fire on us,
> which we did not care for.[43]

Seaman Richards, possibly also serving on *Belliqueux*, wrote to his father
on 2 June, 'we are for more prize money and for our pay when it is won'.[44]
Not all seamen of the fleet were concerned with matters of finance. Joseph
Thomson wrote of 'rights and wages' in a letter to his mother:

> We came from Yarmouth Roads on Saturday morning at two o'clock and
> went to the North Seas and then the men rebelled against our captain and
> the Admiral and then came into the Roads again, then we and three ships
> more set sail on Monday morning for the Noar and got in by six o'clock
> and there was a vast quantity of ships there to receive us sticking out for
> their rights and wages.[45]

John Milam of *Belliqueux*, informed his parents,

> There is at this time at the Nore 14 sail of the line besides sloops &c with
> the bloody Flag hoisted at the fore top mast head, signifying that Seamen
> will have their Rights before they sail. What they intend to have is this: 1st
> that every man belonging to His Majesty's ships shall be paid down to 3
> months, besides all arrears; 2nd that no officer being turned out of any ship
> shall ever come in again without the consent of his ship's company: The
> last article is; That after all things is granted, they will have His Majesty's
> Pardon for every misdemeanor [*sic*] they may have been guilty of since the
> War began. There is many more trifling Articles, which I will give you an
> account of another time. I am in very good spirits hoping that by God's
> grace, everything will be settled to our satisfaction.[46]

Joseph Hismer of *Belliqueux* informed his sister how they were hoping to
achieve these objectives:

> whe histed the bloody flag at the masthead and in the morning whe got on

---

43   Ibid., Letter 6. A seaman of the North Sea Squadron to Ann Broth of North Shields,
2 June 1797, Nore.

44   Ibid., Letter 22. Seaman Richards to his father, Francis Richards of Penzance, 2 June
1797, Nore.

45   Ibid., Letter 13. Seaman Joseph Thompson to the widow Thompson of Yarmouth, 2
June 1797, Nore.

46   Ibid., fol. 1. John Milam, seaman on board *Belliqueux* to his parents, 31 May 1797,
Nore.

the way and came to the Noar and there is two and twenty two-deckers besides cuters and gun boats and they have all got the bloody flag histed and
they will not strike them until they have got all there grievances redressed
and the Kings free pardon for all that has passed and the men have got the
whole command of the ships and they will not so much as let the officers
come on deck without asking the men first and they have stopped all the
provisions they will not so much as let anythings to come on board nor let
any boats go on shore for if they do the solders do take them up and put
them into prison.[47]

Others, however, were neither as expansive nor as eloquent. William Roberts
of *Director* wrote to his wife in the following terms:

Wee poor men are bin fiting against our enemies, and now wee are com
hom, we desire to fit for beter usage; it is a fin thing to bee a solder or seller,
so it is to walk about Birmingham; wee are no captain, we ope he will be
forced to work for his bread. Our captain of Mereens is a fine man, uses
is men well, but our pervidgeins is stoped at the vitlen ofice, firing at some
vessels going up the channel brought some vessels to loaded with buter and
chees. Dear friends, we poor solders and sellers want nothing more than to
be used well.[48]

Similarly, William Higgins of *Belliqueux* wrote to his mother,

We arrived here last night. We came on purpose to join the rest of our
brothers which I suppose you have heard the situation we have at the present. We was out with Admiral Duncan in the North Sea and we took this
ship and came to Yarmouth with her. I think that we will soon be a blight
to grant us our request for all the ships is of one mind and no officer is allowed to take any command but we carry the ship's duty on as usle.[49]

   Beyond wages and seamen's rights another strong message comes through
from these letters – a desire for peace. Clearly, among the seamen of Duncan's
squadron there was a great desire to see an end to the war. In writing to his
brother, John Pickering, a seaman on board *Nassau*, wrote,

I hope you will be kind enough not to charge me with neglect for not writing to you this time past but you may be assured that it has not proceeded
from either indifference or neglect but waiting daily to send you some
satisfactory accounts as we were daily in expectation of peace, but now
such thoughts have almost vanished and nothing prevails but a perpetual

47   Ibid., fol. 1. Joseph Hismer, seaman on board *Belliqueux* to his sister Mrs Presnall of
Whitechapel, London, 31 May 1797, Nore.
48   Ibid., Letter 15. Seaman William Roberts of *Director* to his wife Elizabeth Roberts,
who was living at 18 Water Street, Birmingham. Letter dated 2 June 1797, Nore.
49   Ibid., letter 3. William Higgins, seaman on board *Belliqueux*, to his wife Alice Higgins
of Parkgate near Chester. Letter dated 31 May 1797, Nore.

discontent both by sea and land which in all proabibility can terminate in nothing but a civil war.[50]

On board *Belliqueux*, Devonish wrote,

I wish that every method may be try'd to bring about this long wish'd for Peace, that I may once more hug you to my longing breast, and if it was possible never to part any more, I would most certainly come to you if I had a guinea to pay the expence of waterage and coach hire, for I shall be a most miserable being if kept in this state without seeing you when so near to each other; bread and water to me would be the greatest rarities, when taken with you in contentment. I was told but this very instant that they will not suffer any more woman to come into the ships but such as have been out the cruise with them so that I am debar'd even that pleasure. However, I will try to get money if possible that I may come to see you and content myself withy the hopes of being paid off soon.[51]

Finally, T. G. King, on board *Nassau*, squarely placed the blame on the prime minister, declaring vehemently, 'see what a situation Mr Pitt brought England in'.[52]

While reflecting the opinions of a random group of literate seamen, these letters probably encapsulate the views of a much larger slice of seamen on board the ships of Duncan's squadron. None of these letters, however, appear to show any direct sympathy with the radical, revolutionary or democratic societies of which the government appeared to be so afraid. To a certain extent, this is not surprising. Any self-respecting democrat or revolutionary would take considerable care in not reproducing feelings in a letter that (whatever precautions taken) might fall into government hands. Instead, letters containing such views would be passed on to a trusted colleague for direct conveyance to the intended reader.[53] However, it is not necessary to merely surmise as to the existence of political activists within the assembled ships at the Nore. Instead, there is very real evidence that such individuals were present among the seamen. It would appear that those who were the most active in the mutiny were also those who appeared to have the closest links with various political groupings. At his court martial it was evidenced that James Smart, a pressed landsman and elected seaman delegate serving on board the naval storeship *Grampus*, had not only been a member of the London Corresponding Society

50 TNA, PC1/38/122, p. 1, 29 May 1797, Yarmouth. John Pickering, seaman onboard *Nassau*, to his brother, James Pickering of Northwick, Witton Street, Cheshire.

51 Ibid., fol. 64. 31 May 1797. Joseph B. Devonish, seaman on board *Belliqueux* to his wife, Mrs Jane Devonish of 3 Little Bath Street, Cold Bathfields, Clerkenwell, London.

52 TNA, PC1/38/122, fol. 7. 1 June 1797. T. G. King on board *Nassau* (Onslow's former flagship) to his wife living at 25 Carnaby Street, Carnaby Market, London.

53 John Gale Jones, a leading member of the London Corresponding Society, while making a visit to the naval dockyard town of Chatham in 1795, refused to send any correspondence through the post, fearing that such material would be intercepted by the Post Office. See MacDougall, *John Gale Jones: A Political Tour of Rochester, Chatham, Gillingham &c*, p. vi.

but had spoken to at least one meeting.[54] In addition, James Lewin, the secretary to the committee that met on board *Sandwich*, appears to have been working towards some sort of union with revolutionary France. During the period of the mutiny he requested of James Bray that a hat be supplied for a seaman who was 'about to go on an embassy to France'. Later, Lewin was heard to say, when told that the ship was short of food supplies, that 'we shall go cruize on the coast of France, and there shall get provisions enough'.[55]

Similarly, Thomas Jephson and Charles McCarthy, both of the *Sandwich*, appear to have had close association with the United Irishmen. Having been chosen to head a delegation to Portsmouth, McCarthy, a native of Cork, while in London had a number of secret meetings. Some of these were with others of Irish descent, while he also met Mr Fitzgerald, an attorney at law.[56] Fitzgerald, who lived in Goodman Street, may have been an agent for a political group. Having been informed that McCarthy was proceeding to Portsmouth, he kept the delegation waiting 'for some notes which Mr Fitzgerald was writing for them to take to Portsmouth'. Later, Fitzgerald was known to have met with other Irish seamen delegates from the Nore, it being rumoured in that area of London that 'Fitzgerald always made a point of going into Town previous to giving them an answer'.[57] However, despite his possible association with the United Irishmen, McCarthy himself claimed that there were other more extreme members who formed the elected committees. As part of his defence during his court martial, McCarthy claimed he was expelled from the *Sandwich* committee and that his expulsion 'was nothing but spite because he was not of that violent opinion of which some of the committee were'.[58]

Thomas Jephson, on the other hand, was in London immediately before the mutiny and returned with quantities of literature that called upon Irish seamen to work for the cause of their homeland.[59] However, as this preceded the mutiny, the most damning evidence produced against him at his court martial was that of his refusal, as a bandsman, to play the national anthem. Jephson reputedly called it 'an old stale tune' and then added, 'I care nothing for Kings or Queens – bad luck to the whole of them'.[60]

As a further indication of how some of the most active appear to have

---

54 TNA, ADM1/5340, 12 July 1797, p. 32. The muster returns of *Grampus* (PRO ADM36/15111) indicate that James Smart came from Middlesex, where the London Corresponding Society had been particularly strong, and had been pressed on to *Grampus* on 30 January 1797. While most seamen, whether pressed or not, preferred to subsequently volunteer, receiving payment as a result, Smart chose to reject this, possibly wishing to draw attention to his having been forcibly denied his freedom. Smart, as an active participant in the mutiny, was executed in July 1797.
55 TNA, ADM1/3685. Testimony of William Sandwich, Master of the *Sandwich*.
56 TNA, ADM1/3685, 16 June 1797. Evidence of John and Sarah Carter, ale house keepers of Leman Street, Goodman's Field.
57 Ibid.
58 TNA, ADM1/5340, defence of Charles McCarthy.
59 TNA, PC1/38/122, 29a.
60 ADM1/727 f.393, 25 July 1797. A witness at Jephson's court martial also remembers him saying 'that the Irish and Scotch were in arms to oppose the measures of ministers'. Jephson, who was born in Dublin, received '100 lashes for seditious expression'.

held views that differed from the majority, it is only necessary to consider the work of the committees to which many of the most active were elected. The shipboard committee of the 74-gun *Inflexible* is a particularly good example. One of the ships of Duncan's squadron, she was actually present at the Nore anchorage when the mutiny broke out on 12 May. In giving support to the mutiny, she played a decisive role, enforcing support upon other ships and threatening to fire upon any vessel that attempted to lower the red flag. Parker, the elected president of the fleet, felt that the committee of this particular ship and their supporters were responsible for some of the more extreme aspects of the mutiny.[61] Unfortunately, we know very little about the composition of that ship's committee. A few days before the mutiny ended, at least nine of the committee commandeered a boat and fled to revolutionary France. Here they were accepted as allies and some appear to have entered service onboard privateers. The muster returns for that vessel simply inform us that four of those who fled were Irish, leading to the possibility that they sympathised with the aims of the United Irishmen.[62]

Another ship with a particularly militant committee was *Swan*, a 16-gun sloop. In fact, so committed was this particular vessel, that she was known as 'the little Inflexible'. As with the 74-gun *Inflexible*, the ordnance of this vessel was frequently used upon those ships attempting to escape the cause. As the mutiny entered its final days, the committee determined upon taking the ship to France. However, the majority of the crew, although they accepted many of the commands of the elected committee, baulked at this particular proposal. The president of this ship's committee, Dennis Riordan, seems to have opposed the choice of France, preferring to take her to Ireland. Similarly, on board *Champion*, her committee on 9 June advised their constituents to deliver themselves to the French, who they called the friends to the liberty of mankind. The vote went against them, the delegates having left it wholly to the crew to decide whether they would or would not proceed to France.[63]

Almost certainly, as the mutiny consolidated, the activists who made up the shipboard committees and delegates meeting on *Sandwich* became more resolute. In overseeing the words of those petitions that first indicated the grievances of the seamen, there had been no sign of any concerns beyond that of payment of wages and other related grievances. The petitions submitted by those on board *Nassau* on 18 May or a petition given to Admiral Buckner on that same day, concentrate entirely on pay and conditions at sea. These were being written during the latter days of the mutiny. A petition written

---

61 TNA ADM3/137, 19 June 1797. Report of papers found on board *Inflexible*.

62 TNA, ADM36/12741. According to *Inflexible*'s muster returns, the following seamen were marked 'R' (ran) following the ending of the mutiny: Joseph Turner (Durham), William Reed (Shields), Richard Ryan (Waterford), John Connor (Ware), John Edwards (Liverpool), Thomas Riley (Dublin), William Hodges (London), John Blake (Co. Clare) and Luke Rowe (Armagh). In addition, James Gray (Belfast) was a member of that same committee but was never brought to trial, pardoned following the North Sea Squadron's success at Camperdown.

63 TNA, ADM1/727, fol. 719. A Statement of the behaviour of the crew of His Majesty's sloop Swan, during their mutiny at the Nore.

during the first week of June, and given to Lord Northesk, captain of the
74-gun *Monmouth* for delivery to the King, is largely a polemic against the
government:

> To the Kings Most Excellent Majesty. May it please your Majesty.
>
> We your Majesty's faithful and loyal subjects serving on Bd your
> Majesty's Ships and vessels at the Nore, with the Greatest humility
> beg leave to lay our petition before you, & hope as you always
> avowed yourself to be the father of Your People that our petition
> will be attended to. We have already laid a state of our Grievances
> before your Majesty's Board of admiralty, which Grievances we
> have reason to imagine were never properly stated to you, as we
> are sorry to have reason to remark the Conduct of your present
> ministers seems to be directed to the ruin & overthrow of your
> Kingdom, & as their duty to its good and advantage, a particular
> instance of which is the Council they have given your Majesty
> with regard to us in proclaiming us Rebels, traitors & outlaws,
> this Council if we had not been men particularly attached to your
> Majesty's sacred person & Government, moderate but firm in
> our demands, & resolve with our lives to oppose your enemies
> by Land and Sea would before now have driven into some acts of
> outrage & revenge that might have Shaken the very foundation
> of this Kingdom. We here give you a list of our Grievances
> which list is accompanied by a simple but true Statement of the
> reasons we have of demanding them – and after thus making our
> wants known to your Majesty – We cannot longer ascribe a non
> compliance with those wants to Ministry – with you it now rests
> to determine whether you will or will not get a redress of our
> suffering, Your Majesty may depend that in your Kingdom there
> is not more faithful subjects than we are but at the same time We
> must assure Your Majesty till all those disgraceful proclamations,
> which proscribe outlaws are contradicted, till we have all our
> Grievances redress'd & till We have the same Supply from,
> & communication as usual with the shore, We shall consider
> ourselves masters of Nore shipping. We have already determined
> how to Act & should be extremely sorry We should be forced to
> repose in another country – which must evidently be the case – if
> we are denounced as outlaws in our own.
>
> Your Majesty's minutes seem to build their hopes on Starving
> us into a compliance but this is a wrong Idea. We have as much
> provisions & stores of all kinds as will last months. We were
> aware of their intentions & provided against them but were it
> the reverse & that we had but two days provisions – We would

sooner die in that state sooner than give up the least article of our Demands.

We shall trust to Your Majesty's prudence in chusing such councillors and advisors – in the present and other affairs as will have the good of their country in view, & not like the present ministers its destruction – & with respect to our own Grievances we shall allow 54 hours from 8 o'clock on Wednesday June 7th to know your Majesty's final answer, We shall likewise make known to our fellow subjects on Shore the particulars of this address & Your Majesty's answer so as to Justify to them any measure we may take in Consequence of a refusal.

With loyalty We remain, Your Majesty's dutiful Subjects Seamen at the Nore.[64]

An address to the nation which was also written about this time no longer concentrated entirely upon conditions of service but also dwelt upon natural rights in a style that would have done justice to Rousseau:

Liberty – This invaluable priviledge more particularly inherent to an Englishman – the pride & Boast of a Briton, the natural rights of all have always been denied to us – to us who they allow to be the Bulwark and Glory of Britain and the Gems in the English crown – to us who have by our Services rendered the Kingdom at once the Envy, the Admiration & immitation of all Europe.[65]

In total contrast to the activities of those who were elected to the shipboard committees were a sizeable group of seamen (eventually a majority) who opposed the mutiny. Such an oppositional group had existed from the very outset of the mutiny. The fact that crews on *Venerable*, *Adamant*, *Trent* and *Circe* did not elect to join the cause suggests that these vessels held on board a proportionately higher number of those who wished to remain loyal to Duncan, irrespective of what they felt about prevailing conditions of service on board British warships.[66] In addition, *Agamemnon*, one of the last ships to desert Duncan, may also have had a large oppositional group on board. This is the view of Edward Brenton who, as officer on watch at the time she deserted Duncan, subsequently provided a first-hand account of what took place on board. According to his account, Brenton indicated that he was accused of having given the ship away, the master at arms coming to him,

64 TNA, ADM1/727, papers found on board *Repulse*, No. 1.

65 Ibid., no. 20.

66 It has been suggested it was the charismatic nature of Duncan's leadership that was responsible for persuading those on board the two flagships, *Venerable* and *Adamant*, to remain loyal. See Lloyd, *St Vincent and Camperdown*, p. 110. As regards *Trent*, Nick Slope, in Chapter 14, considers it was a result of a more enlightened captain who built a good relationship with his crew. Morriss in Chapter 6 also suggests that a good relationship between captain and crew averted mutiny on *Minerve*.

and openly, in the presence of others, said, 'Mr Brenton, you have given the ship away; the best part of the men and the marines in your favour.' I replied that I could not act by myself; that the captain had decided, and I feared there was no remedy. I, however, went into the cabin, and in a very clear and distinct manner told Captain Fancourt what the master-at-arms had said, and added my firm conviction that he was right, advising immediate measures to retake the ship, and join the admiral. His answer I shall never forget. 'Mr Brenton, if we call out the marines some of the men will be shot, and I could not see them lying in convulsions on the deck; no, no, no, a little patience and we will all hail unanimity again.' I quitted the cabin, and walked the deck until my watch was out, too much irritated to say a word more.[67]

Brenton was not the only officer who felt that large numbers of seamen were opposed to the mutiny. For his part, Admiral Duncan believed that there 'were many good men … in every ship who were intimidated by others – not necessarily majorities – who were afraid to come forward and speak their mind'.[68]

Among those who posted letters upon the squadron's arrival at the Nore, Devonish expressed himself opposed to the mutiny:

Since my last letter to you we have experienced a general mutiny through the whole fleet, and am sorry to inform you that the crews of the different ships have taken the whole command out of the hands of their officers and the greatest part of Admiral Duncan's fleet are now riding at the Nore, among which number is the Belliqueux, we arrived here yesterday from Yarmouth.[69]

Another letter writer opposed to the mutinies was John Renshaw. He was a seaman on board *San Fiorenzo*, a 38-gun frigate that had slipped her cables on 31 May and actually passed the arriving North Sea Squadron as the passed up the Thames. Upon leaving the Nore, the *San Fiorenzo* was fired upon by a number of ships, one of which was *Swan*. At the time John Renshaw's brother, Abraham, was a supporter of the mutiny and served on board 'the little Inflexible'. He may well have manned one of the guns that fired on his brother's ship. John, however, did not hold this against his brother. In a letter he wrote once *San Fiorenzo* had safely reached the Spithead anchorage, he informed Abraham that he had his full forgiveness:

I write this to inform you that I am safe arrived at Spithead where all is peaceable and quiet, I suppose you think it in general that some of us must be hurt, but thank God there is not one man received the least damage; it was not our intention to come to Spithead, we were to have gone into harbour, but we cut the spring cable too soon and the ship took the wrong way, and that obliged us to come through the fleet. I have heard talk of father against son, brother against brother, but I have now experienced it, I little

67 E. P. Brenton, *Naval History of Great Britain*, 1 (London, 1837), p. 283.
68 TNA, ADM1/524, 17 June 1797.
69 TNA, PC1/38/122, fol. 64.

thought when I left you that ever that would happen, but I forgive even you, supposing you was the foremost of the whole, I do not know what may be the opinion of the fleet at the Nore, but the opinion of the fleet here is, they give us credit, but Curtis' fleet sailed yesterday. Give my respects to George and the cook and Hereward and all your mess mates. Pray write and answer directly and I remain your loving brother until death, John Renshaw.[70]

With the mutiny brought to an end by mid-June, the government investigation began, with magistrates Graham, Williams and Litchfield asked to consider the involvement of revolutionary and radical groups. That they found clear evidence of the involvement of individuals who were sympathetic to such groups has already been shown. What is more surprising, given both the evidence of the magistrates and other details demonstrated, is that later historians have come to dispute the blindingly obvious. While the mutiny was not initiated by political societies, the subsequent direction of the mutinies was clearly influenced by those with either political agendas or experience of having worked with radical or revolutionary societies. In absolutely in every way, the system of representation adopted in each ship participating in the mutiny closely mirrored the organisational structure of the corresponding societies.[71] Similarly there is the wording of the petitions that often adopt the language of democratic societies, and the sympathy towards revolutionary France that was shown by several of the delegates.[72] That these individuals, ultimately, appear to have achieved so little, was due to the existence of a large and constantly growing opposition group. It was their vociferous demand to end the mutiny that finally forced the militants to surrender. Those who may have been members of such organisations as the United Irishmen, United Scots and United Britons were then faced with the choice of either remaining and taking the consequences or of fleeing abroad. We know that those on board *Inflexible* took the choice of going to France while others certainly stayed. Of this latter group, many may have continued organising and may have become involved in several planned single-ship mutinies that were either organised by United Irishmen sympathisers or those involved with other political groups.[73]

---

70 TNA, HO42/212, 6 June 1797. John Renshaw on board *San Fiorenzo* at Spithead to his brother, Abraham Renshaw on board *Swan* at the Nore.

71 London Corresponding Society, *Report of the Committee Appointed to Revise and Abridge a former report of the Constitution of the London Corresponding Society* (London, c.1795).

72 That those who subsequently came to lead seamen involved in the shipboard mutinies of the twentieth century were more politically motivated has been demonstrated by Bell and Elleman. Their explanation is that 'the absence of well-defined leadership provides ample opportunities for the more politically minded sailors to fill the void'. See C. Bell and B. Elleman, eds, *Naval Mutinies of the Twentieth Century: An International Perspective* (London, 2003), p. 270.

73 Evidence of political motivation can be found in mutinies on board *Mars* (1797), *Pompée* (1797), *Grampus* (1797), *Caesar* (1798), *Defiance* (1798), *Diomede* (1798) and *Dreadnought* (1804).

The Influence of 1797 upon the *Nereide* Mutiny of 1809

Jonathan Neale

In 1808 the small naval sloop *Otter* was part of the Indian Ocean fleet, charged with defending the waters between Bombay and the Cape of Good Hope from the French on Isle de France (Mauritius) and Madagascar. As Knight and Wilcox highlight, the East Indies station was the most remote Royal Naval location throughout the 1793–1815 wars: 'The sheer distance from home [a minimum of four months' sailing from England] made co-ordination from England impossible and gave the commander-in-chief on the station considerably greater independence than admirals on stations nearer to home.'[1] On 17 August the ship's company of the *Otter* wrote to Vice Admiral Albermarle Bertie in Cape Town:

> Honured Sir,
>   Your honor being the only person we can apply to this side of the Board of Admiralty, to redress our grievances, humbly implore your protection; ever since Captain Davis left the ship our treatment is cruel & severe, especially the last cruise [we] were out, getting continually starting, and flogging, altho' we were superior in any kind to the Nereide, or Charwell, or in short we were not beat by any ship in the Navy since the Otter has been in Commission.[2]

'Starting' was a naval word for the customary informal beatings to force men to work, to 'start' them working. *Otter* often sailed in company with *Nereide* and *Cherwell*, and her new captain was concerned that his men perform well and his ship sail as fast as the others. The letter continues:

> If a court martial, or any court martial has been passed on these men that have been punished they would not receive a lash but, Captain Willoughby, after he has a man seized up, declares that seeing a man get three, four or six dozen is more satisfaction

---

1 Roger Knight and Martin Wilcox, *Sustaining the Fleet 1793–1815: War, the British Navy and the Contractor State* (Suffolk, UK and Rochester, NY, 2010), p.156.
2 TNA, ADM1/60, L80, enclosures, Otters to Bertie, 17 August 1808. In this chapter I have kept the original spelling and punctuation in all letters, but have changed some of the spelling and punctuation in the clerk's record of court-martial testimony.

to him than going to a good dinner: he has at various times asked the officer of the morning watch how many were started: when told, that there were none deserved it, his reply has been, that he was sorry for it, as by not having ten, or twelve started every morning watch, the officer had not done his duty: since we are in port he declared, to use his own expression that he has flogged like Hell, & would flog like hell, on the least occasion; for flogging a man is only amusement to him.[3]

Nesbit Willoughby was a lieutenant with seventeen years' service. He had been in trouble with his commanding officer twice before. On the second occasion he had been broken in rank and dismissed the service in 1800. Three years later, on the resumption of war in 1803, he rejoined as a volunteer and was immediately promoted to Lieutenant. The *Oxford Dictionary of National Biography* says that at the engagement at Curaçao in 1804 Willoughby 'distinguished himself throughout by his daring and reckless exposure of himself. During his entire service danger seems by itself to have been sufficient lure.'[4]

Otter was Willoughby's first independent command. This was his chance and he wanted to do it properly. That meant running a taut ship, and if his men were slack he intended to whip them into shape, literally.[5] The letter continued:

> We one and all thought it proper to acquaint your honor of this, before we should go out on another Cruize, for if he goes with us again, our treatment will be worse than convicts. We remain, your honors petitioners, the Ships Otters Company, one and all.[6]

This could be read as an implied threat to take collective action on the next voyage. Such things had happened before. Admiral Bertie certainly seems to have read it that way, as we shall see. His first action was to send two captains to investigate *Otter*. This was the traditional form, the correct response to an acceptable petition. Captain Johnson and Captain Tait wrote a report that implied there was some substance to the Otters' complaints. Bertie removed Willoughby from his command, and placed him under arrest on *Grampus* until he could face a court martial.[7] Bertie explained to the Admiralty:

> I did not consider it prudent that Captain Willoughby remain on board of her till his court martial could take place, fearing lest in the face of an Enemy's Port, some ill disposed person should

3 Ibid.

4 J. K. Laughton, rev. M. Duffy, 'Willoughby, Sir Nesbit Josiah', *Oxford Dictionary of National Biography*, accessed online at www.oxforddnb.com, January 2010 edn.

5 Unless otherwise specified, all evidence on the Otters comes from the court martial of Nesbit Willoughby in TNA, ADM1/5392.

6 Otter to Bertie, 17 August 1808.

7 TNA, ADM1/60, L80, enclosures, Johnstone and Tait to Bertie, 24 August 1808, and Bertie to Willoughby, 27 August 1808.

so far influence the rest, as to induce them to depart from that mode of conduct, they had in the first instance adopted, and by which measures most disastrous to the service might be affected.[8]

Bertie commanded a fleet that was rather more at war than the rest of the Royal Navy in 1808. The French and British contested control of Madagascar. Both privateers and French men-of-war were a constant threat. Bertie was chronically short of men, and a sloop like *Otter* was often on detached service. He could not afford to risk losing the ship or its men. Nor could he afford the consequences for discipline on other ships.

So he effectively deprived Willoughby of his command for an indefinite period. A court martial required at least five post-captains, and it was no common event for five captains to be in Cape Town at the same time. Moreover, Willoughby wanted to call in his defence every officer and petty officer on *Otter*, some forty men. Bertie could not spare so many men from duty, so they would have to wait until five post-captains and *Otter* coincided in port. This might be a very long wait indeed.[9]

One detects in the increasingly formal correspondence between Willoughby and Bertie a rising level of personal animosity. This may have contributed to Bertie's decision to hold Willoughby. Be that as it may, what was important was how the matter must have appeared to the Otters themselves. They had appealed to Admiral Bertie for redress, and redress had been forthcoming. They had said they did not want to sail under Willoughby, and now they did not have to.

The Nereides

Otter departed on a cruise to Madagascar under the command of Lieutenant Benge. There her crew will have passed on the news of their victory to other ships, among them *Nereide*. Captain Corbet of *Nereide* was a vicious flogger. According to the *Oxford Dictionary of National Biography*, 'Between August 1806 and March 1807, for example, he ordered fourteen floggings in just 211 days, with an average of seventeen lashes on each occasion. This was a brutal record by contemporary standards.'[10]

Corbet's men also found the starting on board unusually cruel. They had twice written letters to Admiral Pellew at Bombay, but without redress.[11] When they heard the news from *Otter* they seem to have decided that Bertie was a different class of admiral. There is no evidence for this in the documentary record. But it is a fair inference, and it explains what happened next.

8 TNA, ADM1/60, L80, Bertie to Admiralty, 30 September 1808.

9 TNA, ADM1/60, L80, enclosures, Bertie to Willoughby of 27 August and 3 September 1808, and Willoughby to Bertie of 2 September and 5 September 1808; ADM1/2704, Willoughby to Admiralty, 4 October 1808.

10 J. K. Laughton, rev. Tom Wareham, 'Corbet, Robert', *Oxford Dictionary of National Biography*, accessed online at www.oxforddnb.com, January 2010 edn.

11 C. Lloyd, 'The Mutiny of the *Nereide*', *Mariner's Mirror*, 54 (1968), p. 247.

At 7a.m. on 8 January 1809 *Nereide* was anchored off St Mary's Island, Madagascar. The boatswain piped all hands on deck and ordered them to raise the anchor. They gathered forward and announced they would only raise the anchor if the ship was bound for the Cape. Corbet and his officers rushed on to the quarterdeck. First we will let Lieutenant Blight's testimony at the subsequent court martial take up the story:

> Orders were given by Captain Corbet to turn the hands up. 'Up Anchor', and there was a general answer from forward; 'No, No.' The marines were drawn across the quarterdeck, with as I then supposed the immediate determination of forcing compliance.
>
> Captain Corbet remarked that there would be fair play for it, or something to that effect, and called for the ship's books.[12]

Blight was then ordered to take prisoner William Wilkinson, a topman and one of the leaders of the demonstration, and to put him into double irons.

> I found him forward in the crowd but immediately carried him down, under the half deck. On perceiving him to look anxiously about him and supposing he was going to speak, I remarked that it was a very awful time and warned him to hold his tongue.
>
> He instantly answered in a very independent sort of way, 'No sir, but we have written for redress and we will have it.'[13]

Blight was warning Wilkinson that he might be hanged if he called upon the other sailors to rescue him. Blight returned on deck, where Captain Corbet already had the purser calling out the names of the men from the ship's muster books. As each name was called Corbet invited the man to report himself present and loyal, or go forward with the crowd and be considered a mutineer. The great majority of the people went forward. Blight again:

> Captain Corbet took the trumpet and loudly called out that he gave them five minutes to consider before he turned the hands up, 'Up Anchor', which, said he, 'If not obeyed I will fire on you,' ordering me at the same time to note five minutes by the watch.
>
> Some of the people requested to be heard.
>
> Captain Corbet said, 'Come one or two but no more. Recollect, we are now enemies.'
>
> A few men came forward along the narrow gangway that ran from the forecastle to the quarterdeck. Corbet came forward to meet them. They said they wished to go to the Cape.
>
> Corbet said they could not. He told them he wanted to go home himself, and he could not have his wish either. The deputation returned to the forecastle and reported. 'The tenor of all that I [Blight] heard was, "You

---

12   This account of the mutiny is based on the court martial of the mutineers in TNA, ADM1/5391.
13   Ibid.

hear we can't go to the Cape, what do you say? Why don't some of you speak? Say what you want.'"[14]

The men, and their leaders, were clearly at a loss. It seems they had not planned for this moment. They now faced an organised armed force and a captain who was very sure what they were doing. As the delegation were begging men to speak up, Captain Corbet

> loudly called I'll have but two words, obey or not obey, and warned them seriously to recollect what they were about, saying also, 'What the Devil do you take me for, a coward or what?' remarking also that they ought to know him by this time.

John Robinson then returned to the gangway and told Captain Corbet that the ship's company were very ready to obey or go to the cruise, provided they went with any other captain. By this time upwards of four minutes had expired. The captain immediately replied that this was not possible.

> There was a general call forward of 'Obey'.
> When the hands were turned up, 'Up Anchor', there was a partial answer, 'But to the Cape.'
> The marines were then ordered to ready and I immediately remarked that many men were coming to their stations.
> Captain Corbet called aloud, 'Those who choose to obey and go to their stations, go. And those who do not, remain on the forecastle as mutineers and be shot.'
> I believe every person went to his station and the anchor was immediately hove up.[15]

It seems clear the Nereides had planned on a peaceful demonstration, not on taking the ship by force. In refusing to raise the anchor they had followed the tradition of the Spithead mutineers in 1797, twelve years before. But the Spithead mutineers had never forgotten that such a strike had to be backed by the implicit threat of organised force. Corbet had not forgotten it either, and he called the Nereides' bluff.

He had nine men arrested and put into irons with Wilkinson. Then he headed for the Cape. It is not clear if this had been his destination all along. But in any case he could not court-martial his ten mutineers anywhere else. Neither Madagascar nor Bombay could provide five post-captains.

When he arrived at the Cape the ten men were immediately court-martialled. Their defence was that they had been non-violent at all times. All ten men were found guilty and sentenced to death, but the court recommended that the Admiralty show mercy to nine of them. In effect, the captains on the court singled out one man, William Wilkinson, for an exemplary death.

---

14 Ibid.
15 Ibid.

They hanged him the next morning.[16] This was unusual. It was customary to wait while the verdict was referred to the Admiralty. But immediate executions were not unheard of, particularly on distant stations. In 1797 Admiral St Vincent in the Mediterranean had even ordered four men hanged on a Sunday for leading a protest against the execution of two homosexual shipmates. But that had been immediately after the mutiny at Spithead, and St Vincent clearly expected a mutiny by the fleet if swift action was not taken. The speed of Wilkinson's execution does suggest some worry on Admiral Bertie's part.

So does the destination of the other nine defendants. Bertie was short of men. The usual procedure would have been to pardon the nine men upon the occasion of the execution and return them to the ship's company. Instead Bertie sent all nine back to England for disposal by the Admiralty to other ships.[17] Bertie clearly did not want to return the leadership of *Nereide* to the forecastle.

But that was not the end of the story. Wilkinson was hanged on Thursday. On Saturday the Nereides sent a letter to Admiral Bertie. They complained of cruelty and asked for a court martial on Captain Corbet. Seaman John Slade signed the letter with his own name on behalf of the ship's company.[18]

Bertie responded by ordering a court martial on Corbet to begin on the Monday, the first possible day after he received the letter. Bertie may even have encouraged the men to write the letter; we shall return to this question later.

The prosecutor at the court martial was one of the topmen, probably Slade. This was in no way contrary to the laws that governed courts martial. But it was very unusual indeed: I have never found another case in these years where a seaman prosecuted a court martial. It was common, of course, for junior officers to prosecute their seniors. Bertie was now extending this right to the lower deck. This in itself was a major victory for the Nereides and a public humiliation for Corbet.

A stream of lower-deck witnesses came forward to testify against Corbet. They produced considerable evidence of cruel floggings. But they were much more concerned with the startings, the common daily beatings to make men work.

Startings were common practice in the Navy. Lieutenant Thomas Hodgskin was dismissed from the service for insubordination in 1812. The next year he described the practice of starting as

> one man beating another with a piece of rope as hard as he can hit him; the other being perfectly defenseless, and forbid him even to look displeased, as that is contempt or disrespect ... Starting is more generally used for want of alacrity than for any other crime.
>
> [On one ship] In hoisting the topsails to the mast-head, hoisting boats in and out, hoisting in beer and water, and such like duties, when they

---

16 TNA, ADM1/61, L39, Bertie to Admiralty, 18 February 1809.
17 Ibid.
18 There is a copy of the letter in proceedings of the court martial of Corbet in TNA, ADM1/5392. The following section is based on this court martial.

were not done with smartness, the captain stationed the boatswain's mates
at different parts of the deck, each with a rope's end, with orders to beat
every man as he passed them. ... In performing all these little pieces of
duty, every man, almost, as he ran and pulled upon the rope, had to pass.
... Thus, whether good or bad, whether old or young, whether exerting
himself or not, nearly every man in the ship got a beating.[19]

Samuel Leech, who served as a ship's boy on HMS *Macedonian* between
1810 and 1812, described how men were started as they began the day:

[The boatswain's mates] run below, each armed with a rope's end, with
which they belabor the shoulders of any luckless wight upon whose eyes
sleep yet hangs heavily, or whose slow-moving limbs show him to be but
half-awake ...
    A similar rapidity attends the performance of every duty. The word of
command is given in the same manner, and its prompt obedience is enforced
by the same ceremonious rope's end.[20]

Leech and Hodgskin are describing practices of starting they hated, but that
they considered normal in 1812. Captain Corbet's use of starting, however,
was of a different order. The only way to convey the flavour of life under
Corbet is to quote one witness at some length. John Smith, topman:

The first time he ordered me beat was ... I was stowing the hammocks, when
the hands were turned up to loose sails. I went to my station on the yard. While
I was up somebody threw two hammocks into the fore part of the netting.
    Captain Corbet called me off the yard, and when I came down on deck
he enquired, 'Who stowed the hammocks?'
    I said it was me.
    He asked me if I called them hammocks stowed?
    I told him they were two hammocks the people had hove into the netting
whilst I was aloft.
    He then called for a Boatswain's Mate and told him to give me a good
licking which he did with a rope's end. Captain Corbet then made me take
every hammock out of the netting again and stow them afresh and then
sent for the Master's mate and stopped my grog and wine for a week ...
    When setting the foretopmast studding sail I was pulling the jack block
on the main rigging and happened to take the hitch above the sail instead
of under.
    The captain asked who did it.
    I said it was me.
    He then sent for John Allen, Boatswain's Mate, and told him to go beat
me, which he did. The weight of the stick was so heavy that I could not stand.

19 Lieutenant Thomas Hodgskin, *An Essay on Naval Discipline, Shewing Part of its Evil
Effects* (London, 1813), pp. 62–3.
20 Samuel Leech, *Thirty Years from Home, or a Voice from the Main Deck* (Boston, 1843),
pp. 15–16.

Captain Corbet said 'If you don't stand, I'll make you', and then sent for seizings to seize me up to the Jacob's Ladder, which he did and then beat me as long as Captain Corbet thought proper. I was then cast off. My flesh was terribly bruised, but I was not incapable of duty.

Another time I was setting the maintopmast studding sail and was on the main yard. I cast off the main stop of the sail, and the weight of the sail had jammed the other stop so that I could not cast the knot off, it being a new stop. Captain Corbet asked me what had jammed it.

I told him the weight of the sail.

He then called me down off the yard. He asked me what held the stop.

I told him it was tied in a reefknot and being fresh blacked I could not get it off.

He then sent for Moses Veale the Boatswain's mate to beat me. He gave me six or eight strokes. I could not stand. Captain Corbet then told me if I did not stand he would seize me up to the Jacob's ladders. I was then seized up and beat as long as he thought proper.

Another time we were reefing topsails off the Isle of France [Mauritius]. After we taken in the reef a little of the sail showed underneath the yard. Captain Corbet asked who was these?

Somebody told him it was Smith, meaning me.

He called me to him and asked if I saw that.

I said Yes.

He asked me why I had not hauled the sail up.

I told him I thought that I had hauled it up.

Said he, 'I'll make you.'

He sent for a Boatswain's Mate. Moses Veale came aft.

After he had beat me, Captain Corbet sent the topsail yard men up on the yard again to shake the reef out. He then called us down on deck and as soon as we were down he told us aloft again to take the reef in again.[21]

Smith is implying that this was make-work. His testimony continues:

My arm being so sore that I could not tie my points so tight as any other man he asked me whose point was that.

They told him it was mine.

I was then in the top. He called me down on deck and asked me why I did not tie the points taut.

I told him my arm was so sore from the beating I had got I could not.

He sent for a Boatswain's mate. Moses Veale came aft. He told him to give me a damned good licking, which he did. Then he sent the yardmen aloft to shake out the reef again and after the reef was out called us all down again. And then he sent the topsail yardmen up to take the reef in again.[22]

Smith is implying here that Corbet was playing with them. It would take con-

---

21 TNA, ADM1/5391.
22 Ibid.

siderable time to get aloft, reef the sails, and come down again. Each time they were done, only to be ordered aloft again. But let Smith continue:

> He sent the Boatswain on the starboard side to see if the points were all taut. And my arm being so sore [from the beating] I could not tie my points so tight as any other man he asked me who tied them slack points?
>
> The Boatswain told him it was me.
>
> He then called all the topmen down upon the deck. When I came down he called me to him and asked me the reason I did not tie the points tauter.
>
> I told him my flesh was so sore I could not bear my frock [his clothing] to touch it.
>
> He said <u>he</u> would make sore and called for a Boatswain's mate and told him to lick me, which he did according to his orders.
>
> We went up and shook the reefs out and took them in afresh several times after that. And after we had done, my flesh being so sore, I was forced to go to the doctor and he put me on the list.[23]

One can see why Smith joined the protest on the forecastle. His evidence showed a cruel captain, but not a pointlessly cruel one. These punishments were not arbitrary. They were part of a conflict over work. And as on many other ships of the period, a conflict over work meant primarily a conflict with the topmen. Wilkinson, who was hanged, was a topman. The prosecutor was a topman. And Corbet himself felt his problem was 'a cabal of topmen'.

One of the reasons was that other captains could easily notice the speed and precision of the men in reefing topsails or changing tack. Of course, few of them would notice how tightly Smith tied his reef points. Not even Corbet could see that. He had to send the boatswain up to look.

Note that none of the punishments Smith recounts was a flogging. They were all startings. These constant beatings during the course of work were the main complaint of the witnesses at the court martial. Of course most (I suspect almost all) captains had the men started. But the Nereides felt that Corbet was doing it more than the other officers they had served under. And he clearly had some issues of his own.

For instance, William Wiggins, the gunroom cook, was beaten on the loins in front and as a result urinated blood for four months afterwards.

George Scargill, a topman, testified that he had been flogged for not being the first man off the yard. At this point one of the judges intervened to check what Scargill had just said. Many captains, after all, flogged the *last* man off the yard to encourage the others to come down quickly. Scargill repeated his meaning: he had been flogged for *not being the first* man down.

Augustus Dundas, another topman, said Corbet had told him that there was a cat of nine tails marinating in pickle juice for him because he had not been first down from the yard. (The pickle would make the wounds produced by the cat more painful.) In the event Dundas was not flogged, but other men did have pickle juice rubbed into their backs after a flogging.

Dundas also said that once he had been in the maintop when a clue-line (a

---

23 Ibid.

rope holding the sail in place) was let go. Nobody confessed to it, so all were flogged 'most unmercifully'.

Corbet injured their dignity as well as their bodies. Seaman Thomas Cumberledge found some 'dirt' (excrement) on the anchor cables. He 'went for a swab to wipe the nuisance off, when Captain Corbet said he would not allow anything of the kind'.

Corbet forced Cumberledge to wipe the cable clean with his nearly new blue waistcoat. (Cumberledge was proud of that waistcoat.) Then Corbet had Cumberledge put the waistcoat on, and then he had Cumberledge beaten with the waistcoat on.

Cumberledge testified that after the beating Corbet told him that 'if he caught the cable in that state again he would make me lick it off with my tongue. I then went up to the head and threw my waistcoat overboard.'[24]

Verdicts

The prosecutor (probably John Slade) faced a problem in bringing his case against Corbet. Starting was what the people really hated. But this was the most difficult grounds for a conviction. The court-martial judges were all captains, and they might feel sympathetic to Corbet. His actions may have been fierce, but they were only an extreme version of something the other captains did regularly themselves.

So 'Slade' brought another, more serious charge. Corbet and the Nereides had captured several slave ships. 'Slade' produced evidence that Corbet had sold the captured slaves to French merchants on Madagascar.

This was three serious offences in one. Firstly, Parliament had passed the Act for the Abolition of the Slave Trade on 25 March 1807, and the Royal Navy was supposed to enforce the ban. Secondly, the sailors implied that Corbet had pocketed the prize money for the slaves without sharing it with them or the admiral. Thirdly, Corbet had been trading with the enemy. And in addition to selling the slaves he had sold the ships they came in.

Corbet defended himself. He could not say he did not know of the ban on the slave trade, but he was able to prove that at the time he sold the slaves the order forbidding the slave trade had not yet been *officially* conveyed to the fleet. He produced witnesses to show he had kept the books in order. And he argued that the slave ships were not seaworthy enough to send on to the Cape. So when the French merchants came out from Madagascar and offered to buy the slaves, he had faced a choice. Either he had to sell the slaves or forgo the money.

The court accepted Corbet's defence over the slaves. But what did count against him was the 'sticks' used for starting.

The prosecutor had Boatswain's Mate Moses Veale produce the sticks in court. They were much larger than those normally used in the navy for starting, and some of them had been sharpened. Veale admitted that he had also made sticks of sharpened whale bone, but said he had now lost them.

---

24 See the testimonies of Wiggins, Scargill, Dundas and Cumberledge in TNA, ADM1/5391.

The court acquitted Corbet of everything but the sticks. They found: 'The charge of cruelty and oppression has been partly proved by punishment having been inflicted on board the ship with sticks of an improper size and such as are not usual in H.M. service. The court do therefore adjudge the said captain to be reprimanded.'[25]

And reprimanded he was. He remained in command of *Nereide*, of John Slade, John Smith, Thomas Cumberledge and Moses Veale.

The court immediately moved on to the court martial of Nesbit Willoughby, the captain of *Otter*, whose arrest had inspired the Nereides to seek redress in Cape Town.[26] Corbet, of course, moved across the cabin to sit as one of the judges at Willoughby's court martial.

A succession of Otters came forward to prove that Willoughby was not much better than Corbet. Many times he had told his men what a pleasure it was to him to see them punished, and they believed him. William Lot, carpenter's boy, had been flogged with thirteen dozen (156) strokes for stealing liquor. Another boy, Connolly, had been mercilessly flogged for giving his grog away because he did not want it.

But here again most of the violence had been against the topmen, for Willoughby too found his men slack in the tops. As *Otter* sailed together with *Cherwell* and *Nereide*, Willoughby had been timing his men up and down the yards, starting and flogging them if they were not faster than the other ships. The Otters were particularly bitter because they knew they were never bested by other ships. (The Nereides, on the other hand, said the Otters had never beaten them.)

There must have been several times when *Otter* and *Nereide* had run on the same tack, their captains racing each other, their eyes on the set of their sails and the other ship, both beating, beating, beating.

Willoughby was acquitted of all charges but advised by the court not to use such bad language in future. The fleet seems to have returned to a sort of normality.

Admiral Bertie reported to the Admiralty that he had court-martialled the mutineers, hanged one man and tried two officers, and added: 'I trust the example that has taken place, and the fair investigation by which these officers have been acquitted, will operate to the perfect satisfaction of order and subordination.'[27]

There, in a nutshell, is an explanation of the social function of law in this period. The 'example' is William Wilkinson's body. But the merciful pardoning of his nine shipmates is also part of the example. And so is the fair court martial of the officers. The law has three faces: cruelty, mercy and justice. The goal of all three is the same: perfect order and subordination.

Of course true justice was not available to sailors who faced a jury of their captain's peers. But Bertie, in his letter to the Admiralty, clearly felt that justice had been seen to have been done, and that this mattered.

I suggested above that Bertie may have encouraged the topmen of *Nereide* to bring their case. Corbet's court martial certainly fits neatly into the strategy

25 Ibid.
26 TNA, ADM1/5392, Court martial of Willoughby.
27 TNA, ADM1/61, L38, Bertie to Admiralty, 18 February 1809.

Bertie reported to the Admiralty. It also fits with Bertie allowing a topman to prosecute, and with John Slade's confidence in openly signing the letter. But perhaps Bertie only took advantage of an unexpected letter.[28]

Consequences

Corbet retained his command. But the real significance of the mutiny on *Nereide* was what happened afterwards. On 4 August 1809 the Admiralty wrote to every fleet to express their public disapproval of the 'manifest want of management, good order and discipline' in the ship. They added a general prohibition of starting, because it was 'unjustifiable' and 'extremely disgusting to the feelings of the British seaman.'[29]

This did not abolish starting in the navy. The practice continued on many ships, perhaps the great majority. For example, I quoted earlier two descriptions of routine and brutal starting in the navy. One was by Samuel Leech, who served as a ship's boy between 1810 and 1812. The other was by Thomas Hodgskin, who served until 1812, and was writing in 1813 about what he saw as the evils of naval discipline at that time.[30]

Still, the Admiralty's letter in 1809 was a public statement of an ideal, and not without some effect. It was also a signal to the admirals to allow prosecutions of the most flagrantly cruel of the officers. Before 1809 prosecutions of officers for cruelty were extremely rare and were almost all caused by the death of a seaman. But between 1809 and 1813 there were at least twenty-seven courts martial of officers for cruelty.[31] These courts martial usually, but not always, acquitted the defendant. Do these acquittals mean that the Admiralty was forcing unwilling captains to change their ways?

I think not.[32] Serving captains formed an essential link in the process of

28 N. A. M. Rodger, always an acute observer, thinks that 'although Corbet's prosecutors were nominally the men of the *Nereide*, it was obvious that the admiral was behind them'. See Rodger, *The Command of the Ocean: A Naval History of Britain, 1649–1815* (London, 2004), p. 494. It is still important, however, not to forget the theatrical effect of a topman prosecuting and questioning a captain in court.

29 J. K. Laughton, 'Corbet, Robert', *Dictionary of National Biography* (1887), 12, p. 205.

30 Leech, *Thirty Years from Home*, pp. 15–16; Hodgskin, *Naval Discipline*, pp. 62–3.

31 Among others the courts martial of Captain Dundas in TNA ADM1/5393; of Lieutenant Connolly in ADM1/5395; of Lieutenant Richards and of Captain Cuming in ADM1/5397; of Captain Muston and of Lieutenant Westropp in ADM1/5399; of Lieutenant Root in ADM1/5400; of Captain Lake in ADM1/5402; of Midshipman Simmonds in ADM1/5403; of Lieutenant Fynomore, of Captain Scobell and of Surgeon Hamilton in ADM1/5407; of William Murray and of Lieutenant Carr in ADM1/5408; of Captain Watts in ADM1/5412; of Lieutenant Keiley in ADM1/5415; of Lieutenant Grove and of Lieutenant Harvey in ADM1/5416; of Bourne and of Hornsby in ADM1/5417; of the Lieutenant and surgeon of *Hearty* in ADM1/5421; of Major Nicholls in ADM1/5425; of the Boatswain of *Fawn* in ADM1/5426; of Lieutenant Griffon and of Lieutenant Pritchard in ADM1/5430; of Lieutenant Scott in ADM1/5433; and of Lieutenant Burgess in ADM1/5436.

32 For a more detailed argument, see J. Neale, 'Forecastle and Quarterdeck: Protest, Discipline and Mutiny in the Royal Navy, 1793–1814' (unpublished Ph.D. thesis, University of Warwick, 1990), pp. 405–72. Rodger, *Command of the Ocean*, has a very useful discus-

charging an officer. When an admiral received a petition from a ship's company, he could choose to ignore it. If he chose to respond, he did not enquire into the matter himself. When a court martial was a possibility, the correct procedure was to send two or three captains from other ships to investigate the charges. Admirals and post-captains then had the responsibility of adjudicating – the fact that they found some of their fellow captains guilty suggests some ambivalence among them.

After the mutiny on *Nereide* some of these investigating captains began recommending a court martial. They usually said that they had taken evidence from several of the people and there appeared to be a case to answer. The crucial thing, though, must have been how they behaved towards the sailors when they came on board. They could begin by being extremely friendly to the captain. Or they could call the people together and address them, asking for evidence to back up the charges.

In the latter case, everything would depend upon their manner. Sailors were not fools, and the judgement of an officer's true intentions was one of the skills of the trade. In some cases the man who spoke out would find himself court-martialled for writing the first letter of complaint. In other cases the visiting captains could listen carefully, take notes and report back honestly. In 1800 many crews were willing to write letters, but individuals were not willing to step forward. In 1810 many were, and this must have been because the investigating captains wanted them to step forward.

Of course it is likely that many investigating captains still discouraged witnesses. It is in the nature of the records that we encounter only cases where the captains said there was a case to answer. So the most we can be sure of is that some captains now wanted some other captains tried for cruelty.

Moreover, the court martial judges were all captains or admirals. At some level they themselves had to consent to changes in discipline. Of course, that consent was only partial and some may not have consented at all. For in addition to whatever solidarity they felt with the accused officer, there was a real structural problem. Officers alluded to 'the necessities of the service'.

This was not simply a cant phrase. The severity of naval discipline was a response to the process of work on board.[33] Labour that was press-ganged, underpaid and denied shore liberty was unwilling and hostile labour. Unlike an employer on shore, the officers could not threaten the men with the sack. Unlike army officers on shore, they could not call for other troops to put down revolt. Often there was no other ship in sight, and the men heavily outnumbered the officers.

In this situation most officers felt that the men would not work hard unless they were beaten. After all, why should they?

---

sion of the changing attitudes of officers to discipline after 1797. He paints a picture of a steady evolution of feeling, in which officers were always divided between stern traditionalists and gentler reformers, but the reformers gradually became more influential and opinion shifted as a whole. But he does not really tackle the question of why opinion shifted in those years.

33 J. Neale, *The Cutlass and the Lash: Mutiny and Discipline in Nelson's Navy* (London, 1985).

So a whole panoply of punishment was necessary to make the control of the officers seem natural and invulnerable. The flogging, the court martial, the flogging round the fleet, the hangings – all these were formal public rituals, heavy with drama and symbolism. These punishments were not natural features of a brutal age. Merchantmen of the same period enjoyed far lighter discipline. But they were paid four times the wages and unhappy men could leave at the end of a voyage.

After the mutiny on *Nereide* the court-martial records show the judges wrestling with the same problem again and again: how do we satisfy the complaints of the people and yet maintain the customary discipline and control in the fleet? This was not an easy problem to solve, because the contradiction was structural.

But why were the captains themselves wrestling with this problem in a new way after 1809? There is no way of knowing for sure.[34] The problem of controlling the work force was important to all officers at all times. Yet the officers seldom debated or discussed it in print, or even in their private letters. Individual captains who got into serious trouble might be labelled as weaklings or sadists, but even this was largely a matter of gossip, rather than printed record. The question of control was largely taboo. This taboo was part of the control of the officers as a class. Radicals read books and newspapers. So did seamen. If officers began discussing the matter where seamen could overhear them, their control was threatened. There was no place on a ship where officers would not be overheard by at least one servant. Perhaps the only truly private forum was the discussion among the judges at a court martial. Of this, of course, we have no record.

So to understand why so many captains were changing their minds on discipline, we are largely thrown back upon speculation.[35] That said, I think there are three factors which can account for the change.

The first is that the captains of 1810 were, on the whole, not the captains of 1797. They were the midshipmen and lieutenants of 1797. They had lived through the mutinies of that year as relatively junior officers, somewhat closer to the men. As far as one can tell from remarks in later memoirs, their collective retrospective judgement was that the men had been justified in many of their grievances but too forward in their methods. In any case, they had seen the potential power of the people.

Secondly, by 1809 they had lived through up to sixteen years of war. The problems of control in those years had been more severe than the navy had ever faced before. Men were compelled to serve for longer. They were influenced by the revolutionary and trade union movements ashore.[36] And mutiny had been a spo-

---

34 Rodger, *Command of the Ocean*, pp. 488–95, has a very interesting discussion of the evolution of the changing attitudes to discipline after 1793. He paints a picture of a steady evolution of attitude, in which officers were always divided between traditionalists and gentler reformers, but the reformers gradually became more influential and opinion shifted as a whole.

35 But see the excellent Chapter 12 by Brian Lavery in this volume, 'Lower-Deck Life in the Revolutionary and Napoleonic Wars'.

36 The politics of the forecastle in these years has occasioned much debate. For good

radic but regular occurrence throughout these years, and there must have been many more demonstrations that never featured in the court-martial records.[37] All these factors must slowly have combined to change the general climate of opinion among the officer class. In a sense, there had been enough unrest for long enough for the commanders to begin to decide that grievances ought at least to be seen to be addressed, even if they were not always redressed.

Finally, the external world had changed by 1809. The French revolution had lost its influence in Britain and Ireland. The remnants of the United Irishmen had been smashed in 1803. The working-class movement in Britain was at a low ebb. A judicious reform, mostly by a nod and a wink, no longer carried any risk of encouraging conflagration on shore. In 1797 the mutinies had threatened the grip of the ruling class on land. In 1809 they would not have.

And the mutiny on *Nereide* came after Trafalgar. Senior officers in the Royal Navy still had to worry about control of the ocean, but a mutiny in the Mediterranean was now a somewhat less serious strategic threat. Crucially, a mutiny in the home fleet no longer raised the threat of a French invasion of Ireland.

Of course, Trafalgar and the state of the class struggle ashore were not part of the conscious motivations of most captains, if any. Rather, they formed part of the background facts which set historical limits to what men in command were likely to think.

Let me summarise. There was a gradual shift in the attitudes of many officers after 1800. Because it was gradual, and because it was not publicly discussed, it was only partly conscious. After the mutiny on *Nereide* it seemed that new signals were coming from the Admiralty. This enabled the gradual shift in attitudes to crystallise into a rapid shift in behaviour.

But we are in danger of forgetting the actions of individual men in all this speculation about large historical forces. For it is also true that the navy became somewhat less cruel, that some officers stood court martial for killing sailors and that many more officers hesitated at certain brutalities, in part because the people of *Nereide* were prepared to gather on the forecastle and refuse to raise the anchor. And it is certainly true that reforms such as the navy saw do not come unless men like William Wilkinson, topman of *Nereide*, are prepared to give their lives in the fight against cruelty.

summaries see Anthony G. Brown, 'The Nore Mutiny – Sedition or Ship's Biscuits? A Reappraisal', *Mariner's Mirror*, 92, 1 (2006), pp. 60–74; and especially N. A. M. Rodger, 'Mutiny or Subversion? Spithead and the Nore', in Thomas Bartlett, *et al.*, eds, *1798: A Bicentenary Perspective* (Dublin, 2003) pp. 549–64. As Rodgers notes (pp. 557–8), my take on 1797 is unusual in seeing that 'the seamen of the Nore were not an isolated profession needing outsiders to teach them their revolutionary responsibilities, but members of a radical working class quite capable of mounting their own insurrection without the instruction of quota men'.

37 For accounts of all these protests that ended in courts martial between 1799 and 1814 see Neale, 'Forecastle and Quarterdeck'.

Captain Robert Corbet

After the court martial Corbet remained in command of *Nereide*. But the whole navy knew the measure of the man, and a murmuring below decks followed him to his death.

In the spring of the next year, 1810, Corbet was appointed captain of *Africaine*. Her crew wrote a round robin to the Admiralty, refusing to have him aboard. The Admiralty had *Menelaus* drop alongside with her guns ready to fire into *Africaine*, and the Africaines grudgingly accepted their new captain. This suggests some limits to the Admiralty's moral indignation over Corbet's disciplinary habits.

On 13 September *Africaine* went into battle off Madagascar. She had the support of three smaller ships against two French frigates. *Africaine* carried 295 men. She lost 163 killed or wounded, including every officer, before, dismasted, she surrendered. Naval legend later held that her men had refused to fight and stood by their guns to be slaughtered rather than follow such a man. Naval legend also held, variously, that Corbet had been killed by his own men, or that, unable to bear the shame of defeat, he had torn the bandage from his foot and bled to death.[38]

It is impossible to tell how much credence to give these legends. The important thing is that the sailors told these legends. The court martial may have left Corbet in command. The legends testify to the sailors' conviction that the mutiny on *Nereide* had been, in the largest sense, a victory, and that they would no longer stand for men like Corbet.

38 *DNB* (1887), 12, pp. 204–6; J. K. Laughton, rev. T. Wareham, 'Corbet, Robert' in *ODNB* www.oxforddnb.com, January 2010; Lloyd, 'Mutiny of the *Nereide*', pp. 250–1; William James, *Naval History of Great Britain*, V (London, 1859), pp. 183.

Select Bibliography

Adam, P. ed., *Seamen in Society* (London, 1980)

Admiralty, *The Articles of War of 1749 as amended by 19 Geo.III c.17*, in Byrn, *Crime and Punishment in the Royal Navy: Discipline on the Leeward Islands Station, 1784–1812* (Aldershot, 1989), Appendix A.

Admiralty, *Admiralty, Regulations and Instructions Relating to His Majesty's Service at Sea* (1772, 1787)

Alves, H., *The Adam of a New World* (Universidade do Minho, 1985)

Anderson, M. 'Population Change in North-western Europe, 1750–1850', in M. Anderson, ed., *British Population History from the Black Death to the Present Day* (Cambridge, 1996), pp. 199–279

Annual Biography and Obituary, 1834, vol. XVIII (London, 1834)

Annual Register, 1797 (London, 1800)

Aspinall, A., *Politics and the Press: History of 'The Times', c.1780–1850* (London, 1949)

Aspinall, A., and E. A. Smith, eds, *English Historical Documents 1783–1832*, XI (London, 1959)

Atkinson, C. T., ed., *First Dutch War*, V (London, 1905)

Barnes, G. and J. Owen, eds, *The Sandwich Papers*, IV (NRS vol. 78, London, 1938)

Barrow, J., *Life of Earl Howe* (London, 1838)

Barrow, T., 'The Greenlanders at Shield 1760–1830: A Labour Elite', *North East Labour History*, 24 (1990), pp. 4–11

Bartlett, T., David Dickson, Daire Keogh, and Kevin Whelan, eds, *1798: A Bicentenary Perspective* (Dublin, 2003)

Bartlett T. and K. Jeffery, eds, *A Military History of Ireland* (Cambridge, 1996)

Bartlett, T., 'Defence, Counter-insurgency and Rebellion: Ireland, 1793–1803', in T. Bartlett and K. Jeffery, eds, *A Military History of Ireland* (Cambridge, 1996), pp. 247–93

Baugh, D. A., 'The Eighteenth-Century Navy as a National Institution, 1690–1815,' in J. R. Hill, ed., *The Oxford Illustrated History of the Royal Navy* (Oxford, 1995), pp. 120–61

Bellasis, R. O., ed., 'The Trafalgar Order Book of HMS *Mars*', *Mariner's Mirror*, 22 (1936), p. 91

Bell, C., 'The Invergordon Mutiny, 1931', in C. Bell and B. Elleman, eds, *Naval Mutinies of the Twentieth Century: An International Perspective* (London, 2003), pp. 170–92

Bell C. and B. Elleman, eds, *Naval Mutinies of the Twentieth Century: An International Perspective* (London, 2003)

Beedell, A. V., 'John Reeves's Prosecution for Seditious Libel, 1795–6: A Study in Political Cynicism', *Historical Journal*, 36, 4 (1993), pp. 799–824.

Blake, R., *Evangelicals in the Royal Navy 1775–1815. Blue Lights and Psalm Singers* (Woodbridge, 2008)

Booth, A., 'Reform, Repression and Revolution: Radicalism and Loyalism in the North-West of England, 1789–1803' (Ph.D. thesis, University of Lancaster, 1979)

Brailsford, H. N., *The Levellers* and the English Revolution, ed. C. Hill (Nottingham, 1976)

Brenton, E. P., *The Naval History of Great Britain*, I (London, 1837)

Brenton, E. P., *Life and Correspondence of John Earl of St Vincent*, I (London, 1838)

Bromley, ed., J. S., *The Manning of the Royal Navy: Selected Public Pamphlets 1693–1873* (London, 1976)

Bromley, J. S., 'The British Navy and its Seamen: Notes for an Unwritten History' in P. Adam, ed., *Seamen in Society*, II (London, 1980), pp. 36–47

Brown, A., 'The Nore Mutiny – Sedition or Ships' Biscuits? A Reappraisal', *Mariner's Mirror*, 92, 1 (Feb 2006), pp. 60–74

Burke, P., *Celebrated Naval and Military Trials* (London, 1866)

Byrn, J. D., *Crime and Punishment in the Royal Navy: Discipline on the Leeward Islands Station, 1784–1812* (Aldershot, 1989)

Byrn, J. D. ed., *Naval Courts Martial 1793–1815* (NRS vol. 155, London, 2009)

Camperdown, R. A. P. H., *Admiral Duncan* (London, 1898)

Capp, B., *Cromwell's Navy: The Fleet and the English Revolution* (Oxford, 1989)

Capp, B., *Cromwell's Navy: The Fleet and the English Revolution* (Oxford, 1992)

Capper, H. D., *Aft from the Hawse Hole* (London, 1927)

Carew, A., *The Lower Deck of the Royal Navy 1900–39: Invergordon in Perspective* (Manchester, 1981)

Chambers, Liam, 'Fitzgerald, Lord Edward', *Oxford Dictionary of National Biography* (Oxford, 2004) www.oxforddnb.com

Chenevix Trench, C., *Portrait of a Patriot* (London, 1962)

Christie, I. R., *Stress and Stability in Late Eighteenth-Century Britain: Reflections on the British Avoidance of Revolution* (Oxford, 1984)

Christie, I. R., *Wars and Revolutions* (London, 1982)

Coats, A., 'Bermuda Naval Base: Management, Artisans and their Enslaved Workers, 1795–1797 – the Heritage of the 1950 Bermudian Apprentices', *Mariner's Mirror*, 95, 2 (May 2009), pp. 149–78

Coats, A., 'Joyce, Valentine', *Oxford Dictionary of National Biography* (Oxford, 2004) www.oxforddnb.com

Coats, A., 'The Economy of the Navy and Portsmouth: A Discourse between the Civilian Naval Administration of Portsmouth Dockyard and the Surrounding Communities, 1650 to 1800' (D.Phil. thesis, University of Sussex, 2000)

Cock, R., 'Onslow, Sir Richard', *Oxford Dictionary of National Biography* (Oxford, 2004) www.oxforddnb.com

Cock, R., 'Payne, John Willett', *Oxford Dictionary of National Biography* (Oxford, 2004) www.oxforddnb.com

Collingwood, G. L. N., ed., *A Selection from the Public and Private Correspondence of Vice-Admiral Lord Collingwood: interspersed with memoirs of his life* (London, 1828)

Colpoys, Edward Griffiths, *A Letter to Vice Admiral Sir Thomas Byam Martin, K.C.B. Containing an Account of the Mutiny of the Fleet at Spithead* (London, 1825)

Conrad, Joseph, *Heart of Darkness* (London, 1995)

Corbett, J. S., ed., *The Private Papers of George, 2nd Earl Spencer, First Lord of the Admiralty 1794–1801*, I and II (London, 1913, 1914)

Crimmin, P. K., 'Duncan, Adam', *Oxford Dictionary of National Biography* (Oxford, 2004) www.oxforddnb.com

Crimmin, P. K., 'Jervis, John, Earl St Vincent', *Oxford Dictionary of National Biography* (Oxford, 2004) www.oxforddnb.com

Crimmin P. K., 'Patton, Philip', *Oxford Dictionary of National Biography* (Oxford, 2004) www.oxforddnb.com

Croker, T. C., *Popular Songs illustrative of the French Invasions of Ireland* (London, 1845–47)

Crook, M., *Toulon in War and Revolution* (Manchester, 1991)

Cunningham, C., *A Narrative of the Occurrences that Took Place during the Mutiny at the Nore* (Chatham, 1829)

Davies, J. D., *Gentlemen and Tarpaulin: The Officers and Men of the Restoration Navy* (Oxford, 1991)

Davis, R. *The Rise of the Shipping Industry in the Seventeenth and Eighteenth Centuries* (London, 1962)

Deane, J. B., *The Life of Richard Deane* (London, 1870)

Derrick, Charles, *Memoirs of the Rise and Progress of the Royal Navy* (London, 1806)

Dictionary of National Biography (1887)

Divine, D., *Mutiny at Invergordon* (London, 1970)

Donnelly, F. K., 'The Levellers and Early Nineteenth Century Radicalism', *Bulletin for Social Study in Labour History*, 49 (1984), pp. 24–8

Doorne, C. J., 'Mutiny and Sedition in the Home Commands of the Royal Navy, 1783–1803' (Ph.D, University of London, 1998)

Drinkwater-Bethune, Colonel, *A Narrative of the Battle of St Vincent* (London, 1797)

Dugan, James, *The Great Mutiny* (London, 1966)

Elliott, M., *Partners in Revolution* (London, 1982)

Elliott, M., *Wolfe Tone* (London, 1989)

Elliott, M., 'The "Despard Conspiracy" Reconsidered', *Past and Present*, 75 (May 1977), pp. 46–61

Emsley, C. 'Recruitment of Petty Offenders during the French Wars 1793–1815', *Mariner's Mirror*, 66 (1980) pp. 199–208

Emsley, C., *North Riding Naval Recruits: The Quota Acts and the Quota Men 1795–1797* (North Yorkshire, 1978)

Ehrman, J., *The Younger Pitt: The Years of Acclaim* (New York, 1969)

Ehrman, J., *The Younger Pitt: Reluctant Transition* (California, 1983)

Ehrman, J., *The Younger Pitt: The Consuming Struggle* (London, 1996)

Ereira, A., *The Invergordon Mutiny* (London, 1981)

Faller, L. B., *Turned to Account* (Cambridge, 1987)

Feather, J., *A History of British Publishing* (London, 1991)

Featherstone, D, 'Counter-Insurgency, Subalternity and Spatial Relations: Interrogating Court-Martial Narratives of the Nore Mutiny of 1797', *South African Historical Journal*, 61, 4 (December 2009), pp. 766–87

Foreman, A., *Georgiana, Duchess of Devonshire* (London, 1998)

Fresselique, J. J., *Sermon for the Late Victory 1794* (Gosport, 1794)

Fury, C. A., 'Training and Education in the Elizabethan Maritime Community, 1585–1603', *Mariner's Mirror*, 85, 2 (May 1999), pp. 147–61

Fury, C. A., *Tides in the Affairs of Men: The Social History of Elizabethan Seamen, 1580–1603* (Connecticut, 2002)

Gallop, G. I., ed., *Pigs' Meat* (London, 1982)

Gentleman's Magazine, 67, 2 (1797), pp. 1091–3

Gill, C., *The Naval Mutinies of 1797* (Manchester, 1913)

Gilson, J. P., ed., *Correspondence of Edmund Burke and William Windham* (Cambridge, 1910)

Goodwin, A., *The Friends of Liberty* (London, 1979)

Gradish, S. F., *The Manning of the British Navy during the Seven Years War* (London, 1980)

Green, D., *Great Cobbett: The Noblest Agitator* (London, 1983)

Green, M. A. E., ed., *Calendar of State Papers Domestic, Interregnum, 1652–53* (London, 1878)

Grose, *1811 Dictionary of the Vulgar Tongue* (reprinted Stroud, 2008)

Gutteridge, L. *Mutiny: A History of Naval Insurrection* (Annapolis, 1992)

Hall, Basil, *Fragments of Voyages and Travels* (London, 1860)

Hall, C. D., 'Pellew, Edward', *Oxford Dictionary of National Biography* (Oxford, 2004) www.oxforddnb.com

Hall, C. D., 'Pellew, Sir Isaac Israel', *Oxford Dictionary of National Biography* (Oxford, 2004) www.oxforddnb.com

Hannay, D., *Naval Courts Martial* (Cambridge, 1914)

Hannay, D., *Ships and Men* (London, 1910)

Hannay, D., 'The Mutinies of 1797', *Saturday Review* (6 June 1891), pp. 677–8

Hansard, T. C., *The Parliamentary Debates ... from 1803* 2nd series, XIII (London, 1825)

Harvey, C. and J. Press, *Databases in Historical Research: Theory, Methods and Applications* (London, 1996)

Hattendorf, J. B. *et al.*, eds, *British Naval Documents 1204–1960* (London, 1993)

Hawkins, A., and H. Watt, '"Now is our time, the ship is our own, huzza for the red flag": Mutiny on the *Inspector*, 1797', *Mariner's Mirror*, 93, 2 (May 2007), pp. 156–79

Hill, J. R., ed., *The Oxford Illustrated History of the Royal Navy* (Oxford, 1995)

Hill, R., *The Prizes of War* (Stroud, 1998)

History of 'The Times': 'The Thunderer' in the Making 1785–1841 (London, 1935)

Hodges, H. W. and E. A. Hughes, eds, *Select Naval Documents* (2nd edn, London, 1936)

Hodgskin, Lieutenant Thomas, *An Essay on Naval Discipline, Shewing Part of Its Evil Effects* (London, 1813)

Howell, C., and William Twomey, eds, *Jack Tar in History: Essays in the History of Maritime Life and Labour* (Fredericton, 1991)

Howell, T. B. and T. J., *A Complete Collection of State Trials*, XXIII, 1793–4 (London, 1809–28)

Hughes, Edward, ed., *The Private Correspondence of Admiral Lord Collingwood* (NRS vol. 98, London, 1957)

Jackson, G. V., *The Perilous Adventures of a Naval Officer 1801–1812* (London, 1927)

James, W., *Old Oak: The Life of John Jervis* (London, 1950)

James, W., *Naval History of Great Britain*, II (London, 1837)

James, W., *Naval History of Great Britain*, V (London, 1859)

Jamieson, A. G., 'Tyranny of the Lash? Punishment in the Royal Navy during the American War, 1776–1783', *The Northern Mariner/Le Marin du nord*, IX, 1 (January 1999), pp. 53–66.

Journal of the House of Lords, volume 41 (London, 1797)

Jupp, P. J., 'Grenville, William Wyndham', *Oxford Dictionary of National Biography* (Oxford, 2004) www.oxforddnb.com

Keane, J., *Tom Paine: A Political Life* (London, 1995)

Kemp, P., *The British Sailor: A Social History of the Lower Deck* (London, 1970)

Kennedy, A. and D. Ellison, eds, *Pressganged* (Royston, 1984)

Kindleberger, C. P., *Mariners and Markets* (London, 1992)

Knight, Roger, 'Obituary, Alan Pearsall', *Mariner's Mirror*, 92, 3 (2006), pp. 260–1

Knight, R., 'Richard, Earl Howe', *Oxford Dictionary of National Biography* (Oxford, 2004) www.oxforddnb.com

Knight, R. J. B., 'The Introduction of Copper Sheathing into the Royal Navy, 1779–1786', *Mariner's Mirror*, 59, 3 (1973), pp. 299–309.

Knight, R. and Wilcox, M., *Sustaining the Fleet 1793–1815: War, the British Navy and the Contractor State* (Suffolk, UK and Rochester, NY, 2010)

Knock, S., *Clear Lower Deck: An Intimate Study of the Men of the Royal Navy* (London, 1932)

Knox, T. R., 'Thomas Spence: The Trumpet of Jubilee', *Past and Present*, 76 (1977), pp. 75–98

Laird Clowes, W., *The Royal Navy*, II (London, 1996)

Laird Clowes, W. *The Royal Navy*, IV (London, 1997)

Laughton, J. K., ed., 'Letters and Papers of Samuel, First Viscount Hood', *Naval Miscellany*, I (London, 1901), pp. 221–58

Laughton, J. K. ed., *Letters of Lord Barham*, I (London, 1906)

Laughton, J. K., ed., 'Letters of William Cathcart', *Naval Miscellany*, I (London, 1901), pp. 259–332

Laughton, J. K., ed., *The Barham Papers*, I (NRS vol. XXXII, London, 1906)

Laughton, J. K., ed., *The Barham Papers*, II (NRS vol. XXXVIII, London, 1910)

Laughton, J. K., rev. Lambert, A., 'Brenton, Edward Pelham', *Oxford Dictionary of National Biography* (Oxford, 2004) www.oxforddnb.com

Laughton, J. K., rev. Lambert, A., 'Calder, Robert', *Oxford Dictionary of National Biography* (Oxford, 2004) www.oxforddnb.com

Laughton, J. K., rev. Morriss, R., 'Capel, Sir Thomas Bladen', *Oxford Dictionary of National Biography* (Oxford, 2004) www.oxforddnb.com

Laughton, J. K., rev. Wareham, T., 'Colpoys, Sir John', *Oxford Dictionary of National Biography* (Oxford, 2004) www.oxforddnb.com

Laughton, J. K., rev. Wareham, T., 'Corbet, Robert', *Oxford Dictionary of National Biography*, www.oxforddnb.com

Laughton, J. K., rev. Wareham, T., 'Curtis, Sir Roger', *Oxford Dictionary of National Biography* (Oxford, 2004) www.oxforddnb.com

Laughton, J. K., rev. Lambert, A., 'Durham, Sir Philip Charles Henderson Calderwood', *Oxford Dictionary of National Biography* (Oxford, 2004) www.oxforddnb.com

Laughton, J. K., rev. Doorne, C. 'Gardner, Sir Alan', *Oxford Dictionary of National Biography* (Oxford, 2004) www.oxforddnb.com

Laughton, J. K., rev. Morriss, R., 'Hargood, Sir William', *Oxford Dictionary of National Biography* (Oxford, 2004) www.oxforddnb.com

Laughton, J. K., rev. Lambert, A., 'Hotham, William', *Oxford Dictionary of National Biography* (Oxford, 2004) www.oxforddnb.com

Laughton, J. K., rev. Duffy, M., 'Hood, Sir Samuel', *Oxford Dictionary of National Biography* (Oxford, 2004) www.oxforddnb.com

Laughton, J. K., rev. Coats, A., 'Parker, Richard', *Oxford Dictionary of National Biography* (Oxford, 2004) www.oxforddnb.com

Laughton, J. K., rev. Cock, R., 'Payne, John Willett', *Oxford Dictionary of National Biography* (Oxford, 2004) www.oxforddnb.com

Laughton, J. K., rev. Duffy, M., 'Willoughby, Sir Nesbit Josiah', *Oxford Dictionary of National Biography* (Oxford, 2004) www.oxforddnb.com

Lavery, B., *Nelson's Navy: The Ships, Men and Organisation 1793–1815* (London, 1989)

Lavery, B., *Nelson's Fleet at Trafalgar* (Greenwich, 2004)

Lavery, B. *The Ship of the Line, Vol. 1: The Development of the Battlefleet 1650–1850* (London, 1983)

Lavery, B., *The Ship of the Line, Vol. 2: Design, Construction and Fittings* (London, 1984)

Lavery, B., ed., *Shipboard Life and Organisation*, 138 (London, 1998)

Leech, Samuel, *Thirty Years from Home, or a Voice from the Main Deck* (Boston, 1843)

Le Fevre P., and R. Harding, eds, *British Admirals of the Napoleonic Wars. The Contemporaries of Nelson* (Chatham, London, 2005)

Lemmings, David, 'Erskine, Thomas', *Oxford Dictionary of National Biography* (Oxford, 2004) www.oxforddnb.com

Lewis, M., ed., *Dillon's Narrative*, I (NRS vol. XCIII, London, 1953)

Lewis, M., *A Social History of the Navy 1793–1815* (London, 1960)

Lewis, M., *The Navy in Transition, 1814–1864: A Social History* (London, 1965)

Linebaugh, P., and M. Rediker *The Many-Headed Hydra* (London, 2000)

Lloyd, C., *The British Seaman* (London, 1968)

Lloyd, C., ed., *The Health of Seamen* (NRS vol. CVII, London, 1965)

Lloyd, C., ed., *The Keith Papers*, II (NRS vol. XC, London, 1950)

Lloyd, C., 'The Mutiny of the *Nereide*', *Mariner's Mirror*, 54 (1968), pp. 247–60

Lloyd, C., *St Vincent and Camperdown* (London, 1963)

Lloyd, C., 'Victualling of the Fleet in the Eighteenth and Nineteenth Centuries', in J. Watt, E. J. Freeman, W. F. Bynum, eds, *Starving Sailors* (Greenwich, 1981), pp. 9–15

Lodge, Christine, 'Gordon, Jane, Duchess of Gordon', *Oxford Dictionary of National Biography* (Oxford, 2004) www.oxforddnb.com

London Corresponding Society, *Report of the Committee Appointed to Revise and Abridge a former report of the Constitution of the London Corresponding Society* (London, c.1795)

London, David W., 'Manipulation of the Media: Indiscretions, Misrepresentations and Fleet Sightings', *American Journalism*, 24, 4 (2007), pp. 7–36

London, David W., 'Mutiny in the Public Eye: The Role of Newspapers in the Mutiny at Spithead' (Ph.D. thesis, King's College, University of London, 2000)

Lurting, Thomas, *The Fighting Sailor Turn'd Peaceable Christian* (London, 1710)

Lyon, D, *The Sailing Navy List: All the Ships of the Royal Navy – Built, Purchased and Captured, 1688–1855* (London, 1993)

MacDougall, P., 'The English Reign of Terror' in *John Gale Jones: A Political Tour through Rochester, Chatham, Maidstone, Gravesend &c* (Rochester, 1997 edn)

MacDougall, P., 'The Nore Mutiny, Correspondence', *Mariner's Mirror*, 93, 1 (Feb 2007), pp. 96–8.

MacDougall, P., 'The Seamen Have Taken Command', *Bygone Kent*, 17, 12 (Dec 1996), pp. 711–8

MacDougall, P., *Settlers, Visitors and Asylum Seekers* (Portsmouth, 2007)

MacDougall, P., 'The Vilification of Richard Parker', *Journal of Kent History*, 44 (March 1997), pp. 6–7

Mahan, A. T., *Seapower in Its Relations to the War of 1812*, I (London, 1905)

Manwaring G. E. and Bonamy Dobrée, *Mutiny: The Floating Republic* (London, 1987)

Manwaring, G. E. and Bonamy Dobrée, *The Floating Republic* (London, 1935)

Marcus, G. J., *The Age of Nelson* (London, 1971)

Masefield, J., *Sea Life in Nelson's Time* (3rd edn, London, 1971)

McArthur, J., *Principles and Practice of Naval and Military Courts-Martial*, II (London, 1813)

McCord, N. and D. E. Brewster, 'Some Labour Troubles of the 1790s in North East England', *International Review of Social History*, XIII (1968), pp. 365–83

McCracken, J. L., 'The United Irishmen' in T. D. Williams, ed., *Secret Societies of Ireland* (Dublin, 1973), pp. 58–67

McGregor, R., 'Pakenham, Sir Thomas', *Oxford Dictionary of National Biography* (Oxford, 2004) www.oxforddnb.com

Melville, H., *Billy Budd, Sailor* (London, 1995)

Miles, A. A., 'A Letter on the Naval Mutinies of 1797', *Mariner's Mirror*, 78, 2 (May 1992), pp. 200–1

Molloy, J. F., *Court Life Below Stairs*, 2 (2 vols, 1885)

Money, J., 'Birmingham and the West Midlands, 1760–1793: Politics and Regional Identity in the English Provinces in the later Eighteenth Century', *Midland History*, I (Spring 1971), pp. 1–19

Moore, J. P., III, '"The *Greatest Enormity* that Prevails": Direct Democracy and Workers' Self-Management in the British Naval Mutiny of 1786', in Colin Howell and William Twomey, eds, *Jack Tar in History Essays in the History of Maritime Life and Labour* (Fredericton, 1991)

Moorhouse, E. H., ed., *Letters of the English Seamen: 1587–1808* (London, 1910)

Morriss, R., *Cockburn and the British Navy in Transition: Admiral Sir George Cockburn 1772–1853* (Exeter, 1997)

Morriss, R., *The Channel Fleet and the Blockade of Brest, 1793–1801* (London, 2001)

Morriss, R., *Guide to British Naval Papers in North America* (Greenwich, 1994)

Morriss, R., 'Hood, Alexander, Viscount Bridport', *Oxford Dictionary of National Biography* (Oxford, 2004) www.oxforddnb.com

Morriss, R., *Naval Power and British Culture, 1760–1850: Public Trust and Government Ideology* (Aldershot, 2004)

Murtagh, H., 'Irish Soldiers Abroad, 1600–1800', in T. Bartlett and K. Jeffery, eds, *A Military History of Ireland* (Cambridge, 1996), pp. 248–314

Nastyface, J. *Nautical Economy* (London, 1836)

Neale, J., *The American War: Vietnam, 1960–1975* (London, 2001)

Neale, J. *The Cutlass and the Lash: Mutiny and Discipline in Nelson's Navy* (London, 1985)

Neale, J. 'Forecastle and Quarterdeck: Protest, Discipline and Mutiny in the Royal Navy 1793–1814', Ph.D, University of Warwick (1990)

Neale, J., *Stop Global Warming: Change the World* (London, 2008)

Neale, J., *Tigers of the Snow* (London, 2002)

Neale, W. J., [Roberts], *History of the Mutiny at Spithead and the Nore: With an Enquiry into Its Origin and Treatment and the Suggestions for the Prevention of Future Discontent in the Royal Navy* (London, 1842)

Nichelson, W., *A Treatise of Seamanship and Navigation* (London, 1796)

Nicolas, N. H., ed., The Dispatches and *Letters of Vice Admiral Lord Viscount Nelson*, II (7 volumes, London, 1845)

Nicolas, N. H., ed., *The Dispatches and Letters of Vice Admiral Lord Viscount Nelson*, VII (7 volumes, London, 1844–6)

Norris, David, ed., '*Captain's Orders for HMS* Superb', *Mariner's Mirror*, VII (1921), p. 345

O'Brien, P., 'Agriculture and the Home Market for British Industry, 1660–1820, *Economic History Review*, 100 (1985), pp. 773–800

Olson, A. G., *The Radical Duke* (Oxford, 1961)

Oprey, C. 'Schemes for the Reform of Naval Recruitment 1793–1815' (MA thesis, Liverpool, 1961)

Orde, D. A., 'Orde, Sir John', *Oxford Dictionary of National Biography* (Oxford, 2004) www.oxforddnb.com

O'Toole, F., *A Traitor's Kiss* (London, 1997)

Oxford Dictionary of National Biography (2004)

Owen, C. H. H., 'Collingwood, Cuthbert', *Oxford Dictionary of National Biography* (Oxford, 2004) www.oxforddnb.com

Pakenham, T., *The Year of Liberty* (London, 1969)

Parkinson, C. N., *Portsmouth Point: The Navy in Fiction 1793–1815* (London, 1948)

Parliamentary History (1840), Wiley Interscience

Patterson, A. Temple, *The Naval Mutiny at Spithead*, Portsmouth Paper, 5 (Portsmouth, 1978)

Perpetual Berthing and Watch Bill Book, The (London, 1797), transcribed in B. Lavery, *Shipboard Life and Organisation*, 138 (London, 1998), pp. 257–62

Perrin, W. G. ed., *The Keith Papers*, I (NRS vol. LXII, London, 1927)

Pitcairn Jones, C. G., 'On the Identity of Jack Nastyface', *Mariner's Mirror*, 39 (1953), pp. 136–8

Pitt, W., 'The Mutiny at the Nore', *Orations of the French War to the Peace of Amiens* (London, n.d.)

Pope, D., *Life in Nelson's Navy* (London, 1981)

Powell, J. R. and E. K. Timings, eds, *Documents Relating to the Civil War 1642–1648* (London, 1963)

Price, A., *The Eyes of the Fleet* (London, 1992)

Prickett, S., *England and the French Revolution* (London, 1989)

Rediker, M., *Between the Devil and the Deep Blue Sea* (Cambridge, 1989)

Regulations and Instructions Relating to His Majesty's Service at Sea, 1st edn (London 1772)

Reid, S., *Redcoat Officer 1740–1815* (London, 2002)

Rhys, E., ed., *Orations of the French War by William Pitt* (London, n.d.)

Richmond, Rear Admiral H. W., *The Private Papers of George, 2nd Earl Spencer, First Lord of the Admiralty 1794–1801*, III and IV (1923, 1924, London)

Richmond, H., *Statesmen and Sea Power* (Oxford, 1946)

Robinson, William, *Jack Nastyface* (reprinted Annapolis, 1973)

Rodger, N. A. M., *Articles of War* (Havant, 1982)

Rodger, N. A. M., *Command of the Ocean* (London, 2004)

Rodger, N. A. M., 'Considerations on Writing a General Naval History', in J. B. Hattendorf, ed., *Doing Naval History* (Naval War College Press, Newport, Rhode Island, 1995), pp. 117–28

Rodger, N. A. M., 'Jolly Tars Were Our Men?' in *Mutiny on the Bounty 1789–1989* (Greenwich, 1989), pp. 11–17

Rodger, N. A. M., 'Mutiny or Subversion? Spithead and the Nore' in Thomas Bartlett, David Dickson, Daire Keogh, and Kevin Whelan, eds, *1798: A*

Bicentenary Perspective (Dublin, 2003), pp. 549–64

Rodger, N. A. M., Review: C. Bell and B. Elleman, eds, 'Naval Mutinies of the Twentieth Century: An International Perspective', in *Journal of Military History*, 68, 1 (January 2004), pp. 297–8

Rodger, N. A. M., 'The Inner Life of the Navy, 1750–1800: Change or Decay?' *Guerres et paix 1660–1815* (Vincennes, 1987), pp. 171–80

Rodger, N. A. M., *The Safeguard of the Sea* (London, 1997)

Rodger, N. A. M., *The Wooden World: An Anatomy of the Georgian Navy* (Glasgow, 1990)

Rogers, Woodes, *A Cruising Voyage Round the World* (London, 1928)

Rose, R. B., 'Red Flag over Liverpool: 1775 – A Liverpool Sailors' Strike in the Eighteenth Century', in B. Blick and L. Patsouras, eds, *Rebels against the Old Order* (Ohio, 1994), pp. 63–70, originally published in *Transactions of the Lancashire and Cheshire Antiquarian Society*, 68 (1958), pp. 85–92

Rosebery, Earl of, ed., *The Windham Papers*, II (London, 1913)

Ross, Daniel, *The Perpetual Berthing and Watch Bill Book* (London, 1797)

Rudé, G., *Wilkes and Liberty* (London, 1983)

Sainsbury, A. B., 'Duckworth, Sir John Thomas', *Oxford Dictionary of National Biography* (Oxford, 2004) www.oxforddnb.com

Sainsbury, A. B., 'Keats, Sir Richard Goodwin', *Oxford Dictionary of National Biography* (Oxford, 2004) www.oxforddnb.com

Saxby, R., 'Lord Bridport and the Spithead Mutiny', *Mariner's Mirror*, 79, 2 (May 1993), pp. 170–8

Statutes Revised, III (London, 1872)

Schomberg, I, *Naval Chronology*, vol. III (5 vols, London, 1802)

Sharpe, J. A. '"Last Dying Speeches": Religion, Ideology and Public Execution in Seventeenth-Century England', *Past and Present*, 107 (May 1985), pp. 144–67

Sherrard, O. A., *A Life of Lord St Vincent* (London, 1933)

Slight, Julian, *A Narrative of the Loss of the Royal George* (Portsea, 1841)

Slope, N., 'Royal Navy Officer Development in the Age of Nelson', *The Bicentennial Edition of the Nelson Dispatch* (2005), pp. 914–23

Slope, N., 'Serving in Nelson's Navy: A Social History of Three Amazon Class Frigates Utilising Database Technology, 1795–1811' (Ph.D. thesis, Thames Valley University, 2006)

Slope, N., *Volunteer Landsmen Recruits to the Royal Navy 1795–1811: The Case of Three Thames-built Frigates* (West Wickham, 2004), pp. 123–35

Smith, L. V., 'Review of Leonard F. Gutteridge, *Mutiny*', *Journal of Military History* 58, 3 (July 1994), p. 523

Smyth, W. H., *The Sailor's Word-Book: An Alphabetical Digest of Nautical Terms* (London, 1991)

Stevenson, J., *Popular Disturbances in England 1700–1832* (London, 1992)

Syrett D., and R. L. DiNardo, *Commissioned Sea Officers of the Royal Navy 1660–1815* (London, 1994)

Syrett, D., *Admiral Lord Howe* (Stroud, 2006)

Taylor, P., *Munitions of the Mind* (Wellingborough, 1990)

Temple Patterson, A., *The Naval Mutiny at Spithead* (Portsmouth, 1978)

Thale, M., *Correspondence of the London Corresponding Society* (Cambridge, 1983)

Thiers, M. A., *Histoire de la révolution française*, V (Paris, 1850)

Thompson, E. P., *The Making of the English Working Class* (Harmondsworth, 1968)

Thompson, E. P., *The Making of the English Working Class* (Harmondsworth, 1978)

Thompson, E. P., *The Making of the English Working Class* (Harmondsworth, 1982)

Thursfield, H. G., ed., *Five Naval Journals* (vol. XCI, London, 1951)

Tucker, J. S. ed., *Memoirs of Earl St Vincent*, I (2 volumes, London, 1844)

Tunstall, B., *The Anatomy of Neptune* (London, 1936)

Uring, N., *Voyages and Travels* (London, 1928)

Vere White, T. de, 'The Freemasons', in T. D. Williams, ed., *Secret Societies of Ireland* (Dublin, 1973)

Vipont, Charles, *Blow the Man Down* (London, 1939)

Wells, R., *Insurrection: The British Experience, 1795–1803* (Gloucester, 1983)

Werkmeister, L., *A Newspaper History of England* (Nebraska, 1967)

Wharam, A., *The Treason Trials* (Leicester, 1992)

Williams, F., *Dangerous Estate: The Anatomy of Newspapers* (London, 1958)

Williams, G. and Ramsden, J., *Ruling Britannia: A Political History of Britain 1688–1988* (London, 1990)

Williams, J., *A History of English Journalism to the Foundation of The Gazette* (London, 1908)

Williams, T. D. ed., *Secret Societies of Ireland* (Dublin, 1973)

Wilson, K., 'Inventing Revolution: 1688 and Eighteenth-Century Popular Politics', *Journal of British Studies*, 28, 4 (October 1989), pp. 349–86

Wilson, T., *Flags at Sea* (London, 1986)

Winfield, R., *British Warships in the Age of Sail: 1714–1792, Design, Construction, Careers and Fates* (Barnsley, 2007)

Yexley L., *Our Fighting Seamen* (London, 1911)

Primary Sources

British Library

Add. MS. 34,906   Correspondence and papers of Admiral Horatio Nelson, Baron Nelson (1798), Viscount Nelson and Duke of Bronte (1801)

Add. MS. 34,907   Correspondence and papers of Admiral Horatio Nelson, Baron Nelson (1798), Viscount Nelson and Duke of Bronte (1801)

Add. MS. 35,143   Autobiography, correspondence and papers of Francis Place, of Westminster

Add. MS. 35,197   Bridport Papers: General correspondence of Lord Bridport, consisting chiefly of official orders and letters to him. Vol. VII, Jan. 1796–June, 1797

Add. MS. 35,197, fol. 90   Bridport Papers March 1797

Add. MS. 35,197, fol. 85   Bridport Papers March 1797

Add. MS, 35,197, fol. 109   Bridport Papers April 1797 The Spirit of
   Kempenfeldt
Add. MS. 37,877   Windham Papers, vol. XXXVI, Aaron Graham: 'Hints',
   folios 72–73v, May 1797
Add. MS. 38,355   Official Papers of the 1st Earl of Liverpool, vol. CLXVI,
   1798–1800, fol. 21, 1798
Althorp Papers, G187   Pakenham to Spencer, 11 December 1796, Spencer to
   Pakenham, 12 December 1796
Althorp Papers, G191   Bridport to Spencer, 30 March 1797; 23 April 1797;
   24 April 1797
Althorp Papers, G191   Spencer to the Board of Admiralty, 6 May 1797
Althorp Papers, G195   2 June 1797
Althorp Papers, G195   Keith to Spencer, 3 June 1797
Althorp Papers, G195   Keith to Spencer, 6 June 1797
Althorp Papers, G196   Letter from Sir Edward Newenham to Earl Spencer,
   28 April 1797
Althorp MS. G197   W. Payne to Spencer, 18 April 1797
Althorp Papers, G197   Declaration of Richard Parker executed 30th June
   1797
Althorp Papers, G14560   Richard Parker, 'An Impartial and Authentic
   Account of the Life of Richard Parker', 1797

Newspapers
Belfast News Letter
Cobbett's Political Register
Dublin News Letter
Ipswich Journal
Kentish Chronicle
Kentish Gazette
London Chronicle
London Evening Post
London Gazette
London Gazette Extraordinary
Maidstone Journal
Morning Chronicle
Morning Herald
Morning Post
Naval Chronicle
Newcastle Chronicle
Norfolk Chronicle
Oracle and Public Advertiser
Penny Magazine
Portsmouth Gazette and Weekly Advertiser
Saturday Review
Star
The Times
True Briton

Library of Congress
George Cockburn Papers

Portsmouth Central Library
Gentleman's Magazine

National Museum of the Royal Navy, Portsmouth
VG25   J. J. Fresselique, *Sermon for the Late Victory 1794* (J. Watts,
     Gosport, 1794)
1993.453(2)   Address made by Thomas Preston and William Lee, *Royal
     Sovereign*, 4 September 1797
1988.500(294)   'Address from the Seamen at Spithead to their Brethren at
     the Nore', 4 June 1797
1988.500(295)   Address from the seamen on board ships in Hamoaze to
     Nore, 6 June 1797
1988.500 (297)   'Resolutions of a numerous and respectable meeting
     of merchants, ship-owners, insurers'. London merchants at the Royal
     Exchange, resolution to raise subscriptions to end the Nore Mutiny, 7 June
     1797
2007.49   Papers of Lionel Yexley c.1907–1932
8/1996, 19598, 6.10.3   The Seamen's Manifesto 'To a Loyal and Discerning
     Nation'

The National Archive, Kew

Admiralty
ADM1/58   Admiralty In-Letters from C-in-C, Cape of Good Hope, 1804
ADM1/60   Letters from Commander-in-Chief / Senior Officer at the Cape
     of Good Hope, 1808, L80, enclosures, Otters to Bertie, 17 August 1808
ADM1/61   Letters from Commander-in-Chief / Senior Officer at the Cape
     of Good Hope, 1809, L39, Bertie to Admiralty, 18 February 1809
ADM1/107   Letters from Flag Officers, Channel Fleet, 1797
ADM1/136   Letters from Flag Officers, Channel Fleet, 1808
ADM1/524   Letters from Commanders-in-Chief, North Sea, 1797
ADM1/579   Letters from Commanders-in-Chief, Portsmouth, 1797
ADM1/727   Letters from Commanders-in-Chief, Nore, 1797; Papers found
     on board *Repulse*
ADM1/728   Letters from Commanders-in-Chief, Nore, 1797
ADM1/737   Letters from Commanders-in-Chief, Nore, 1804, C359
ADM1/811   Letters from Commanders-in-Chief, Plymouth, January–May
     1797
ADM1/812   Letters from Commanders-in-Chief, Plymouth, June–
     December 1797
ADM1/982   Letters from Commanders-in-Chief, Portsmouth, January–
     May 1783
ADM1/1022   Letters from Commanders-in-Chief, Portsmouth: 1797

ADM1/1023 Letters from Commanders-in-Chief, Portsmouth: 1797
ADM1/2062 Letters from Captains, Surnames L, letter L259, fols 112–3, 25 May 1797
ADM1/2152 Letters from Captains, Surnames M, 1806
ADM1/2704 Letters from Captains, Surnames W, Willoughby to Admiralty, 4 October 1808.
ADM1/3685 Letters from the Solicitor of the Admiralty and other Crown legal officers, 1797; Courts Martial Papers: Nore Mutiny
ADM1/3773 Letters from the Transport Board 1795–1800, riotous marines on a transport ship 12 May 1797
ADM1/3974 Intelligence Papers, 1782–1800: 1797
ADM1/4172 Letters from Secretaries of State, April–June 1797
ADM1/5125 Petitions together with a related instruction from George III to Admiral Howe, 1797 papers of *Queen Charlotte* (Lord Howe's flagship), *Royal George* (Lord Bridport's flagship)
ADM1/5189 Orders in Council, 1797
ADM1/5321 Courts Martial Papers, Aug–Nov 1782, Captain Waghorn, 7 September 1782
ADM1/5338 Courts Martial Papers, Jan–Mar 1797
ADM1/5339 Courts Martial Papers, Apr–June 1797: *Calypso, Artois, Pompée*, June 1797
ADM1/5340 Courts Martial Papers, July 1797: 12 July 1797
ADM1/5360 Courts Martial Papers, Jan–Mar 1802: Captain Sir Edward Hamilton, HMS *Trent* for 'gross cruelty'
ADM1/5391 Courts Martial Papers, Jan 1809
ADM1/5392 Courts Martial Papers, Feb 1809: Captains Corbet, Willoughby
ADM1/5393 Courts Martial Papers, 1809: Captain Dundas
ADM1/5395 Court Martial Papers, Apr 1809: Lieut. Connolly
ADM1/5397 Courts Martial Papers, June–July 1809: Lieut. Richards and Capt. Cuming
ADM1/5399 Courts Martial Papers, Aug–Sept 1809: Capt. Muston and Lieut. Westropp
ADM1/5400 Courts Martial Papers, Oct–Dec 1809: Lieut. Root
ADM1/5402 Courts Martial Papers, Feb 1810: Capt. Lake
ADM1/5403 Courts Martial Papers, Mar 1810: Midshipman Simmonds
ADM1/5407 Courts Martial Papers, July 1810: Lieut. Fynomore, Capt. Scobell, Surgeon Hamilton
ADM1/5408 Courts Martial Papers, Aug 1810: William Murray, Lieut. Carr
ADM1/5412 Courts Martial Papers, Jan 1811: Captain Watts
ADM1/5415 Courts Martial Papers, Apr 1811: Lieut. Keiley
ADM1/5416 Courts Martial Papers, May–June 1811: Lieut. Grove, Lieut. Harvey
ADM1/5417 Courts Martial Papers, July–Aug 1811: Bourne, Hornsby
ADM1/5421 Courts Martial Papers, Dec 1811: Lieutenant and surgeon of *Hearty*

ADM1/5425   Courts Martial Papers, Apr 1812: Major Nicholls

ADM1/5426   Courts Martial Papers, May 1812: Boatswain of *Fawn*

ADM1/5430   Courts Martial Papers, Sept 1812: Lieuts Griffon and Pritchard

ADM1/5433   Courts Martial Papers, Dec 1812: Lieut. Scott

ADM1/5436   Courts Martial Papers, May–June 1813: Lieut. Burgess

ADM1/5486   Courts Martial Papers: Nore Mutiny, 1797: Vol. XXIV, Court martial of Thomas Jephson, 27 July 1797, evidence of Thomas Phipps Hewson

ADM1/6033   Intelligence Papers, 1796–1798: April 1797

ADM2/133   Admiralty Orders and Instructions, 1797, including 1 May 1797

ADM2/151   Admiralty Orders and Instructions, 28 April 1806.

ADM2/607   Admiralty Secretary's Letters: Public Officers and Flag Officers, September–November 1794

ADM2/608   Admiralty Secretary's Letters: Public Officers and Flag Officers, November 1794–January 1795

ADM2/617   Admiralty Secretary's Letters: Public Officers and Flag Officers, Mar–June 1797

ADM2/1117   Courts Martial Papers: 1789–February 1797

ADM2/1352   Secret Letters, Jan–Nov 1797

ADM3/136   Board of Admiralty Rough Minutes, Jan–April 1797, 'The Seamen's Reply', 19 April 1797

ADM3/137   Board of Admiralty: Rough Minutes, May–June 1797, including Report on Nore Mutiny, May 1797

ADM7/343   Memorials and Reports, 1787–1799

ADM7/361   Return of men raised at the Port of London, 1795: Quota Act Returns

ADM7/362   Return of men raised in Essex, 1796–1797: Quota Act Returns

ADM8/73   List Book (showing the disposition of Ships, names of Officers, &c., Jan–June 1797

ADM8/74   List Book (showing the disposition of Ships, names of Officers, &c., July–Dec 1797

ADM12   Admiralty Index and Digest to Admiralty In-letters, Vols 58 and 62, Section 28.3.Richard Parker

ADM30/63/8   Description list of volunteers under the Quota Acts from the Isle of Wight, 1795: Quota Act Returns

Muster Books	Ships	Dates
ADM36/11634	*Terrible*	May–Dec1796
ADM36/11704	*Royal George*	Jan–Oct1797
ADM36/11715	*Glory*	Mar–Nov 1797
ADM36/11724	*Queen Charlotte*	July 1795–Apr 1797
ADM36/11752	*Monarch*	Jan–Dec 1797
ADM36/11759	*Marlborough*	Sept 1796–June 1797
ADM36/11769	*London*	Nov 1796–Apr 1797
ADM36/11865	*Ramillies*	Feb 1793–Apr 1797

Muster Books	Ships	Dates
ADM36/11908	*Defiance*	Aug 1794–Apr 1797
ADM36/11911	*Defiance*	Nov 1796–Oct 1797
ADM36/11978	*Royal Sovereign*	June 1796–Apr 1797
ADM36/12233	*Mars*	Jan–Oct 1797
ADM36/12345	*Duke*	Mar–Oct 1797
ADM36/12387	*Defiance*	Mar 1794–Aug 1797
ADM36/12482	*Pompée*	Sept 1796–June 1797
ADM36/12741	*Inflexible*	Dec 1796–Oct 1797
ADM36/12824	*Impétueux*	July 1797–Feb 1798
ADM36/12830	*Minotaur*	Apr 1797–Mar 1798
ADM36/13083	*Meleager*	July 1794–Oct 1795
ADM36/13135	*Minerve*	Nov 1796–Feb 1798
ADM36/13164	*Nymphe*	May 1796–Aug 1797
ADM36/13253	*Trent*	Mar 1796–July 1797 Captain Bowater
ADM36/13816	*Minerve*	May 1800–Apr 1801
ADM36/14344	*Defence*	Feb–Sept 1797
ADM36/14794	*Robust*	Mar–Oct 1797
ADM36/15226	*Trent*	July 1797–Dec 1798: Captain Bagot July 1797–12 June 1798; Captain Otway June–Dec 1798
ADM36/15227	*Trent*	Jan 1799–Apr 1800 Captain Otway
ADM36/15228	*Trent*	May 1800–June 1801: Captain Otway May–31 Oct 1800; Captain Hamilton Oct 1800–June 1801
ADM36/15229	*Trent*	Mar 1801–June 1802: Captain Hamilton Mar 1801–23 Jan 1802; Captain Brisbane Jan–June 1802
ADM36/15230	*Trent*	July 1802–June 1803: Captain Brisbane July 1802–4 May 1803; Captain Hatton May 1803–June 1803

Logbooks	Ships	Captains	Dates
ADM51/1130	Culloden	Captain Troubridge	Nov 9 1794–Nov 8 1795
ADM51/1167	Trent	Captain Bowater	Apr 5 1796–July 25 1797
ADM51/1305	Trent	Captain Otway	Aug 29 1798–Aug 29 1799
ADM51/1352	Trent	Captain Hamilton	Nov 1 1800–Oct 31 1801
ADM51/1397	Trent	Captain Hamilton	Nov 1 1801–Jan 23 1802
		Captain Brisbane	Feb 2 1802–Apr 5 1802
ADM51/1429	Trent	Captain Otway	Sept 1 1799–Oct 31 1800
ADM51/1439	Trent	Captain Hatton	Apr 6 1802– June 14 1803
ADM51/4226	Janus	Captain O'Hara	Sept 20 1780–Apr 12 1783
ADM51/4510	Trent	Captain Bagot	May 9 1797–12 June 1798
		Captain Otway	June 1798–29 Jan 1799

ADM106/1866   Portsmouth Commissioners, 1790–1794
ADM106/1867   Portsmouth Commissioners, 1795–1796
ADM178/111   Report of Admiral Sir John D. Kelly, Commander-in-Chief,
   Atlantic Fleet: 'State of Discipline in the Atlantic Fleet', 9 November 1931
ADM178/133   Lieut Commander J. H. Owen, 'Mutiny in the Royal Navy'
   (unpublished, Admiralty, 1933) 1932–1937 Insubordination in the Navy:
   instruction to officers on handling insubordination. Staff monograph of
   history of naval mutinies

Home Office
HO42/27   George III Letters and Papers, Nov–Dec 1793: John Heriot to
   Evan Nepean, 10 December 1793
HO42/41   Domestic Correspondence, George III, Dec–June 1797: Report
   on the Nore Mutiny by Aaron Graham and Daniel Williams to the Home
   Office Minister Duke of Portland, 24 June 1797
HO42/212   George III Letters and Papers, 1797: Letters addressed to the
   Fleet at the Nore June 1797

Privy Council
PC1/38   Privy Council, 27 June 1797
PC1/38/122   Papers relating to mutiny at the Nore, near Sheerness, Kent:
   Letters addressed to the Fleet at the Nore May, June 1797
PC1/42/A   Privy Council
PRO/30/8/51   Duke of Norfolk to Pitt, 12 January 1760
PRO/30/8/54   Duke of Bedford to Pitt, 11 February 1760

The National Maritime Museum
Philip Patton, *Strictures on Naval Discipline and the Conduct of a Ship of
   War, Intended to Produce a Uniformity of Opinion among Sea Officers*
   (c.1807).
WYN/109/7/14   Philip Patton, 'Observations on Naval Mutiny Presented
   April 1795' drafted in 1790
NE4   St Vincent to Nepean, 27 May 1797
ADM/L/M/145   Lieutenant's log *Meleager*
HOL/77   Sir Home Popham's Order Book
WYN/109/3   Admiral Sir Charles Morice Pole, 'Return of Irish Seamen and
   Marines in the Squadron', c.1797, Miscellaneous papers on naval matters
   1778–1829

Portsmouth City Museum
'Lines Composed on Board His Majesty's Ship LONDON', owned by John
   Pounds, Old Portsmouth, loaned to Portsmouth City Museum for the
   Spithead Mutiny Exhibition, 1997

Index

Acts of Parliament: Abolition of
the Slave Trade, 25 March 1807,
273; Census, 1800, 3; felony to
communicate with mutinous ships,
June 1797, 156, 172, 222; Fox's Libel,
1792, restored to juries the right to
decide what was libel, 70; Habeas
Corpus Suspension, 1794–5, 180;
Increase to Seamen's Pay, 9 May 1797,
27, 52, 53, 55, 61, 65, 70, 72, 74, 103,
108, 165; Insurrection, 1796, 135; Port
Quota Act for procuring a Supply
of Men, 1795, 16; Quota Acts (five),
1795–6, 3, 59, 180, 182, 182–3, 184,
186, 236; Seditious Meetings, 1795,
one of the 'Gagging Acts' or 'Two
Acts', 128, 129, 180; Treasonable and
Seditious Practices, 1795, one of the
'Gagging Acts' or 'Two Acts', 128,
129, 180; Unlawful Oaths 1797, 15
n. 71, 55–6
Adams, Michael, Spithead delegate, 44
Admiralty, The: Board of, 63, 83, 93, 95,
117, 125, 135, 248; commissioners,
2, 23, 25, 64, 67, 83, 84, 92, 155, 173;
enquiries into seamen's complaints, 98;
First Lord of, 2, 14, 15, 23, 48, 61, 73,
80, 140, 213; instructions, orders, 14,
61, 67, 71, 118 n. 35, 145, 229; letter
on starting, 1809, 275; letters to, 24,
51, 56, 98164, 274; minutes, 153–4;
Navy and Admiralty Committees, 40;
neglect in answering seamen's letters
of complaint, 1, 6, 99, 106, 215, 216;
Order of 1 May 1797, 55, 72, 74, 217;
pay offers, 27; proclamations, 14;
reforms, nineteenth century, xi, 14, 37,
100, 144, 145, 205, 207, 278; removal
of Thames buoys following an Order-
in-Council, 156, 221; responses to 1783
mutinies, 47–9; responses to mutiny
generally, 31, 33, 40, 64, 268, 279;
responses to Invergordon mutiny, 1931,
20; responses to Nore mutiny, 209, 224,
252; responses to Spithead mutiny, 35,

36, 50, 53, 54, 58, 65, 66, 68, 73, 74,
91, 103, 120, 130, 131, 140, 153, 154,
155, 156, 172, 214, 217, 218; visit to
Portsmouth, 25–6, 83–4, 86–7; visit to
Sheerness, 173, 174, 220, 252
Age of Reason, 121, 129, 189, 247
Agitators, 39
alcohol, 24, 66, 229, 233
Allen, John, boatswain's mate, *Nereide*,
1809, 270
Allen, Thomas, Spithead delegate, 44
America, 134
Americas, 43, 47; possible destination of
Nore mutineers, 156
American Independence, War of (1775–
83), 12, 31, 43; republicanism, 16, 39,
129; revolutionary ideas, 120
Americans, 9; impressed into the navy, 213
amnesty, 158
Anderson, William, Spithead delegate, 44
Arden, Lord *see* Perceval, Hon. Charles
George
Army, 31, 33, 39, 40, 149, 228, 276
Articles of War (1749), 2, 15, 28, 33, 40,
126, 206, 212, 229, 232
Ashley, Thomas, *Pompée* mutineer, 56
Assize of Bread, 43
Atlantic Ocean, 1
Atchison, Samuel, Plymouth delegate, 45
Atkinson, Thomas, Nore delegate, 147,
148, 151

Bagot, Captain Richard, *Trent*, 239, 240
Baltic Sea, 43
Bantry Bay (Ireland), 81; battle of, 23
December 1796, 81, 122, 187
Bastille, fall of, 14 July 1789, 128
Barham, Lord *see* Middleton, Captain
Charles
Batavian Republic (Napoleonic
Netherlands 1795–1806), 31, 120

Beaver, Lieutenant Philip (later Captain), 22, 50

Bedford, Duke of *see* Russell, Francis

Bedford, Captain William (later Vice Admiral) *Royal Sovereign*, 1797, 104

Belfast (Ireland), suggested destination for Nore mutineers, 222

Benge Lieutenant Edward, acting commander of *Otter*, 1808 during Willoughby's arrest, 266

Bennet, John, Spithead delegate, 44

Benny, David, Quota man flogged on *Trent*, 236

Berehaven Harbour (Bantry Bay, County Cork, Ireland) near Castletownbere in southwest coast of Ireland, 8

Berry, Charles, Spithead delegate, 44

Bertie, Vice Admiral Albermarle, commander-in-chief of the Cape, 1808–10, (later Admiral Sir), 264, 265, 266, 269, 274

Bethell, John, Spithead delegate, 44

Berwick, James, Spithead delegate, 44

Binns, John, London Corresponding Society delegate who visited Portsmouth 1796, 129

Blake, Admiral Robert, 40

Blane, Sir Gilbert, physician of the fleet, 1780, 198

Bligh, Captain William (later Vice Admiral) of *Director*, Nore Mutiny, 153–4

Blight, Lieutenant William, *Nereide*, 1806–9 (later Captain), 267

Blithe, James, Spithead delegate, 44

bloody flag *see* red flag

blue (loyal) flag, 157

Blue Lights, naval evangelicals, 13, 14

Bombay (Mumbai, India), important historical trading port and East India Company Dockyard used by the Royal Navy on the west coast of India, 264, 268

Bone, John, London Corresponding Society delegate who visited Portsmouth 1797, 130

bounty men, bounties, 180, 236

Bourne, W. S., founder of the *Observer* in 1791, at first independent, then with his brother W. H. Bourne, pro-government, 88

Bover, Lieutenant Peter Turner (later Captain), 71, 72, 75, 76–7

Bowater, Captain Edward, *Trent* (later Admiral), 239–40

Brenton, Lieutenant Edward, *Agamemnon* North Sea Fleet (later Captain), 7, 22, 261–2

Brest (France), 22, 23, 69, 124, 161; blockade of, from 1759, 196

Bridport, Admiral Sir Alexander, Viscount, acting, subsequently commander-in-chief of the Channel Fleet during the mutiny, 1, 2, 7, 23–4, 25, 27, 28, 47, 53, 64, 69, 70, 79, 80, 81, 91, 92, 93, 95, 104, 105, 164, 190, 191, 214, 215, 216–7

Brice, Lieutenant on *Royal Sovereign*, 1797, 105

Brisbane, Captain Charles *Trent* (later Rear Admiral Sir), 240, 242

Brompton Hill (Kent) overlooks Chatham Dockyard and the River Medway, 171

Broth, Anne, North Shields, letter from a seaman, North Sea Fleet, 255

Bruix, Étienne Eustache, French Minister of the Marine, 1798, 124

Buckner, Vice Admiral Charles (later Admiral) commander-in-chief at the Nore, 1797, 150, 152, 153, 169, 172, 191, 212, 252, 253, 259

bumboat men and women rowed small boats from river or shore to sell provisions to moored ships, 222

Burdett, Sir Francis, 19

Burdon, Rowland, County Durham MP, 1790–1806, 46

Burke, Edmund, MP, 1756–94, political theorist, 57, 59, 129, 140

Cadiz (Spain), 8, 22, 23, 30, 224

Calder, Captain Sir Robert (later Rear Admiral), 7

Calais (France), 191

Camperdown, Battle of, 11 October 1797, 137, 158, 243, 247

Cape St Vincent (Portugal), battle of, 14 February 1797, 111–12

Cape of Good Hope, established at Cape Peninsula on the south Atlantic African coast by the Portuguese from 1488 and the Dutch East India Company from 1652. Rear Admiral Elphinstone captured the Cape in 1795 and held it (battle of Saldanha Bay) in 1796. The colony and naval base at Cape Town in Table Bay was restored to the Dutch by the Peace of Amiens (1802), but in 1806 it was again captured by the British, possession ratified by the Treaty of Paris in 1814, 266, 267, 268, 273, 274

Capel, Lieutenant Sir Thomas Bladen (later Captain), 7

Carhampton, Lord see Luttrell

Carnegie, Captain William, 7th Earl of Northesk, Monmouth (later Admiral), who took a Nore petition to the Admiralty, 185, 260

Carr, Hugh, Plymouth delegate, 45

Carter, Sir John, Whig opposition Mayor of Portsmouth, 1796–7, 32, 34, 180–1

Cass, William, Spithead delegate, 44

Castlereagh, Lord Robert Stewart, 2nd Marquess of Londonderry, Foreign Secretary, 1813, 213

Cavanagh, Edward, Spithead delegate, 44

Cavendish-Bentinck, William Henry see Portland, 3rd Duke of

Cawsand Bay, anchorage on the east coast of Rame Head, on the west side of Plymouth Sound, 216

celebrations, 74, 147, 219

Channel Fleet, 1, 2, 3, 7, 9, 22, 23, 30, 31, 33, 39, 41, 55, 61, 63, 64, 67, 73, 78, 80, 83, 106, 107, 120–41, 142, 143, 144
    Admiral's command style, 139, 214; grievances, 150; officers of, 214, 218; seamen of, 147, 149, 152, 157, 166, 180, 192, 193, 216, 219, 224; ships of, 149, 162, 183, 184, 186, 190, 191

chaplains, 30, 125

Charles II, 51, 53, 130, 180

Charlotte of Mecklenburg-Strelitz, Queen Consort of George III, 79

Chatham (Kent), 48, 170, 182

cheering, 24, 49, 50, 54, 69, 99, 150, 219

civil rights, 78

Clarence, Vice Admiral HRH William Henry, Duke of (later Admiral of the Fleet, Lord High Admiral, King William IV), 68, 120, 206

Clarke, J. S. chaplain, Impétueux, 1797, 125

class warfare, 6, 278

cleaning: of ship, 199–201; of clothes, 198, 199–201; of person, 199–201

cleanliness, 196, 198, 199–201

Clear, George, Spithead delegate, 44

clothing, seamen's, 198, 273

Cobbett, William loyalist, later reformist journalist, MP, 1832, 88, 94

Cockburn, Captain George of Minerve, 1796–1802 (later Admiral Hon. Sir), MP, 35, 108–19, 239

Cole, John, Plymouth delegate, 45

collectivism, 126

colliers, 43, 170

Collingwood, Captain Baron Cuthbert (later Rear Admiral), 7, 27, 182–3, 190

Colpoys, Captain Edward Griffith (later Rear Admiral) in London, nephew of Vice Admiral Colpoys, 75, 103

Colpoys, Vice Admiral Sir John, 8, 25, 33, 52, 56, 61, 67, 69, 70, 71, 72, 74–5, 76, 103, 104, 136, 165, 166, 215, 217, 218

Colville, First Lieutenant, Eurydice, 1796, 205

commander-in-chief, 7, 98, 101, 117, 150, 154, 180, 195, 218, 224, 264, 266

committees: Nore, 148, 150, 151, 155, 157, 181, 245, 258, 261; North Sea Fleet, 243, 251, 254, 259; seamen's, 125

Commonwealth, seventeenth century, 29, 126

complaints: against officers, 98–106; against petty officers, 98–106

Compton, Lieutenant William (later Captain), *Minotaur*, 1797, 100

Conner, William, marine private, *Trent*, sentenced to death, 232

Conrad, Joseph, 78

conspiracy, 58, 180, 181, 193

conspiracy theory, 73, 78, 143, 179–193

Connolly, carpenter's boy, *Otter*, 1809, 274

convoys, 108, 110, 215

Cooke, Captain John, *Nymphe*, 1797, 100

Cook, Patrick, Plymouth delegate, 45

copper sheathing (of ships' hulls), 136

Corbet, Captain Robert, *Nereide*, 1806–9, 7, 10, 100 n. 9, 207, 266, 267, 268, 269, 270, 271, 272, 273, 274, 275, 279

Cork (Ireland) suggested destination for Nore mutineers, 222

corresponding societies, 126, 129, 143, 175, 177, 179, 182, 245

Cosby, Phillip, at Dublin Castle, 135

county associations, 1770s, 126

court(s) martial, xiii, 7, 8, 10, 14, 30, 41, 109, 117, 158, 199, 212, 224, 226, 229, 230, 234, 249, 264, 265, 266, 268, 269, 272, 273, 274, 277, 279; of officers for cruelty, 275, 276, 278

Cowper, William, 'On the loss of the Royal George', 1782, 95

Cristell, John, Spithead delegate, 44

Cromarty Firth, 5

Crossland, George, Spithead delegate, 44

Crown and Anchor Tavern in the Strand, London, 224

Culverhouse, Lieutenant Jonathan: on *Meleager*, 1794–6, *Minerve*, 1796–1802, 111

Cumberledge, Thomas, seaman, *Nereide*, 1809, 273

Cumby, Captain William Pryce, *Hyperion*, 1811, 206

Curaçao, siege of, 1804, to take the Dutch island, 265

Curtis, Rear Admiral Sir Roger (later Vice Admiral), 7, 31, 44, 143, 219

Dartmouth (Devon), 115

Dashwood, Lieutenant Charles (later Vice Admiral Sir), *Defiance*, 1797, 103

D'Auvergne, Captain Philippe, Prince de Bouillon (later Vice Admiral), agent in Jersey, 123–4

Davie, Captain John, wrote book on ship organisation, 1804, 202

Davies, member of *Sandwich* committee at the Nore, 152, 175

Davies, Captain John, *Otter*, 1805–7, 264

Day, seaman, *Sandwich*, Nore, letter, 249

Deal (Kent), ancient port and shipyard near the Downs anchorage and Goodwin Sands whose boatmen maintained good trade links across the Channel, 172

death, 145, 158, 180, 209, 226–42, 275; accidental drowning, 228; after flogging, 233; penalty, 232; for communicating with mutinous ships at the Nore, 172

de Bouëxic, Luc Urbain, Admiral Comte de Guichen, lost 15 transports to Admiral Kempenfeldt in the second battle of Ushant, 12 December 1781, 83

Defenders, 21, 121, 122, 132, 135

de Guichen *see* de Bouëxic, Luc Urbain, Admiral Comte de Guichen

delegates : alleged to have been paid money, 168; articles, 52, 152–3, 216, 253, 255; convention on *London*, 70, 71, 75; Downs, 171; elected representatives, 247; general assembly, 25; Irish, 133, 137; language, 76; London Corresponding Society, 129–30; Nore, 2, 147–9, 150, 151, 152, 167, 172, 174, 177, 181, 182, 245, 252, 253; North Sea, 169, 253; Plymouth, 216, 218; rules and orders, 24, 49, 125, 151; Spithead, 1, 4, 25, 32, 33, 39–60, 61, 65, 66, 85, 126, 162, 166, 215, 218, 219; strategy, 130;

democracy, democratic, 40, 41, 49, 60, 257

demotion of *Trent* seamen, related to flogging, 239

Deptford (Dockyard, Kent), 114

Devonish, Joseph P., seaman, *Belliqueux*, Nore, letter to wife, 252, 257, 262

'difference of opinion' *see* 'discontent',

Diggers, seventeenth century, 126

'Discharged Dead', from ships' books, 228

'Discharged Sick', from ships' books, 233, 234

discipline: of seamen, desired by the authorities, 67, 101, 144, 180, 190, 196, 198, 199, 202, 224, 276–7; naval officers', xi, 35, 42, 81–2, 83, 92, 213, 216; naval seamen's self-discipline, 24, 29, 31, 42, 56, 61, 64, 66, 85, 165, 216; overall, xi, 11, 78, 145, 226–42, 279

'discontent', 29, 61, 66, 67, 78, 148, 176

dissenters, 128

'disturbance' *see* 'discontent'

divine service, 197

divisional system, 82, 83, 195

divisions, 196, 198

Dixon, Captain, offered to get rid of Parker, 221

Dock (Plymouth), early name for Plymouth/Devonport Dockyard, 218

Downs, anchorage (Kent) near the Goodwin Sands, 40, 190; squadron, 195

Drake, Vice Admiral Sir Francis, 42

drinking, 195

drunkenness, 195

Dublin Castle (Ireland), centre of British rule until 1922, 123

Duggan, Patrick, Spithead delegate, 44

Duke of York *see* Frederick Augustus, Prince, Duke of York and Albany

Duncan, Adam, Admiral Lord, commander-in-chief North Sea Fleet, 1795–1800, 2, 7, 8, 13, 143, 145, 154, 155, 158, 190, 191, 192, 222, 243, 249–51, 254, 259, 261–3; crews' loyalty to, 261

Dundas, Augustus, topman, *Nereide*, 1809, 272–3

Dundas, Henry, *see* Melville, Lord

Durham, Captain Sir Philip, 7

Durnford, seaman and committee member, *Nassau*, North Sea Fleet, letter, 254

duty, 27, 58, 81, 92, 125

East India Company, 42, 221

East Indies, 47; Station, 264

Easter: Sunday (16 April 1797), 1, 24, 164; Monday (17 April 1797), 2, 25

economic indices, 130

education, 58

Edwards, Henry, Spithead delegate, 44

Elphinstone, George, Plymouth delegate, 45

Elphinstone, Captain George *see* Keith, Admiral George Elphinstone

Elizabethan traditions, 4

Erskine, Thomas, radical, barrister (later Lord Chancellor, 1806–7), opposition Whig MP, 126, 211

Essex, 170

excrement, 273

execution, 158, 209, 222, 223

eyewitnesses, 69

Fancourt, Captain Robert Devereux, *Agamemnon*, North Sea Fleet (later Admiral), 262

Faversham (Kent) ancient port on the River Swale, near the Isle of Sheppey, 191

feu de joye, fire of joy or salute of guns fired successively by each man along a line and back on occasions of public rejoicing, 219

Field, Colonel Cyril, RMLI, published 'Mutiny at the Nore – Ill-treatment of Officers' in *Britain's Sea-Soldiers*, 1924, 210–1, 223

fireships against the mutinous Nore ships, suggested by Vice Admiral Keith, 221

firing into mutinous ships, 53–4, 279

Fitzgerald, Lord Edward, cousin of Charles James Fox, United Irishman, 122, 123, 132

Fitzgerald, London attorney in Goodman Street, met Nore delegates, 258

flag of defiance *see* red flag

Fleming, John, Spithead delegate, *London*, 41 n. 16, 44, 58, 77

floating republic, 179, 245 *see also* Republic, The Floating

food *see* provisions

Fort Monckton, part of the western defences of Portsmouth Harbour, overlooks Spithead from the west, 86

Fountain Inn, Portsmouth High Street, proprietor George Fielding 1797, 83, 86

Fox, Charles James, leader of opposition Whigs, 24, 129, 186, 211, 215

France, 2, 10, 31, 55, 56, 84, 121, 134, 141, 192, 247, 251, 258; destination of *Inflexible* mutineers, 259; possible destination of Nore mutineers, 259

Freeling, Francis, Secretary of the Post Office, 116 n. 116

Frederick Augustus, Prince, Duke of York and Albany, 88

French: Directory, 123, 137; dockyards, 123; influence upon the mutinies, 84, 247; invasion, 123; merchants, 273; navy, 65, 69, 80, 83, 83, 122, 123, 123, 279; prisoners' cartel, 112; prizes, 83; republicanism, 129; Revolution, 78, 127, 278; revolutionaries, xi, 16, 33, 39, 55, 135; revolutionary ideas, 120, 121, 179; Terror, 144; wars, 194, 226, 227

Fresselique, J. J., chaplain, 30, 213–4, 219

fresh water for washing, 199, 200, 201

'From the Spirit of Kempenfeldt', 86, 91, 93, 95

Gallaway, George, Spithead delegate, 44

Galloway, Admiral George Stewart, Earl of, called Lord Garlies, MP admiralty commissioner, 1805–8, 213

Gambier, Admiral Sir James (later Admiral Baron James), 197

Gardner, Vice Admiral Sir Alan, second-in-command of the Channel Fleet, 7, 24, 25, 52, 53, 54, 63, 64–6, 68, 73, 74, 104–5, 125, 164, 215, 217

Garrison invalid corps, Portsmouth, 58

General Chamber of Manufacturers of Great Britain, 130

George I, 128

George III, 2, 8, 25, 47, 58, 60, 67, 83, 92, 120, 127, 128–9, 157, 185, 218, 260; 'God Save the King', 185; Nore ships flew the Union flag for the Stuart restoration in his honour (with the red flag), 29 May 1797, 171; North Sea delegates fired salute for the Stuart restoration in his honour, 29 May 1797, 169; porphyria, 89; proclamations, 173, 175, 221; responses to the mutinies, 220, 224; seamen's loyalty to, 189; seditious threats against, 185

George Augustus Frederick, Prince of Wales, 79

George Inn, Portsmouth High Street, 79, 87

Gibraltar, 111, 114

Gibson, James, marine private, *Trent*, flogged, 239

Gilder, John, Spithead delegate, 44

Glorious First of June, 1794, 30, 51

Glorious revolution, 1688, 126

Glynn, Patrick, Spithead delegate, 44, 56

Gosport (Hampshire), naval supply port and military base opposite Portsmouth on the west entrance to Portsmouth harbour, 219

governor's house Portsmouth (demolished 1826) was next to the ex-royal hospital, Domus Dei, now the Garrison Church, close to the Square Tower and the Parade, 219

government: control of the press, 170; duty to, 40; financial problems, xii, 31, 60; intelligence, 120, 123; legislation *see* Acts of Parliament; ministers, 61, 67, 70, 72, 173; newspapers, 87–9, 90; proclamations, 33; propaganda, 173, 247; responses to mutinies, 63, 68, 73, 78, 91, 93, 120, 130, 131, 132, 135, 141, 144, 149, 153, 170, 172, 180; surveillance, 21, 59, 140; use of newspapers at the Nore, 122

Gower, Captain Erasmus (later Admiral Sir), *Triumph*, 1797, 103–4

Graham, Aaron, Home Office magistrate sent to investigate sedition in the mutinies: Portsmouth 14 n. 60, 21, 32, 57, 58, 60, 131, 180, 181, 219–20; Sheerness, 180, 181–2, 187, 245, 263

Gravesend (Kent) on the south bank of the River Thames, opposite Tilbury Fort on the north bank, marks the entrance to the Port of London, 170, 176, 177, 221

Great Nore anchorage see Nore anchorage

Green, Joseph, Spithead delegate, 44

Green, William, seaman, Montagu, Nore, letter from parents, 177

Gregory, member of Sandwich committee at the Nore, 152

'Gregory, James', seaman, Montagu, Nore, letter from Charlotte Osbaldeston, 177, 178

Greenland, 43

Greenland, Benjamin, Plymouth delegate, 45

Greenwich (Kent in 1797)

Greenwich Hospital see Royal Hospital for Seamen at Greenwich

Grenville, Lord see Wyndham, William

Grey, General Sir Charles, commander of Sheerness garrison, 173, 211

Griffith, Captain see Colpoys, Edward Griffith

Griffiths, Captain Anselm John (later Rear Admiral), 109, 203–4, 205, 207–8

Groignard, Antoine, leading French eighteenth-century naval architect and engineer, 124

Groves, Joseph, printer Kentish Chronicle, 163

Guthrie, William, Pompée mutineer, 55, 56

Haddock, Captain Richard (c.1581–1660, later Vice Admiral), 40

Hall, Captain Basil, 204

Hallowell, Captain Benjamin (later Admiral Sir Benjamin Hallowell Carew), Lively, 1797, 109

Hamilton, Captain Edward (dismissed and restored 1802, later Admiral Sir), 145, 230, 239, 240, 242

hammocks, 270

Hamoaze (Plymouth), 26, 219 n. 59

handbills, 46, 60, 76, 109, 175, 211

Hanoverian monarchy, 128

Harding, Alexander, Spithead delegate, 41 n. 16, 44

Hardy, Lieutenant Thomas Masterman (later Vice Admiral Sir) on Meleager 1794–6, Minerve 1796–1802, 111, 117

Hardy, Thomas, secretary London Corresponding Society, 127

Hargood, Captain Sir William, 7

Hartwell, Captain Francis John, Commissioner of Sheerness Dockyard, 1797–1800, 253

Haslar Hospital (Gosport, Hampshire), 56

Haton, Captain James, Trent, 239, 240, 242

Hay, John, marine private, Trent, flogged, 229

health, crew's, 196, 197, 198

Heriot, John, pro-government founder-editor of the Sun and the True Briton newspapers, 87–93

Hervey, Captain Lord John Augustus, 48

Hewson, Thomas Phipps, supernumerary Sandwich, Nore, gave evidence against Jephson, 185–6

Higgins, William, seaman, Belliqueux, North Sea Fleet, letter to his mother, 256

Hines, Edward, Nore delegate, 147, 148, 151

Hismer, Joseph, seaman, Belliqueux, North Sea Fleet, letter to his parents, 255

historians: economic, 130; Irish, 122–3; Marxist, 3, 144–5; naval, xii, 3–7, 33, 107, 112, 145, 150, 191, 213, 214, 226, 236–7, 246–8, 250–1; social, xii, 3, 107–8, 121–5, 132, 136, 141, 142–3, 150, 179, 180, 180, 182, 191, 193, 226, 237, 243, 246–7, 250–1; socialist, xii, 3, 107, 179, 180, 181, 193, 243, 246–8; Whig, 211

Hoche, General Louis Lazare,
    commanding French troops assisting
    United Irishmen in 1796, 122
Hockless, member of *Sandwich*
    committee at the Nore, 152
Hodgskin, Lieutenant Thomas,
    description of starting, 269–70, 275
Hoggan, George, Plymouth delegate, 45
Hollister, Matthew, Nore delegate, 147,
    148, 149, 150, 151, 152, 158
Holloway, Captain John (later Admiral),
    Duke, 1797, 105
Hollowood, John, Spithead delegate, 44
Holmes, Lieutenant, *Amphitrite*, 1797, 102
holystoning, seamen on their knees
    scoured ships' wooden deck with a
    piece of soft sandstone about the size
    of a Bible, 205, 229
Honeyman, Captain Robert (later
    Admiral), *Tisiphone*, 1797, MP, 162
Holt, Daniel, Newark publisher
    convicted of seditious libel, 1793, 126
Home Fleet, 5, 278
Home Office, 57, 254; magistrates, 14
    n. 60, 21, 32, 57, 58, 60, 131, 143, 180,
    181, 245, 263; spies, 127
Home Secretary *see* Portland, 3rd Duke of
homosexual, 269
Hood, Captain Sir Samuel (later Vice
    Admiral Sir), 7
Hoop and Horseshoe Tavern, Little
    Tower Hill, London, where Richard
    Parker's body was displayed, 225
Horser, George, Spithead delegate, 44
Hotham, Admiral Lord William, 7, 8
House of Commons, 46, 51, 73, 74, 90,
    128, 215–6; Committee of Secrecy,
    appointed by William Pitt, 20, 59, 127,
    132
House of Lords, 67, 69, 70
Houses of Parliament, 8, 33, 39, 41, 53,
    55, 61, 65, 69, 70, 72, 74, 88, 130, 156,
    172, 213
Howard, Lord Charles, 1st Earl of
    Nottingham, Lord High Admiral,
    1585–1619, 42
Howe, Captain Richard, then Admiral

Earl, First Lord of the Admiralty,
    1783–88, commander-in-chief of
    the Channel Fleet, 1790–7, 79, 95,
    148, 153, 213; 'Black Dick', 147,
    148; printed signal book 1758,
    197; representative of George III in
    Spithead celebrations, 9, 74, 140, 218,
    219; role in 1783 mutinies, 12, 39, 47–
    8; role in initial seamen's and marines'
    petitions, 1, 7–8, 17, 22–3, 28, 35, 50,
    64, 66, 67–8, 136, 218; sailor's friend,
    197; standing orders 1776, 196
Huddlestone, John, Spithead delegate, 44
Hughes, member of *Sandwich*
    committee at the Nore, 152
Husband, John, Spithead delegate, 44
Hyland, John, Spithead delegate, 44

'idlers': craftsmen and servants on board
    naval ships, 201, 229, 237
Île de France (Mauritius), from 1715 a
    French island colony in the south-west
    Indian Ocean east of Madagascar,
    captured by the British in 1810, 264, 271
impressed, 175, 183, 190; more likely to
    be flogged on *Trent*, 236
impressment, 14, 30, 46, 112, 133, 135,
    180, 213, 236
Impress Service, 46
Indian Ocean, 1; Fleet, 264
inflammatory language, 181
inflation, 43, 130, 215, 254
information technology in naval history,
    227
Inglis, Alexander, Plymouth delegate, 45
Ingram, William, Spithead delegate, 44
invasion, threat, 11, 107, 120, 123, 161, 278
Ireland, 31, 107, 122, 123, 134, 137, 247,
    278; possible destination of Nore
    mutineers, 156, 259
Irish: born, 3, 59, 136, 137, 184; anti-
    British campaigns, 124, 185, 186;
    Catholics, 121, 122, 179, 184; marines,
    135, 184; protestants, 124, 179;
    republicanism, 3, 16, 57, 121, 179, 184;
    revolutionary ideas, 120, 184; seamen,
    3, 6, 8, 9, 21, 22, 123, 133, 134, 135,
    136, 138, 184, 187, 191, 193, 259

Isle of Grain (Kent), an island at the head of the Hoo Peninsula where the River Medway meets the Thames, opposite Sheerness, 155

Isle of Sheppey (Kent), island off the north Kent coast separated from the mainland by the River Swale; the main towns are Sheerness and Queenborough, 170, 172

Isle of Wight, 7, 23

Jackson, George Vernon, midshipman, *Trent*, 1800–2 (later Admiral), 239

Jacobins, Jacobinism, 19, 41, 78, 86, 186, 212, 236

Jacob's ladder, a rope ladder used to climb from the lower mast to the top mast rigging, around the top platform, 271

Jane, Duchess of Gordon, 79

Jefferson, Michael, surgeon, *Vanguard*, 1797–8, 200

Jephson, Thomas, formerly an Irish Belfast shoemaker, seaman delegate *Sandwich*, Nore, 177, 184–6, 258

Jervis, Sir John, *see* St Vincent

Johnson, Captain, investigated the Otters' complaints of Captain Willoughby, 1808, 265

Johnstone, John, Plymouth delegate, 45

Jones, John Gale, member of the London Corresponding Society, visited Chatham in 1795, 257

Joyce, Valentine, quarter master's mate, delegate *Royal George*: alleged Belfast clubman, tobacconist, Quota man, 21, 57, 58, 140, 166; alleged to have travelled to Sheerness, 162; born Jersey, 58; family kidnapped by A. Graham, 180; father Valentine Joyce, 58; mother Elizabeth Joyce, 58; Spithead delegate and spokesman, 4, 8, 13, 20, 21, 44, 56, 57–8, 77

jurisprudence, 15

Keats, Captain Sir Richard Goodwin (later Admiral), 8, 206

keelmen, 43

Kelly, Admiral Sir John, 5

Kempenfeldt, Captain Richard (later Rear Admiral) 79, 82–3, 95–6, 139

Kent, North, 142, 147, 148, 170

Keppel, Admiral the Hon. Augustus, Viscount, 48

Keith, Admiral George Elphinstone, 1st Viscount, formerly Captain George Elphinstone, 47 n. 46, 209, 211, 212, 221, 222

King, John, boatswain of *Jason*, 1797, 101

King, John, under-secretary of state at the Home Office, 129

King, T. G., seaman, *Nassau*, North Sea Fleet, letter to brother, 257

King Lear, 141

King, Vice Admiral Sir Richard, commander-in chief, Plymouth, 1797 (later Admiral), 216, 218

King, Thomas, seaman, *Nassau*, North Sea Fleet, letter to his wife, 254

Knowles, Captain Sir Charles (later Admiral), 197; signal and order books, 197

labour dispute, 78, 272

'Launched into Eternity', 209

law: and customs of the sea, 232; and order ashore, 226; social function of, 274

Lawler, Dennis, Spithead delegate, 44

Lawson, Captain John (later Admiral Sir), 23

Lee, William, mutineer seaman, *Royal Sovereign*, executed September 1797, 222

Leech, Samuel, ship's boy, *Macedonian*, 1810–2, description of starting, 270, 275

Leeward Islands (Lesser Antilles, Caribbean Sea), 114

Leghorn (Livorno, Tuscany, Italy), 114

Lemon, John, Plymouth delegate, 45

Lennox, Charles, 3rd Duke of Richmond, 3rd Duke of Lennox, 3rd Duke of Aubigny, 122 n. 8; 1780 Reform Bill, 127, 128–9

letters written by/to seamen and mutineers at the Nore, 144, 175–8, 249, 253–7, 262–3

Levellers, seventeenth century, 40, 126

Lewin, James, secretary to the committee meeting on *Sandwich* at the Nore, 258

Lewins, Edward, United Irish agent, 123,

liberty, 24, 52, 56, 134, 135, 195, 203, 261

liberty of the press, 90

Lilburne, John, Leveller leader, 40

Linden, James, printer *Hampshire Chronicle*, 163

Linsday, John, Spithead delegate, 44

liquor *see* alcohol

Litchfield, Henry, Home Office magistrate sent to Sheerness to investigate sedition the Nore mutiny and attended Parker's court martial, 245, 249, 263

literacy, 4, 125, 257, 277

Liverpool (Lancashire), 43

Lock, Captain Walter (later Vice Admiral), 54

Lock, Captain Charles, *Inspector*, the Nore, 1797, 167, 251

Locke, John, political philosopher, secretary to the Board of Trade and Plantations 1670s, 129

log books, xiii, 98, 229, 232, 233, 236, 240

London, 43, 148, 149, 156, 171; responses to Nore mutiny, 176

London Corresponding Society, 11, 40, 127, 128, 148, 177, 211, 257; Portsmouth branch, 129; remonstrance, 1795, 128

Long, Henry, wrote a note addressed to the Board of Admiralty, found on *Repulse*, Nore, 189

Long Reach, a point on the River Thames near Gravesend, 176, 212, 221

longevity of service on a ship: reducing flogging on *Minerve*, 113, 239; reducing flogging on *Trent*, 239–40

Lot, William, carpenter's boy, *Otter*, 1809, 274

Loughborough, Lord, (Alexander Wedder-burn) Lord Chancellor, 1793–1801, 26

lower deck, xiii, 6, 7, 8, 12, 13, 35, 36, 59, 83; actions, 98–106, 113, 145;

attitudes, 145, 159, 175; life, 194–208, 227; voices from, 98–106, 269

loyalists, 49, 55

Lukin, Captain William (later Vice Admiral Windham), 109–10

Luttrell, Henry Lawes, 2nd Earl of Carhampton, commander-in-chief Ireland, 1796–8, 58, 166

MacCarthy, Neil, Plymouth delegate, 45

MacDonough, seaman, *Eurydice*, 1796, 205

Mackenzie, Andrew, Plymouth delegate, 45

Madagascar, a large island kingdom off the southeast of Africa, strategic within Indian Ocean trade routes, an important base for pirates and slave traders, its control contested by the French and British until the British won the Battle of Tamatave off western Madagascar in 1811, 264, 266, 268, 273, 279

Madeira (Portuguese archipelago in the North Atlantic Ocean), 108

magistrates: borough, 183, 225, *see also* Home Office

Maitland, Agnes, Leith, wrote letter to Hardwick Richardson, seaman, *Inflexible*, Nore, 176

Malden (also Maldon, Essex), port, 170

management practices/tools, 108, 230, 240

Manchester, 179

marines, 24, 53, 55, 65, 69, 71, 75, 85, 135, 136, 166, 217, 227, 228, 253, 256; conditions, 27; interests shared with seamen, 41; flogged, 231, 233, 234, 235, 241, 242; removed during the mutinies, 102; 'ships' policemen', 136, 231, 267, 268

Margate, Kent, 170

Marsden, William, second secretary to the Admiralty, 1795–1804 (later first secretary), 173

martial law, 135

McCann, Thomas, Nore mutineer, 158

McCarthy, Charles from Cork, Nore delegate, 9, 147, 148, 149, 150, 151, 152, 158, 258

McCloud, master's mate, *Eurydice*, 1796, 205

Medway, River, 2, 147, 150, 155, 161

Mediterranean Sea, 1, 43, 115

Mediterranean Fleet, 23, 115, 135, 180, 269, 278

messes, 196: right to change, 203–5; size and number, 203–5

Mein, Thomas, Plymouth delegate, 45

Melville, Herman, *Billy Budd*, begun in 1888, refers to the 1797 mutinies, 223

Melville, Lord, secretary of state for the Home Department, 1791–94; minister for war, 1794–1801, 8

Melvin, James, Spithead delegate, *Pompée*, 44, 56

merchant seamen, 4, 29, 33, 43, 126, 130, 180, 184, 190, 214, 221, 277

merchant officers, 4

Methodism, Methodists, 14

Microsoft Access database, 227; methodology, 230, 241

Middleton, Captain Charles (later Admiral Sir, Lord Barham), 14, 82, 196, 206

middle-class views, 162, 177, 178

Milam, John, seaman *Belliqueux*, North Sea Fleet, letter to his parents, 255

militia, 31

Monaghan (Ireland), 123; militia, 123

Monke, Commander G. P., 198–9

Montagu, Admiral Sir John, Portsmouth port admiral, 48

morale, crew's, 196

Morrice, John, Spithead delegate, 44

Mosse, Captain James Robert of *Sandwich*, Nore, 1793–7, 212, 224

Moulton, Captain Robert (later navy commissioner 1651–2), 40

Mumford, Richard, Plymouth delegate, 45

murmuring, 56, 279

muster books, 9, 22, 43, 115, 241

mutineers, indecision among, 222

mutiny: *Bounty*, (1789), (11); Cadiz Fleet (1797, 1798), 220, 223; Channel Fleet, 149, 223; Channel Fleet (1798), 187; Downs, 171; East Coast, 147–59; Ely militia (1809), 88 n. 36; fleet, 8, 12, 31; general, 133, 213; *Hermione* (1797), 11; individual ships, 84, 223; Invergordon (1931), 5, 6, 17, 20, 37, 223; keelmen(seventeenth century), 43; multiple-ship, 4, 153; *Nereide* (1809), 264–79; Nore (1797), 2, 10, 12, 14, 15, 17, 21, 22, 35, 41, 118, 119, 131, 137, 140, 142–5, 147–59, 167, 168, 175, 177, 179–93, 220, 223, 225, 249, 252; North Sea (1797), 2, 3, 13, 169, 249–63; number of, 2–3, 61, 69, 70; *Otter* (1808), 7, 264–6, 274–5; Plymouth (1628), 42; Plymouth (1797), 85–6, 216, 219, 220; *Pompée* (June 1797), 55, 132, 219; Portsmouth (1628), 42; royalist (1648), 40; second Spithead (1797), 61, 166; Spithead (1783), 9, 12, 47, 48, 133; Spithead (1797), 1, 2, 3, 7–8, 10, 12, 13, 14, 15, 17–37, 39, 43, 49, 55, 59, 60, 67, 69, 78, 79, 85, 90, 91, 108, 118, 119, 131, 133, 137, 140, 147, 148, 151, 152, 153, 154, 175, 213, 216, 219, 220, 223, 268, 269; single-ship, 5, 6, 12, 22, 31, 48, 144, 195; South Africa, 223; theory, xi, 4–5, 9–10; twentieth-century typology, 10, 11; West Indies (1797), 223; Yarmouth (1797), 8

Nastyface, Jack, pseudonym for William Robinson, 102; meaning of name, 204

Naval Instructions 1775, 195

naval officers, in general: arbitrary power, 11; careers, 8; complaints against, 99–106,; conduct, 98–106; cruelty, 6, 12, 35, 40, 48, 100–1, 133–4, 136, 205, 269, 274, 278; discipline, 82, 119, 139, 214, 225; gentlemanly behaviour, 102, 275; yearly election, 40; leadership, xi, 8, 10, 11, 15, 214; ratio of commissioned officers to men, 228; removals, 27, 35, 40, 74, 101, 102, 103, 104, 105, 106, 145, 147, 148, 218; responses to 1797 mutinies, 219, 277; royalist, 40; seamen's respect for, 104, 105, 106; sympathy for 1797 mutinies, 15, 144, 218, 277; worship, 13

naval officers, commissioned: admirals, 98, 195, 217, 264, 266, 273, 275; captains, 98, 100, 101, 102, 103, 104, 105, 195, 196, 200, 201, 202, 205, 207, 213, 220, 228, 229, 230, 232, 236, 239, naval officers, commissioned: (*cont.*) 241, 242, 254, 272, 273, 274, 275, 277, 278, benefits for the ship's company, 101–2, clerk, 111, followers, 110, impartiality in courts martial, 158, inexperience, 139, letters, 9, logbooks, 145, multiplicity of business, 115, responsibility, 115; first lieutenant removed from *Amphitrite*, 102; generals, 40; lieutenants, 102, 103, 106, 111, 161, 205, 205, 206, 254, 277; midshipmen, 41, 102, 111, 195, 237, 277; petty officers, 13, 106, 196, 206, 213, 216

naval officers, warrant, 206; boatswains, 111, 157, 267, 272; master at arms, 118, 206; on *Minerve/Meleager*, 110, Fellows, Charles, 111, Galway, Robert, 116, Gregory, James, 116, Henley, John, 116, Hobbs, Richard, 116, Mooney, Patrick, 116, Thompson, John, 116, Taylor, Robert, 116; surgeons, 114, 115, complaints against, 102, 103, seamen's requests for removal, 102, threats against, 167, writings, 194

naval punishment: abusive language, frequent use of, 35, 101, 274; carrying hammock on the back, 102; cat-o'-nine-tails, 100, 106, 171, 230, 233, marinated in pickle juice, 272; complaints regarding, 99–106; drinking a pint of salt water, 206; execution, 15; flogging, 15, 35, 99, 100, 109, 111, 114, 117, 118, 205, 206, 226, 229, 230, 231, 232, 233, 234, 236, 237, 238, 239–42, 266, 269, 272–3, 274, 277, round the fleet, 234, used as a punishment by mutineers, twelve lashes only, 242; hanging, 15, 223, 269; imprisonment, 15; informal, 206–7; inconsistence, 158; lashed to guns/rigging, 230; numbers of lashes, 100, 101; physical, 2, 12; records, 35, 113, 117, 229–34, 241; returns began 1811, 14; running the gauntlet, 13, 118 n. 35; running the gauntlet abolished in 1806, 100, 118 n. 35, 207; starting/beating with a rope's end, rattan cane, 14, 100, 101, 102, 106, 118 n. 35, 206, 207, 229, 264, 269–70, 272, 273, 274, 275; starting abolished 1809, 100, 207, 275; with-holding the daily rum or wine ration, 101, 102, 200; wooden collar, 197, 206

naval seamen: able, 27, 41, 42, 111, 217, 237; allotment, 49, 86; American, 59; arrears of pay, 11, 16, 30, 179, 191; boatswain's mate, 111, 157, 206, 270, 271, 272, 273–4; boys, 111, 227, 235; captain of the forecastle, 216, 219; carpenter's mate, 111; caulker, 111; celebratory dress, 54; characteristics, 125, 228; cook, 111, 272; collective memory, 12, 70, 94, 279; communities, 43; complaints against officers, 98; conditions, 8, 60; continuity of service, 113; corporal, 111; coxswain, 111; crews, 227, 228; deaths, 4, 32, 33, 49, 103; demands, 2, 27, 41, 63, 65, 143, 147, 180, 218, 253; disabled; disease, 4; execution, 144; foreign, 235; French, 59; Dutch, 59; German, 59; grievances, 12, 15, 37, 40, 41, 52, 53, 54, 60, 64, 67, 78, 80, 83, 93, 99–106, 165, 219, 259; gunner, 111; gunner's mate, 41; indecision at the end of the Nore mutiny, 259; injured, 27, 42, 52, 72, 75; Irish *see* Irish seamen; landsmen, 27, 207, 237; language, 76; loyalty, xi, 6, 12, 15, 56, 92, 109, 157, 192, 207, 219; master's mate, 111, 205, 170; *Minerve*, Brady, Charles, Brady, John, Evett, Jonathan, Fellows, Charles, Fells, Jonathan, Johnson, Thomas, Knapp, Jonathan, Lawson, Theodosius, Markey, William, Morrison, Henry, Nugent, William, Renoux, Jonathan, Slaper, Robert, Taylor, Robert, Wilson, Richard; moderation, 246; money paid to further mutiny, 168; nationality, 234–5, 241; numbers, 4, 30, 31, 39, 43, 46, 59, 143, 180; ordinary, 27, 111, 217, 237; organisation, 40, 41, 42, 191, 219; pensions, 27, 165; political aims, 40, 59, 188–9, 246, 248, 257; public support for, 176; recruitment, 42, 235–6; round robin, 33, 42, 279; Russian, 59; Scandinavian, 59; Scottish, 235; senior rates, 8, 11, 15, 31, 32, 213; sick and wounded, 27, 42, 52, 60; strategy, 172, 218; surgeon's mate, 116; topmen, 267, 269, 270, 272, 274, 278; topsail yardmen, 271; traditions, 4, 22, 33, 41, 42, 43; voices, 42, 98–106, 144; volunteers, 112, 135, 180, 183, 227,

235, 236; Welsh, 235; West Indian, 59; wounded in action, demand for wages to be paid to, 99; yeoman of the powder room, 41; yeoman of the sheets, 40, 111, 116

Navy: alphabets, 115; Board, 47, 96, 115; bounties, 28, 30; complements, 110, 112; debt, 23, 213; divisional system, 29; merchant, 15, 29, 30, 33, 42, 43, 214, 228; Royal, 15, 17, 22, 30, 31, 39, 42, 43, 66, 78, 92, 106, 118, 119, 136, 141, 180, 190, 203, 226, 228, 241, 272

Neale, Captain Sir Harry Burrard (later Admiral), MP, 155

'necessaries', see provisions

Nelson, Rear Admiral Viscount Horatio (later Vice Admiral) 22, 108, 109, 120, 224

Nepean, Edmund, First Lieutenant, Atlas, Plymouth, 216 n. 36

Nepean, Evan, under-secretary at the Home Office, 1782–94, secretary for the Department of War and Colonies, 1794, secretary to the Admiralty, 1795–1804, MP, 1 n. 3, 24, 25, 46, 56, 80–1, 92, 129, 188, 212, 215, 216, 223

Netherlands (Dutch), 192

New Model Army, 126; grievances, 39; officers expelled, 39

Newenham, Sir Edward, Irish protestant Whig MP, letter to Earl Spencer 1797, 184, 186

Newmarket (Suffolk), 39

newspapers, 31, 32, 33, 55, 59, 68, 69, 76, 88, 94, 125, 277; controlled by the government during the mutinies, 170; county: Hampshire, Kentish, East Anglian, 144, 163, 166, 167, 168, 171, 174, 178; Dublin News Letter, 163 n. 5, 172 n. 41; Evening Post (London), 171; Hampshire Chronicle, 164, 165, 168, 172; Ipswich Journal, 168. 169; journalists, 161, 163; Kentish Chronicle, 157, 167, 168, 169, 171, 172, 173, 174, 175; Kentish Gazette, 161, 162, 167, 168, 173–4; local correspondents, 161, 162, 166, 173; London, 61, 163, 165, 166; London Chronicle; ministerial, 67, 70, 76, 91;

Moniteur, 88; Maidstone Journal, 167; Morning Herald, 61, 67, 69, 95; Morning Post, 70; Norfolk Chronicle, 168, 169, 175, 177; Northern Star, 123; opposition, 67, 76; Observer, 88; Oracle and Public Advertiser, 71, 74–5; Portsmouth Gazette and Weekly Advertiser, 22, 57, 164, 165, 166, 168, 172, 177; presses, 123; provincial newspapers, 161–78, 175, 178; Saturday Review, 25 n. 38; stamp duty increase, 1797, 90; Star, 64, 69–70, 71, 86, 165; Sun, 57, 88, 89, 87, 90, 91, 93, 166; Times, The, 25, 33, 64, 78, 89, 90, 141; True Briton, 89, 90–3; used at the Nore by the government to control information, 122

Nichelson, William, master attendant Portsmouth Dockyard, 1770–83, 96–7

Nicholls, Captain Henry (later Admiral), Marlborough, 1797, 101–2

nonconformists, nonconformity, 13, 128

Nore (Great): anchorage near the Nore sandbank at the mouth of the Thames estuary, near Sheerness, 2, 142, 143, 155, 157, 161, 172, 185, 243, 252, 253, 254, 255, 259, 262; Fleet, 157, 168, 190, 217, 221; seamen at, 174, 219

Northesk, Lord see Carnegie, Captain William

North Foreland (Kent), cliff headland in the Isle of Thanet forming Kent's most easterly point, 156

North Sea Fleet, 2, 3, 143, 145, 150, 154, 155, 157, 169, 183, 190, 191, 243–63

Nows, John, Spithead delegate, 44

oaths : Defenders', 21, 132; marines', 41, 130; merchant seamen's, 131; seamen's, 12, 16, 24, 33, 49, 55–6, 64, 130, 131, 132; Spithead, 130; soldiers', 127, 131; trade unions', 130, 131; United English, 132; United Irish, 21, 57, 132

O'Connell, Daniel, Irish political leader, barrister, campaigner for Catholic Emancipation and political reform, renounced freemasonry after the 1826 Papal Bull against secret societies, 131

O'Connor, Arthur, United Irishman, arrested and tried (acquitted) in 1798 and rearrested, 123, 132

offences, naval: absent without leave, 231; attempting to desert, 231, 240; breaking leave on shore, 112, 117; contempt, 113, 117, 231, 232; desertion, 4, 112, 145, 180, 203, 226–242; desertion rates, 228; disobedience of orders, 113, 212, 236, 240; drawing upon a superior officer, 114; drunkenness, 111, 113, 206, 231, 232, 236, 240; enticing others to desert, 240; fighting, 113, 231, 232; going ashore without leave, 112; impertinence, 117; indecent familiarity, 114; insolence, 114, 117, 231, 232, 240; mutinous assembly, 40, 117, 199, 212; mutinous behaviour, 231, 232; mutinous expressions, 117; mutinous language, 117; mutiny, 113, 114, 117; neglect of duty, 111, 113, 231, 232, 240; negligence, 231; quarrelling, 113, 114, 231, 232, 240; recorded, 113, 114, 231, 238; sleeping on watch, 239; striking a superior officer, 114; swearing, 197, 206; theft, 113, 114, 231, 233, 236, 240; treating superior officers with disrespect, 212; uncleanliness, 114, 200, 206, 231, 233

Oliver, William, Spithead delegate, 44

Onslow, Vice Admiral Sir Richard, second-in-command North Sea Fleet (later Admiral), 249

Orde, Rear Admiral Sir John, commander-in-chief Plymouth, 7

order, 274

order-in-council, 172, 221

Ormskirk (Lancashire), 43

Osbaldeston, Charlotte, wrote letter to Gregory, James, seaman, *Montagu*, Nore, 177, 178

Otway, Captain Robert Waller (later Admiral Sir), *Trent*, 239, 240, 242

Pakenham, Captain the Hon. (later Admiral Sir) Thomas, 6, 8, 23, 36, 213

Paine, Thomas, *Rights of Man* (1791); *Age of Reason* (I, 1794; II, 1795; III, 1807), 21, 120, 126, 129, 141, 247

Palermo (Sicily), 114

pardon, 269, 274; royal, 2, 8, 14, 25, 27, 52, 54, 61, 65–6, 74, 165, 175, 219

Parker, Admiral Sir Peter, Portsmouth port admiral, 23, 25, 80, 105, 164

Parker, Richard Nore, mutineer: background and career, 8, 224; burial, 225; court martial, 158, 159, 211, 212, 245, 249; death, 2, 13, 209, 224–5; met the Admiralty commissioners, 253; moderation, 151, 152; North Sea Fleet under his command, 252; President/leader of the Nore Mutiny, 2, 13, 151, 152, 174, 175, 187, 188, 191, 192, 220, 247, 259; Quota man, 151; suggested removal of, 221; wife Ann, 224

Parkinson, James, Plymouth delegate, 45

Parliament Ship, 2, 151

Pasley, Vice Admiral Sir Thomas (later Admiral), president of Richard Parker's court martial, 212, 224

paternalism, 15, 114

Patman, member of *Sandwich* committee at the Nore, 152

patriotism, 88, 92

Patton, Captain, Charles, Transport Board Agent, 23, 29

Patton, Captain (later Admiral) Philip, 4, 8, 13, 15, 29, 53, 130, 132, 198, 199, 201, 213

Pay, naval: allotment, 115; arrears, 143, 179, 191, 249, 254, 255; back, 115; books, 115; bounty, 115, 180, 236; increase, 27, 33, 36, 41, 51, 55, 60, 64, 78, 80, 84, 90, 93, 108, 130, 145, 154, 180, 213, 214, 215, 253, 259; for those wounded in action, 27; per lunar month, 27; rates, 4, 6, 8, 11, 13, 23, 24, 29, 30, 33, 47, 51, 64, 78, 214, 215; remittance, 115; tickets, sick, dead, remove, 115

Payne, James, Plymouth delegate, 45

Payne, Captain John Willett (later Rear Admiral), MP 1787–96, 79, 83–7, 94, 97

peace, xi, 55, 60

Peage, James, Plymouth delegate, 45

Pearce, Nicholas, Plymouth delegate, 45

Pellew, Captain Sir Edward, then Rear Admiral and East Indies commander-in-chief, 1804–9, based at Bombay (Mumbai) (later Admiral), 7, 8, 266

Pellew, Israel, 7

Penrose, Sir Charles, 14

'people', the, 48, 54, 276

perseverance statements, 32, 39, 51, 52, 53, 54

'Per order' seamen transferred with a captain to a new ship, 110

Perceval, Hon. Charles George, admiralty commissioner, 1783–1801, 173

petitions: to the Admiralty, 215; Downs, 171; to the House of Commons, 215; London Corresponding Society, 128; marines', 102, 136; Nore, 169, 260; North Sea Fleet, 249–50; seamen's, xiii, 33, 35, 98–106, 133, 136, 159, 164, 200, 205–6, 247, 248, 263, 276

Pompée, 55; Spithead, 9, 17, 22, 23, 24, 40, 42, 49, 50, 51, 52, 59, 64, 80, 92, 215, 216

Peyton, Admiral Joseph, 104

Pickering, John, seaman, *Nassau*, North Sea Fleet, letter, 254, 256

Pigot, Captain Hugh, *Hermione* whose crew mutinied and murdered him on 21 September 1797, 145

Pitt, William, chancellor of the exchequer, 1782–3, 1783–1801, 1804–6, prime minister, 1783–1801, 1804–6, 8, 19, 33, 59, 60, 63, 67, 120, 127–8, 130, 141, 143, 170, 211, 213, 257; actions against the mutineers, 221, 245; 'Reign of Terror', 180; threats against, 185

Pitt, Sir William Augustus, governor of Portsmouth, 1794–1810, 219

Plantain, Alexander, Plymouth delegate, 45

Plymouth (Dockyard, Devon), 2, 7, 22, 31, 45, 59, 218; Sound, 216; Squadron, 147, 217, 218

Pole, Rear Admiral Sir Charles Morice, 25, 52, 54, 137 n. 118, 217

political reform, 41, 55, 179

Popham, General-at-Sea Edward, 40

Popham, Captain Sir Home Riggs (later Rear Admiral): signal and order books, 197

port admiral, 48, 164, 236

Port Mahon (Mahón, Minorca), 114

Porter, William, Spithead delegate, 44

Portland, 3rd Duke of, Home Secretary (1794–1801), 32, 33, 59, 181, 245

Porto Ferrajo (island of Elba), 112

Portsmouth (Hampshire), 2, 7, 21, 22, 23, 25, 32, 48, 54, 57, 69, 74, 80, 84, 90, 91, 92, 93, 94, 114, 147, 148, 149, 151, 152, 155, 164, 180, 199, 216, 219, 258

Portsmouth Corporation, 60, 180

Post Office, 215, 254

Potts, William, Spithead delegate, *Pompée*, 44, 56

Preed, Ryan, Plymouth delegate, 45

'Pressed', 'Prest' in ships' books *see* impressed *and* impressment

Preston, Thomas, mutineer seaman, *Royal Sovereign*, executed September 1797, 222

prime minister, 170, 257

Prince of Wales *see* George Augustus Frederick, Prince of Wales

Pritchett, Samuel, letter to brother on *Serapis*, Nore, 177

privateers, 29, 42, 259

Privy Council, 26

prize money: distribution, 2, 12, 13, 27, 219–20, 253, 273; making, 117, 139, 273; payment, 47; proclamation (1808), 13, 55

promotion of *Trent* seamen, related to flogging, 238

Protestant Ascendancy, 122, 179

provisions, 52; bedding, 115; beer, 233; butter, 256; cheese, 170, 256; complaints about the quality, 12, 13, 28, 35, 40, 49, 99; condemned, 114; demand for additional for the sick, 52, 99; demand that no flour to be served in port, 25, 52, 99, 165; flour, 52, 170; fresh vegetables, 25, 52, 99, 165, 180; fruit, 115; full allowance of, from 20 May 1797, 27, 52, 99, 147, 154, 180, 217; grog, 274; lemons, 115; nutritional value, 114, 194; onions,

provisions: (*continued*)
115; porter, 170; ships' biscuits, 49, 143, 179, 243; shoes, 115; slop clothing, 115; spirits, 233; wine, 233; withheld, 103, 187, at the Nore, 252

Pulteney, William, 87

purser, naval: allowed deduction of an eighth of provisions since 1776 to cover wastage, 27, 215; *Nereide*, 267

Pye, Admiral Sir Thomas, Portsmouth port admiral, 47, 48

Queen Charlotte *see* Charlotte of Mecklenburg-Strelitz, Queen Consort of George III

Quota men, 3, 4, 6, 9, 15, 19, 20, 21, 22, 28, 30, 57, 58, 59, 124, 136, 139, 183, 186, 190; accused of being sent from gaols, 236–7, 241; blamed as fomenters of the mutinies, 236, 241; low chance of being flogged on *Trent*, 236; numbers entering the navy, 236

radicals, radicalism, 9, 39, 40, 41, 49, 179, 182, 186, 191, 192, 193, 194, 257, 263, 277

Ramsay, James, Spithead delegate, 44

reconciliation: at Spithead, 219–20

Redpath, Thomas, Spithead delegate, 44

red flag, 2, 24, 25, 33, 43, 49, 66, 126, 150, 155, 157, 171, 191, 255, 259

refusal to weigh anchor, 24, 64, 217

Regency crisis 1788–9, 79

regulations made by seamen during the mutinies, 195, 198–9

Regulations and Instructions Relating to His Majesty's Service at Sea 1772, 100, 233

Reinhard, Charles-Frédéric, diplomat of the French Directory and Consulate (later of the Bourbon Restoration), 123

Renshaw, John, seaman, *San Fiorenzo*, Nore, letter to his brother, 162–3

Republic, The Floating, 20 n. 8 *see also* floating republic

republicanism, 75, 120

Remonstrance of the Navy, 1649, 40

retribution, 58, 158, 209, 222, 223, 225, 226; mutinous ships to be fired upon by naval ships, 48, 104

'Returned Sick' in ships' books, seamen discharged but returned to their ship when recovered, 235

revolution: threat of in 1797, 78, 85, 107, 120–41, 141, 143; English, 59; French, 144, 259

revolutionary, 41, 58, 59, 119, 141, 179, 186, 191, 192, 193, 243, 246, 257, 278; societies, 128, 180, 182, 263

Richards, seaman, North Sea Fleet, letter to his father, 255

Richardson, Hardwick, seaman, *Inflexible*, Nore, letter from Agnes Maitland, Leith, 176

Richardson, John, Spithead delegate, 44

Richmond, Duke of *see* Lennox, Charles, 3rd Duke of Richmond

Riou, Captain Edward, 197, 204

Rights of Man, Thomas Paine (1791), 126

Riley, William, Spithead delegate, 44

Riordan, Dennis, president of *Inflexible*'s committee, Nore, 259

Roberts, John, Plymouth delegate, 45

Roberts, John (2), Plymouth delegate, 45

Roberts, William, seaman, *Director*, Nore, letter to his wife, 256

Robertson, William, seaman, *Brilliant*, Nore, letter from his father Patrick, 176

Robespierre, Maximilien, Jacobin leader of the French Revolution during the Terror, 174

Robinson, John, seaman, *Nereide*, 1809, 268

Rochester (Kent) has the lowest bridge on the River Medway, therefore a strategic crossing point, 170–1, 172, 174, 225

Ross, Daniel, master Royal Navy, 204

Rousseau, Jean-Jacques, philosopher who influenced the French Revolution, 261

Rowley, Captain William (later Rear Admiral), *Cumberland*, 1797, 101

Royal Exchange in the City of London,

centre of commerce for London
merchants, 221
Royal Hospital for Seamen at
Greenwich, 42, 108, 116
Russell, Francis, 5th Duke of Bedford,
opposition Whig politician, 67–8,
72–3, 185, 186
Russell, Lord John, MP 1788–1802, 63, 66

Saffrey, Surgeon Stephen, Sheerness, 167
St Fiorenza Bay (Corsica), 12
St Helen's anchorage (Isle of Wight), 2, 54,
61, 69, 71, 75, 91, 104, 165, 166, 217, 219
St Mary Matfelon, Whitechapel, London,
where Richard Parker was buried, 225
St Mary's Island (Île Sainte-Marie off
the north-east coast of Madagascar),
a sheltered base for pirates throughout
the seventeenth and eighteenth centuries close to maritime routes of ships
returning from the East Indies, 267
St Vincent, Admiral Lord, 8, 22, 23, 82,
83, 108, 136, 139, 180, 195, 200, 201,
214, 223, 224, 269
St Vincent, battle of, 14 February 1797,
for whose success Jervis was created
Earl St Vincent, 247
Salked, George, Spithead delegate, 44
Sally Port, gate through Portsmouth
fortifications near the Tudor Square
Tower, by the junction of High Street
and Broad Street, a landing and
embarkation point for small ships, 119
sandbanks, 156, 157
Sandwich, Earl of (John Montagu), 83
Sané, Jacques-Noël, noted French eight-
eenth-century shipbuilder, maritime
agent at Brest Dockyard, 1797, 124
Saunders, John, Spithead delegate, 44
scapegoat, 209, 222, 225
Scargill, George, topman, Nereide, 1809,
272
Scotland, possible destination of Nore
mutineers, 156
Screaton, William, Spithead delegate, 44
Scrivener, John, Spithead delegate, 44
Scully, James, Spithead delegate, 44

scurvy, 115
Seamen's Manifesto, 74–6
Secretary of State, 103
sedition, 140
sexuality, 113, 269
Seven Years' War, 43
Seymour, Rear Admiral Lord Hugh,
Admiralty commissioner, 23, 35
Sheerness (Kent), dockyard and harbour
near the Nore anchorage, 76, 149, 155,
157, 167, 168, 169, 170, 172, 173, 209,
220–1, 224, 251, 252; responses to the
Nore mutiny, 173, 174
Sheffield, 179
Sheridan, Richard Brinsley, playwright
and opposition Whig MP, 1780–1812,
73–4, 75, 140
ships, merchant: Derby, 43; Weymouth,
115
ships, Royal Navy: Adamant, 7, 154, 227,
243, 250, 251, 254, 261; Africaine, 279;
Agamemnon, 261; Albion, 169; Amazon, 202; Amphitrite, 102; Ariadne, 200;
Ariel, 118 n. 35; Artois, 41 n. 19; Atlas,
2, 47 n. 46; Audacious, 22; Beaulieu,
171; Bellerophon, 22; Belliqueux, 169,
252, 255, 256, 262; Blanche, 199; Bombay Castle, 47 n. 45; Bounty, 11, 12, 31,
195; Brilliant, 176; Ça Ira, 112; Caesar,
44; Calypso, 41 n. 19; Cambridge, 47
n. 45; Champion, 259; Cherwell, 164,
274; Circe, 227, 243, 251, 261; Clyde,
151, 155; Culloden, 6, 8, 11, 12, 22, 31,
39, 48, 49, 70, 214; Cumberland, 101;
Defence, 14, 15, 24, 44, 99 n. 2, 138;
Defiance, 44, 49, 53, 99 n. 2, 103, 131;
Director, 153, 157, 212, 256; Duke, 41,
44, 49, 53, 54, 55, 99 n. 2, 102, 105, 131,
138; Edgar, 26, 45, 216 n. 37; Egmont,
47 n. 45; Espion, 149 n. 5; Ethalion, 200;
Eurydice, 104, 105, 205; Firm, 149 n. 5;
Formidable, 22, 44; Galatea, 8, 45; Ganges, 44, 47 n. 45; Garland, 32; Gibraltar,
26, 45; Gladiator, 199; Glatton, 104;
Glory, 44, 99 n. 2, 104, 138; Goliath, 47
n. 45; Good Intent, 191; Grampus, 10,
165; Hebe, 111; Hector, 44; Hermione,
6, 145, 195; Hind, 102; Hyperion, 200,
206; Impétueux, 8, 44, 79, 99 n. 2, 138;

ships, Royal Navy: (*continued*)

Inflexible, 150, 151, 155, 157, 161, 176, 191, 192, 259, 263; *Inspector*, 167, 250–1; *Intrepid*, 31 n. 70; *Iris*, 149 n. 5; *Isis*, 176; *Janus*, 46, 47; *Jason*, 101; *Juste*, 22, 44; *Lancaster*, 176; *Leopard*, 7, 151, 157, 212, 249; *Leviathan*, 26, 45; *Lion*, 169, 252; *Lively*, 109; *London*, 2, 24, 32, 33, 41 n. 16, 44, 50, 51, 53, 54, 55, 56, 58, 61–78, 99 n. 2, 137, 138, 166, 215, 217; *Macedonian*, 270; *Magnanime*, 196; *Majestic*, 99 n. 2; *Marlborough*, 2, 44, 55, 99 n. 2, 101, 103, 104, 138, 166, 223; *Mars*, 21, 44, 55, 99 n. 2, 136, 138, 148, 149, 165, 200; *Martin*, 46; *Megaera*, 50; *Meleager*, 110, 111, 112, 113; *Menelaus*, 279; *Minerve*, 35, 107–19, 239, 240; *Minotaur*, 2, 22, 44, 54, 99 n. 2, 100, 138; *Monarch*, 41 n. 16, 44, 47 n. 46, 50, 136, 137, 138; *Monmouth*, 159, 212, 260; *Montagu*, 177, 178, 251; *Nassau*, 7, 249, 251, 252, 253, 254, 256, 259; *Neptune*, 212; *Nereide*, 7, 14, 100 n. 9, 144, 206, 264–74, 276, 277, 278; *Niger*, 217; *Nymphe*, 2, 49, 50, 53, 55, 59, 100, 131, 138; *Otter*, 7, 14, 202, 264, 266, 274; *Overyssel*, 171; *Pearl*, 102; *Pégase*, 47 n. 45; *Perseverance*, 58; *Pompée*, 21, 32, 41 n. 19, 44, 49, 55–6, 99–100, 131, 138, 148, 149, 219; *Porcupine*, 2, 54 n. 72, 216, 217; *Portland*, 47 n. 45; *Prince*, 44, 148; *Prince George*, 8, 44, 201; *Princess Royal*, 47 n. 45; *Proserpine*, 200; *Pylades*, 104; *Queen*, 47 n. 45; *Queen Charlotte*, 1–2, 17, 22, 23, 24, 25, 41, 44, 49, 50, 51 n. 67, 53, 54, 56, 65, 85, 86, 93, 99 n. 2, 120, 138, 162; *Raisonable*, 47 n. 45, 48; *Ramillies*, 2, 22, 44, 99 n. 2, 102, 138; *Repulse*, 151, 157, 189, 212, 252, 253; *Reunion*, 200; *Revenge*, 102 n. 16; *Robust*, 43, 99, 138; *Romney*, 56, 215; *Royal George*, 22, 24, 44, 50, 53, 54, 57, 58, 85, 95–7, 99 n. 2, 138, 219; *Royal Sovereign*, 23, 24, 44, 85, 99 n. 2, 104, 105, 138, 222; *Royal William*, 50; *Russell*, 44; *St George*, 223; *Sandwich*, 2, 150, 151, 156, 157, 161, 167, 168, 171, 175, 177, 183, 185, 186, 190, 191, 192, 209, 219, 224, 245, 247, 249, 252, 258, 259; *San Fiorenzo*, 151, 155, 262; *Sans Pareil*, 22; *Saturn*, 26, 45; *Serapis*, 177, 222; *Shannon*, 133; *Standard*, 169, 222, 252, 253; *Superb*, 206; *Surprise*, 145; *Swan*, 259, 262; *Tarleton*, 115 n. 23; *Terrible*, 8, 11, 12, 31, 44, 48, 49, 99 n. 2, 103, 138, 214; *Thames*, 35, 44, 108, 109; *Theseus*, 22; *Tisiphone*, 162; *Trent*, 145, 226–42, 243, 251, 261; *Triumph*, 22, 47 n. 45, 103, 104; *Vanguard*, 200, 201; *Venerable*, 13, 154, 227, 243, 250, 151, 254, 261; *Venus*, 215; *Windsor Castle*, 8, 11, 12, 48, 49, 214

ship seaworthiness, 12, 49, 70

ships' size, 195, 196

shore leave, 112, 194, 276; demand for, 13, 35, 56, 99, 139, 147, 159, 180

shutter telegraph, Portsmouth, 24

sick seamen: on board ship, 234; more attention for, 99, 102, 147, 159

sickness, 203

signal books, 83

Sims, lieutenant of marines, *London*, 166

Sinclair, Robert, Spithead delegate, 44

sinking of *Royal George* (29 August 1782), 95–7

Sittingbourne (Kent), 162

Slade, John, topman, *Nereide*, 1809, 269, 273, 274, 275

slave trade, 273

slop sellers, 23

Smart, James/Samuel, pressed seaman and delegate *Grampus*, Nore, alleged to be a member of the LCS, addressed a corresponding society meeting, 177, 257–8,

Smith, John, topman, *Nereide*, 1809, 270–2, 274

Smith, Vice Admiral Thomas (later Admiral), 82 n. 15; *Naval Instructions 1775*, 195; *see also* divisional system; training in gunnery and sail handling, 195

Sneeden, Thomas, captain of the forecastle *Raisonable*, 1783, 48

Snowdon, John, Plymouth delegate, 45

soap, 198, 201

Society for Constitutional Information, 126, 127, 224

soldiers, 115, 228

Solent (strait separating the Isle of Wight from the south of England), 115

Southsea (Hampshire), in 1797 a fortified coastal common and marsh to the south of Portsea Island, used for military exercises and hunting birds, 219

Spence, Thomas, radical author, 126

Spencer, Earl George, First Lord of the Admiralty 1794–1801, 2, 8, 13, 15, 23, 24, 33, 53, 61, 67, 73, 80, 83, 86, 132, 134, 173, 211, 213, 213, 215, 216, 220–1, 224, 225

Spithead, anchorage in the Solent, 1, 23, 95, 114, 147, 172, 217, 262

Stanhope, Lady Hester Lucy, niece of Prime Minister William Pitt, 141

Steward, James, Quota man flogged on *Trent*, 236

Stonehouse (Devon) shipbuilding and residential neighbourhood near Plymouth Dockyard, 218

strike, 4, 10, 11, 16, 35, 43, 159, 190, 219, 247

Stuart: monarchy, 128; restoration 29 May 1660, 127, 169, 171

subordination, 274

Sweet, John, sergeant of marines, *Pompée*, 56

Tagus, River (Spain), 114

Talbot, Captain John (later Admiral Sir), *Eurydice*, 1797, 104

Tait, Captain James Haldane, *Grampus*, 1806–9, investigated the Otters' complaints against Captain Willoughby, 1808, 265

Tate, Colonel William, Irish-American who led the unsuccessful French invasion of Fishguard (Wales) 22 February 1797, 124

Tees, River (County Durham, Yorkshire, Westmorland), 43

Texel (Netherlands), Frisian island and harbour, site of the Battle of Camperdown, 11 October 1797, 7, 8, 137, 154, 161, 243

Thames, River, 2, 147, 150, 156, 243; blockade by mutineers, 156, 169, 187, 252–3; removal of buoys by the government, 192, 221; boom across the river

suggested by Pitt, 221; watermen to be used against the Nore mutineers, 221

Thoroughgood, Captain Charles (later master attendant Portsmouth Dockyard 1654–60), 40

Thorn, William, Plymouth delegate, 45

Thurlow, Edward, Lord Chancellor (1778–92), 28

Tilbury (Essex), ancient River Thames crossing point, fortified since the reign of Henry VIII to crossfire with fortifications at Gravesend to protect the entrance to the Port of London, 221

tilt boat, a two-masted Thames vessel with a canvas tilt to cover passengers and cargo, 176, 177

Thomson, Joseph, seaman, North Sea Fleet, letter to his mother, 255

Tone, Wolfe, 123, 132, 133, 134, 135, 136, 179

Tooke, John Horne, radical politician, tried (acquitted) for high treason 1794, 127–8

Torbay anchorage (Devon), 22, 54

Toulon (Dockyard France), 124

trade union, 130

Trafalgar, battle of, 1805, 205, 278

Transport Board, 23, 29

treason, 63, 276

troops, 45, 46, 123, 170, 171, 172

Trotter, Dr Thomas, 194

'Turned Over' in ships' books, seamen entered from another ship before being paid and without being given leave, 235

Turner, Mark, Spithead delegate, 44

Tutton, Alexander, patient in Haslar Hospital, 56

Tyne, River (Northumberland, Cumbria), 43, 46

typology, mutiny, 11

Ulster (Ireland), 122, 185

Union flag, 171

Unitarian, 58

United Britons, 179, 263

United Englishmen, 179; oaths, 132

United Irishmen, 3, 22, 55, 118, 121, 123, 129, 132, 135, 136, 149, 179, 180, 184, 248, 258, 259, 263, 278; revolutionary involvement, 21, 22, 41, 121, 187

United Scotsmen, 179, 263

unity statements, xi, 32, 39, 41, 50, 51, 53, 54

Ushant (Ouessant, France), island which marks the southern west point of the English Channel, 83; second battle of, 12 December 1781, 83

Vassie, John, Spithead delegate, 44

Veale, Moses, boatswain's mate, *Nereide*, 1809, 271, 273–4

victuals *see* provisions

Victualling Board, 114

violence during the mutinies, 168, 169, 216, 252

Waghorn, Captain Martin, of *Royal George* in 1782, 95–6

Wallace, William, North Sea Fleet delegate, *Standard*, 253

Wallis, Captain James, *Tisiphone*, 162

Walpole, Horace Whig MP, 129

Walter, George, Plymouth delegate, 45

Walter, John, founder editor and publisher of the paper named *The Times* in 1788, 88–9

wars : for American Independence, 1776–83, 190, 246; French revolutionary, 1793–1801, 194, 246; Napoleonic, 1803–14, 1815, 226, 227

washing, 198, 200; clothes, 200; decks, 200

watches, two or three, 196, 201–3

Watson, Thomas Bailey, supernumerary, *Sandwich*, Nore, gave evidence against Jephson, 185–6

Watson, Dr Robert, London Corresponding Society delegate who visited Portsmouth 1797, 130

West Indies, 43, 83, 85, 110

West, Thomas, seaman, *Isis*, Nore, letter from his parents, 176

Western Approaches, area of the

Atlantic west of the British Isles, 201

Whig Club, 126

Widgery, Samuel, North Sea Fleet delegate, *Nassau*, 253

Wiggins, William, gunroom cook, *Nereide*, 1809, 272

Wilberforce, William, 8

Wilkinson, William, topman, *Nereide*, 1809, 267, 272, 274, 278

William, Prince of Orange, nephew and son-in-law of James II, landed at Torbay 5 November 1688, crowned William III 1689, 128

Williams, Daniel, Home Office magistrate sent to investigate sedition at Sheerness, 131, 180, 181–2, 187, 245, 263

Williams, Edward, Plymouth delegate, 45

Willoughby, Captain Sir Nesbit, *Otter*, 1807, 7, 202, 265; court martial, 274; *Otters* complained of cruelty, 264–5; investigation by Admiral Bertie, arrest, 265, 266

Wills, seaman *Leopard*, North Sea Squadron, letter to his wife, 249

Willson, James, Spithead delegate, 44

Wilson, David, Spithead delegate, 44

Wilson, John, Plymouth delegate, 45

Wilson, Robert, seaman, 204

Wishart, John, Plymouth delegate, 45

Witney, John, Spithead delegate, 44

women: in bum boats, selling provisions to moored ships, 23; on board, 24, 197, 216, 257

working class, 3, 137–9, 278; views of the mutinies from newspapers, 175–8

Wyndham, William, Baron Grenville, Foreign Secretary, 1791–1801, 68, 72, 73

Yarmouth (Great) Roads, Norfolk, port and anchorage on the North Sea coast, 150, 153, 155, 167, 169, 172, 251, 252, 254, 255, 256

Yexley, Lionel, 6

Young, Admiral William, admiralty commissioner, 1795–1801, 173